Penguin Modern Economics Readings

General Editor

B. J. McCormick

Advisory Board

K. J. W. Alexander
R. W. Clower
G. R. Fisher
P. Robson
J. Spraos
H. Townsend

Wealth, Income and Inequality

Selected Readings

Edited by A. B. Atkinson

Penguin Education

Penguin Education
A Division of Penguin Books Ltd,
Harmondsworth, Middlesex, England
Penguin Books Inc, 7110 Ambassador Road,
Baltimore, Md 21207, USA
Penguin Books Australia Ltd,
Ringwood, Victoria, Australia

First published 1973
This selection copyright © A. B. Atkinson, 1973
Introduction and notes copyright © A. B. Atkinson, 1973

Copyright acknowledgements for items in this
volume will be found on page 405

Made and printed in Great Britain by
Richard Clay (The Chaucer Press) Ltd, Bungay, Suffolk
Set in Monotype Times

Contents

Introduction

The unequal distribution of personal income and wealth is one of the most prominent features of our society and one which has a profound effect on economic and social relationships. It raises many important questions. How is it that the gap between the rich and the poor has come to exist? What forces are at work to widen or narrow the gap? How is inequality in income and wealth related to economic and social institutions? What has been the impact of measures designed to reduce inequality? Despite the importance of these questions, they have not been among those with which economists have been most concerned in the postwar period. As was argued in the first issue of the *Review of Radical Political Economics*, 'Inequality is what economics should be all about. But, in fact, economics as it is taught and practised by economists deals very little with inequality'. It is in the hope of partly redressing the balance that this set of readings has been compiled.

To suggest that economists have completely neglected distributional questions would not, of course, be fair. For classical writers, the distribution of national income among factors of production was a central concern. Ricardo (1821), for example, opened the Preface to his *Principles of Political Economy and Taxation* with a statement which was supported by many other nineteenth century economists:

The produce of the earth . . . is divided among three classes of the community, namely, the proprietor of the land, the owner of the stock or capital necessary for its cultivation, and the labourers by whose industry it is cultivated. . . . To determine the laws which regulate this distribution is the principal problem in Political Economy.

It is important to emphasize, however, that the question of the distribution among factors of production – such as land, capital and labour – is rather different from some of the questions raised in the first paragraph. We have to distinguish between the *distribution by factor shares* (Ricardo's division among three classes of the community) and the *distribution by persons*. The former distribution clearly influences the latter but is not the only important consideration. A theory which explained the total share of wages in national income would not tell us why some workers earned ten times as much as others. Similarly, an understanding of the behaviour of the share of capital is only relevant when we know how capital is distributed among persons. The personal distribution of income and wealth has however received very much less attention than the distribution by factor shares. In 1920, Dalton commented

that most 'theories of distribution' were almost wholly concerned with distribution as between 'factors of production'. Distribution as between persons, a problem of more direct and obvious interest, was either left out of the textbooks altogether, or treated so briefly as to suggest that it raised no question which could not be answered either by generalizations about the factors of production or by plodding statistical investigations.

Similarly, Fisher (1912) said of the distribution of personal income that 'no other problem has so great a human interest as this, and yet scarcely any other problem has received so little scientific study'. The same remains very much true today.

During the twentieth century, interest even in the problem of factor shares has tended to decline. Bronfenbrenner (1971) has suggested that 'reaction against what we have called the classical stress on distribution seems to have set in shortly before the Second World War'. This loss of interest in distributional questions can be attributed in part to the concentration on full employment and growth and a belief that these would provide benefit to everyone. Typical of American views of this kind is the statement by an American businessman that 'it is quite obvious that over a period of years, even those who find themselves at the short end of inequality have more to gain from faster growth than from any conceivable income redistribution' (Galbraith, 1960). In Britain, high levels of employment after the Second World War, coupled with improvements in the social services, were believed to have produced a levelling of incomes. As described by Titmuss, in 1960 'inequality, as a subject of political discourse, was less in evidence everywhere and what remained of poverty in Britain was thought to be either eradicable through the "natural" process of growth or as constituting a permanent residue of the unfortunate and irresponsible. The rich, it was further argued, were no longer with us; they had been taxed out of existence' (Titmuss, 1964). In the past decade, however, interest in questions of income distribution has begun to revive. The renewed concern reflects the growing realization that full employment and growing per capita incomes do not by themselves lead to the steady reduction of inequality and the 'discovery' of the persistence of poverty in advanced countries. It is on studies emerging from this new wave of interest that this volume is focused.

Economic inequality is an extremely complex phenomenon; and it is impossible to cover all aspects of the distribution of income and wealth in one volume of readings. It may, therefore, be helpful to indicate some of the principles of selection, and to explain the emphasis on certain aspects and the exclusion of others.

The readings in this volume focus on two main aspects. The first is the presentation of evidence about the personal distribution of income and wealth. Everyone is aware of the existence of inequality, but its precise extent is difficult to determine. The rich are naturally reluctant to reveal their affairs; the poor are not often covered by government statistics; the middle classes are more willing to talk about their sex lives than about their salaries. Official statistics about the distribution of income and wealth are of considerably lower quality than those in other fields – a state of affairs which may well reflect a low priority attached by governments to distributional questions. Without such statistical information, however, it is impossible to assess the magnitude of the problem and to throw any light on the causes of inequality. While Tawney (Reading 1) was quite right to stress that 'there are other sides of the truth about mankind and its behaviour than those . . . expressed in . . . logarithms', he himself drew heavily on statistical studies of the distribution of income and wealth and they must provide an important foundation for any modern enquiry. One of the principal aims of this volume is, therefore, to collect the main information available about the degree of concentration of income and wealth.

The second aspect emphasized in this volume is the analysis of the major economic factors influencing the distribution of income and wealth. Part Three presents a selection of the theories advanced to explain the observed inequalities in earnings. The questions which these theories seek to answer include the following: How far can occupational differences in earnings be explained by differences in the training required? What is the relationship between organizational hierarchies and the distribution of earnings? What are the causes of low pay? In Part Four, similar questions are considered in relation to the distribution of wealth. What are the forces leading to its concentration in a few hands? How does the pattern of inheritance influence the distribution of wealth? The readings selected are principally concerned with the role of *economic* factors. This should not, however, be taken as reflecting a view that these are the sole (or indeed the most important) forces at work. The aim is rather to allow the reader to assess the relevance of economic explanations of inequality, which can then be considered in the light of broader social and political theories. In asking, for example, how far the earnings of doctors can be explained by their long period of training, there is no presumption that this is the only factor of importance, and to obtain a complete picture one would certainly have to examine the social and political role of the medical profession.

The editor of any selection of readings is faced with the problem of deciding whether to attempt to cover the whole field or whether to concentrate on certain topics. I have chosen the latter approach and most of the readings are concerned with the two aspects discussed above – the evidence about inequality in the personal distribution of income and wealth, and the analysis of economic factors influencing the distribution. This decision has inevitably meant that important topics have been left uncovered. Four major omissions should be particularly mentioned here. Firstly, there are no readings concerned with the distribution by factor shares. While the behaviour of factor shares is of importance for understanding the distribution among persons, it has, as was pointed out earlier, received much more attention from economists than the personal distribution, and it seemed reasonable to concentrate on the latter, relatively neglected subject. Moreover, the fact that many more economists have written on the subject of factor shares means, in turn, that there are a correspondingly larger number of opinions and one or two readings would be insufficient to cover the different views which have been put forward. (For good surveys of the field, see Scitovsky (1964), Bronfenbrenner (1971), Phelps Brown (1969) and Kaldor (1956).) Finally, readings on factor shares are in general more accessible than those on the personal distribution, and a number of the major articles have already appeared in the Penguin Modern Economics series.[1] Secondly, no attempt has been made to cover measures designed to reduce or eliminate inequality. The range of possible measures is extremely wide – from tax reform to revolution – and the scope of one volume is insufficient to do justice to this range. To take one example, adequate coverage of the proposals for a negative income tax to reduce poverty in the United States would require at least two readings (one in favour and one against) and possibly as much as a whole section. Some of the readings selected here (such as that by Abel-Smith and Townsend on poverty in Britain) do make reference to the policy implications of their findings, but no readings dealing solely with policy measures have been included. Thirdly, at least half the readers will have been struck by the absence of any reading on inequality between the sexes. This does not reflect discrimination on the editor's part, but rather the absence of any extract suitable for the volume. Some indication of the distance we are at present from equal pay is provided by the New Earnings Survey in Britain, which showed that whereas 17 per cent of adult men working full-time earned less than £20 a week, the corresponding percentage for women was 80 per cent. Similarly, in the United States in 1969 the median earnings of white women full-time workers was only 57 per cent of that of white men (and 85 per cent

1. Readings on factor shares have been included in the volumes on *The Labour Market* (edited by B. J. McCormick and E. Owen Smith, Penguin, 1968), on *Growth Economics* (edited by A. K. Sen, Penguin, 1968), and on *The Theory of the Firm* (edited by G. C. Archibald, Penguin, 1971).

of that of black men). The final omission is that of any reading on the world distribution of income. This subject warrants a volume in its own right, and it did not prove possible to find extracts which in the space available would have brought out the magnitude of the inequality between rich and poor countries. This should not, however, allow the importance of this problem to be forgotten. Beckerman and Bacon (1970) have presented estimates of the distribution of per capita real consumption in different countries and showed that the poorest 50 per cent of the world's population enjoyed only 10 per cent of total world consumption in 1962–3. Moreover, since these figures relate only to average per capita income, the inequality within countries causes the overall degree of inequality to be even greater. As Beckerman and Bacon say, 'if the average annual consumption of the poorest 20 per cent of the world population is only about $84 per head (1962–3) it is left to the imagination what it must be for the poorer people in the poorest countries' (1970).

The reader will probably have noted that all the readings date from this century and in fact over half of the twenty-four were published in the past ten years. This reflects the aim of concentrating on work arising from the recent revival of interest in this field. It has, however, meant that a number of 'classic' sources have had to be excluded for lack of space. At the same time, recency of publication has not been an over-riding principle and in a number of cases 'pioneering' articles have been selected in preference to the more up to date, but often less easily read, alternatives. For example, the reading on poverty in America is taken from the 1964 *Economic Report of the President* rather than from sources giving more recent figures, or more extended analysis. This is because the former provides (in my view) a better overall perspective of the problem. In some cases, I have attempted to bring the statistical evidence up to date and the relevant figures will be found in an Editor's Note or in the introduction to the Part concerned.

References

BECKERMAN, W., and BACON, R. (1970), 'The international distribution of incomes' in P. Streeten (ed.) *Unfashionable Economics*, Weidenfeld & Nicolson.

BRONFENBRENNER, M. (1971), *Income Distribution Theory*, Macmillan.

DALTON, H. (1920), *Some Aspects of the Inequality of Incomes in Modern Communities*, Routledge & Kegan Paul.

FISHER, I. (1912), *Elementary Principles of Economics*, Macmillan.

GALBRAITH, J. K. (1960), *The Affluent Society*, Houghton Mifflin, reprinted in Penguin, 1962.

KALDOR, N. (1956), 'Alternative theories of distribution', *Rev. econ. Stud.*, vol. 23, pp. 83–100.

KUZNETS, S. (1963), 'Quantitative aspects of economic growth of nations: VIII distribution of income by size', *Econ. Devel. cult. Change*, vol. 11, part 2.

NEW EARNINGS SURVEY (1970), Department of Employment, HMSO.

PHELPS BROWN, E. H. (1969), *Pay and Profits*, Manchester University Press.

RANADIVE, K. R. (1965), 'The equality of incomes in India', *Bull. Oxford Inst. Econ. Stats.*, vol. 27, pp. 119–134.

RICARDO, D. (1821), *Principles of Political Economy and Taxation*, Cambridge University Press.

SCITOVSKY, T. (1964), 'A survey of some theories of income distribution', in *The Behaviour of Income Shares*, Princeton University Press.

TITMUSS, R. M. (1964), 'Introduction', to fourth edition of R. H. Tawney, *Equality*, Allen & Unwin.

Part One
The Concept of Inequality

The readings in this first section deal with different aspects of two fundamental questions: why are we concerned about inequality and what exactly does inequality mean?

The first reading is taken from chapter 1 of Tawney's classic essay on *Equality*. In this chapter Tawney bases the case for greater equality principally on the grounds that:

What a community requires ... is a common culture, because, without it, it is not a community at all. ... But a common culture cannot be created merely by desiring it. It must rest upon practical foundations of social organization. It is incompatible with the existence of sharp contrasts between the economic standards and educational opportunities of different classes. ... It involves, in short, a large measure of economic equality.' (page 22).

He then proceeds to examine the arguments advanced against any move to establish greater equality. As he points out, 'the word "Equality" possesses more than one meaning, and ... the controversies surrounding it arise partly, at least, because the same term is employed with different connotations'. He emphasizes that the case for equality rests in no sense on the assumption that people are identical in their natural endowments of character and intelligence. As a corollary, economic equality does not necessarily involve an identical level of money incomes or provision of public services, rather it requires 'equality of consideration'.

The translation from the concept of 'consideration' to the actual measurement of living standards raises many methodological questions. Should we be concerned with the individual, the family or the household? Should we look at their income, their expenditure or their wealth? What allowance should be made for the needs of families of different sizes? In Reading 2, Morgan examines a number of these questions with particular reference to the position of old people in the United States at the beginning of the 1960s. He shows that what might appear to be unimportant questions of definition (such as the choice between the household and the nuclear family as a unit of measurement) may make a major difference to the assessment of economic status: 'the mean income of the very young and very old are substantial if one counts the total income of the extended family with which they live, whereas the actual income of the adult units at extreme ages is much smaller'. Of particular importance is the range of economic resources taken into consideration. As has been emphasized by Kaldor (1955), Titmuss (1962) and others, the definition of income commonly used in studies of inequality (particularly those based on income tax statistics) falls a long way short of a comprehensive definition such as that advanced by Simons (1938).[1] In the third section of his article, Morgan discusses some of the items which should be included. Besides money income, Morgan considers the role of income in kind, wealth and leisure, but there are strong grounds for interpreting the concept of economic resources even more widely and including, for example, the benefits derived from government expenditure (as argued by Townsend, 1970).

In Reading 1, Tawney warns against confusing economic 'laws' about how people tend to behave with statements about how people should behave (referring particularly to the 'proof' of the impossibility of redistribution derived from the observation of Pareto that the income distribution tends to take a particular form). Reading 3 is similarly concerned with the relationship between the measurement of inequality and social values about the desirability of redistribution. When information has been collected about the distribution of income or other economic resources, it is frequently convenient to be able to attach some measure to the degree of inequality: for example, when comparing the distribution of income in different countries. The conventional approach to this measurement is to adopt some summary measure such as the Gini coefficient and use this as the basis for comparison. (This practice is in fact followed by Morgan (page 36) and by four other authors in this volume.) In Reading 3, Atkinson examines these conventional summary measures and argues that implicit in the use of any such measure are values about a desirable distribution of income and that there is no reason to believe that the values embodied in the measures most frequently employed would be widely acceptable. In view of those conclusions, he argues that these conventional summary measures should be rejected in favour of direct consideration of the distributional values to be adopted, and suggests a new measure which would allow this to be done. (Since the argument in the original article is set out mathematically, a summary for non-mathematical readers is given on pp. 64–68).

1. Defined as the sum of '(a) the market values of rights exercised in consumption and (b) the change in the value of the store of property rights between the beginning and end of the period in question'. The definition of income for the purpose of equity in taxation is discussed in Readings 1–3 in the parallel volume on *Public Finance*, edited by R. Houghton, Penguin, 1970.

References

KALDOR, N. (1955), *The Expenditure Tax*, Allen & Unwin.
SIMONS, H. (1938), *Personal Income Taxation*, University of Chicago Press.
TITMUSS, R. M. (1962), *Income Distribution and Social Change*, Allen & Unwin.
TOWNSEND, P. (ed) (1970), *The Concept of Poverty*, Heinemann.

1 R. H. Tawney

The Religion of Inequality

Excerpts from chapter 1 of R. H. Tawney, *Equality*, Allen & Unwin, 1964, pp. 33–56.

Discoursing some sixty years ago on the text, 'Choose equality and flee greed', Matthew Arnold observed that in England inequality is almost a religion. He remarked on the incompatibility of that attitude with the spirit of humanity, and sense of the dignity of man as man, which are the marks of a truly civilized society. 'On the one side, in fact, inequality harms by pampering; on the other by vulgarizing and depressing. A system founded on it is against nature, and, in the long run, breaks down' (Arnold, 1903).

Much has changed since Arnold wrote, and not least what he called the Religion of Inequality. The temper which evoked his criticism, the temper which regarded violent contrasts between the circumstances and opportunities of different classes with respectful enthusiasm, as a phenomenon, not merely inevitable, but admirable and exhilarating, if by no means extinct, is no longer vociferous. Few politicians today would dwell, with Mr Lowe, on the English tradition of inequality as a pearl beyond price, to be jealously guarded against the profane. Few educationalists would seek, with Thring, the founder of the Headmasters' Conference and one of the most influential figures in the educational world of his day, to assuage the apprehension felt by the rich at the extension of education by arguing that 'the law of labour' compels the majority of children to work for wages at the age of ten, and that 'it is not possible that a class which is compelled to leave off training at ten years of age can oust, by superior intelligence, a class which is able to to spend four years more in acquiring skill'. Few political thinkers would find, with Bagehot, the secret of English political institutions in the fact that they have been created by a 'deferential people'; or write, as Erskine May wrote in his *Democracy in Europe*, of the demoralization of French society, and the paralysis of the French intellect, by the attachment of France to the bloodstained chimera of social equality; or declare, with the melancholy assurance of Lecky, that liberty and equality are irreconcilable enemies, of which the latter can triumph only at the expense of the former. When Taine published his *Notes sur l'Angleterre* in 1872, he could describe it, by contrast with France, as still haunted by the ghost of the feudal spirit, a country governed by 100,000 to 120,000 families with an income of £1000 a year and upwards, in which 'the lord provides for the needs of his dependent, and the dependent is proud of his lord'. It is improbable that, if he analysed the English scene today, even the relentless exigencies of historical antithesis would lead him to regard it as gilded with quite the same halo of haughty benevolence and submissive gratitude (Thring, 1864, pp. 4–5; Bagehot, 1867, pp. 50–4; Erskine May, 1877, vol. 2, p. 333; Lecky, 1899, vol. 1, pp. 256–7; Taine, 1863, 1872).

Institutions which have died as creeds sometimes continue, nevertheless, to survive as habits. If the cult of inequality as a principle and an ideal has declined with the decline of the aristocratic society of which it was the accompaniment, it is less certain, perhaps, that the loss of its sentimental credentials has so far impaired its practical influence as to empty Arnold's words of all their significance. It is true, no doubt, that, were he writing today, his emphasis and illustrations would be different. No doubt he would be less impressed by inequality as a source of torpor and stagnation, and more by inequality as a cause of active irritation, inefficiency and confusion. No doubt he would say less of great landed estates, and more of finance; less of the territorial aristocracy and the social system represented by it, and more of fortunes which, however interesting their origin, are not associated with historic names; less of the effects of entail and settlement in preventing the wider distribution of property in land, and more of the economic forces, in his day unforseen, which have led to a progressive concentration of the control of capital; less of the English reverence for birth, and more of the English worship of money and economic power. But, if he could be induced to study the statistical evidence accumulated since he wrote, it is probable that he would hail it as an unanticipated confirmation of conclusions to which, unaided by the apparatus of science, he had found his way, and, while noting with interest the inequalities which had fallen, would feel even greater astonishment at those which had survived. Observing the heightened tension between political democracy and a social system marked by sharp disparities of circumstance and education, and of the opportunities which circumstance and education confer, he would find, it may be suspected, in the history of the two generations since his essay appeared a more impressive proof of the justice of his diagnosis than it falls to the lot of most prophets to receive. 'A system founded on inequality is against nature, and, in the long run, breaks down.'

[. . .] An indifference to inequality, as the foreign observers remark, is less the mark of particular classes than a national characteristic. It is not a political question dividing parties, but a common temper and habit of mind which throws a bridge between them. Hence even those groups which are committed by their creed to measures for mitigating its more repulsive consequences rarely push their dislike of it to the point of affirming that the abolition of needless inequalities is their primary objective, by the approach to which their success is to be judged, and to the attainment of which other interests are to be subordinated. When the press assails them with the sparkling epigram that they desire, not merely to make the poor richer, but to make the rich poorer, instead of replying, as they should, that, being sensible men, they desire both, since the extremes both of riches and poverty are degrading and anti-social, they are apt to take refuge in gestures of deprecation. They make war on destitution, but they sometimes turn, it seems, a blind eye on privilege.

The truth is that, in this matter, judged by Arnold's standard, we are all barbarians, and that no section or class is in a position to throw stones at another. Certainly a professional man, like the writer of these pages, is not.

High Heaven rejects the lore
Of nicely calculated less and more

And how, when he accepts an income five times as large as that of the average working-class family, can he cavil at his neighbours merely because their consciences allow them to accept one twenty, or thirty, or fifty times as large? Certainly the mass of the wage-earners themselves, in spite of the immense advance which they have achieved since Arnold wrote, are but little better entitled to adopt a pose of righteous indignation.

What the working-class movement stands for is obviously the ideal of social justice and solidarity, as a corrective to the exaggerated emphasis on individual advancement through the acquisition of wealth. It is a faith in the possibility of a society in which a higher value will be set on human beings, and a lower value on money and economic power, when money and power do not serve human ends. But that movement is liable, like all of us, to fall at times below itself, and to forget its mission. When it does so, what it is apt to desire is not a social order of a different kind, in which money and economic power will no longer be the criterion of achievement, but a social order of the same kind, in which money and economic power will be somewhat differently distributed.

Its characteristic fault is not, as is sometimes alleged, that the spirit behind it is one of querulous discontent. It is, on the contrary, that a considerable number among those to whom it appeals are too easily contented – too ready to forget fundamental issues and to allow themselves to be bought off with an advance in wages, too willing to accept the moral premises of their masters, even when they dispute the economic conclusions which their masters draw from them, too distrustful of themselves and too much disposed to believe that the minority which has exercised authority in the past possesses a *mana*, a mysterious wisdom, and can wield a *karakia*, a magical influence bringing prosperity or misfortune (De Man, 1927,

p. 89). Their sentiment is just, but their action is timid, because it lacks a strong root of independent conviction to nourish and sustain it. If leaders, their bearing not infrequently recalls, less the tribune, than the courtier; they pay salaams of exaggerated amplitude to established proprieties, as though delighted and overawed by the privilege of saluting them. If followers, they are liable, with more excuse, to behave on occasion in a manner at once docile and irritable, as men who alternately touch their hats and grumble at the wickedness of those to whom they touch them.

Heaven takes, to paraphrase Homer, half the virtue from a man, when, if he behaves like a man, he may lose his job; and it is not for one who has not experienced the wage-earners' insecurity to be critical of the wage-earners' patience. But it would be better, nevertheless, both for them and for the nation as a whole, if they were more continuously alive, not only to their economic interests, but to their dignity as human beings. As it is, though they resent poverty and unemployment, and the physical miseries of a proletariat, they do not always resent, as they should, the moral humiliation which gross contrasts of wealth and economic power necessarily produce. While they will starve for a year to resist a reduction in wages, they still often accept quite tamely an organization of industry under which a dozen gentlemen, who are not conspicuously wiser than their neighbours, determine the conditions of life and work for several thousand families; and an organization of finance which enables a handful of bankers to raise and lower the economic temperature of a whole community; and an organization of justice which makes it difficult, as Sir Edward Parry has shown 1914, for a poor man to face the cost of obtaining it; and an organization of education which still makes higher education inaccessible to the great majority of working-class children, as though such children had, like anthropoid apes, fewer convolutions in their brains than the children of the well-to-do.

They denounce, and rightly, the injustices of capitalism; but they do not always realize that capitalism is maintained, not only by capitalists, but by those who, like some of themselves, would be capitalists if they could, and that the injustices survive, not merely because the rich exploit the poor, but because, in their hearts, too many of the poor admire the rich. They know and complain that they are tyrannized over by the power of money. But they do not yet see that what makes money the tyrant of society is largely their own reverence for it. They do not sufficiently realize that, if they were as determined to maintain their dignity as they are, quite rightly, to maintain their wages, they would produce a world in which their material miseries would become less unmanageable, since they would no longer be under a kind of nervous tutelage on the part of the minority, and the determination of their economic destinies would rest in their own hands.

Thus inequality, as Arnold remarked, does not only result in pampering one class; it results also in depressing another. But what does all this mean except that the tradition of inequality is, so to say, a complex – a cluster of ideas at the back of men's minds, whose influence they do not like to admit, but which, nevertheless, determines all the time their outlook on society, and their practical conduct, and the direction of their policy? And what can their denial of that influence convey except that the particular forms of inequality which are general and respectable, and the particular arrangement of classes to which they are accustomed, so far from being an unimportant detail, like the wigs of judges or the uniform of postmen and privy councillors, seem to them so obviously something which all right-thinking people should accept as inevitable that, until the question is raised, they are hardly conscious of them? And what can the result of such an attitude be except to inflame and aggravate occasions of friction which are, on other grounds, already numerous enough, and, since class divisions are evidently far-reaching in their effects, to cause it to be believed that class struggles, instead of being, what they are, a barbarous reality, which can be ended, and ended only, by abolishing its economic causes, are permanent, inevitable or even exhilarating.

The foreign critics, therefore, can console themselves with the reflection that they have not, after all, aimed so wide of the mark. But to those who cannot regard the fate of their fellow-countrymen with the detachment of foreigners, these proofs of their predilection for worshipping images are less consoling. They will observe that the ritual of the cult is even more surprising than the albs and chasubles and aumbries, which so shocked the late Lord Brentford and the House of Commons a few years ago. They will note that its own devotees do not seem to find in it a source of unmixed gratification, since it keeps them in a condition of morbid irritation with each other, so that, however urgent the need for decisive action may be, such action is impossible, because, as has repeatedly been seen in the twenty years since 1918, defence and attack neutralize each other, as in trench warfare, and the balance of forces produces a state of paralysis. They will reflect that such a paralysis, which is the natural result of a divided will, is less noticeable in nations where classes are less sharply divided, and that, since a united will can no longer today be secured, as it was secured in the past, by restricting political power to the classes endowed with social power and opportunity, the time may have come, perhaps, to increase the degree in which the latter, as well as the former, are a common possession. They will ask, in short, whether one condition of grappling more effectively with the economic difficulties of the nation – not to mention its intellectual and moral deficiencies – may not be, in the words of Arnold, to 'choose equality'.

Psychologists tell us that the way to overcome a complex is not to suppress it, but to treat it frankly, and uncover its foundations. What a community requires, as the word itself suggests, is a common culture, because, without it, it is not a community at all. And evidently it requires it in a special degree at a moment like the present, when circumstances confront it with the necessity of giving a new orientation to its economic life, because it is in such circumstances that the need for cooperation, and for the mutual confidence and tolerance upon which cooperation depends, is particularly pressing. But a common culture cannot be created merely by desiring it. It must rest upon practical foundations of social organization. It is incompatible with the existence of sharp contrasts between the economic standards and educational opportunities of different classes, for such contrasts have as their result, not a common culture, but servility or resentment, on the one hand, and patronage or arrogance, on the other. It involves, in short, a large measure of economic equality – not necessarily in the sense of an identical level of pecuniary incomes, but of equality of environment, of access to education and the means of civilization, of security and independence, and of the social consideration which equality in these matters usually carries with it.

And who does not know that to approach the question of economic equality is to enter a region haunted, not, indeed, 'by hobgoblins, satyrs, and dragons of the pit', yet by a host of hardly less formidable terrors – 'doleful voices and rushings to and fro', and the giant with a grim and surly voice, who shows pilgrims the skulls of those whom he has already despatched, and threatens to tear them also in pieces, and who, unlike Bunyan's giant, does not even fall into fits on sunshiny days, since in his territory the sun does not shine, and, even if it did, he would be protected against the weaknesses that beset mere theological ogres by the inflexible iron of his economic principles? Who does not recognize, when the words are mentioned, that there is an immediate stiffening against them in the minds of the great mass of his fellow-countrymen, and that, while in France and Scandinavia, and even in parts of the United States, there is, at least, an initial sympathy for the conception, and a disposition to be proud of such economic equality as exists, in England the instinctive feeling is one, not of sympathy, but of apprehension and repulsion, as though economic equality were a matter upon which it were not in good taste to touch? And who does not feel that, as a consequence of this attitude, Englishmen approach the subject with minds that are rarely more than half open? They do not welcome the idea, and then consider whether, and by what means, the difficulties in the way of its realization, which are serious enough, can be overcome. They recite the difficulties with melancholy, and sometimes with exultant satisfaction, because on quite other grounds – grounds of history, and social nervousness, and a traditional belief that advantages which are shared cease to be advantages at all, as though, when everybody is somebody, nobody will be anybody – they are determined to reject the idea.

So, when the question is raised whether some attempt to establish greater economic equality may not be desirable, there is a sound of what Bunyan called 'doleful voices and rushings to and fro'. They rear, and snort, and paw the air, and affirm with one accord that the suggestion is at once wicked and impracticable. Lord Birkenhead, for example, declared that the idea that men are equal is 'a poisonous doctrine', and wrung his hands at the thought of the 'glittering prizes' of life being diminished in value; and Mr Garvin, with his eye for the dangers of the moment, and the temptations to which his fellow-countrymen are most prone to succumb, warns us against the spirit that seeks the dead level and ignores the inequality of human endowments; and Sir Ernest Benn writes that economic equality is 'a scientific impossibility', because Professor Pareto has shown, he says, that 'if the logarithms of income sizes be charted on a horizontal scale, and the logarithms of the number of persons having an income of a particular size or over be charted on a vertical scale, then the resulting observational points will lie approximately along a straight line', and that, if only this were more generally known, the poor, like the wicked, would cease from troubling. A great industrialist, like Sir Herbert Austin, and a distinguished minister of religion, like Dean Inge, rehearse, in their different ways, the same lesson. The former implores us to 'cease teaching that all men are equal and entitled to an equal share of the common wealth', and 'enrich the men who make sacrifices justifying enrichment', and 'leave the others in their contentment, rather than try to mould material that was never intended to withstand the fires of refinement'. The latter complains, in an address at Oxford – with a view, perhaps, to mitigating the class feeling which he rightly deplores – that 'the Government is taking the pick of the working classes and educating them at the expense of the ratepayers to enable them to take the bread out of the mouths of the sons of professional men'. This deplorable procedure, he argues, cannot fail to be injurious to the nation as a whole, since it injures 'the upper middle classes', who are 'the cream of the community'.[1]

When he hears this comminatory chorus directed against the idea of equality by men of such eminence, the first impulse of the layman is to exclaim with Moses, 'Would God that all the Lord's people were prophets!'

1. See Lord Birkenhead, *The Times*, September 30, 1927; November 17, 1928. J. L. Garvin, *Observer*, July 1, 1928. E. J. P. Benn, *The Confessions of a Capitalist*, 1926, pp. 188–9. Sir H. Austin, *Daily Herald*, May 13, 1930. D. Inge, *Evening Standard*, May 8, 1928.

He wishes that he himself, and all his fellow-countrymen, were capable of charting logarithms on horizontal and vertical scales in the manner of Sir Ernest Benn, and of escaping with confidence the dead-level of mediocrity so justly deprecated by Mr Garvin, and of being moved by the righteous indignation which fills Dean Inge when he contemplates those vessels of wrath, the working classes. But he knows, to his dismay, that these gifts have been denied to ordinary men, and that it would, indeed, be a kind of presumption for ordinary men to desire them, for to do so would be to aspire to an impious and unattainable equality with their betters. So he is bewildered and confounded by the perversity of the universe; he is oppressed by the weight of all this unintelligible world. If only the mass of mankind were more intelligent, they would realize how unintelligent their pretensions are. But they are condemned, it seems, to be unaware of their inferiority by the very fact of their inferiority itself.

When an argument leads to an *impasse*, it is advisable to re-examine the premises from which it started. It is possible that the dilemma is not, after all, quite so hopeless as at first sight it appears to be. Rightly understood, Pareto's law is a suggestive generalization; and the biological differences between different individuals are a phenomenon of great interest and significance, and Dean Inge is, doubtless, more than justified in thinking that the working classes, like all other classes, are no better than they should be, and in telling them so with the apostolic fervour which he so abundantly commands. It is the natural disposition of clever and learned people to attack the difficult and recondite aspects of topics which are under discussion, because to such people the other aspects seem too obvious and elementary to deserve attention. The more difficult aspects of human relations, however, though doubtless the most interesting to nimble minds, are not always the most important. There are other ways than that of the eagle in the air and the serpent on the rock, which baffled the author of the Book of Proverbs. There are other sides of the truth about mankind and its behaviour than those which are revealed by biological investigation, or expressed in the logarithms which delight the leisure of Sir Ernest Benn.

It is these simpler and more elementary considerations that have been in the minds of those who have thought that a society was most likely to enjoy happiness and goodwill, and to turn both its human and material resources to the best account, if it cultivated as far as possible an equalitarian temper, and sought by its institutions to increase equality. It is obvious, indeed, that, as things are today, no redistribution of wealth would bring general affluence, and that statisticians are within their rights in making merry with the idea that the equalization of incomes would make everyone rich. But, though riches are a good, they are not, nevertheless, the only good; and because greater production, which is concerned with the commodities to be consumed, is clearly important, it does not follow that greater equality, which is concerned with the relations between the human beings who consume them, is not important also. It is obvious, again, that the word 'Equality' possesses more than one meaning, and that the controversies surrounding it arise partly, at least, because the same term is employed with different connotations. Thus it may either purport to state a fact, or convey the expression of an ethical judgment. On the one hand, it may affirm that men are, on the whole, very similar in their natural endowments of character and intelligence. On the other hand, it may assert that, while they differ profoundly as individuals in capacity and character, they are equally entitled as human beings to consideration and respect, and that the well-being of a society is likely to be increased if it so plans its organization that, whether their powers are great or small, all its members may be equally enabled to make the best of such powers as they possess.

If made in the first sense, the assertion of human equality is clearly untenable. It is a piece of mythology against which irresistible evidence has been accumulated by biologists and psychologists. In the light of the data presented – to mention only two recent examples – in such works as Dr Burt's admirable studies of the distribution of educational abilities among schoolchildren, or the Report of the Mental Deficiency Committee (Burt, 1917; HMSO, 1929), the fact that, quite apart from differences of environment and opportunity, individuals differ widely in their natural endowments, and in their capacity to develop them by education, is not open to question. There is some reason for holding, for instance, that, while 80 per cent of children at the age of ten fall within a range of about three mental years, the most backward may have a mental age of five, while the most gifted may have one of as much as fifteen.

The acceptance of that conclusion, nevertheless, makes a smaller breach in equalitarian doctrines than is sometimes supposed, for such doctrines have rarely been based on a denial of it. It is true, of course, that the psychological and political theory of the age between 1750 and 1850 – the theory, for example, of thinkers so different as Helvétius and Adam Smith at the beginning of the period, and Mill and Proudhon at the end of it – greatly underestimated the significance of inherited qualities, and greatly overestimated the plasticity of human nature. It may be doubted, however, whether it was quite that order of ideas which inspired the historical affirmations of human equality, even in the age when such ideas were still in fashion.

It is difficult for even the most sanguine of assemblies to retain for more than one meeting the belief that Providence has bestowed an equal measure of intelligence upon all its members. When the Americans declared it to be a self-evident truth that all men are created equal, they were thinking less of the admirable racial qualities of the inhabitants of the New World than of their political and economic relations with the Old, and would have remained unconvinced that those relations should continue even in the face of proofs of biological inferiority. When the French, who a century and a half ago preached the equalitarian idea with the same fervent conviction as is shown today by the rulers of Russia in denouncing it, set that idea side by side with liberty and fraternity as the motto of a new world, they did not mean that all men are equally intelligent or equally virtuous, any more than that they are equally tall or equally fat, but that the unity of their national life should no longer be torn to pieces by obsolete property rights and meaningless juristic distinctions. When Arnold, who was an inspector of schools as well as a poet, and who, whatever his failings, was not prone to demagogy, wrote 'choose equality', he did not suggest, it may be suspected, that all children appeared to him to be equally clever, but that a nation acts unwisely in stressing heavily distinctions based on birth or money.

Few men have been more acutely sensitive than Mill to the importance of encouraging the widest possible diversities of mind and taste. In arguing that 'the best state for human nature is that in which, while no one is poor, no one desires to be richer', and urging that social policy should be directed to increasing equality, he did not intend to convey that it should suppress varieties of individual genius and character, but that it was only in a society marked by a large measure of economic equality that such varieties were likely to find their full expression and due need of appreciation (Mill, 1865, book 4, ch. 6; 1909, p. 133). Theologians have not, as a rule, been disposed to ignore the fact that there are diversities of gifts and degree above degree. When they tell us that all men are equal in the eyes of God, what they mean, it is to be presumed, is what Jeremy Taylor meant, when he wrote, in a book today too little read, that 'if a man be exalted by reason of any excellence in his soul, he may please to remember that all souls are equal, and their differing operations are because their instrument is in better tune, their body is more healthful or better tempered; which is no more praise to him than it is that he was born in Italy'. It is the truth expressed in the parable of the prodigal son – the truth that it is absurd and degrading for men to make much of their intellectual and moral superiority to each other, and still more of their superiority in the arts which bring wealth and power, because, judged by their place in any universal scheme, they are all infinitely great or infinitely small. And, when observers from the Dominions, or from foreign countries, are struck by inequality as one of the special and outstanding characteristics of English social life, they do not mean that in other countries differences of personal quality are less important than in England. They mean, on the contrary, that they are more important, and that in England they tend to be obscured or obliterated behind differences of property and income, and the whole elaborate façade of a society that, compared with their own, seems stratified and hierarchical.

The equality which all these thinkers emphasize as desirable is not equality of capacity or attainment, but of circumstances, institutions and manner of life. The inequality which they deplore is not inequality of personal gifts, but of the social and economic environment. They are concerned, not with a biological phenomenon, but with a spiritual relation and the conduct to be based on it. Their view, in short, is that, because men are men, social institutions – property rights, and the organization of industry, and the system of public health and education – should be planned, as far as is possible, to emphasize and strengthen, not the class differences which divide, but the common humanity which unites them.

Such a view of the life which is proper to human beings may, of course, be criticized, as it often has been. But to suppose that it can be criticized effectively by pointing to the width of the intellectual and moral differences which distinguish individuals from each other is a solecism, an *ignoratio elenchi*. It is true, of course, that such differences are important, and that the advance of psychology has enabled them to be measured with a new precision, with results which are valuable in making possible both a closer adaptation of educational methods to individual needs and a more intelligent selection of varying aptitudes for different tasks. But to recognize a specific difference is one thing; to pass a general judgment of superiority or inferiority, still more to favour the first and neglect the second, is quite another.[2] The nightingale, it has been remarked, was placed in the fourth class at the fowl show. Which of a number of varying individuals is to be judged superior to the rest depends upon the criterion which is applied, and the criterion is a matter of ethical judgment. That judgment will, if it is prudent, be tentative and provisional, since men's estimates of the relative desirability of initiative, decision, common sense, imagination, humility and sympathy appear, unfortunately, to differ, and the failures and fools – the Socrates and St Francis – of one age are the sages and saints of another. Society would not be the worse, perhaps, if idiots like Dostoevsky's were somewhat less uncommon, and the condemnation passed on those who offend one of these little ones was not limited to offenders against children whose mental ratio is in excess of eighty-five.

It is true, again, that human beings have, except as regards certain elementary, though still sadly neglected, matters of health and development,

2. See the *Report of Consultative Committee of Board of Education on Psychological Tests of Educable Capacity*, 1924, p. 71: 'All our witnesses are agreed that intelligence does not cover temperament or character, and that, therefore, the important personal qualities of will, feeling and emotion are not dealt with by tests of intelligence.'

different requirements, and that these different requirements can be met satisfactorily only by varying forms of provision. But equality of provision is not identity of provision. It is to be achieved, not by treating different needs in the same way, but by devoting equal care to ensuring that they are met in the different ways most appropriate to them, as is done by a doctor who prescribes different regimens for different constitutions, or a teacher who develops different types of intelligence by different curricula. The more anxiously, indeed, a society endeavours to secure equality of consideration for all its members, the greater will be the differentiation of treatment which, when once their common human needs have been met, it accords to the special needs of different groups and individuals among them.

It is true, finally, that some men are inferior to others in respect of their intellectual endowments, and it is possible – though the truth of the possibility has not yet been satisfactorily established – that the same is true of certain classes (Ginsberg, 1930, pp. 47–54). It does not, however, follow from this fact that such individuals or classes should receive less consideration than others, or should be treated as inferior in respect of such matters as legal status, or health, or economic arrangements, which are within the control of the community.

It may, of course, be deemed expedient so to treat them. It may be thought advisable, as Aristotle argued, to maintain the institution of slavery on the ground that some men are fit only to be living tools; or, as was customary in a comparatively recent past, to apply to the insane a severity not used towards the sane; or, as is sometimes urged today, to spend less liberally on the education of the slow than on that of the intelligent; or, in accordance with the practice of all ages, to show less respect for the poor than for the rich. But, in order to establish an inference, a major premise is necessary as well as a minor; and, if such discrimination on the part of society is desirable, its desirability must be shown by some other argument than the fact of inequality of intelligence and character. To convert a phenomenon, however interesting, into a principle, however respectable, is an error of logic. It is the confusion of a judgment of fact with a judgment of value – a confusion like that which was satirized by Montesquieu when he wrote, in his ironical defence of slavery:

The creatures in question are black from head to foot, and their noses are so flat that it is almost impossible to pity them. It is not to be supposed that God, an all-wise Being, can have lodged a soul – still less a good soul – in a body completely black.

Everyone recognizes the absurdity of such an argument when it is applied to matters within his personal knowledge and professional competence.

Everyone realizes that, in order to justify inequalities of circumstances or opportunity by reference to differences of personal quality, it is necessary, as Professor Ginsberg observes, to show that the differences in question are relevant to the inequalities (1926, p. 14). Everyone now sees, for example, that it is not a valid argument against women's suffrage to urge, as used to be urged not so long ago, that women are physically weaker than men, since physical strength is not relevant to the question of the ability to exercise the franchise, or a valid argument in favour of slavery that some men are less intelligent than others, since it is not certain that slavery is the most suitable penalty for lack of intelligence.

Not everyone, however, is so quick to detect the fallacy when it is expressed in general terms. It is still possible, for example, for one eminent statesman to ridicule the demand for a diminution of economic inequalities on the ground that every mother knows that her children are not equal, without reflecting whether it is the habit of mothers to lavish care on the strong and neglect the delicate; and for another to dismiss the suggestion that greater economic equality is desirable, for the reason, apparently, that men are naturally unequal. It is probable, however, that the first does not think that the fact that some children are born with good digestions, and others with bad, is a reason for supplying good food to the former and bad food to the latter, rather than for giving to both food which is equal in quality but different in kind, and that the second does not suppose that natural inequality of men makes legal equality a contemptible principle. On the contrary, when ministers of the Crown responsible for the administration of justice to the nation, they both took for granted the desirability and existence at any rate on paper of legal equality. Yet in the eighteenth century statesmen of equal eminence in France and Germany and in the nineteenth century influential thinkers in Russia and the United States, and, indeed, the ruling classes of Europe almost everywhere at a not very distant period, all were disposed to think that, since men are naturally unequal, the admission of a general equality of legal status would be the end of civilization.

Our modern statesmen do not agree with that view, for, thanks to the struggles of the past, they have inherited a tradition of legal equality, and, fortified by that tradition, they see that the fact that men are naturally unequal is not relevant to the question whether they should or should not be treated as equal before the law. But they have not inherited a tradition of economic equality, for that tradition has still to be created. Hence they do not see that the existence of differences of personal capacity and attainment is as irrelevant to the question whether it is desirable that the social environment and economic organization should be made more conducive to equality as it is to the question of equality before the law, which itself, as we have said, seemed just as monstrous a doctrine to conservative thinkers in the past as the suggestion of greater economic equality seems to them today.

And Sir Ernest Benn, who says that economic equality is a scientific impossibility, is quite unconscious, apparently, of the ambiguities of his doctrine. He ignores the obvious fact that, in some economic matters of the first importance – protection by the police against violence and theft, and the use of the roads, and the supply of water, and the provision of sewers, and access to a minimum of education and medical attendance, all of which were once dependent on the ability of individuals to pay for them – all members of civilized communities are now secured equality irrespective of their personal attainments and individual economic resources. He fails to see that the only question is whether that movement shall be carried forward, or rather, since in fact it is carried forward year by year, how quickly society will decide to establish complete environmental equality in respect of the external conditions of health, education and economic security. So he behaves like the countryman who, on being for the first time introduced to a giraffe at a circus, exclaimed indignantly, 'There ain't no such animal'. He says that equality is a scientific impossibility, and draws a sharp line between the natural and, as he thinks, the healthy state of things, under which each individual provides all his requirements for himself, and the unnatural and morbid condition, under which the community, consisting of himself and his fellows, provides some of them for him.

Such a line, however, is quite arbitrary, quite fanciful and artificial. Many services are supplied by collective effort today which in the recent past were supplied by individual effort or not supplied at all, and many more, it may be suspected, will be so supplied in the future. At any moment there are some needs which almost everyone is agreed should be satisfied on equalitarian principles, and others which they are agreed should be met by individuals who purchase what their incomes enable them to pay for, and others, again, about the most suitable provision for which opinions differ. Society has not been prevented from seeking to establish equality in respect for the first by the fear that in so doing it may be perpetrating a scientific impossibility. Nor ought it to be prevented from moving towards equality in respect of the second and third, if experience suggests that greater equality in these matters also would contribute to greater efficiency and to more general happiness.

'But', it will be said, 'you are forgetting Pareto's law, and the logarithms and the observational points. These are hard realities. No ingenious sophistry will enable you to make light of *them*'. It is wrong, as we all know, to speak disrespectfully of the equator; and if the equator, which is a simple idea, deserves to be approached in a spirit of deference, how much more is such deference incumbent on those who venture within the awful ambit of economic law? There is, however, as St Paul says, one glory of the sun and another glory of the moon; there are powers celestial and powers terrestrial; there are laws and laws. There are scientific laws which state the invariable relations between phenomena, and there are juristic laws which state how men should conduct themselves, and there are laws which are neither juristic nor, in the full sense, scientific, though they belong, no doubt, to the same category as the latter. Such laws neither state invariable relations nor prescribe conduct, but describe how, on the whole, under given historical and legal conditions, and when influenced by particular conventions and ideas, particular groups of men do, as a rule, tend to behave.

It is evident that, as economists have often reminded us, many economic laws are of the third class, not of the first or second. They indicate the manner in which, given certain historical conditions, and a certain form of social organization, and certain juristic institutions, production tends to be conducted and wealth to be distributed. They are not the less instructive and useful on that account, to those, at least, who know how to interpret them. But those who, though successful and rich, are not fully alive to the pitfalls which yawn for the unwary, and who are delighted when they hear of a law which jumps, as it seems to them, with their own instinctive preference for success and riches, sometimes find in economic laws a source of intellectual confusion, which it is distressing to all persons of humanity, and in particular, it may be suspected, to economists to contemplate. They snatch at elaborate formulae in order to demonstrate that the particular social arrangements that they have been accustomed to admire are the product of uncontrollable forces, with which society can tamper only at its peril. They run to the fashionable nostrum of the moment, in order to shuffle off their responsibilities upon some economic automaton. Like a drunkard who pleads an alcoholic diathesis as an excuse for drinking, they appeal to economic laws, the majority of which are merely a description of the manner in which, in a certain environment and in given circumstances, men tend to behave, as a proof that it is impossible for them to alter their behaviour.

How men in given circumstances tend to behave, and how, as a consequence, wealth tends in such circumstances to be distributed, are subjects about which valuable and illuminating, if necessarily tentative, generalizations have been produced by economists. But their behaviour, as economists have often told us, is relative to their circumstances; and the distribution of wealth depends, not wholly, indeed, but largely, on their institutions; and the character of their institutions is determined, not by immutable economic laws, but by the values, preferences, interests and ideals which rule at any moment in a given society.

These values and preferences are not something fixed and unalterable. On the contrary, they have changed repeatedly in the past, and are changing today; and the distribution of wealth has changed, and is changing with them. It was of one kind in France and of the old régime, where a large part of the wealth produced was absorbed by the privileged orders, and quite another in France after the Revolution, where wealth previously paid in taxation and feudal dues was retained by the peasantry. It is of one kind in Denmark today and of another kind in England. Thanks largely to changes in fiscal policy and to the development of the social services, which Sir Ernest Benn finds so distasteful, it is different in the England of 1937 from what it was in the England of 1857, and, if experience may be trusted, it will be different again in the England of 1957. To suppose, as he supposes, that it must necessarily be wrong to aim at greater economic equality, because Pareto suggested that, under certain conditions, and leaving the effects of inheritance, fiscal policy and social services out of account, the curve of distribution in several different countries and ages tended, as he thought, to conform to a certain shape, is a pardonable error, but an error none the less. It implies a misunderstanding of the nature of economic laws in general, and of Pareto's laws in particular, at which no one, it is probable, would have been more amused than Pareto himself, and which, indeed, he expressly repudiated in a subsequent work (see Pigou, 1929, 645–53). It is to believe in economic Fundamentalism, with the New Testament left out, and the Books of Leviticus and Deuteronomy inflated to unconscionable proportions by the addition of new and appalling chapters. It is to dance naked, and roll on the ground, and cut oneself with knives, in honour of the mysteries of Mumbo-Jumbo.

Mumbo-Jumbo is a great god, who, if he is given his head, is disposed to claim, not only economics, but the whole world as his kingdom, and who is subtle enough to deceive even the elect; so that Sir Ernest Benn is to be pitied, rather than blamed, for yielding to his seductions, and for feeling the same kind of reverence for Mumbo-Jumboism as was inspired in Kant by the spectacle of the starry heavens and by the moral law. But the power of Mumbo-Jumbo, like that of some other spirits, depends on the presence of an initial will to believe in the minds of his votaries, and can, if only they are not terrified when he sends forth his thunders and his lightnings – the hail of his logarithms and the whirlwind of his economic laws – be overcome. If, when he tells them that a certain course will result in the heavens falling, they summon up the resolution to pursue it all the same, they will find that, in a surprising number of cases, though they may have succeeded in improving the earth, the heavens, nevertheless, remain much where they were. And, when his prophets are so much alarmed by the symptoms of increasing equality, and by the demand for its still further increase, that they declare that equality is a scientific impossibility, they ought not, indeed, to be treated unkindly, or hewn in pieces before the Lord, like the prophets of an earlier Mumbo-Jumbo; but they should be asked to undergo, for the sake both of themselves and of their neighbours, what to nimble minds, with a gift for quick and sweeping generalization, is sometimes a hardly less painful discipline. They should be asked to study the facts. The facts, they will find, show that the distribution of wealth in a community depends partly, at least, upon its organization and institutions – its system of property rights, its economic structure, its social and financial policy – and that it is possible for it to give these matters a bias either towards greater equality or towards greater inequality, because different communities, at different times, have done, in fact, both the one and the other.

Perhaps, therefore, the remote Victorian thinkers, like Arnold and Mill, who dealt lightly with Mumbo-Jumbo, and who commended equality to their fellow-countrymen as one source of peace and happiness, were not speaking so unadvisedly as at first sight might appear. They did not deny that men have unequal gifts, or suggest that all of them are capable of earning, as the author of *The Confessions of a Capitalist* tells us that he earns, £10,000 a year, or of making a brilliant show when their natural endowments are rigorously sifted and appraised with exactitude. What they were concerned to emphasize is something more elementary and commonplace. It is the fact that, in spite of their varying characters and capacities, men possess in their common humanity a quality which is worth cultivating, and that a community is most likely to make the most of that quality if it takes it into account in planning its economic organization and social institutions – if it stresses lightly differences of wealth and birth and social position, and establishes on firm foundations institutions which meet common needs, and are a source of common enlightenment and common enjoyment. The individual differences of which so much is made, they would have said, will always survive, and they are to be welcomed, not regretted. But their existence is no reason for not seeking to establish the largest possible measure of equality of environment, circumstance and opportunity. On the contrary, it is a reason for redoubling our efforts to establish it, in order to ensure that these diversities of gifts may come to fruition.

It is true, indeed, that even such equality, though the conditions on which it depends are largely within human control, will continue to elude us. The important thing, however, is not that it should be completely attained, but that it should be sincerely sought. What matters to the health of society is the objective towards which its face is set, and to suggest that it is immaterial in which direction it moves, because, whatever the direction, the goal must always elude it, is not scientific, but irrational. It is like using the impossibility of absolute cleanliness as a pretext for rolling in a manure heap, or denying the importance of honesty because no one can be wholly honest.

It may well be the case that capricious inequalities are in some measure inevitable, in the sense that, like crime and disease, they are a malady which the most rigorous precautions cannot wholly overcome. But, when crime is known as crime, and disease as disease, the ravages of both are circumscribed by the mere fact that they are recognized for what they are, and described by their proper names, not by flattering euphemisms. And a society which is convinced that inequality is an evil need not be alarmed because the evil is one which cannot wholly be subdued. In recognizing the poison it will have armed itself with an antidote. It will have deprived inequality of its sting by stripping it of its esteem.

References

ARNOLD, M. (1903), 'Equality', in *Mixed Essays*, Murray.

BAGEHOT, W. (1867), *The English Constitution*, Chapman & Hall.

BURT, C. (1917), *The Distribution and Relations of Educational Abilities*, LCC.

DE MAN, H. (1927), *Au Delà du Marxisme*, p. 89.

ERSKINE MAY (1877), *Democracy in Europe*, Longmanns Green & Co.

GINSBERG, M. (1926), 'The problem of colour in relation to the idea of equality', *J. of Phil. Studs.*, supp. to vol. 1, p. 14.

GINSBERG, M. (1930), 'The inheritance of mental characters', *The Rationalist Ann.*, pp. 47–54.

HMSO (1929), *Report of the Mental Deficiency Committee*, HMSO.

LECKY, W. E. H. (1899), *Democracy and Liberty*, Longman.

MILL, J. S. (1865), *Principles of Political Economy*, Reader & Dyer.

MILL, J. S. (1909), *Autobiography*, Longman.

PARRY, E., Sir (1914), *The Law and the Poor*, Smith, Elder & Co.

PIGOU, A. C. (1929), *Economics of Welfare*, Macmillan.

TAINE, H. A. (1863), *Histoire de la Littérature Anglaise*, Hachette.

TAINE, H. A. (1872), *Notes sur l'Angleterre*, Hachette

THRING, E. (1864), *Education and School*, Macmillan.

2 J. N. Morgan

Measuring the Economic Status of the Aged

J. N. Morgan, 'Measuring the economic status of the aged', *International Economic Review*, vol. 6, 1965, pp. 1–12.

Over the years those interested in quantitative assessment of the economic status of the aged, or of any other groups in society, have been concerned about the problems of measurement. A variety of improved measures has been tried, and here and there comparisons made between the results of different methods. I should like to report some of our work at the Survey Research Center in developing better measures and then to point out remaining inadequacies and problems yet to be tackled.

Epstein in her excellent paper before the Fifth Congress of Gerontology pointed out clearly the need for attention to the unit of analysis and to the measure or measures of economic status (Epstein, 1960; see also Fisher, 1963, pp. 103–13). One can summarize her suggestions, and what we have tried to do with our own data, as follows:

1. Look at distributions rather than means or aggregates.
2. Use a proper unit, small enough so that poverty cannot be hidden by units living together.
3. Develop a better measure of income or resources.
4. Relate that income to a budget standard that takes account of differing family size, structure and basic needs.
5. Take some account of non-current resources such as assets, insurance, potential help from relatives and other rights.

In summarizing our own work, we shall concentrate not only on presenting some improved estimates but also on providing some evidence as to what difference the improvements really made in the data for the United States.

Averages versus distribution

Averages tend to be deceptive, particularly when the underlying distributions are skewed, as in the case of income. More than half the people are below the average (mean). What is more important, this skewness in the distribution is substantially greater among the aged in the United States. This is true of incomes and still more of assets. The spending units headed by someone aged 65 or older have higher average liquid assets than other age groups, but a larger proportion of them also have few or no liquid assets. Even when one looks at a broader measure of net worth, the aged have medians only slightly less than those in the age group 45–64, but more of them (23 per cent) have less than $1000 (Katona, Lininger and Kosobud, 1963, p. 129).

A summary measure of inequality is the Gini index (or Lorenz coefficient), which varies from 1.0 if one unit has all the income to 0.0 if each unit has the same income as every other one. For a national cross section of spending units in the United States, if we use only the wage income of the head, this index is 0.48 for the whole population and 0.86 for units headed by someone 65 or older. For total spending unit incomes the coefficients are 0.41 for all units and 0.52 for units headed by someone 65 or older. These are extremely large differences, since the index is quite stable under many other kinds of changes (Morgan, 1962, p. 273).

If we take a more inclusive income measure, gross disposable income and a more basic unit, each adult couple or unmarried individual, the coefficients range between 0.30 and 0.39 for units under 65 compared with 0.47 for units headed by people 65 or older.

In addition, there are two major subgroups among the aged, single females and all other units. Steiner and Dorfman pointed out some years ago that it was the old women who were usually in the most difficult economic circumstances (Steiner and Dorfman, 1957). Our own data for 1959 incomes indicate that in the United States 35 per cent of adult units headed by males 65 or older had total money incomes of $3000 or more, and only 5 per cent of the units headed by women 65 or older had incomes of $3000 or more.

These comments on the need for distributional data may seem obvious, were it not that a substantial fraction of the numbers quoted in the United States to prove that old people are not so badly off as to need medical care coverage included in their retirement benefits under social security, rely upon averages. While levels of income vary between countries, the same patterns of inequality may well exist in other countries.

The unit of analysis

We have already used one or more units of analysis in discussing the need for distributions. We shall have to employ several different measures of income in discussing the impact of different units of analysis.

The way to approach the problem of the best unit of analysis is to assume that one wants to make comparisons either over long periods of time or between countries with wide differences in living patterns. In this case, it becomes obvious that there is a major problem with family obligations, particularly when they involve people other than husband, wife and minor children living in the same housing unit. If one used the family (all related people living in the same dwelling unit), then families classified according to the age of the head would not include in the '65 or over' category families providing a home for impoverished parents. Even if an ingenious computer managed to separate all families containing anyone 65 or older, the poverty of the parents would be hidden in the combined family income.

Since families can combine and separate over time, and since there are wide differences between countries in the extent to which each adult or adult couple has its own dwelling unit, estimates on a family basis are unstable and inadequate. In the United States, the extent of doubling up has been decreasing steadily and is relatively small. About 17 per cent of adults or adult couples (nuclear families) live in a relative's home; about a third of these are separate spending units with their own finances and are tabulated separately in most of the Survey Research Center's economic studies. A substantial number of those who live in a relative's home are children aged 18 or older who have not yet left the parental home, an obviously temporary situation of convenience and one likely to be affected by changes in housing costs, employment conditions for young people and the like. (Nearly six tenths of adult units living in relatives' homes are headed by someone under 35 and less than one fifth of them are headed by someone 65 or older.)

Popular attitudes in the United States are overwhelmingly opposed to older people living with their children. The heads of 3000 spending units were asked in early 1960:

Some people move in with their children. Others try to keep a separate household, even if it means pinching pennies. Do you think that it is a good idea or a bad idea for older people to live with their children? Why is that?

Six in ten were unqualified in their opposition, and fewer than one in ten clearly in favor. The opposition was even stronger among heads who were already retired (Morgan *et al.*, 1962, p. 160; Shanas, 1961).

While people do not like to live with relatives, they still have a sense of family responsibility, a feeling which is reinforced by varying state laws in the United States as to the responsibility of relatives. The same sample was asked in 1960:

If the older people don't have enough money, do you think their relatives should support them, or should the government take care of them, or what? Why do you say so?

A majority said the relatives should have the responsibility.

Given some differences over time and between countries both in these attitudes, and in the actual amount of aid to relatives, we must decide upon some systematic treatment. Since the vast bulk of aid to relatives, at least in the United States, takes the form of providing housing (and other things simultaneously), there appears a strong argument for separating related adults or adult couples into more basic adult units or nuclear families and estimating the amount of free housing and other help provided in each case.

Why should we not go further and use the adult individual as the unit? The answer is that husbands and wives form a close economic union, and that we are unable to measure the real income produced by housework. Hence, distributions of individuals, in which wives on the whole show up with no income, are misleading and inappropriate. One could, of course, make distributions of total adult unit income per capita, using individuals as units. This would mean splitting the unit's income evenly between husband and wife. Once one goes from the individual to the adult unit or nuclear family, it becomes difficult to define '65 or older', since husband or wife or both may be 65 or older. Even this, however, is much less serious for the nuclear family, given the high correlation between the ages of husband and wife and the tendency for the husband to be the older of the two, than when a more extended family definition is used, and any one of several adults may be 65 or older.

The effects of living with relatives on income estimates for the United States can be summarized by giving two mean income figures: the mean income of the adult unit including transfers, (free rent, etc.) and the family income, using in both cases an inclusive income measure defined in the next section. Table 1 shows that even the mean 'incomes' of the very young and very old are substantial if one counts the total income of the extended family with which they live, whereas the actual income of the adult units at extreme ages is much smaller, even when one includes non-money incomes and the value of the free rent and food received by those who live with relatives.

The unit of analysis is the adult unit, but in column three it is the total gross disposable income of the family in which the unit lives which is counted. Hence, a family with three adult units has its family income counted three times in that column, and items in the column should not be used to estimate aggregates. Gross disposable income includes non-money incomes: imputed rent on net equity in a home, value of free rent or housing and food provided by relatives, money saved by own home repairs and food grown, plus money incomes minus estimated federal income taxes. For adult units the free housing and food received while living with relatives is included; for families, such intrafamily transfers are, of course, omitted.

Another way to look at the importance of the unit is to go all the way to the ultimate measure, that is, the ratio of the most inclusive income defini-

Table 1 Mean gross disposable income by age of adult unit head in the United States, 1959

Age of adult unit heads	Percentage of all adult units	Adult unit gross disposable income* $	Family gross disposable income $	Percentage of adult units who live in a relative's home
18–24	12	2602	6315	61
25–34	19	5562	6485	14
35–44	21	6441	6998	6
45–54	18	5977	6794	6
55–64	14	5306	6445	8
65–74	10	3452	4711	16
75 and older	6	1935	3731	29
Total	100			

* Gross disposable income includes the value of food and housing received by those living in a relative's home.
Sample size: 3396 adult units.
Source: Morgan *et al.*, Table 14–30, p. 177, and Table 14–6, p. 164. See also Morgan and David (1961, appendix 4, pp. 188–99); also Morgan and David (1962).

tion to a budget standard defined below. Here we find that when we use the more basic adult unit some 28 per cent of the population and 48 per cent of the aged are below 85 per cent of the standard budget. If we use families and family income and budget needs, only 20 per cent of the population and 39 per cent of the aged have gross disposable incomes less than 0·85 of the standard budget. The differences measure the extent to which poverty (remaining even after family aid) is hidden by looking only at family incomes when units live together.

The use of the adult unit or nuclear family requires estimates of intra-family transfers between units living together. It does not entirely eliminate the problem of defining '65 or older', nor that of taking account of differences in the number of people, their sex and age. Yet it appears a more basic unit, more appropriate for comparisons over time when undoubling is going on, or between countries with different patterns of housing and family life. It is doubtful that two women happily occupy the same kitchen in very many cultures, and in any case it is better to use a unit that brings intrafamily aid out where one can see it. It is clear that a sufficiently extensive system of extended family responsibility might hide almost all poverty, even if it produced all sorts of inequities and disincentives at the same time.

The measure of economic status

While there may be impoverished old people who live with relatives and are thus hidden in family income distributions, there may also be ways in which the economic resources of older units are understated. They have lower taxes, paid-for homes in which they live rent-free, smaller families and lower food and clothing requirements. The last two of these we shall leave until the next section on budget standards. The other two raise questions of the measure of income or resources.

Among the sources of financial strength in addition to money income are some which can be estimated, and which vary greatly from one unit to another. They were, therefore, included in our definitions of gross disposable income.

We asked people how much they saved growing their own food or repairing their own homes. Note that the question asked not how much the food or repair would have cost otherwise, but how much they thought they saved. The amounts were generally small, but in other countries they might be quite large. This was combined with other earnings of head and wife and children and the estimated wage component of business or farm income (total minus 6 per cent return on capital) to get 'real earnings'.

To this we added income from capital, including 6 per cent on investments in a home, farm, or business, to get gross factor income of the unit. We then added money and non-money transfers: pensions, annuities, unemployment compensation, free rent and food less any payments made in return, large gifts of food, clothing or money from relatives or institutions, free medical care, free child care.

Deducting estimated federal income taxes from this cumulative total gave us our most inclusive income estimate: gross disposable income. Some of its components are subject to reporting errors and estimating errors, but most of those components are small.

It may be instructive to note what components of a theoretically complete definition of income were not included even in this measure. Capital gains were not included, since they are for the most part not realized, difficult to estimate and of doubtful total importance. There may also be previous capital gains on the same asset sufficiently large so that the potential capital gains taxes inhibit realization of the gain. The real income created and consumed immediately in the form of housework and child care was omitted because it is difficult to estimate and may not vary much from one unit to another, at least among the aged. Finally, the amount of leisure time left after earning the money and real income and doing the housework and child care was not included, even though it may vary greatly from person to person. One reason is that some differences in leisure are involuntary and unwanted, because the individual is unemployed, or disabled, or too old to work. Moreover, not only do some people enjoy their work and others hate leisure, but it is not clear how one would evaluate leisure time in dollars even if it were measured in hours.

International comparisons might well be distorted, however, by failure to take account of differences in leisure time. According to traditional marginalist economic theory, the marginal utility of leisure, where it is voluntary, must be equal to the marginal rewards from extra work, where such extra work is available. Intramarginal units of leisure would presumably be worth more, producing a kind of consumers' surplus. Hence, one estimate could be made by valuing a man's leisure at his average wage rate. How then does one compare units with and without a wife, and with and without children? In any case, the probability that leisure is excessive becomes so great for older people as to make the exercise in estimation unprofitable, and we did not attempt it.

The mean incomes, as one moves to a more and more inclusive income measure, for each age group in the United States are given in Table 2. We used means for simplicity, in spite of our own warnings about the need for distributions. The importance of transfers and non-money income for the aged are obvious in the differences between gross disposable income and gross factor income. Again, it is necessary to keep in mind that the distribution of income is much more unequal among the aged, so that the proportions below some levels are higher than the means would indicate. Those proportions are less exaggerated than they are with younger people, since the incomes of the aged are more stable over time. The proportion of

Table 2 **Cumulative adult unit income components by age of adult unit head in the United States, 1959**

Age of unit head	Percentage of all units	Average wage income of unit head $	Average real earnings of unit[a] $	Average gross factor income of unit[b] $	Average gross disposable income of unit[c] $	Average value of welfare ratio of unit[d] %
18–24	13	1939	2294	2326	2602	100
25–34	19	4457	5677	5915	5562	150
35–44	20	4836	6336	6967	6441	160
45–54	18	4357	5862	6741	5977	170
55–64	14	3669	4826	5891	5306	180
65–74	10	983	1472	2524	3452	140
75 and older	6	141	271	868	1935	90
All adult units	100	3486	4560	6258	4986	150

Sample size: 3396 adult units.

[a] Includes money earnings of wife and children, wage component of business or farm income, money saved by home repair or production of own food.

[b] Includes income from capital, including own home, farm, or business.

[c] Includes transfer income, money and non-money, contributory and non-contributory, minus Federal income taxes.

[d] Adult unit gross disposable income as a per cent of the budget requirement.

any 'low income' group who might expect to remain in that income bracket in the future is much larger among older people. Estimates of the number of low income units among younger groups are thus exaggerated more by the inclusion of temporarily low incomes.

It is clear then that both the unit of analysis and the measure of income are important. The measure itself may seem to involve the unit, where we use the family income relative to family needs even when looking at adult units. On the other hand, the unit may seem to involve a measure, when we use adult individuals as the unit but distribute them according to the income, assets, or insurance of a whole unit.

When measures of inequality are computed for a whole national cross-section, the move from the larger family unit to the basic adult unit or nuclear family leads to *increased* inequality, but the change from narrower definitions of income to the more inclusive gross disposable income leads to *decreased* inequality estimates. Adjustment for needs leads to a welfare ratio which, if treated as a number, gives still lower inequality estimates because so many low income units contain only one or two persons (Morgan *et al.*, 1962, p. 315; Ferge, 1962). Similar analyses should be made for other countries.

Income relative to budget estimate of needs: adjustment for family composition

Gross disposable income may be about as good an estimate of income as we can make; but it has meaning only against some standard, and clearly that standard should be different for adult units of different sizes. It is

Table 3 **Distribution of adult unit welfare ratios by age of adult unit head in the United States, 1959**

Adult unit welfare ratio (gross disposable income as of budget standard)	Age of adult unit head							
	18–24	25–34	35–44	45–54	55–64	65–74	75 and older	All
0–44	22	8	6	10	19	12	18	11
45–64	14	5	5	7	9	13	28	9
65–84	11	5	7	7	6	13	11	8
85–104	11	11	8	7	10	10	9	9
105–124	9	11	10	9	7	9	9	9
125–154	13	16	18	13	9	8	12	14
155–204	13	24	20	19	18	15	7	18
205 and over	7	20	26	28	32	20	6	22
Total	100%	100%	100%	100%	100%	100%	100%	100%
Per cent of sample	12	19	21	18	14	10	6	100

Sample size: 3396 adult units.
Source: Morgan *et al.* (1962).

frequently argued that we exaggerate the problems of older units, since the units are generally smaller and their needs fewer.

A wide variety of equivalent adult scales have been developed. The detailed precision of such scales or budgets is much less important if one provides distributional data on the ratio of actual individual incomes to the budget standard. This avoids the necessity of defining 'poverty' or setting an absolute standard in a world where such standards properly increase over time with the increase in general living standards and vary from country to country.

It is mainly important that such a needs budget take account of the employment status of head and wife, of the ages of children and of some economies of scale in housing costs. Indeed, once we take account of the composition of the unit, then the problem of whether to use adult unit, spending unit, or family becomes less serious. We used a budget adapted from the Community Council of Greater New York's Budget Standard Service and computed for each unit the ratio of its gross disposable income to its 'needs', as estimated from the current costs of such a standard budget (see Table 3).[1]

Non-current resources

The question of assets, insurance, potential additional help from relatives and other rights becomes particularly important in a discussion of the ability of the aged to pay for their own medical care. Older people are more likely to have accumulated various assets. Where the income from these assets is part of current income, it is impossible to use them without foregoing some income in the future. On the other hand, it is obvious from Table 4 that the units with the most adequate incomes are also those most likely to have assets and insurance as well. Since the incidence of illness pertains to individuals, Table 4 is a distribution of individuals by age groups according to the income and assets and insurance of the adult unit to which that individual belongs.

On the other hand, Table 4 overstates the resources of units with more than one person because the same assets cannot cover two adults. A couple, indeed, has more than twice the chance of an individual of having total medical bills above a certain size, because that total can be reached if either of them has a sufficiently expensive illness, or if each of them has an illness half as expensive. If one had accurate data on the costs of medical insurance for families of different sizes and ages and on the adequacy of the

1. See Morgan *et al.* (1962, p. 189) 20 per cent of all families and 39 per cent of all families headed by someone 65 or older had an income less than 85 per cent of that standard. Details, on an adult unit basis, are given in Table 3.

Table 4 **Adult unit welfare ratio by savings, health insurance and age**
(percentage distribution of *persons* 55 and older)

Adult unit welfare ratio (gross disposable income as a % of budget standard)	Savings, Health Insurance and Age						All persons 55 and older	Family welfare ratio of all persons 55 and older*
	$5000 or more in savings		Less than $5000 in savings, health insurance		Less than $5000 in savings, no health insurance			
	55–61	62 and over	55–61	62 and over	55–61	62 and over		
0–44	4	4	3	12	21	20	12	7
45–84	3	15	11	16	22	39	21	18
85–124	8	14	16	15	25	24	18	18
125–204	21	26	29	39	19	13	24	29
205 and over	64	41	41	18	13	4	25	28
Total	100	100	100	100	100	100	100	100
Number of persons (in millions)	2·8	3·8	4·7	5·0	3·1	7·9	27·3	27·3
Number of cases	134	183	239	238	188	409	1391	1391

* For a similar table of individuals distributed according to *family* welfare ratio, savings and insurance, see Morgan *et al.* (1962, p. 206).

insurance carried for the possible multiple exposures, some better assessment of the meaning of Table 4 would be possible. It is not safe to use medical insurance premium rates in the United States for this purpose, since policies carry more serious limitations on benefits for older people and/or may involve redistribution in favor of the aged (as with Blue Cross). Both of these result in premiums that understate the actuarial costs. In the case of disability, older people who are working have frequently the option of retiring, so that the income costs of the disability risk may be smaller than they seem.

If the assets of the aged in the United States must be sold for any reason, a differential overstatement results from the much greater amount of capital gains locked into them and subject to tax upon realization.

This is as far as we have gone statistically: we have looked at the numbers of people in the older age groups who have both low income relative to current needs, few assets and no medical insurance. Another way to get at the provision for risk is to ask people directly. In the 1961 Survey of Consumer Finances we asked 1981 heads of spending units:

Suppose your family had to pay a very large medical bill equal to about two months' income and not covered by insurance. How would you handle such a major medical expense?

Most of those under 65 talked about borrowing, going into debt, or mortgaging the house, but the proportion declined with age from 82 per cent to 44 per cent and finally, for those 65 or older, to 26 per cent. On the other hand, the proportion who mentioned using savings, or assets, or investments increased from 16 per cent to 33 per cent, and finally, to 38 per cent for those 65 or older. Another fifth of those 65 or older said, however, that they would have to depend on help from relatives, friends, government or charity. It is well known that older people are both less able and less willing to borrow. In the 1962 Survey of Consumer Finances, 2117 heads of spending units were asked:

Did you and your family have any large medical expenses during 1961 for doctors, nurses, hospitals and things like that, including expenses covered by medical insurance? If yes: To take care of these expenses, did you take anything out of your savings? Do you still owe part of it? Did you borrow money? Did you pay any out of current income? Did you raise any money any other way? What was that?

The reports on actual medical expenditures followed a pattern similar to the earlier reports of a different sample as to what they might do: the major source was current income, even for those 65 or older, perhaps because they were talking about somewhat smaller bills. Beyond this, younger people were more likely to report still owing and older more likely to report having taken money from savings. Of course, those 65 and older were less likely to have had medical insurance and more likely to report a large medical expenditure.

References

EPSTEIN, L. (1960), 'Some problems in measuring the economic status of the aged' paper presented to the Fifth Congress of the International Association of Gerontology, mimeographed.

FERGE, Z. (1962), 'Which indicator is the best for featuring the standard of living', in M. Mód *et al.* (eds.), *The Standard of Living*, Publishing House of the Hungarian Academy of Sciences.

FISHER, J. (1963), 'Measuring the adequacy of retirement incomes', in H. Orbach and C. Tibbitts (eds.), *Aging and the Economy*, University of Michigan Press.

KATONA, G., LININGER, C., and KOSOBUD, R. (1963), *1962 Survey of Consumer Finances*, Institute for Social Research, Michigan.

MORGAN, J. N. (1962), 'The anatomy of income distribution', *Rev. Econ. Stats.*, vol. 44, p. 273.

MORGAN, J. N., *et al.* (1962), *Income and Welfare in the United States*, McGraw-Hill.

MORGAN, J. N., and DAVID, M. (1961), 'The aged and their economic position – some highlights of a survey taken early in 1960', in *Retirement Income of the Aging*, US Senate, 87th Congressional Session, appendix 4, pp. 188–99.

MORGAN, J. N., and DAVID, M. (1962), 'The aged: their ability to meet medical expenses', appendix A of *Financing Health Care of the Aged*, part 1, American Hospital Association.

SHANAS, E. (1961), 'Family relationships of older people', research series 20, *Health Information Foundation*, National Opinion Research Centre.

STEINER, P., and DORFMAN, R. (1957), *The Economic Status of the Aged*, University of California Press.

3 A. B. Atkinson

On the Measurement of Inequality

A. B. Atkinson, 'On the measurement of inequality', *Journal of Economic Theory*, vol. 2, 1970, pp. 244–263; and non-mathematical summary.

Introduction

Measures of inequality are used by economists to answer a wide range of questions. Is the distribution of income more equal than it was in the past? Are underdeveloped countries characterized by greater inequality than advanced countries? Do taxes lead to greater equality in the distribution of income or wealth? However, despite the wide use of these measures, relatively little attention has been given to the conceptual problems involved in the measurement of inequality and there have been few contributions to the theoretical foundations of the subject. In this paper, I try to clarify some of the basic issues, to examine the properties of the measures that are commonly employed, and to discuss a possible new approach. In the course of this, I draw on the parallel with the formally similar problem of measuring risk in the theory of decision-making under uncertainty and make use of recent results in this field.[1]

The problem with which we are concerned is basically that of comparing two frequency distributions $f(y)$ of an attribute y which for convenience I shall refer to as income. The conventional approach in nearly all empirical work is to adopt some summary statistic of inequality such as the variance, the coefficient of variation or the Gini coefficient – with no very explicit reason being given for preferring one measure rather than another. As, however, was pointed out by Dalton fifty years ago in his pioneering article (1920), underlying any such measure is some concept of social welfare and it is with this concept that we should be concerned. He argued that we should approach the question by considering directly the form of the social welfare function to be employed. If we follow him in assuming that this would be an additively separable and symmetric function of individual incomes, then we would rank distributions according to[2]

1. My interest in the question of measuring inequality was originally stimulated by reading an early version of the paper by Rothschild and Stiglitz (1970), to which I owe a great deal.

2. It is assumed throughout that $U(y)$ is twice continuously differentiable. The restriction of the incomes under consideration to a finite range $0 \leqslant y \leqslant \bar{y}$ is mathematically convenient and not very limiting as far as the problem is concerned.

$$W \equiv \int_0^{\bar{y}} U(y)f(y)\,dy. \qquad\qquad 1$$

My main concern in this paper is to explore the implications of adopting this approach and its relationship to the conventional summary measures of inequality.

It may be helpful to distinguish two objectives that we may have in seeking to compare distributions. Firstly, we may want simply to obtain a ranking of distributions – to be able to say, for example, that post-tax income is more equally distributed than pre-tax income. On the other hand, we may want to go further than this and to quantify the difference in inequality between two distributions. In particular, we may want to separate 'shifts' in the distribution from changes in its shape and confine the term inequality to the latter aspect. Now it is clear that the conventional summary measures are chiefly directed at the second of these problems. For the economist, however, it is more natural to begin by considering the ordinal problem of obtaining a ranking of distributions, since this may require less agreement about the form of the social welfare function.

The ranking of distributions

In order to arrive at any ranking of distributions, we clearly have to make some assumption about the form of the function $U(y)$. As a first step, let us consider what can be said if we restrict our attention to the class of functions $U(y)$ that are increasing and concave – which seem quite acceptable requirements. Under what conditions can we then rank two distributions without specifying any further the form of the function $U(y)$?

Fortunately, at this point we can draw on recent work on the economically unrelated but formally similar problem of decision-making under uncertainty. As should be quite clear, ranking income distributions according to **1** is formally identical to ranking probability distributions $f(y)$ according to expected utility, and the assumption that $U(y)$ is concave is equivalent to assuming that a person is risk averse. Since the field of decision-making under uncertainty has attracted more attention recently than that of measuring inequality, I intend to exploit the parallel by making use of the results that have been reached. In particular, a number of authors have proved the following result (see Rothschild and Stiglitz, 1970; Hadar and Russell, 1969; Hanoch and Levy, 1969):

A distribution $f(y)$ will be preferred to another distribution $f^*(y)$ according to criterion **1** for all $U(y)$ ($U' > 0$, $U'' \leqslant 0$) *if and only if*

$$\int_0^z [F(y) - F^*(y)]\,dy \leqslant 0 \quad \text{for all } z \quad (0 \leqslant z \leqslant \bar{y})$$

$$\text{and} \quad F(y) \neq F^*(y) \quad \text{for some } y, \qquad\qquad 2$$

where $F(y) = \int_0^y f(x)\,dx$.

This condition **2** provides the answer to our question, but as it stands it is very difficult to interpret. It can, however, easily be shown to have a straightforward interpretation in terms of the familiar Lorenz curve – an interpretation which has been overlooked by those working in the field of uncertainty. Let us suppose for the moment that we are comparing distributions with the same mean – as when considering a redistribution of a given total income. The Lorenz curve (which shows the proportion of total income received by the bottom x per cent) is defined implicitly by

$$\varphi(F) = \frac{1}{\mu} \int_0^{y_1} yf(y)\,dy, \qquad F = \int_0^{y_1} f(y)\,dy,$$

where μ denotes the mean of the distribution.

Integrating the expression for φ by parts, we obtain

$$\mu\varphi[F(y_1)] = y_1 F(y_1) - \int_0^{y_1} F(y)\,dy. \hspace{2cm} 3$$

If we now compare the Lorenz curves for two distributions $f(y)$ and $f^*(y)$ at a point $\bar{F} = F(y_1) = F^*(y_1^*)$, then

$$\mu[\varphi(\bar{F}) - \varphi^*(\bar{F})] = [y_1 - y_1^*]\bar{F} - \left[\int_0^{y_1} F(y)\,dy - \int_0^{y_1^*} F^*(y)\,dy \right]$$

$$= -\int_0^{y_1^*} [F(y) - F^*(y)]\,dy + \left[\int_{y_1}^{y_1^*} F(y)\,dy - (y_1^* - y_1)F(y_1) \right].$$

Applying the first mean-value theorem, the second term is positive, so that it follows that condition **2** implies that the Lorenz curve corresponding to $f(y)$ will lie everywhere above that corresponding to $f^*(y)$. From **3** we can also write

$$-\int_0^{y_1} [F(y) - F^*(y)]\,dy = \mu[\varphi(F\{y_1\}) - \varphi^*(F^*\{y_1\})] - y_1[F(y_1) - F^*(y_1)].$$

But from the definition of the Lorenz curve, $\mu\varphi(\bar{F}) = \int_0^{\bar{F}} y\,dF$ so that

$$-\int_0^{y_1} [F(y) - F^*(y)]\,dy = \mu[\varphi(F\{y_1\}) - \varphi^*(F\{y_1\})] +$$

$$+ \left[\int_{F^*(y_1)}^{F(y_1)} y\,dF^* - y_1(F - F^*) \right].$$

Again applying the first mean-value theorem to the second term, we can see that it is positive, so that if the Lorenz curve for $f(y)$ lies above that for $f^*(y)$ for all F, then condition 2 will be satisfied. We have shown, therefore, that, when comparing distributions with the same mean, condition 2 is equivalent to the requirement that the Lorenz curves do not intersect. We can deduce that if the Lorenz curves of two distributions do not intersect, then we can judge between them without needing to agree on the form of $U(y)$ (except that it be increasing and concave); but that if they cross, we can always find two functions that will rank them differently. If we consider distributions with different means, then condition 2 clearly implies that the mean of $f(y)$ can be no lower than that of $f^*(y)$. Conversely, if $\mu \geqslant \mu^*$ and the Lorenz curve of $f(y)$ lies inside that of $f^*(y)$ then 2 will hold.

In the literature on decision-making under uncertainty it has been shown that there are a number of conditions equivalent to 2, and by making use of one of these equivalences we can throw further light on the problem of ranking income distributions. In his article, Dalton (1920) argued that any ranking of distributions should satisfy what he called *the principle of transfers*: If we make a transfer of income d from a person with income y_1 to a person with a lower income y_2 (where $y_2 \leqslant y_1 - d$), then the new distribution should be preferred. In terms of Figure 1, the distribution $f(y)$ should be preferred to $f^*(y)$. This principle of transfers turns out, however, to be identical to the concept of a mean preserving spread introduced by

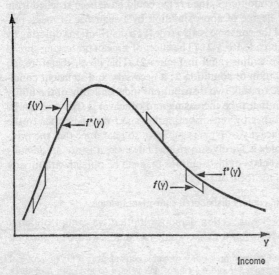

Figure 1 The principle of transfers

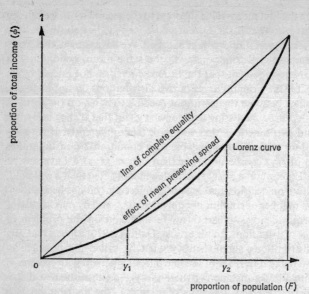

Figure 2 Effect of mean-preserving spread on Lorenz curve

Rothschild and Stiglitz (1970).[3] Now they have shown that where two distributions satisfy condition **2**, then $f^*(y)$ could have been reached from $f(y)$ to any desired degree of approximation by a sequence of mean preserving spreads, and the converse is also true (two distributions differing by a mean preserving spread satisfy **2**). (The effect of a mean preserving spread on the Lorenz curve is illustrated in Figure 2). This gives, therefore, an alternative interpretation of condition **2**: a necessary and sufficient condition for us to be able to rank two distributions independently of the utility function (other than that it be increasing and concave) is that one can be obtained from the other by redistributing income from the richer to the poorer. That the concavity of $U(y)$ is sufficient to guarantee that the principle of transfers holds is hardly surprising; however, it is not so obvious that this is the widest class of distributions that can be ranked without any further restriction of the form of $U(y)$.

Complete ranking and equally distributed equivalent income

The results of the previous section demonstrate that we cannot obtain a complete ordering of distributions according to **1** unless we are prepared to

3. Using their notation, a mean preserving spread is equivalent to a tax of d on a of those with incomes between $a+d$ and $a+t+d$ which is used to give e to β of those with incomes between b and $b+t$.

specify more precisely the form of the function $U(y)$. It is in fact clear that for a complete ranking we need to specify $U(y)$ up to a (monotonic) linear transformation. In the rest of the paper, I consider the implications of alternative social welfare functions and their relation to the summary measures that are commonly used.

The specification of the function $U(y)$ will provide a ranking of all distributions; it will also, however, allow us to meet the second objective of quantifying the degree of inequality. Dalton (1920), for example, suggested that we should use as a measure of inequality the ratio of the actual level of social welfare to that which would be achieved if income were equally distributed:

$$\frac{\int_0^{\bar{y}} U(y)f(y)\,dy}{U(\mu)}. \qquad\qquad 4$$

This normalization is not, however, invariant with respect to linear transformations of the function $U(y)$; for example, in the case of the logarithmic utility function, Dalton's measure is

$$\frac{\int_0^{\bar{y}} \log(y)f(y)\,dy + c}{\log(\mu) + c},$$

the value of which clearly depends on c (Dalton, 1920, p. 350). So that although two people might agree that the social welfare function should be logarithmic – and hence agree on the ranking of distributions – their measures of inequality would only coincide if they agreed also about the value of c. For this reason, the measure suggested by Dalton is not very useful.[4]

We can, however, obtain a measure of inequality that is invariant with respect to linear transformations by introducing the concept of the *equally distributed equivalent* level of income (y_{EDE}) or the level of income per head which if equally distributed would give the same level of social welfare as the present distribution,[5] that is,

$$U(y_{EDE}) \int_0^{\bar{y}} f(y)\,dy = \int_0^{\bar{y}} U(y)f(y)\,dy.$$

4. Dalton's approach has been applied by Wedgwood (1939), who calculated that in the case of the logarithmic function the level of welfare associated with the actual distribution of income in Great Britain in 1919–20 was only 77 per cent of what it would have been had income been equally distributed. A similar approach has been adopted by Aigner and Heins (1967). For the reason described in the text, however, the particular numerical values calculated by these authors have no meaning.

5. This line of approach was suggested to me by discussions with David Newbery. It also resembles the work of Mirrlees and Stern in a quite different context (1972).

We can then define as our new measure of inequality

$$I = 1 - \frac{y_{\text{EDE}}}{\mu}$$

or 1 minus the ratio of the equally distributed equivalent level of income to the mean of the actual distribution. If I falls, then the distribution has become more equal – we would require a higher level of equally distributed income (relative to the mean) to achieve the same level of social welfare as the actual distribution. The measure has, of course, the convenient property of lying between 0 (complete equality) and 1 (complete inequality). Moreover, this new measure has considerable intuitive appeal. If $I = 0.3$, for example, it allows us to say that if incomes were equally distributed, then we should need only 70 per cent of the present national income to achieve the same level of social welfare (according to the particular social welfare function). Or we could say that a certain plan for redistributing income would raise social welfare by an amount equivalent to an increase of 5 per cent in equally distributed income. This facilitates comparison of the gains from redistribution with the costs that it might impose – such as any disincentive effect of income taxation – and with the benefits from alternative economic measures. Finally, it should be clear that the concept of equally distributed equivalent income is closely related to that of a risk premium or certainty equivalent in the theory of decision-making under uncertainty. y_{EDE} is simply the analogue of the certainty equivalent and I is equal to the proportional risk premium as defined by Pratt (1964).[6] This parallel conveniently allows us once more to borrow results.

Before examining the implications of specific measures, it may be helpful to discuss some of the general properties that we should like such measures to possess. In particular, I should like to consider the relationship between inequality *per se* and general shifts in the distribution. Nearly all the measures conventionally used are concerned to measure inequality independently of the mean level of incomes; so that if the distribution of income in country A is simply a scaled up version of that in country B, $f_A(y) = f_B(\theta y)$, then we should regard them as characterized by the same degree of inequality. Now suppose that we were to require that the equally distributed measure I were invariant with respect to such proportional shifts, so that we could consider the degree of inequality independently of the mean level of incomes. Then by applying the results of Pratt (1964), Arrow (1965),

6. The proportional risk premium is defined as the amount π^* such that a person with initial wealth W would be indifferent between accepting a risk Wz (where z is a random variable) and receiving the non-random amount $E(Wz) - W\pi^*$. In the present case, $W = \mu$ and $z = \frac{(y - \mu)}{\mu}$.

and others, we can see that this requirement (which may be referred to as *constant (relative) inequality-aversion*) implies that $U(y)$ has the form

$$U(y) = A + B \frac{y^{1-\varepsilon}}{1-\varepsilon}, \quad (\varepsilon \neq 1)$$

and $\quad U(y) = \log_e (y), \quad (\varepsilon = 1),$ 5

where we require $\varepsilon \geqslant 0$ for concavity. On the other hand, it might quite reasonably be argued that as the general level of incomes rises we are more concerned about inequality – that I should rise with proportional additions to incomes. In other words, the social welfare function should exhibit *increasing (relative) inequality-aversion*. In that event, the measure of inequality I can only be interpreted with reference to the mean of the distribution.

The previous paragraph was concerned with the effect of equal *proportional* additions to income; we may also consider the effect of equal *absolute* additions to incomes (denoted by θ). We can then define a measure of *absolute* inequality-aversion (which is again parallel to the measure of risk-aversion in the theory of uncertainty):[7] Absolute inequality-aversion is increasing/constant/decreasing according as

$\partial y_{\mathrm{EDE}}/\partial \theta$ is less than/equal to/greater than 1.

It has been argued by a number of writers that equal absolute additions to all incomes should reduce inequality; if one looks at the effect on I, this has the sign of

$$(1-I) - \frac{\partial y_{\mathrm{EDE}}}{\partial \theta}.$$

From this we can see that I may fall with equal absolute additions to income even if absolute inequality-aversion is increasing.

Specific measures of inequality

So far I have discussed general principles without considering specific measures of inequality. In this section, I examine some of the implications of different measures, beginning with the conventional summary statistics.

The conventional summary measures

The measures most commonly used in empirical work include the following:

7. This definition can be seen to be parallel to that for the uncertainty case since y_{EDE} is equal to $\mu - \pi$, where π is the *absolute* risk premium (for an absolute gamble $y - \mu$ and initial assets μ).

1. The variance, V^2;

2. The coefficient of variation, $\dfrac{V}{\mu}$;

3. The relative mean deviation, $\displaystyle\int_0^{\bar{y}} \left|\frac{y}{\mu} - 1\right| f(y)\, dy$;

4. The Gini coefficient, $\dfrac{\left(\displaystyle\int_0^{\bar{y}} [yF(y) - \mu\varphi(y)]f(y)\, dy\right)}{2\mu}$;

5. The standard deviation of logarithms, $\displaystyle\int_0^{\bar{y}} \left[\log\left(\frac{y}{\mu^*}\right)\right]^2 f(y)\, dy$,

where μ^* is the geometric mean.

The implications of the earlier discussion for the use of these summary measures can be seen as follows. If we consider distributions with the same mean and apply one of the measures 1–4, then we are guaranteed to arrive at the same ranking as with an arbitrary concave social welfare function if and only if condition 2 is satisfied.[8] For example, if condition 2 holds (and the distributions have the same mean), then the Gini coefficient will give the same ranking as any concave social welfare function (this is clearly the case since it represents the area between the Lorenz curve and the line of complete equality); but if 2 does not hold, we can always find a function $U(y)$ such that the distribution with the *higher* Gini coefficient is preferred. With these measures it follows, therefore, that they will give the same ranking of distributions satisfying 2, but where this condition is not met, they may give conflicting results.[9] Dalton suggested that 'in most practical cases' the measures would in fact give the same ranking, so that we could rely on the 'corroboration of several'. However, as the work of Yntema (1933), Ranadive (1965) and others has demonstrated, this expectation is not borne out and in practice the measures give quite different rankings. Much of the

8. In the case of the variance, this follows directly – see Rothschild and Stiglitz, (1970). For the other measures, the restriction to distributions with the same mean is important. In the case of measures (2) and (3), we can write them in the form

$$\int_0^{\bar{y}} V(y, \mu) f(y)\, dy,$$

where V is convex in y (NB the integral is minimized to give the least inequality). While the Gini coefficient cannot in general be written in this form (as shown by the example of Newbery (1970)), the same result can be shown to hold.

9. The relationship between cases where the conventional measures give conflicting rankings and the crossing of the Lorenz curves was suggested by Ranadive (1965); the results given earlier provide a proof of this.

early literature was in fact concerned with the problem of choosing between the different summary measures, and such properties were discussed as ease of computation, ease of interpretation, the range of variation, and whether they required information about the entire distribution. However, as I have emphasized earlier, the central issue clearly concerns the underlying assumption about the form of the social welfare function that is implicit in the choice of a particular summary measure. It is, therefore, on this aspect that I shall concentrate here.

The first issue is one discussed in the previous section – the dependence of the measures on the mean income. With the exception of the variance, all the measures listed above are defined relative to the mean, so that they are unaffected by equal proportional increases in all incomes. In the case of the variance, we know from the theory of uncertainty that ranking distributions according to mean and variance is equivalent to assuming that $U(y)$ is quadratic, and that this in turn implies increasing relative and absolute inequality-aversion. As argued earlier, increasing relative inequality-aversion may be a quite acceptable property of the social welfare function. Increasing absolute inequality-aversion, however, may be less reasonable: it means that equal absolute increases in all incomes cause the equally distributed equivalent income to rise by less than the same amount. While the objections to this property are less strong than the corresponding objections in the uncertainty case, it may be grounds for rejecting the quadratic. In any event, it is the mean independent measures 2–5 that have received most attention, and for this reason I shall concentrate on them here.

The second point is one made by Dalton, but apparently neglected since then. He argued that if we make a strictly positive transfer from a richer person to a poorer person, this ought to lead to a strictly positive reduction in the index of inequality (and not merely leave it unchanged). If we accept this requirement, which seems quite reasonable, it provides grounds for rejecting measures which are not *strictly* concave – in particular the relative mean deviation–as well as other measures such as the interquartile range. As is clear from the definition of the relative mean deviation, it is unaffected by transfers between people on the same side of the mean. This is illustrated by Figure 3. The distributions characterized by φ and φ^* have the same relative mean deviation, although φ would be preferred for all strictly concave utility functions (and has a lower Gini coefficient). This view is not, however, shared by two recent supporters of the relative mean deviation – Éltetö and Frigyes (1968). In their article, these authors put forward three measures which are simple transforms of the relative mean deviation and argue that these are preferable to the Gini coefficient. They suggest, in particular, that their measure is more 'sensitive' than the Gini coefficient because it

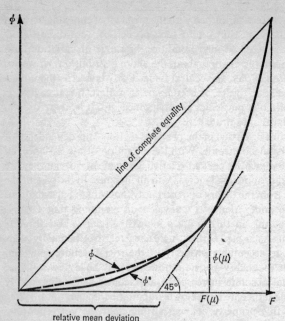

Figure 3 Effect of transfers on the relative mean deviation (note: the relative mean deviation is given by $2(F(\mu) - \varphi(\mu))$)

has a wider range of variation, but ignore the fact that it is completely insensitive to transfers between people on the same side of the mean.[10]

The three remaining measures – the coefficient of variation, the Gini coefficient, and the standard deviation of logarithms – are sensitive to transfers at all income levels; however, it is important to examine the *relative* sensitivity of the measures at different income levels. Suppose that the Lorenz curves for two distributions intersect once (as shown in Figure 4) so that country A has a more equal distribution at the bottom and country B is more equal at the top. Now it is clear that we could redistribute income in A in such a way that the distribution was the same as in B. We should (broadly) take some from the poor and give it to the middle income class and take some from the rich and give it to those in the middle. In this way, we can see the choice between distributions A and B in terms of the weight attached to redistributive transfers at different points of the income

10. Schutz (1951) also argued that the relative mean deviation is preferable to the Gini coefficient. He pointed out that 'the shape of the Lorentz curve may be infinitely varied without any change in the Gini coefficient'. However, as we have just seen, the same objection applies even more strongly to the relative mean deviation.

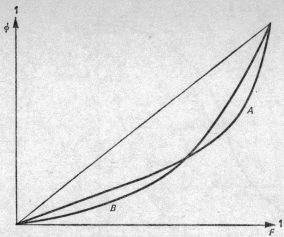

Figure 4

distribution. If we are ranking distributions according to $\int_0^{\bar{y}} V(y)f(y)\,dy$,

then the effect of an infinitesimal redistribution from a person with income y_1 to a person with income $y_1 - h$ is given by $V'(y_1 - h) - V'(y_1)$. In the case of the coefficient of variation, this would be constant for all y_1. The effect of a transfer would be independent of the income level at which it was made. If, therefore, one wanted to give more weight to transfers at the lower end of the distribution than at the top, this measure would not be appropriate. In the case of the standard deviation of logarithms, $V' = \{\log(y/\mu^*)\}/y$ which does attach more weight to transfers at the lower end, but which also of course ceases to be concave at high incomes. Finally, in the case of the Gini coefficient the effect of an infinitesimal transfer can be shown to be proportional to $F(y_1) - F(y_1 - h)$.[11] This suggests that for typical distributions more weight would be attached to transfers in the centre of the distribution than at the tails (see Figure 5). It is not clear that such a weighting would necessarily accord with social values.

The results of this examination of five of the conventional summary measures have shown that

1. The use of the variance implies increasing inequality-aversion; all the other measures imply constant (relative) inequality-aversion;

11. This does not follow directly, but can be shown by taking a discrete mean preserving spread (as defined in Rothschild and Stiglitz (1970)) and allowing the size of the transfer to tend to zero.

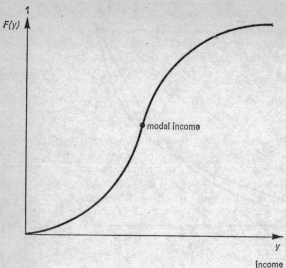

Figure 5

2. The relative mean deviation is not strictly concave and is not sensitive to transfers on the same side of the mean;

3. The coefficient of variation attaches equal weight to transfers at different income levels, the Gini coefficient attaches more weight to transfers affecting middle income classes and the standard deviation weights transfers at the lower end more heavily.

The social welfare function approach

In the previous section, I examined the implicit assumptions about the form of the social welfare function embodied in the conventional summary measures and suggested that a number of these assumptions were unlikely to command wide support. In any case, it seems more reasonable to approach the question directly by considering the social welfare function that we should like to employ rather than indirectly through these summary statistical measures. While there is undoubtedly a wide range of disagreement about the form that the social welfare function should take, this direct approach allows us to reject at once those that attract no supporters, and also serves to emphasize that *any* measure of inequality involves judgements about social welfare.

The social welfare function considered here is assumed to be of the form 1 that we have been discussing throughout; that is, it is symmetric and additively separable in individual incomes – although this is, of course, restrictive. Now we have seen that nearly all the conventional measures are defined relative to the mean of the distribution, so that they are invariant with respect to proportional shifts. If we want the equally distributed equivalent measure to have this property, then this restricts us still further to the class of homothetic functions **5**, which in the case of discrete distributions imply a measure

$$I = 1 - \left[\sum_i \left(\frac{y_i}{\mu} \right)^{1-\epsilon} f(y_i) \right]^{1/(1-\epsilon)}.$$

In this case, the question is narrowed to one of choosing ϵ, which is clearly a measure of the degree of inequality-aversion – or the relative sensitivity to transfers at different income levels. As ϵ rises, we attach more weight to transfers at the lower end of the distribution and less weight to transfers at the top. The limiting case at one extreme is $\epsilon \to \infty$ giving the function $\min_i \{y_i\}$ which only takes account of transfers to the very lowest income group (and is therefore not strictly concave); at the other extreme we have $\epsilon = 0$ giving the linear utility function which ranks distributions solely according to total income.[12]

An illustration

To illustrate the points made in the previous section about the conventional summary measures and the use of the equally distributed equivalent measure, I have taken the data collected by Kuznets (1963) covering the distribution of income in seven advanced and five developing countries. This data has been used by both sides in the recent controversy as to whether incomes are more unequally distributed in the developing countries – see, for example, Ranadive (1965). I should emphasize, however, that my use of the figures is purely illustrative; their well-recognized deficiencies make any concrete conclusion difficult to draw.

Our earlier discussion suggested that the first step in the analysis should be an examination of the Lorenz curves corresponding to the distributions. If we consider all the pairwise comparisons of the twelve countries, then in only sixteen out of sixty-six cases do the Lorenz curves not intersect, so that we can arrive at a ranking without specifying the form of the social welfare function in only some quarter of the cases.[13] This explains the finding of Kuznets and others that the application of the conventional summary

12. It should be noted that the measure is readily decomposable if it is desired to measure the contribution of inequality *within* and inequality *between* subgroups of the population.

13. I assume throughout this section that we are ranking distributions independently of the mean level of income.

Table 1 Conventional and equally distributed equivalent measures of inequality

Country	Year	1 Gini coefficient		2 Standard deviation of logarithms		3 Coefficient of variation		Equally distributed equivalent measure					
								4 $\varepsilon = 1 \cdot 0$		5 $\varepsilon = 1 \cdot 5$		6 $\varepsilon = 2 \cdot 0$	
India	1950	0·410	(8 =)	0·305	(3)	0·901	(11)	0·297	(7)	0·359	(5)	0·399	(3)
Ceylon	1952–3	0·427	(10)	0·341	(6)	0·876	(10)	0·311	(10)	0·395	(6)	0·457	(6)
Mexico	1957	0·498	(12)	0·395	(12)	1·058	(12)	0·401	(12)	0·492	(12)	0·550	(12)
Barbados	1951–2	0·436	(11)	0·383	(10)	0·842	(9)	0·315	(11)	0·433	(10)	0·524	(10)
Puerto Rico	1953	0·394	(4)	0·317	(4)	0·783	(8)	0·256	(4)	0·341	(4)	0·408	(4)
Italy	1948	0·378	(3)	0·301	(2)	0·748	(3)	0·241	(2)	0·319	(2)	0·379	(1)
Great Britain	1951–2	0·356	(1)	0·304	(1)	0·673	(1)	0·224	(1)	0·311	(1)	0·384	(2)
West Germany	1950	0·410	(8 =)	0·369	(8)	0·773	(6)	0·299	(8)	0·411	(8)	0·498	(8)
Netherlands	1950	0·406	(6 =)	0·355	(7)	0·781	(7)	0·290	(5)	0·395	(7)	0·478	(7)
Denmark	1952	0·401	(5)	0·381	(9)	0·751	(4)	0·292	(6)	0·418	(9)	0·521	(9)
Sweden	1948	0·406	(6 =)	0·393	(11)	0·752	(5)	0·303	(9)	0·435	(11)	0·540	(11)
United States	1950	0·372	(2)	0·325	(5)	0·705	(2)	0·242	(3)	0·339	(3)	0·421	(5)

Source of columns 1–3 is Ranadive (1965), p. 122.
Source of columns 4–6 is calculated from data in Kuznets (1963, Table 3).

measures yields conflicting results. In the first three columns of Table 1, I have summarized the results obtained by Ranadive using three of the conventional summary measures. This shows clearly the discrepancies that arise; for example, India would be ranked as more unequal than West Germany on the basis of the coefficient of variation, as less unequal on the basis of the standard deviation of the logarithms of income, and ranks equally when we take the Gini coefficient. In fact the three measures agree in only forty out of sixty-six cases, which subtracting those where the Lorenz curves do not intersect means that no more than half the doubtful cases would be agreed. The differences in ranking are in fact such that no clear conclusion emerges with regard to the relative degree of inequality in advanced and developing countries. The Gini coefficient and the coefficient of variation suggest that income is more unequally distributed in developing countries (four out of five come right at the bottom), but this is not borne out by the standard deviation of logarithms.

The last three columns in Table 1 show the effect of adopting the equally distributed equivalent measure (for the iso-elastic function with different values of ε). If we look first at the absolute value of the measure, then in the United States, for example, the measure of inequality I for $\varepsilon = 1.5$ is 0.34. In other words, if incomes were equally distributed, the same level of social welfare could be achieved with only two thirds of the present national income – which is a striking figure. For most other countries, the figure is even lower and in the case of Mexico it is only one half. These figures relate to one particular value of ε and it is clearly important to examine their sensitivity to changes in ε. In Figure 6, I have shown how I varies with ε in

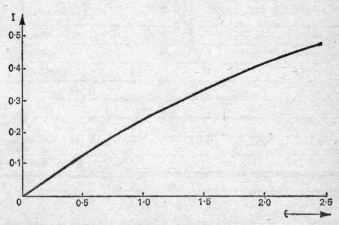

Figure 6   Sensitivity of I to variation in ε – United States

A. B. Atkinson   61

the case of the United States. The range of variation is considerable, but I is less sensitive than one might at first have expected; for example, if we could agree that ε should be between 1·5 and 2·0, then I would lie between 0·42 and 0·34. It is also interesting to note that the potential gains from re-distribution are considerable over most of the range: for $\varepsilon > 0·2$ they are greater than 5 per cent of national income and for $\varepsilon > 0·8$ they are greater than 20 per cent.

Turning to the relative ranking of different countries, we may note first of all that the last column ($\varepsilon = 2·0$) gives a ranking *identical* with that based on the standard deviation of logarithms, but one which is very different from that given by the Gini coefficient and the coefficient of variation. Of the 50 pairwise comparisons where the Lorenz curves intersect, the equally distributed equivalent measure with $\varepsilon = 2·0$ would disagree with the Gini coefficient in 17 cases and with the coefficient of variation in no fewer than 26 cases. If we take $\varepsilon = 1·0$, which implies a lower degree of inequality-aversion, then the ranking is closer to that of the Gini coefficient (only in 5 cases would it be different), but is still quite a lot different from that of the coefficient of variation (14 disagree). The sensitivity of the ranking to ε is shown more clearly in Figure 7, which covers the range $\varepsilon = 1·0$ to $\varepsilon = 1·5$. This indicates that if we could agree, for example, that ε should lie between 1·5 and 2·0, then only five rankings would remain ambiguous.

It appears from this example that 2 of the conventional measures (the

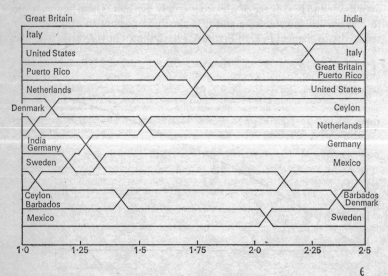

Figure 7 Ranking of income distributions for different values of ε

Gini coefficient and the coefficient of variation) tend to give rankings which are similar to those reached with a relatively low degree of inequality-aversion – ε of the order of 1·0 or less. This accords with the analysis of these measures in the previous section. It also appears that the conclusions reached about the relative degree of inequality in advanced and developing countries depend on the degree of inequality-aversion. It is clear why this is the case. The distribution of income in the developing countries is typically more equal at the bottom and less equal at the top than in the advanced countries, and as the degree of inequality-aversion increases, we attach more weight to the distribution at the lower end of the scale. It is striking that in Figure 7 none of the reversals of ranking as ε increases involve a developing country falling relative to an advanced country.

Concluding comments

In this paper I have examined the problem of measuring inequality in the distribution of income (alternatively consumption or wealth).[14] At present this problem is usually approached through the use of such summary statistics as the Gini coefficient, the variance or the relative mean deviation. I have tried to argue, however, that this conventional method of approach is misleading. Firstly, the use of these measures often serves to obscure the fact that a complete ranking of distributions cannot be reached without fully specifying the form of the social welfare function. Secondly, examination of the social welfare functions implicit in these measures shows that in a number of cases they have properties which are unlikely to be acceptable, and in general there are no grounds for believing that they would accord with social values. For these reasons, I hope that these conventional measures will be rejected in favour of direct consideration of the properties that we should like the social welfare function to display.

14. In this paper I have not referred to other applications of measures of inequality in economics, such as to the degree of industrial concentration or to concentration in foreign trade. The underlying considerations of social welfare are likely to be very different in these cases.

References

AIGNER, D. J. and HEINS, A. J. (1967), 'A social welfare view of the measurement of income inequality', *Rev. Income Wealth*, vol. 13, pp. 12–25.

ARROW, K. J. (1965), *Aspects of the Theory of Risk Bearing*, Helsinki.

DALTON, H. (1920), 'The measurement of the inequality of incomes', *Econ. J.*, vol. 30, pp. 384–61.

ÉLTETÖ, O., and FRIGYES, E. (1968), 'New income inequality measures as efficient tools for causal analysis and planning', *Econometrica*, vol. 36, pp. 383–96.

HADAR, J., and RUSSELL, W. R. (1969), 'Rules for ordering uncertain prospects', *Amer. Econ. Rev.*, vol. 59, pp. 25–34.

HANOCH, G., and LEVY, H. (1969), 'The efficiency analysis of choices involving risk', *Rev. Econ. Studs.*, vol. 36, pp. 334–46.

KUZNETS, S. (1963), 'Quantitative aspects of economic growth of nations: VIII distribution of income by size', *Econ. Devel. Cultural Change*, vol. 11, pp. 1–80.

MIRRLEES, J. A., and STERN, N. H. (1972), 'On fairly good plans', *J. Econ. Theory*, vol. 4, pp. 268–88, 2, p. 264.

NEWBERY, D. M. G. (1970), 'A theorem on the measurement of inequality', *J. Econ. Theory*, vol. 4, p. 268–88.

PRATT, J. W. (1964), 'Risk aversion in the small and large', *Econometrica*, vol. 32, pp. 122–36.

RANADIVE, K. R. (1965), 'The equality of incomes in India', *Bull. Oxford Inst. Econ. Stats.*, vol. 27, pp. 119–34.

ROTHSCHILD, M., and STIGLITZ, J. E. (1970), 'Increasing risk: a definition and its economic consequences', *J. econ. Theory*, vol. 2, pp. 225–43.

SCHUTZ, R. R. (1951), 'On the measurement of income inequality', *Amer. Econ. Rev.*, vol. 41, pp. 107–22.

WEDGWOOD, J. (1939), *The Economics of Inheritance*, Penguin.

YNTEMA, D. B. (1933), 'Measures of inequality in the personal distribution of income or wealth', *J. Amer. stat. Assoc.*, vol. 28, pp. 423–33.

Non-mathematical summary

The basic problem considered in Reading 3 concerns the conditions under which we can say that one distribution (of, say, income) is more unequal than another. Is it possible to compare the degree of inequality between countries, or between different periods in the same country? The usual approach to these questions is to employ one of a range of summary measures of inequality (such as the variance, the coefficient of variation or the Gini coefficient), but very little attention has been paid to their underlying justification. The aim of Reading 3 is to clarify these issues.

The conclusions reached in Reading 3 may best be illustrated with the aid of a simple example. Suppose that we are interested in comparing the degree of income inequality in the United Kingdom, West Germany and the Netherlands on the basis of the data set out in Table 1. The data are presented in terms of the shares of total income received by the bottom 10 per cent, 20 per cent, etc. (it is assumed that differences in average incomes between the countries are not relevant to the comparison).

The approach adopted in Reading 3 is to consider the Lorenz curve for each distribution. Suppose first that we use the data from Table 1 to draw the Lorenz curves for the United Kingdom and Netherlands. It can readily be checked that they have the form shown in Figure 1 and in particular that the Lorenz curve for the United Kingdom lies everywhere inside that for the Netherlands (in terms of Table 1 this is equivalent to the share of the bottom x per cent being larger in each case for the United Kingdom). This means that we can apply the first result given in Reading 3 (page 49) that *if the Lorenz curves for two distributions do not intersect, we can say*

Table 1

Cumulative share of bottom %	United Kingdom 1964	Netherlands 1962	West Germany 1964
10	2·0	1·3	2·1
20	5·1	4·0	5·3
30	9·3	8·2	10·0
40	15·3	14·0	15·4
50	22·8	21·4	21·9
60	31·9	30·0	29·1
70	42·9	40·0	37·5
80	55·8	51·6	47·1
90	70·7	66·2	58·6

Source: Economic Commission for Europe (1967).

unambiguously that the distribution closer to the diagonal is more equal than the other. Moreover, any of the summary measures usually employed (those listed on page 54) will give the same ranking: the Gini coefficient, the variance, the coefficient of variation will all indicate a higher degree of inequality in the Netherlands than in the United Kingdom.

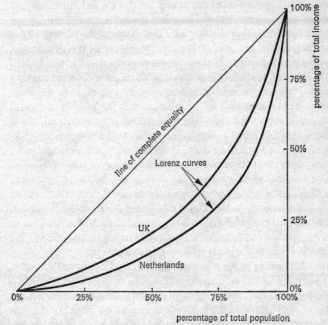

Figure 1

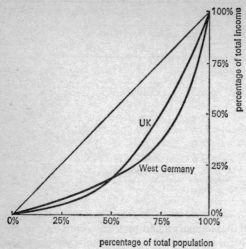

Figure 2

If, however, the Lorenz curves are drawn for the United Kingdom and West Germany (see Figure 2), it is clear that the same conclusion cannot be drawn since the Lorenz curves intersect. The shares of the bottom 10 per cent, 20 per cent, 30 per cent and 40 per cent are higher in West Germany, but above that point the distributions becomes more equal in the United Kingdom. In such a situation it is quite possible to get a different ranking from different summary measures. We can see by eye that the Gini co-efficient (which ranks according to the area between the Lorenz curve and the diagonal) will show that the United Kingdom is less unequal, but a measure which attaches more weight to inequality at the bottom may indicate less inequality in West Germany. This illustrates the principal conclusion of the paper: that *the degree of inequality cannot, in general, be compared without introducing values about the distribution*. Summary measures such as the Gini coefficient are often presented as purely 'scientific', but in fact they implicitly embody values about a desirable distribution of income. Moreover, when one examines the values implicit in such measures (as in the section on specific measures of inequality), there are no grounds for supposing that the values are likely to be widely acceptable.

In the latter part of the paper it is argued that the conventional measures should be rejected in favour of direct consideration of the values we should like to see embodied. One method through which this can be achieved is the 'equally distributed equivalent measure' suggested on page 51. In this formula, the parameter ε represents the weight attached by society to inequality in the distribution: high values of ε mean that the society is particularly averse to inequality, whereas a zero value means that it is indifferent to inequality. The meaning of different values of ε can be seen from the following 'mental experiment'. Suppose that there are two people, one with twice the income of the other, and that we are considering taking £1·00 from the richer man and giving £x to the poorer (the remaining £1 – £x being lost in the process – e.g. in administering the transfer). How far can £x fall below £1·00 before we cease to regard the redistribution as desirable? (Clearly if we are at all concerned with inequality £x = £1·00 is considered desirable.) The answer to this question determines the value of ε. For example, $\varepsilon = 1$ corresponds to our regarding it as 'fair' to take £1·00 from the richer man and give £0·50 to the poorer; and $\varepsilon = 2$ to it being regarded as fair to take £1·00 and give £0·25p to the poorer man.

Returning to the comparison of the United Kingdom, West Germany and the Netherlands, we can calculate the value of the equally distributed equivalent measure (I) for different values of ε (Table 2).

Table 2

Equally distributed equivalent measure (I)*			
Value of ε	United Kingdom	Netherlands	West Germany
0·5	0·12	0·15	0·17
1·0	0·24	0·29	0·29
1·5	0·34	0·42	0·38
2·0	0·43	0·52	0·45
3·0	0·55	0·66	0·54

* Calculated according to the formula given on page 59.
A higher value of I denotes greater inequality.

The value taken by I has a straightforward interpretation: a value of 30 per cent means that if incomes were equally distributed we should need only (100 per cent — 30 per cent) = 70 per cent of the present national income to reach the same level of social welfare – or alternatively that the gain from redistribution to bring about equality is equivalent to raising national income by 30 per cent. ($I = 0$ corresponds to the case of complete equality.) In this way the measure I provides an index of the potential gains from redistribution. It also allows us to compare the different distributions, and it can be seen, for example, that the United Kingdom is only regarded as being less unequal than West Germany where ε is less than 3·0 and that for higher values of ε the ranking is the reverse of that given by the Gini coefficient.

The use of the equally distributed equivalent measure involves a decision being made about the value of ε. However, without introducing such judgements it is impossible to measure the degree of inequality. That no such decision has to be made with the conventional measures simply obscures the fact that they embody quite arbitrary values about the distribution of income.

Reference

ECONOMIC COMMISSION FOR EUROPE (1967), *Incomes in Postwar Europe: A Study of Policies, Growth and Distribution*, United Nations.

Part Two
The Distribution of Income in Britain and the United States

It is obvious to everyone that incomes are unequally distributed; however, the extent of inequality can only be seen if we examine the available statistical evidence. Such statistics are in fact in notoriously short supply, but this section presents a selection from the information that is available about income inequality in Britain and the United States. The kinds of question which they try to answer include: How unequal are incomes in these countries? Is income inequality increasing? Are incomes in the United States more unequally distributed than in Britain?

Evidence about inequality is inevitably statistical; however, Pen (Reading 4) succeeds in presenting the statistical picture in a way which will be painless for even the least numerate reader. As the author describes it, the purpose of his 'parade' is to give a first impression of the distribution of income and it does so in a very graphic way. The following readings look at the distribution of income in Britain in more detail. Soltow (Reading 5) is concerned with the long-run trend in inequality and includes such fascinating pieces of information as the annual income of 'vagrants, beggars, gypsies, thieves and prostitutes' in 1688. The more recent trends are taken up by Nicholson (Reading 6) who examines the period 1949–63 (extended to 1967 in the following note). The conclusion which he draws is that it is 'doubtful whether the trend in the distribution of incomes for the immediate future is set in the direction of greater equality'. Rather similar findings are described in the case of the United States by Miller (Reading 7), who examines the period 1929–62 and argues that 'the statistics show no appreciable change in income shares for nearly twenty years'. He concludes that the 'figures hardly support the view held by many Americans that incomes in our society are becoming more evenly distributed'.

Comparison of the degree of income inequality in different countries is fraught with difficulties arising from different sources of data, differing real incomes, etc. Reading 8 presents one of the few attempts at a systematic comparison between Britain and the United States, and although now rather dated (relating to the early 1950s), it is of considerable interest. As far as incomes are concerned, the principal conclusion is that 'pre-tax income per spending unit is, in general, very similarly distributed in the two countries'. It may be interesting to include here comparative figures for a number of European countries, although it should be stressed that the basis for collection may be rather different:

Table 1 Share in total personal income before tax

	Top 10%	Bottom 30%
Norway 1963	24·9	9·8
Sweden 1963	27·9	8·5
United Kingdom 1964	29·3	9·3
Finland 1962	32·5	5·9
Netherlands 1962	33·8	8·2
France 1962	36·8	4·8
West Germany 1964	41·4	10·0

Source: Economic Commission for Europe (1967).

The research described in the Readings in this section has contributed greatly to our knowledge about the distribution of income. At the same time, the authors would be the first to admit that their conclusions need to be treated with caution. Two principal factors need to be borne in mind: Firstly, the basic data on incomes is deficient in a number of significant respects. In Britain, this is particularly important since the main source is the income tax statistics as used in Readings 5 and 6. Apart from the obvious problems of tax evasion, these statistics leave out such sources of income as capital gains, income in kind, imputed rent on owner-occupied houses, fringe benefits and pension contributions. These omissions are very likely to bias the measurement of inequality: for example, the study by Prest and Stark (1967) showed that the inclusion of capital gains led to a significant increase in inequality in 1959. It has been argued (e.g. by Nicholson on page 100) that the deficiencies of the data are less important when *trends* in income distribution are considered. This would, however, only be correct if the omitted sources of income had maintained the same relationship to recorded income. In fact, there are good grounds for expecting that the relative importance of 'missing' income increased during the postwar period: for example, the significance of capital gains undoubtedly increased over the 1950s and various fringe benefits (such as those from occupational pension schemes) have increased in importance. It is quite possible, therefore, that the income tax data may provide a misleading impression of the trends in income distribution.

Secondly, the observed pattern of inequality needs to be interpreted in the light of structural changes in society – changes in work habits and relative importance of different sources of income, changes in marriage patterns and in the age structure of the population, changes in the level of unemployment, the development of private and state social security systems, etc. The effect of changes in the age composition of the population may be taken to illustrate this point. If old people tend to have below-average incomes, and the proportion of old people is growing, then the observed degree of inequality will increase, without there having been any change in individual circumstances. (The importance of this factor in the United States is discussed by Miller at the end of Reading 7.) If a life-cycle approach were adopted, with inequality being assessed in terms of each person's lifetime income, this problem would be overcome; however, the necessary data is not in general available.

In the case of Britain, the role of these two factors has been documented at length by Titmuss (1962)[1], and his concluding comments should be borne in mind when assessing the evidence presented in this section

No conclusion which takes account of an ageless individual and forgets the family, which measures 'income' and omits 'wealth', which disregards the unit of time, in command-over-resources, which fails to inquire into the meaning of power which avoids investigating the interlocking connections between social and economic institutions, and which is oblivious of the key role now played by the educational system in the social distribution of 'life chances', can be relied upon in the context of the social changes we have depicted. Ancient inequalities have assumed new and more subtle forms; conventional categories are no longer adequate for the task of measuring them (pp. 198–9).

1. It had been hoped to include a passage from this important study, but the editor felt that there was no extract which, taken by itself, would adequately reflect the author's views. It is a book to be read in whole and not in part.

References

ECONOMIC COMMISSION FOR EUROPE (1967), *Incomes in Postwar Europe: A Study of Policies, Growth and Distribution*, United Nations.

PREST, A. R., and STARK, T. (1967), 'Some aspects of income distribution in the UK since World War II', *Manchester School*, 1967, pp. 217–43.

TITMUSS, R. M. (1962), *Income Distribution and Social Change*, Allen & Unwin.

4 J. Pen

A Parade of Dwarfs (and a Few Giants)

Excerpt from J. Pen, *Income Distribution*, Allen Lane the Penguin Press, 1971, pp. 48–59.

Before we embark on theoretical reflections we must have a survey of the facts of distribution. The aim of this chapter is to give a provisional and rough impression of these facts. It brings us up against the problem of presentation. Suppose that we know exactly how much each individual of the mass of income recipients earns. In reality that is not so, but thanks to the work of pioneers like S. Kuznets in the United States and A. L. Bowley in the United Kingdom, and through the availability of tax data, quite a lot of figures are nevertheless known. The question is how to marshal this enormous quantity of material. This should preferably be done in such a way that the presentation really tells us something. A chaotic mountain of detached figures or a tiring series of tables must be transformed into a coherent, manageable whole. That can be done in a variety of ways.

In this section we are concerned with a first impression. For this purpose we shall organize a parade in which everyone takes part who gets money. We could give all the marchers a sign to hold stating his or her pay, but it is more spectacular if we make everyone's size proportionate to his income. To achieve that we call in Procrustes, a cruel host whose custom it was to adapt the height of his guests to the size of the bed in the guest room. We shall ask him to stretch or to contract every income recipient in such a way that his height corresponds to his income. The average income recipient gets the average height. Anyone who earns more than average becomes taller; anyone who earns less than average shrinks (let's hope that the proportions of the victims, and their health, remain intact). The average income is computed by adding all incomes together and dividing by the number of income recipients. Taxes are not deducted, but social benefit, family allowances, pensions, etc., are thrown in. We can therefore see by looking at people what they earn.

It is worth mentioning that in this procedure we consider individual incomes. We ignore wealth, and we concern ourselves with *individual* remuneration. This is not the most decisive criterion of prosperity; usually family incomes are more important. We shall presently come across tiny women, but before we pity them we must bear in mind that perhaps they have a husband who is also earning, so that the wife merely supplements the family income. And young girls are as a rule reduced to pygmies without being bowed down by that; they live with their parents and earn plenty of pocket-money. (Unfortunately, other young girls must live on their wages and rent expensive rooms, and some women have to support families and really ought to earn more and not less than the men.) Old people are sometimes small without this troubling them overly; but fathers of large families who have been stretched to more than average height by Procrustes may be financially pinched to a considerable degree. The smallest of all are schoolchildren and students, who work for money for a few months a year; on an annual basis that income is minuscule, but that does not affect their enjoyment of life. These restrictions disappear from sight in our approach. We observe only tall and short human beings. Before passing judgement on their prosperity we ought to know more about them, but we are not attempting that.

The procession is now forming up; just as when a school marches in from the playground, the smallest ones are in the van. The parade moves on at uniform speed in such a way that it is past in one hour, which means that the marchers are going to have to move in double-quick time. They *flash* past. You and I, two persons of average height,[1] watch the strange spectacle. What do we see?

In the first seconds a remarkable thing already happens. If we have superhuman powers of observation (and why shouldn't we confer them upon ourselves?) we see a number of people of negative height passing. On closer inspection they prove to be businessmen who have suffered losses and whose capital is reduced. They are not necessarily short people. In fact, right in the front we spot a few very tall men, with their feet on the ground and their heads deep in the earth. The first one may be as tall as ten yards – he must be rich to indulge in that kind of thing. It's an unhealthy way of carrying on, and most of them don't keep it up long. This vanguard is not so small in number either; we live in a rough world, where many are attracted by the successes of private enterprise which, however, pass them by. A third to half of all retail businesses close down within two years of their start[2] – and all this mortality is not without losses.

After this tragi-comic opening we see tiny gnomes pass by, the size of a matchstick, a cigarette. We think we see among them housewives who have worked a short time for some money and so have not got anything like an annual income, schoolboys with a paper round and once again a few entrepreneurs who didn't make it (though without their having applied for

1. I'm just assuming. I can hardly know your income; mine is far above the Dutch average.

2. The figure applied to the United States. See Samuelson (1964, p. 78).

National Assistance). It takes perhaps five minutes for them to pass. We should bear in mind that those who have no income and don't want one either – children, non-working housewives – are not taking part in the parade at all.

Suddenly we see an increase by leaps and bounds. The people passing by are still very small ones – about three feet – but they are noticeably taller than their predecessors. They form a heterogeneous group; they include some young people, especially girls who work regularly in factories, but above all people who are not in paid employment: very many old-age pensioners without other means of support, some divorced women without alimony, people with a physical handicap. Among them are owners of shops doing poor trade. They supply the smooth transitions. And we see artists – they may include geniuses, but the public does not understand their work and the market does not reward their capacities. Unemployed persons also belong to this heterogeneous company, but only in so far as they received a low wage, while they were working (otherwise they would be coming later). Some members of this group receive National Assistance. It takes them at least five or six minutes to pass by.

After them – the parade has been going on for about ten minutes – come the ordinary workers about whom there is nothing out of the ordinary except that they are in the lowest-paid jobs. Dustmen, Underground ticket collectors, some miners. The unskilled clerks march in front of the unskilled manual workers. Precisely among these lower-paid categories each group applies the principle of ladies first – particularly in Britain equal pay is far from being a reality. We now also see large numbers of coloured persons. These groups take their time to pass; we have ample opportunity to observe them at our leisure. It takes almost fifteen minutes before the passing marchers reach a height of substantially more than four feet. For you and me this is a disturbing sight; fifteen minutes is a long time to keep seeing small people pass by who barely reach to our midriff. More than a third of them are women, dwarf-like human beings. In embarrassment we avert our gaze and look in the direction of the approaching parade to catch sight at long last of normal people.

But a new surprise awaits us here. *We keep on seeing dwarfs*. Of course they gradually become a little taller, but it's a slow process. They include masses of workers, just ordinary people with not inconsiderable technical knowledge, but shorties. After we have waited another ten minutes small people approach who reach to our collar-bones. We see skilled industrial workers, people with considerable training. Office workers, respectable persons so to see. We know that the parade will last an hour, and perhaps we expected that after half-an-hour we would be able to look the marchers straight in the eye, but that is not so. We are still looking down on the tops of their heads, and even in the distance we do not yet see any obvious improvement. The height is growing with tantalizing slowness, and forty-five minutes have gone by before we see people of our own size arriving. To be somewhat more exact: about twelve minutes before the end the average income recipients pass by.

We are of course interested as to who they are. Now, they prove to include teachers, executive-class civil servants, clerical workers, older NCOs, grown grey in the services. Of course we also encounter shopkeepers, together with sales representatives and insurance agents (a number of *them* do not come along until later). This group also includes people in overalls and rubber boots and with callouses on their hands; they are a number of foremen, superintendents and technicians, and a few farmers.

After the average income recipients have passed, the scene changes rather quickly. The marchers' height grows; six minutes later we see the arrival of the top 10 per cent, a group that will turn up again repeatedly in the following pages. The first to arrive are around six feet six inches, but to our surprise we see that they are still people with modest jobs. Headmasters, Assistant Principals and Principals. (Our parade is being held in Britain; in other countries the exact order is sometimes a little different, but the picture is the same.) University graduates, but most of them are very young. Small contractors who lend a hand themselves. Seamen too. And once again farmers; in Britain their income is higher than the national average (in this respect this country differs from the United States and from all countries of Continental Europe!). Again office staff, department heads, but certainly not yet genuine top executives. They are people who had never thought that they belonged to the top 10 per cent.

In the last few minutes giants suddenly loom up. A lawyer, not exceptionally successful: eighteen feet tall. A colonel, also of much the same height. Engineers who work for nationalized industries. The first doctors come into sight, seven to eight yards, the first accountants. There is still one minute to go, and now we see towering fellows. University professors, nine yards, senior officers of large concerns, ten yards, a Permanent Secretary thirteen yards tall, and an even taller High Court judge; a few accountants, eye surgeons and surgeons of twenty yards or more. This category also includes managers of nationalized concerns; the Chairman of the National Coal Board is likewise a good twenty yards.

During the last seconds the scene is dominated by colossal figures: people like tower flats. Most of them prove to be businessmen, managers of large firms and holders of many directorships, and also film stars and a few members of the Royal Family. There prove to be towers and towers, and we cannot describe them all. To mention a few examples of persons whose salaries have been published: we note, with due respect, Prince Philip, sixty yards (too short to play polo), and the senior managing director of Shell, David Barran, who measures more than twice as much.

Now these giants are still people with salaries (the interest on their wealth makes them still taller – how much so we do not know), and the yard is still a practical measure of their height. But the rear of the parade is brought up by a few participants who are measured in miles. Indeed, they are figures whose height we cannot even estimate: their heads disappear into the clouds and probably they themselves do not even know how tall they are. Most of them are men of venerable age, but they also include women; these are as a rule younger, and we even think that we can see a few babies and adolescents. (Their ranks include Tom Jones; nearly a mile high.) These super-rich people are almost all heirs, and the tallest of them have managed to multiply their inheritance. The last man, whose back we can still see long after the parade has passed by, is John Paul Getty (though as a rule we have not invited American guests, Getty lives for much of his time in Britain and is an Oxford B.A.) At the time of writing he is almost 80 years old and made his money in oil. Few know what he earns (perhaps nobody does); his fortune is estimated at 1000 to 1500 million dollars. His height is inconceivable: at least ten miles, and perhaps twice as much.

Suddenly the parade is gone – the income recipients disappear from sight and leave the spectators behind them with mixed feelings. We have watched a dramatic spectacle, full of unexpected scenes.[3] It is worth while summarizing a few of our impressions.

1. A striking fact is that we have to wait so long for the average income recipient. The reason lies in the fact that a number of colossal people are bringing up the rear. Not only do they attract the attention of the spectator so much, but they also raise the average; it shifts to well above the great mass of income recipients. For that reason by far the greater part of the parade consists of small men and women, not to say dwarfs. If we were to exclude from the parade those who bring up the rear, say during the last minute, the average height – that is to say your height and mine – would drop considerably. Those remaining in the parade would not become any taller as a result, but the impression would be removed that we have organized a parade of dwarfs. After just over half-an-hour we would

3. Honesty compels me to admit that I have intensified the effect because spectators usually pay attention not only to height but also to width of shoulders, size of chest and volume. In our case they should not do so, because a person's volume increases with the third power of his height. You and I must therefore consider only the distance between soles and crown, and ignore the frightening effect of volume. If you think that we are asking too much of our capacity for abstraction, we ought to ask Procrustes *not* to leave the proportions intact; a thirteen-yard general then acquires a very weedy figure, and the gnomes look like soup plates. Getty becomes as thin as gossamer, relatively speaking.

already be able to look the marchers in the eye. People desirous of assessing income distribution should bear such things in mind.

Incidentally, we could also have brought the height of the participants closer to the average if we had considered family income instead of individual incomes. That would have removed many women and young people from the procession; their husbands and fathers would have grown taller and many dwarfs would have risen to almost average height. The marchers of the first five minutes would almost all have remained at home. The parade would have been less colourful and less dramatic. A few giants might have grown still taller: wealthy people who have set fortunes aside for their wives and children.

2. The end of the parade makes a shattering impression. The marchers' height increases with incredible speed in the last minutes, and above all *within* the last minute. It therefore makes a great deal of difference whether we watch the marchers of the last minute (the top 1·7 per cent) or whether we consider those of the last seconds. There is not just a great difference in height: the last minute starts with six yards or so, and the last second we see people of five to ten miles; but there is also difference in the nature of income. A member of the top 1·7 per cent need not necessarily be fabulously rich. He may be wealthy, but this fortune is not essential. His top income may consist in a salary: a senior civil servant, a professor, a manager. It may also be a professional income, earned with the hands: the surgeon. These people have such generous incomes that they can save. This of course breeds wealth, and we consequently see that the top 1 per cent almost always have some wealth in reserve. But this is not a *sine qua non* for their high incomes – the interest is nice to have, but this 'private income' is not essential to their position in the parade.

That is where they differ from the participants of the last seconds. They may also have salaries, but at the same time they are immensely rich. In their case the salary is often subordinate. Their main income consists of interest and profit (these two components of personal income cannot always be sharply distinguished from one another. Their source is different, and consequently we shall at all times keep profit and interest apart in this book. But when the dividend reaches the income recipient it sometimes begins to look like interest). The top fortunes are not only a welcome supplementation to income from work – the capital is the essential basis of the economic position of the financial giants. Their wealth is not always invested in a wide portfolio of shares – it is often deliberately invested in their own firms, in which they have a say.[4] Considerable misunderstanding occurs through

4. Needless to say, considerable attention has been drawn to the significance of wealth to inequality. This was done with great emphasis by Dalton (1920). Incidentally,

confusion of these two groups – the last minute and the last seconds – though it is of course true that there are smooth transitions between them. The top 1 per cent (and even the top 10 per cent!) are too often identified with the very wealthy capitalists. The latter group is tiny.[5]

The question is how these enormous fortunes are accumulated. The answer is a straightforward one: the source is always formed by profits. You can save a modest little capital from a salary, and so become well-to-do, but if you really want to build up a huge fortune you cannot leave it at that. (It is of course easier to inherit the money, but that passes over the manner in which the testator came by the money.) Savings from wage and salary may form a springboard, but ultimately the aspiring Croesus will have to rely on the rewards of entrepreneurship. The best thing is to have the disposal of a good, brand-new product (with the necessary patents) and to start producing it with drive. You might come a financial cropper, but you might bring it off. The survivors cross a threshold after which their profits accumulate, and so the lucky ones join the rear ranks of our parade.

The process of getting rich sometimes goes faster than you might think. It does not always take generations; the list of the enormously wealth is growing. The theory that it is impossible to become colossally wealthy nowadays and that the big fortunes are at least a generation old is unrealistic. A well-known example in support of the contrary is that of Dr Edwin H. Land, who invented the sixty-second camera in the Forties. At first the public did not see much in it, but took a second look and found this way of photography attractive after all. Incidentally, Dr Land has many other optical inventions to his name. In 1968 he was number 4 on *Fortune*'s list of the Super-Rich, that is to say behind J. Paul Getty (oil), Howard Hughes (aircraft, among other things) and H. L. Hunt (oil), but ahead of the old families like the Duponts, the Fords, the Mellons and the Rockefellers. Land's fortune is estimated at $500 to 1000 million. Chester Carlson is another example of an inventor (Xerography; he started as a lawyer!); he is said to be worth $150 to 200 million. According to *Fortune* there were 153 people in the United States with a net worth of above $100 million in 1968 (including wealth held by spouses, minor children, trusts and foundations). A third of these 153 were not yet really wealthy ten years

it is not so easy to state exactly which part of the inequality is caused by wealth distribution. That requires sophisticated quantitative methods.

5. Anyone desirous of getting to know this group's American counterpart should read the informative book by Lundberg (1968). He tells us who the rich are, how they acquired their money, how they spend it, how they solve their tax problems, their relations with politics, arts and science and with each other. No such book exists for Britain. Although I have some criticism of Lundberg's view, I can strongly recommend the reading of his 1000-page paperback.

before. Of course the big heirs with the familiar names are still to be found on the list of 153. They have been displaced from top position by the *nouveaux riches*, but they're keeping their end up very nicely (*Fortune*, 1968).

3. The head of the procession naturally also deserves closer attention. We must make a distinction between the part-time workers and casual earners on the side on the one hand and the shocking social emergency cases on the other. Recently more has become known about the latter group: the cumulative processes operating at the bottom end of income distribution have been brought to light in particular by M. Harrington in his book on the American poor. This group is of importance to social policy (minimum wages, social security, tax exemption limit, negative income tax). Some are inclined to make this very group the principal objective of distribution policy, and I heartily agree. In my opinion they form a more urgent problem than the very rich.

4. Also of interest is the great difference in predictability and determinateness of the incomes. People are marching in our parade whose earnings we know within narrow limits. That applies to all wage-earners whose incomes are laid down in collective agreements, to civil servants, to many other salary-earners: a good 80 per cent of the population. But the fact that someone is called a rentier or capitalist (depending on the observer's preference) tells us nothing at all about his place in income structure. He may scrape together a small income from interest, just enough to supplement his pension slightly; he may also belong at the end of the procession. We already know much more about him if he tells us how great his wealth is – then his income can be predicted within certain limits.

But this predictability does not apply to profits. The man who lives on profit may pop up anywhere in the procession. Even further information on the size of a person's business is no criterion of his income. Firstly because there are flourishing and highly profitable small businesses that place their owners in the last minute of the parade, and there are large firms that make a loss. In the second place because the distribution of a firm's profit may differ so greatly. Three brothers may each pocket one third of the profit made by the family business, but that may also be arranged quite differently. The very large firm has again a wider variation in its arrangements: shareholders, top executives and staff may share in the profit in accordance with different criteria. And then there are profits whose volume it is difficult to estimate. If a wealthy shipowner wants to know how much he earns and how that income is made up, he has to ask his accountant. We, as inquisitive outsiders, certainly cannot find out. It is profit that often escapes our understanding and at the same time creates the tremendous inequality.

5. Our procession has the attractive property that we can see and recognize the participants. We saw men with boots on and dirty hands, respectable gentlemen with briefcases, striking figures and ordinary ones. We saw with our own eyes the richest man in the world. We saw great numbers of very small women, an appalling sight. The other side to this dramatic effect is that our procession is an imaginary one. It is not the custom to organize such shows, and they would in any case meet with opposition from the participants, if only because of the preliminary treatment by Procrustes.[6]

In a highly watered-down form we can achieve something similar by a graph that hurts no one. (Incidentally, this graph is about as rare as the parade – I've never yet seen it in a book or an article.) On the horizontal axis of this graph (Figure 1) minutes are plotted, and on the vertical the

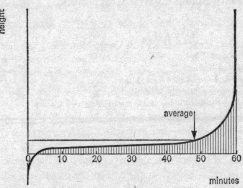

Figure 1 A parade

height of the income recipients. The curve illustrates the dwarf-like nature of most people; the average is indicated by the arrow. The recognizability of the individuals has now disappeared. Nor does the graph lend itself to accurate reading-off, because the right-hand part rises so steeply that small inequalities in the drawing lead to great differences in income. The last millimetre comprises, on a reduced scale, a top manager of a good 100 yards and the super-rich capitalist of ten miles. The vertical axis ought in fact to be well over 200 yards long. Is this perhaps why the graph does not appear in the books?

And yet this drawing suggests one of the most striking properties of income structure: the huge inequality illustrated by the right-hand part of the

6. On paper the operation is painless but it is not performed either. The transformation of incomes into heights is not to be found in the books, with, as far as I know, only one exception: a casual remark by Mrs Barbara Wootton (1955, p. 18). I have never come across the parade in economic literature.

curve. Other drawings conceal this property. In the next section we shall encounter the frequency distribution, a curve that is very usual in statistics; the income classes are plotted horizontally and the number of income recipients in every bracket vertically. As we shall see, this presentation is useful and stimulating, but it spirits away the very rich. All the same, the frequency distribution also shows reality. The Lorenz curve, yet another technique, shows us the same facts through yet other eyes, so that yet other properties strike us. This illustrates my argument that income distribution (and even the narrower subject of *personal* income distribution) has many different faces. It depends on the temperament, the intellectual structure and the political preference of the reader which face he recognizes best. If I may speak for myself, I am rather struck by the presentation in this section. The inequality that emerges from it colours my view of the problem.

References

DALTON, H. (1920), *Some Aspects of the Inequality of Income in Modern Communities*, Routledge & Kegan Paul.
Fortune (1968), 'America's centimillionaires'.
LUNDBERG, F. (1968), *The Rich and the Super Rich*, Stuart.
SAMUELSON, P. A. (1964), *Economics*, 6th edn Macmillan.
WOOTTON, B. (1955), *The Social Foundations of Wage Policy*, Allen & Unwin.

5 L. Soltow

Long-Run Changes in British Income Inequality

L. Soltow, 'Long-run Changes in British Income Inequality', *Economic History Review*, vol. 21, 1968, pp. 17–29.

It is difficult to measure the extent of improvement of various social and economic groups during the Industrial Revolution. There seems to be a growing body of evidence showing that lower-income segments shared in economic growth.[1] However, the idea still prevails that a dynamic industrial group developed in the eighteenth and nineteenth centuries which made the rich richer even if the poor did not become poorer. The consequence of such a movement would mean that relative inequality among all income groups would increase. This belief is often accepted in the United States because of the large body of literature dealing with the era of the robber baron. It is accepted by economists as being true for Germany mainly because of the study of annual income distributions available for the years from 1873 to 1913 and the one year 1854 (Procopovitch, 1926; Kuznets, 1963).

There is a degree of silence about the British experience, even though income-tax distributions exist for various income years since 1801. (See, Parliamentary Accounts and Records, 1801–2, vol. 4, pp. 152–5, also 1852 vol. 9, p. 463; Josiah Stamp 1916, 1922; Inland Revenue reports beginning in 1857). This stems from the fact that from 1803 to 1910 there were no comprehensive definitions of income. Distributions were available only for Schedule D income, that is, income from trade or business, the professions and some miscellaneous items including small interest payments. The large amounts of property income, including interest and rents, were subject to separate flat rates so that any exact statements about income were difficult to make. It is the purpose of this paper to bring together available distributions before and after the Industrial Revolution in an attempt to make those data that are available more meaningful within the context of a long period of economic growth. This will involve the use of distributions for 1962–3, 1801, 1688, and, brazenly, for 1436.

1. See Taylor (1960), which lists four major works supporting this thesis. The list is headed by the remarkable work of George (1966).

Distributions for the total labour force

For 1688 there are Gregory King's well-known estimates. He gives the number and average incomes of twenty-six classes of persons in England and Wales as follows:

No. of families in class	Class	Yearly income per family (£)
160	Temporal lords	3200
26	Spiritual lords	1300
800	Baronets	880
600	Knights	650
3000	Esquires	450
12,000	Gentlemen	280
5000	Persons in greater offices and places	240
5000	Persons in lesser offices and places	120
2000	Eminent merchants and traders by sea	400
8000	Lesser merchants and traders by sea	198
10,000	Persons in the law	154
2000	Eminent clergymen	72
8000	Lesser clergymen	50
40,000	Freeholders of the better sort	91
120,000	Freeholders of the lesser sort	55
150,000	Farmers	$42\frac{1}{2}$
15,000	Persons in liberal arts and sciences	60
50,000	Shopkeepers and tradesmen	45
60,000	Artisans and handicrafts	38
5000	Naval officers	80
4000	Military officers	60
35,000	Common soldiers	14
50,000	Common seamen	20
364,000	Labouring people and out-servants	15
400,000	Cottagers and paupers	$6\frac{1}{2}$
30,000 (persons)	Vagrants, beggars, gipsies, thieves and prostitutes	2 (per head)

Phyllis Deane, who has used King's data as the basis of an estimate of national income for 1688, states that King had access in some main respects to better data than we do (Deane, 1955–6, pp. 3–38).

By ordering King's twenty-six average incomes from lowest to highest, and weighting each by the number of families involved, data may be obtained for the Lorenz curve given in Figure 1. A measure of relative inequality, Gini's coefficient of concentration or R, is calculated by determining the area between the actual Lorenz curve and the straight-line curve of perfect equality. This area as a ratio of the triangular area under the line of perfect equality was 0·551 in 1688. This procedure neglects dispersion within each economic class which, if accounted for, might increase R by 5 or 10 per cent.

Patrick Colquhoun was the next person to make a serious estimate of annual income distribution in England and Wales, considering data from 1801 to 1803. Superficially at least, he used King's framework.

No. of families in class	Class	Yearly income per family (£)
287	Peers	8000
26	Spiritual lords	4000
540	Baronets	3000
350	Knights	1500
6000	Esquires	1500
20,000	Gentlemen	700
2000	In high civil offices	800
11,000	Persons of the law	350
1000	Eminent clergymen	500
10,000	Lesser clergymen	120
120,000	Better freeholders	200
120,000	Lesser freeholders	90
160,000	Farmers	120
16,300	Liberal arts and sciences	260
74,500	Shopkeepers	150
445,726	Artisans, mechanics, labourers	55
3000	Naval officers	347
5000	Military officers	363
50,000	Common soldiers	110
38,175	Marines	129
67,099	Seamen	107
340,000	Labourers	31
40,000	Labourers in mines	40
260,179	Paupers	26
222,000	Vagrants	10

Colquhoun significantly added twenty more classes to this list (Colquhoun, 1806, p. 23). Some of these were classes emerging as a result of industrialization so that, with a few exceptions, these additions could perhaps be thought of as a partial accounting for the effects of eighteenth century economic growth:

No. of families in class	Class	Yearly income per family (£)
1	The Sovereign and Queen	200,000
5000	Ship-owners letting ships	500
25,000	Manufacturers	800
500	Wholesalers	800
300	Employing capital in ship-building	700
25,000	Employing capital in textiles	150
5000	Engineers	200
30,000	Clerks and shopmen	75
2500	Dissenting clergymen	120
500	Educators in universities	600
20,000	In education	150
500	Families in theatrical pursuits	800
800	Hawkers and pedlars	125
2000	Debtors in prisons	43
40	Lunatic keepers	500
2500	Lunatics	30
50,000	Innkeepers	100
2000	Part military	45
30,500	Pensioners	20
50,000	Having trusts	100

The Lorenz curve for these forty-five classes is given in Figure 1. There is some little tendency to show betterment among lower-income classes, but vagaries associated with subsistence non-cash income perhaps make it advisable to conclude that there is no evidence of change in the eighteenth century. The concentration coefficient, R, for the 1801–3 data is 0·555. A further elaboration of the above lists obtained by weighting families by size does not materially alter the calculations.

Colquhoun's total for annual national income in 1801–3 of £222 million for England and Wales is almost the same as might be expected on the basis of later research. Phyllis Deane and W. A. Cole estimated total gross national income for Great Britain to be £232 million in 1801. Colquhoun again made estimates of income for social and economic classes for 1812. This time his total of £430 million was for Great Britain and Ireland. This can be compared to a Deane–Cole estimate for Great Britain (Mitchell, 1962, pp. 8, 11, 366) of £301 million for 1811. It thus seems that Colquhoun's data are not unreasonable. One may construct the Lorenz curve for the 1812 data of Colquhoun in the manner already described. It is not surprising that it is similar to that for 1801 and has a concentration coefficient of 0·536. A list of findings to this point is given in Table 1.

Table 1 Summary information concerning complete distributions of income of persons in Great Britain for eight selected years

Year	Name of investigator	Region	Use of income-tax data	No. of persons in data	Arithmetic mean, x̄ (£)	Concentration coefficient R
1688	Gregory King	England and Wales	No	1,350,000 families and single individuals	32·2	0·551
1801–3	Patrick Colquhoun	England and Wales	No	2,210,000 families and single individuals	99·8	0·555
1812	Patrick Colquhoun	GB and Ireland	No	4,379,000 families and single individuals	98·0	0·536
1867	R. Dudley Baxter	England and Wales	Yes	5,229,000 men	112·0	0·500
1867	R. Dudley Baxter	GB and Ireland	Yes	13,720,000 men, women, and children with income	59·3	0·521
1880	Arthur Bowley	United Kingdom	Yes	14,770,000 with occupations and assessments	76·2	0·474–0·629
1913	Arthur Bowley	United Kingdom	Yes	20,700,000 with occupations and assessments	105·0	0·467–0·588
1962–3	Inland Revenue	United Kingdom	Yes	22,242,000 married couples* and single	853·0	0·338

Sources: Davenant (1771, vol. 2, p. 184). Slight variants of these figures will be found in King (1936), and in Chalmers (1804); Colquhoun (1806, p. 23); Colquhoun (1815, pp. 124, 125); Baxter (1868, frontispiece, p. 60, appendix 1); Bowley (1920, pp. 13, 16); Report of the Commissioners of Her Majesty's Inland Revenue (1965, p. 83); Mitchell (1962, pp. 8, 11).

* A married couple (whether separately assessed for tax or not) is counted as one person.

One now turns to distributions based on income-tax data for at least the upper-income classes. The first of these is by R. Dudley Baxter, who presented 1867 estimates to the Statistical Society of London. The frequency table for England and Wales based on family income unweighted by family size is

Lower limit of income class (£)	No. in class[2]	Lower limit of income class (£)	No. in class[2]
5000	4609	52	582,000
1000	25,812	46	1,028,000
300	92,188	36½	260,360
100	522,401	33	1,148,500
73	616,433	30	73,400
60	42,200	20	34,500
60	798,600		

2. See Baxter (1868, p. 60, appendix 1). Use has been made of the fact that 62 per cent of men, women and children in the upper- and middle-income classes were males twenty years old and over.

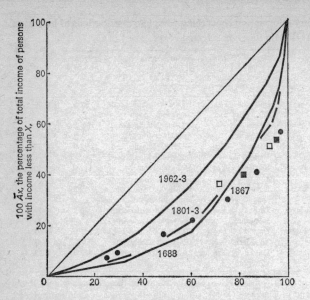

100$\bar{N}x$, the percentage of persons with incomes less than income X

- ▬▬▬ 1962-3, $R = 0.34$
- ■ 1913, $R = (0.48-0.63)$
- □ 1880, $R = (0.47-0.59)$
- ● 1867, $R = 0.52$
- ▬ ▬ 1801-3, $R = 0.56$
- ▬▬▬ 1688, $R = 0.55$,

Figure 1 Lorenz curves of frequency distributions of income of persons in Great Britain in selected years from 1688 to 1963 (Source : Table 1)

The Lorenz curve for this case, as presented in Figure 1 and stated in Table 1, yields a concentration coefficient of 0.500. A similar calculation considering the number of income earners per family gives an R of 0.521. Examination of Figure 1 shows greater equality in the lower portion of the curve in 1867 than in 1801–3. The upper portion of the 1867 distribution has greater inequality than in 1801–3. At least part of this is due to the fact that Schedule D income-tax data were used in the latter but not in the former year. Information for the upper tail based on income-tax data will be presented shortly. It is best to hold in abeyance any conclusion that the rich got richer from 1801 to 1867.

Professor Bowley (1920) made estimates for three income classes in 1880 and 1913, using income-tax data for the highest class with incomes over £160.

Income class	1880		1913	
	No. of persons (*millions*)	Income (*£ millions*)	No. of persons (*millions*)	Income (*£ millions*)
Wages	12·30	465	15·20	770
Income under £160	1·85	130	4·31	365
Income over £160	0·62	530	1·19	2165

It is difficult to compute R measures with only three classes. If one assumes perfect equality in the modal class, R is 0·48 in 1880 and 0·47 in 1913. If one assumes a Pareto distribution within each based on the relationship between the three points, R is 0·63 in 1880 and 0·59 in 1913. The main point to note is that there is no indication of increased inequality in the third of a century before the First World War.

One completes the final half-century by comparing the 1962–3 distribution for families and single individuals, as compiled by the Inland Revenue, with the earlier distributions of 1913 and 1867. The concentration coefficient of 0·34 is at most two thirds of that in 1867 and probably two thirds of that in 1913. The tentative hypothesis is that long-run inequality did not change in the eighteenth and nineteenth centuries. Only since the First World War has there been a decrease, and this decrease has been substantial.

Distributions limited to high-income groups

It is possible to add three more important distributions which have a bearing on inequality changes. These distributions, based on income-tax data, are for upper-income groups in 1436, 1801 and 1911–12. These data are summarized in Table 2 and presented graphically in Figure 2 in conjunction with the eight distributions previously described.

Unfortunately, one cannot use a Lorenz curve approach as such when dealing with incomplete distributions, since the total income and perhaps even the total labour force are not known. The alternative approach, using Pareto curves, will be employed because certain estimates from these curves have attractive ramifications. Although Pareto curves may be considered inappropriate by some for distributions today, they can be used to make effective generalizations if handled with care. It must continually be borne in mind that these curves put an emphasis upon the incomes of high-income and upper-income groups and neglect the poor.

One might begin by examining the 1962–3 cumulative curve in Figure 2, where X is defined as the income variate, and L_X is the number of persons having an income greater than X. It may be seen that a straight line unfolds

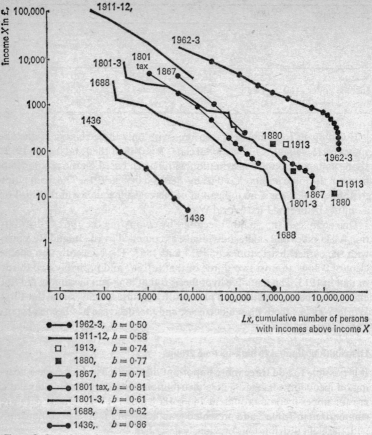

Figure 2 Cumulative frequency distributions of income of persons in Great Britain for selected years from 1436 to 1963 (Source : Table 2)

for incomes above £400 or £500 which encompasses 75–80 per cent of the cases. One may fit a straight line of the form $X = aL_x^{-b}$ to the data by the method of least squares with the following results

1962–3, £500 $\leqslant X \leqslant$ £20,000, $N = 11$ points or classes,
$\log X = 5 \cdot 0226 - 0 \cdot 435 \log L_x$, $b = 0 \cdot 435$, implied lower
$\qquad$ (0·009)

limit = £499, implied arithmetic mean = £883, implied concentration coefficient = 0·278.

It is of interest to know some of the properties of this distribution were it to continue to be distributed below £500 in logarithmic fashion to an L_x equivalent to the total number of cases. The implied lower limit may be obtained by substituting the total number of cases ($L_x = 22,242,000$ in 1962–3), in the formula. It can be demonstrated by using a continuous distribution that the implied arithmetic mean for this inverse Pareto curve is $\bar{X}$ = (implied lower limit)/$(1 - b)$ and its concentration coefficient is $R = b/(2 - b)$ (Soltow, 1965). This procedure thus yields an $\bar{X}$ = £883 and an R of 0·278 which differ from the actual $\bar{X}$ = £853 and R = 0·338. The theoretical R is less than the actual R because lower-tail incomes have been raised with an implicit lower limit of £499 instead of the actual lower limit of £180.

If the inverse Pareto line had been fitted to all points, one would have obtained

1962–3, £180 $\leqslant X \leqslant$ £20,000, N = 16 points or classes,
$\log X = 5\cdot2265 - 0\cdot503 \log L_x, b = 0\cdot503$, implied lower
$\qquad\qquad$ (0·032)
limit = £345, implied arithmetic mean = £694, implied concentration coefficient = 0·336.

The point to be emphasized is that when the procedure is applied only to upper-tail income for a distribution like that in 1962–3, $\bar{X}$ has an upward bias. The estimate for R has a downward bias but the slope of the line, b, is a measure of inequality with a larger value being associated with a larger R.

We are now in a position to examine the ramifications of the various slopes which are presented in Figure 2 and Table 2. H. L. Gray has made estimates for six income classes in the year 1436, obtaining

Class	No. of families in class	Yearly income family (£)
Barons	51	865
Knights	183	208
Lesser knights and other men of government	750	60
Esquires (who were beneath the squirearchy,	1200	24
including gentlemen, merchants, artisans,	1600	12
but largely artisans)	3400	5–9

When the inverse Pareto curve is fitted to these six classes the slope, b, is 0·86 (0·042). One might consider the extension of the curve to an L_x of 750,000 persons,[3] shown as a dot at the bottom of Figure 2. Such a distribu-

3. Gregory King used approximately 1,350,000 as the number of adult families and single adult individuals in 1688. He further estimated the total population in the year 1400 as 60 per cent of the total population in the year 1700.

Table 2 British income data featuring upper-income groups

| Year | Name of investigator | Region | No. of persons in data | Lower limit of smallest class (£) | % of total persons covered by data | No. of classes used | Inverse Pareto curve | | | | Standard error of b | Correlation coefficient squared and adjusted, R^2 |
							Slope b	Implied R for all persons	Implied mean $\bar{X}$, of all persons (£)	Implied income of top person when $L_x = 1$ (£)		
1436	H. L. Gray	England and Wales	7184 men	5	1	6	0·856	0·748	0·78	12,000	0·042	0·99
1688	Gregory King	England and Wales	1,350,000 families and single persons	2	100	26	0·616	0·446	33·8	77,000	0·040	0·94
1801–3	Patrick Colquhoun	England and Wales	2,210,000 families and single persons	10	100	45	0·610	0·438	105	320,000	0·023	0·94
1812	Patrick Colquhoun	GB and Ireland	4,379,000 families and single persons	25	100	12	0·520	0·351	109	150,000	0·028	0·96
1801	Parliamentary returns	GB	320,759 persons	65	15	33	0·807	0·677	64·2	1,600,000	0·008	0·99
1867	R. Dudley Baxter	England and Wales	5,229,000 men	20	100	13	0·705	0·544	94·2	1,500,000	0·027	0·98
1867	R. Dudley Baxter	GB and Ireland	13,720,000 men, women, and children with income	15	100	8	0·726	0·570	27·6	570,000	0·036	0·98
1880	Arthur Bowley	UK	14,770,000 with occupations and assessments	below 160	100	3	0·772	0·629	76·2	4,600,000	0·033	0·99
1913	Arthur Bowley	UK	20,700,000 with occupations and assessments	below 160	100	3	0·740	0·588	105	4,900,000	0·038	0·99
1911–12	Josiah Stamp	UK	12,399 assessed persons	5000	0·1	11	0·575	0·403	—	1,200,000	0·009	0·99
1913–14	Josiah Stamp	UK	13,231 assessed persons	5000	0·1	11	0·575	0·403	—	1,300,000	0·013	0·99
1962–3	Inland Revenue	UK	22,242,000 married couples* and single	180	100	16	0·503	0·336	694	170,000	0·032	0·95
			15,981,000 married couples* and single	500	72	11	0·435	0·278	883	110,000	0·009	0·99

Sources: Gray (1934, pp. 607–39); Davenant (1771, p. 184); Colquhoun (1806, p. 23); Colquhoun (1815, pp. 124, 125); *Parliamentary Accounts and Records*, 1801–2; 4, pp. 152–5, pp. 4–7; Baxter (1868, frontispiece, p. 60, appendix 1); Bowley (1920, p. 16); Stamp (1916, p. 338); Report of the Commissioners of Her Majesty's Inland Revenue (1965, p. 83); Mitchell (1962, pp. 8, 11).

* A married couple (whether separately assessed for tax or not) is counted as one person.

tion has an implicit R of 0·75, which is larger than any other implied or actual income R computed in this study. It will be remembered that the implied R is more likely to be a minimum than a maximum R. The author has never found a complete distribution with an R less than the implied R of the upper tail having a substantial number of classes.

The next upper-tail distribution is that stemming from the income tax in 1801. This included

Lower limit of income class (£)	No. in class	Lower limit of income class (£)	No. in class
5000	1020	200	42,694
2000	3657	150	33,554
1000	6927	100	70,381
500	14,762	60	147,764

The slope, b, of 0·81 is substantially greater than the $b = 0·61$ from Colqu-
$\quad\quad\quad\quad\quad\quad$ (0·008) $\quad\quad\quad\quad\quad\quad\quad\quad\quad\quad\quad\quad\quad\quad\quad$ (0·023)
houn's data, and one should try to resolve the discrepancy if he is to link 1436 to 1801, and 1801 to 1867 [$t(0·81, 0·61) = 3·67$; $t_{05} = 1·67$].[4] At least part of the difference can be explained by statistical calculations. Let us reshuffle the Colquhoun data by granting a modest dispersion within each socio-economic class by assuming within each class a Pareto distribution with an R of 0·25. When this is done, some persons in each class spill over into higher- or lower-income classes, yielding an overall cumulative curve with a slope, b, of 0·68, based on a laborious calculation involving 14 points. The value 0·68 is substantially higher than that value without internal class dispersion, 0·61. One might argue, then, that at least one third of the inequality discrepancy between Colquhoun's 1801–3 data and the 1801 income-tax data can be explained by the statistical formulation.

The 1801 tax data are criticized because they are considered to account for only a small part of national income. High evasion is suspected. If one uses the concepts of implied lower limit and implied $\bar{X}$, however, average income from the income-tax data is calculated to be £64·2. This was 64 per cent of Colquhoun's annual average income in the 1801–3 period.

One is left to make judgements about inequality. These might be

1. No change occurred from 1688 to 1801–3. This is based on the King–Colquhoun data with $b_{1688} = 0·62$, and $b_{1801-3} = 0·61$.
[$t(0·62, 0·61) = 0·10$; $t_{05} = 1·67$]

4. The t-statistics stem from the standard error of the difference between two sample slopes. In this and subsequent comparisons of two slopes, it is assumed that the standard errors of estimate for the two universes are the same. One-tail tests are employed, using the 5 per cent level.

2. Income inequality in 1436 was perhaps a little greater than in 1801 (and, thus, than in 1688). This is based on the income-tax data of Gray and the parliamentary returns with $b_{1436} = 0.86$, and $b_{1801} = 0.81$.

$[t(0.86, 0.81) = 1.83; t_{05} = 1.68]$

3. Inequality in 1867 and 1880 was similar to that in 1801. This stems from the parliamentary returns of 1801, the Baxter estimates for 1867, and the Bowley estimates of 1880. All are based on income-tax returns with $b_{1801} = 0.81$, $b_{1867} = 0.71$, and $b_{1880} = 0.77$. One might conclude that there is evidence that inequality was less in 1867 and in 1880 than in 1801. However, Colquhoun's estimates might dampen one's ardour.

$[t(0.81, 0.71) = 4.46; t_{05} = 1.68]$
$[t(0.81, 0.77) = 1.36; t_{05} = 1.69]$

4. Inequality was not greater in 1911 and 1913 than it was in 1867 and 1880. It might even have been 10 per cent less. These results are based on $b_{1867} = 0.71$, $b_{1880} = 0.77$, and $b_{1913} = 0.74$, coupled with additional data yielding $b_{1911-12} = 0.58$ and $b_{1913-14} = 0.58$. These latter two coefficients, coming from data of Sir Josiah Stamp, are rather startling. The Stamp 1911–12 cumulative curve is given in Figure 2. Particular details are listed in Table 2.

$[t(0.71, 0.74)$ has wrong sign$]$
$[t(0.71, 0.58) = 3.56; t_{05} = 1.73]$
$[t(0.71, 0.58) = 3.47; t_{05} = 1.73]$
$[t(0.77, 0.74) = 0.63; t_{05} = 2.92]$
$[t(0.77, 0.58) = 2.69; t_{05} = 1.81]$
$[t(0.77, 0.58) = 6.12; t_{05} = 1.81]$

5. Inequality decreased substantially from 1911–13 to 1962–3, with $b_{1962-3 \text{ above £500}} = 0.44$.

$[t(0.74, 0.44) = 7.56; t_{05} = 1.80]$
$[t(0.58, 0.44) = 9.44; t_{05} = 1.73]$
$[t(0.58, 0.44) = 8.40; t_{05} = 1.73]$

6. Upper-tail income-tax data show evidence of continuous decline in inequality based on the 1436, 1801, 1911–12, and 1962–3 data, where $b_{1436} = 0.86$, $b_{1801} = 0.81$, $b_{1911-12} = 0.58$, and $b_{1962-3 \text{ above £500}} = 0.44$.

Economic growth and inequality

Emphasis in this paper is placed on upper-income groups and their relative income shares. In traditional society, property income was the more substantial portion of total income. If the Industrial Revolution had not taken place, incomes in 1873 might have been distributed in the fashion shown in Table 3. The concentration coefficients for gross rentals are not quite as high as they would have been had sorting been by rentals rather than by acres. With this allowance, one can say that the concentration coefficients are substantially greater than those of Figure 1 and Table 1. The inverse Pareto slopes are close to unity. A continuous geometric distribution of this shape would lead to perfect inequality. The 1688 peers and great landowners owned almost 50 per cent of the land. The 10,207 persons having landholdings of 500 acres or more had two thirds of private landholdings and 40 per cent of gross estate rentals.

This is probably the element determining the configuration of the 1436 data and the element dominating that of the 1801 tax data. It was noted that there could have been a slight lessening of inequality from 1436 to 1688. One might engage in somewhat questionable calculations to demonstrate that economic growth took place during this period and, thus, that property income might not have been as dominant in the latter year. The implicit arithmetic mean for 1436 was given earlier as £0·78. The King average for 1688 was £32·2. If prices doubled in this 253-year period, the average annual rate of growth was 1·2 per cent. If prices quadrupled, it was 0·9 per cent.[5] It will be recalled that the implicit arithmetic mean projected internally from the 1436 figures is more a maximum than a minimum estimate. One may still question the absolute level of the 1436 figures.

It would seem that the onslaught of the Industrial Revolution, with growth in profits from trade and professional income, could not have introduced an element of greater inequality than that existing with property income. Two pieces of evidence which have some bearing on this point can now be introduced.

Table 3 **British landownership 1873–5** (a) in England, 1873

Class	No. of owners	Acres (000s)
Peers and peeresses	400	5728
Great landowners	1288	8497
Squires	2529	4319
Greater yeomen	9585	4782
Lesser yeomen	24,412	4144
Small proprietors	217,049	3931
Cottagers	703,289	151
Public bodies	14,459	1443
Waste		1524
Total	973,011	34,519

Concentration coefficient, R, of private holders is 0·817 excluding cottagers and 0·944 including cottagers.

5. Wheat prices at Exeter in 1688 as a ratio of those in 1436 were 3·84 (Mitchell, 1962, p. 484).

(b) in England and Ireland, 1874–5

Lower class limit (in acres)	No. of persons	Acreage (000s)	Gross revenue estimates (£000)
100,000+	1	181	161
50,000+	3	194	188
20,000+	66	1917	2331
10,000+	223	3098	4337
5000+	581	3974	5522
2000+	1815	5529	9579
1000+	2719	3799	7914
500+	4799	3317	6427
100+	32,317	6827	13,680
50+	25,839	1791	4302
10+	72,640	1750	6509
1+	121,983	478	6438
0+	703,289	151	29,127
Total	966,275	33,006	96,515

The concentration coefficient for acreage was 0·858 for those holding 1 acre or more, and 0·774 for those holding 10 acres or more. The concentration coefficients of gross revenues based on these same classifications were 0·697 and 0·678.

Sources: Table 3 (a): Bateman (1883, p. 515); this table is culled from *The Modern Domesday Book* and correspondence to correct for variation in spelling of landowners holding land in several counties. Table 3 (b): Spahr (1893, p. 162), as taken from the Domesday Book for 1874–5. Bateman suggests several changes above 2000 acres showing greater concentration (lower class limit in acres – frequency): 100,000 – 44; 50,000 – 71; 20,000 – 299; 10,000 – 487; 6000 – 617; 3000 – 982; 2000 – 1320. There is some question of Irish holdings.

First, as mentioned earlier, Colquhoun's estimates for 1801 had 20 socio-economic classes listed which were not stated in King's 1688 data. These 20 classes, given earlier, included shopowners, manufacturers, merchants, etc. which in general might be considered as the emerging groups. The analysis from Lorenz curves for the 1801–3 data yields

	Number of families and single individuals	$\bar{X}$ (£)	R
25 classes similar to those of King	1,958,000	87·9	0·545
20 classes including those emerging with economic growth	252,000	198·1	0·501
45 classes	2,210,000	99·8	0·555

The new element at this stage has not increased total inequality, even though its income average is higher. Its internal relative dispersion is less than that for more traditional classes.

Secondly, the introduction of evidence from British 1812 and 1849 income-tax data, using Schedule D income from trade and the professions, shows the following results

1812, $X \geqslant$ £150, 13 income classes, $b = 0.85$
1849, $X \geqslant$ £150, 13 income classes, $b = 0.74$
$[t(0.85, 0.74) = 7.31; t_{05} = 1.72]$

Inequality in the developing trade and professional sector in 1812, as measured by $b = 0.85$, was at least as large as that of the total taxable income inequality in 1801, with $b = 0.82$. By 1849, Schedule D income had a slope b of 0.74. This was sufficient to elicit the conclusion in the Parliamentary Papers, 'this remarkable fact that the incomes have increased more under the smaller classes of income than the larger ones' (Parliamentary Papers, 1852, vol. 9, p. 593). It will be recalled that R. Dudley Baxter's data for 1867 employ Schedule D income, yielding a b of 0.72. One has access again to a concept of total income in 1911 where the slope is 0.58. From 1811 to 1911 the number of males employed in the agricultural sector with its great inequality remained relatively unchanged while the male labour force expanded more than five times in other endeavours with less inequality (Mitchell, 1962, p. 60).

The argument is thus one that there was a continued widening of opportunity for non-propertied income groups. Statistical evidence indicates that income inequality, particularly in upper-income groups, has decreased for several centuries. This trend has been accelerated in the twentieth century.

References

BATEMAN, J. (1883), *The Great Landowners of Great Britain and Ireland*, Harrison.
BAXTER, R. D. (1968), *National Income, the United Kingdom*, Macmillan.
BOWLEY, A. (1920), *The Change in the Distribution of the National Income, 1880–1913*.
CHALMERS, G. (1804), *An Estimate of the Comparative Strength of Great Britain*, J. Stockdale.
COLQUHOUN, P. (1806), *A Treatise on Indigence*, J. Hatchard.
COLQUHOUN, P. (1815), *A Treatise on the Wealth, Power and Resources of the British Empire*.
DAVENANT, C. (1771), in Sir Charles Whitworth (ed.) *The Political and Commercial Works*, vol. 2, p. 184.
DEANE, P. (1955–6), 'The implications of early national income estimates for the measurement of long-term economic growth in the United Kingdom', *Econ. Devel. cult. Change*, vol. 4, pp. 3–38.
GEORGE, D. M. (1966), *London Life in the Eighteenth Century*, Penguin.
GRAY, H. L. (1934), 'Incomes from land in England in 1436', *Eng. hist. Rev.*, vol. 49 pp. 607–39.
KING, G. (1936), in G. Barnett (ed.) *Two Tracts*.
KUZNETS, S. (1963), 'Quantitative aspects of the economic growth of nations', *Econ. Devel. cult. Change*, vol. 11, pp. 1–80.

MITCHELL, B. R. (1962), *Abstract of British Historical Statistics*, Cambridge University Press.

PROCOPOVITCH, S. N. (1926), 'The distribution of national income', *Econ. J.*, vol. 36, pp. 69–82.

Report of the Commissioners of Her Majesty's Inland Revenue (1965), *Report 107*, p. 83, HMSO.

SOLTOW, L. (1965), 'The share of lower income groups in income', *Rev. Econ. Stats.*, vol. 47, pp. 429–33.

SPAHR, C. B. (1893), in R. T. Ely (ed.) *The Present Distribution of Wealth in the United States*, Library of Economics and Politics, Crosswell and Co.

STAMP, J. (1916), *British Incomes and Property*, King & Son.

STAMP, J. (1922), *Wealth and Taxable Capacity*, King & Son.

TAYLOR, A. J. (1960), 'Progress and poverty in Britain in 1780–1850; a reappraisal', *History*, vol. 45, p. 17.

6 R. J. Nicholson

The Distribution of Personal Income

R. J. Nicholson, 'The distribution of personal income', *Lloyds Bank Review*, no. 83, 1967, pp. 11–21, and editor's note.

In 1957, Professor F. W. Paish contributed an article to this *Review* in which he examined the changes in the distribution of personal income over the years 1938 to 1955, and two years later Dr H. F. Lydall made a more detailed study of the changes over the longer period 1938 to 1957. These writers showed that the concentration of personal income, both before and after tax, in the hands of the top 5 per cent of income recipients was substantially reduced after the war, compared with 1938, and that this tendency towards greater equality continued during the postwar years which their analyses covered. Indeed, Lydall found that 'If anything the tendency towards reduced inequality of pre-tax income seems to have been accelerating.' The present article, linking up with this earlier work, examines the distribution of personal income in the period 1949–63 to see what light more recent data shed on the trends found for the earlier postwar years.

Defining personal income

Both Paish and Lydall used the estimates of personal income as set out and tabulated in the national income and expenditure accounts for the UK. These figures have been criticized, however, particularly by Titmuss (1962), as being inadequate for studying changes in the distribution of incomes. A further analysis based on these data thus requires some preliminary justification.

First, it is argued that the number of incomes in the national income tabulations is a compromise between the number of family incomes and the number of individual incomes, since it is derived from Inland Revenue records in which the incomes of husband and wife are counted as one, and all other incomes are counted separately. Hence, the distribution of personal income could be affected by changes in the age of marriage and by changes in the proportion of the total population married and of married women going out to work. These changes may be important when prewar and postwar distributions of income are compared, because considerable sociological movements took place as a result of the war, and it was in connection with such comparisons that Titmuss made his sharpest criticisms.

However, these demographical and sociological changes have been less rapid since 1949 and would not distort comparisons of income distributions over the last decade.

Secondly, this definition of personal income is criticized on the ground that certain claims on wealth are excluded: for instance, undistributed profits and 'tax avoidance' incomes which fall outside income-tax regulations. The effect of extending the definition of personal income to include these other claims on wealth is by no means certain and there are, anyway, differences of opinion as to what the appropriate definition should be, e.g. whether companies' undistributed profits should be included. It is probable that the shape of the income distribution, i.e. the proportionate shares of different income groups, might be modified but it does not follow that the *trend of changes* in income distribution derived from the national income tables would be discredited. Indeed, even in prewar/postwar comparisons, Lydall's estimates suggest that the trends would not be fundamentally altered. In the national income figures of personal income we do, at least, have a consistently defined aggregate which must account for a major proportion of total income on any definition and one which is adequate for picking out changing trends in the distribution of incomes in postwar years.

In the following tables, comparisons are made between various levels of income and shares of particular groups in terms of incomes ranged in order of size. For example, the top 1 per cent of incomes all receive more than a certain amount, those in the top 5 per cent are all above a lower figure, those in the top 30 per cent are above a still smaller figure, and so on. Thus, Table 1 shows that the top 1 per cent of incomes were all above £1861 in 1949 and exceeded £3364 in 1963, while the top 40 per cent of incomes had a minimum of £304 and £773 in these two years. These money incomes which divide off the top 1 per cent, top 5 per cent, top 10 per cent and so on of incomes may conveniently be referred to as 'percentile incomes'.[1] Secondly, the distribution of incomes can be considered in terms of percentage shares. From Table 3 on page 102, for example, it will be seen that in 1963 the top 1 per cent of incomes received 7·9 per cent of the total, the next 4 per cent received 11·2 per cent, and those in the range from the 11th to the 40th percentage bands from the top shared 39 per cent of the total.

1. This method of using 'percentiles' was that employed by Lydall. Alternatively, using Paish's method, the comparisons could be made in terms of the shares of specified *numbers* of incomes. In view of the gradual increase in the number of incomes over the years the percentile-income method is preferable. All the numerical results given in the present article have been obtained by logarithmic interpolation into the published distributions.

Incomes before tax

Percentile incomes before tax are shown in Table 1 and index numbers derived from them in Table 2.

Table 1 **Incomes before tax**

		1949 (£)	1957 (£)	1959 (£)	1960 (£)	1961 (£)	1962 (£)	1963 (£)
Top	1% at least	1861	2545	2839	3039	3162	3255	3364
,,	5% ,,	763	1198	1350	1442	1526	1592	1697
,,	10% ,,	565	940	1068	1151	1215	1273	1357
,,	20% ,,	427	773	844	909	966	1028	1067
,,	30% ,,	353	667	718	776	828	865	899
,,	40% ,,	304	577	613	653	719	742	773
,,	50% ,,	259	491	514	543	612	621	645
,,	70% ,,	122	304	315	331	374	378	400

Table 2 **Index numbers of incomes before tax**

	1957 (1949 = 100)	1959 (1957 = 100)	1960	1961	1962	1963
			(1959 = 100)			
Top 1%	137	112	107	111	115	119
,, 5%	157	113	107	113	118	126
,, 10%	166	114	108	114	119	127
,, 20%	181	109	108	115	122	126
,, 30%	189	108	108	115	121	125
,, 40%	190	106	107	117	121	126
,, 50%	190	105	106	119	121	126
,, 70%	249	104	105	119	120	127

Between 1949 and 1957, the lower the income the greater the rate of increase of income (first column, Table 2). Without exception, the growth-rate increases as one moves from the upper to the lower income ranges. These trends, which have been studied in detail by Lydall and Paish, indicate some reduction in the inequality of incomes in the postwar years up to 1957.

The next column, however, shows a different picture. Between 1957 and 1959 the top three percentile incomes increased most rapidly, the rates of increase of the lower ranges being progressively less, so that the lowest pre-tax incomes show the least rate of growth. This represents a movement away from equality, the higher incomes pulling away from the lower ones. Over the period 1959–63 all incomes, except the top one, increased in about the same proportion. It is clear, therefore, that since 1957 the trend towards equality in incomes before tax has ceased.

An alternative way of showing these trends, and one which brings out clearly the changes in the distribution of incomes over time, is to set out the percentages of total income held by selected groups of income-recipients, counting from the richest to the poorest.

Table 3 **Percentage distribution of incomes before tax**

| Group of income recipients | 1949 | 1957 | 1959 | 1960 | 1961 | 1962 | 1963 |
	%	%	%	%	%	%	%
Top 1%	11·2	8·2	8·4	8·5	8·1	8·1	7·9
2%–5%	12·6	10·9	11·5	11·4	11·1	11·1	11·2
6%–10%	9·4	9·0	9·5	9·8	9·7	9·7	9·6
11%–40%	34·9	37·6	38·4	38·5	37·6	38·6	39·0
41%–70%	19·2	23·1	22·5	22·1	23·5	22·6	22·6
Bottom 30%	12·7	11·3	9·7	9·8	10·0	9·8	9·7

The most considerable change is that which took place between 1949 and 1957. Between these two years the proportion of pre-tax income accounted for by the top 10 per cent of incomes fell from over 33 per cent to 28 per cent, while that of the middle 11–70 per cent increased from 54 per cent to nearly 61 per cent. The share of the bottom 30 per cent fell slightly, so that, as Paish has noted, the redistribution was from the extremes to the middle ranges. The percentage shares from 1957 onwards, however, show no continuation of these trends. Apart from a reduction in the proportion going to the bottom 30 per cent, the distribution since 1957 has not significantly changed.

Incomes after tax

Because of the stability that we have just noted in the distribution of pre-tax incomes since 1957, changes in rates of income tax and surtax may be important in affecting the distribution of incomes at the actual disposal of persons. Table 4 will serve to summarize the way tax rates have changed. It shows, in the form of index numbers for two specimen families of different composition, the amounts of earned income taken in tax at different levels of income for the tax years 1956–7 to 1962–3.

Clearly, there has been a general reduction in rates of direct taxation, but the most considerable fall has been in the rates on higher incomes since 1960–61. On an income of £1000, a married couple with three children paid in tax in 1960–61 rather less than threequarters of what they paid in 1956–7, and two thirds of this sum in 1962–3. If their income had been £5000, however, while in 1960–1 they would still have paid 79 per cent of their 1956–7 tax total, in 1962–3 their tax liability would have dropped sharply to 59 per cent. This greater proportionate reduction was, in fact, experienced by all those with annual incomes of about £3000 and upwards, i.e. incomes in the top ranges.

Under a progressive tax system, the effect of reductions in tax rates can be offset by the effect of inflation on money incomes. As Paish pointed out

During a period of rising prices, a man who succeeds in increasing his income before tax by an amount just enough to offset the rise in the cost of living, so that his *real* income before tax remains constant, is continually tending to move into higher tax brackets. With a system of progressive taxation, he will therefore pay in tax a constantly increasing proportion of a constant real income, even if rates of tax are not raised.

To show how tax changes have affected the distribution of incomes Tables 5 and 6 on page 104 repeat the foregoing analysis for percentile incomes (as defined on page 100) and the shares of groups of income-recipients for incomes after tax.

Table 4 **Index numbers of amounts taken in income tax and surtax**

| | *Married couple without children* | | | | | *Married couple with three children* | | | |
| | *(Pre-tax earned income £)* | | | | | | | | |
	600	1000	2000	5000	10,000	1000	2000	5000	10,000
1956–7	100	100	100	100	100	100	100	100	100
1957–8	100	100	100	89	92	84	97	85	89
1958–9	100	100	100	89	92	84	97	84	89
1959–60	88	91	91	83	87	73	88	79	84
1960–61	88	91	91	83	87	73	88	79	84
1961–2	88	91	91	61	66	73	88	59	64
1962–3	77	87	90	61	66	66	87	59	64

Incomes after tax over the period 1949–57 (except that at the 50 per cent mark) show the same trend towards equality as incomes before tax. The changes between 1957 and 1959, similarly, bring this trend to an end with higher post-tax incomes increasing more than those in the lower ranges. Between 1959 and 1963 all incomes increase by about the same amount. This pattern of change is confirmed by the distribution of incomes after tax, as given in Table 7.

Whether taken before tax or after tax, therefore, the distribution of incomes shows the same general trends, with the tendency towards greater equality ceasing after 1957. However, some slight difference between the two cases is shown by the results for the very high incomes. Before tax, the

Table 5 Incomes after tax

		1949 £	1957 £	1959 £	1960 £	1961 £	1962 £	1963 £
Top	1% at least	1270	1822	2073	2161	2327	2406	2545
,,	5% ,,	660	1038	1212	1292	1357	1427	1480
,,	10% ,,	520	860	965	1036	1087	1164	1205
,,	20% ,,	382	701	787	831	868	933	973
,,	30% ,,	317	593	655	711	761	794	819
,,	40% ,,	277	526	557	588	633	667	699
,,	50% ,,	250	439	478	508	540	557	576
,,	70% ,,	115	281	287	305	333	336	356

Table 6 Index numbers of incomes after tax

		1957 (1949 = 100)	1959 (1957 = 100)	1960	1961 (1959 = 100)	1962	1963
Top	1%	144	114	104	112	116	123
,,	5%	157	117	107	112	117	122
,,	10%	165	112	107	113	121	125
,,	20%	183	112	106	110	119	124
,,	30%	187	110	109	116	121	125
,,	40%	190	106	107	114	120	126
,,	50%	176	109	106	113	117	121
,,	70%	245	102	106	116	117	124

Table 7 Percentage distribution of incomes after tax

Group of income-recipients	1949 %	1957 %	1959 %	1960 %	1961 %	1962 %	1963 %
Top 1%	6·4	5·0	5·2	5·1	5·5	5·5	5·2
2%–5%	11·3	9·9	10·6	10·5	10·5	10·7	10·5
6%–10%	9·4	9·1	9·4	9·4	9·1	9·4	9·5
11%–40%	37·0	38·5	39·8	39·8	38·9	39·2	39·5
41%–70%	21·3	24·0	23·7	23·5	24·3	23·6	23·5
Bottom 30%	14·6	13·4	11·2	11·7	11·9	11·7	11·8

highest percentile income (i.e. that relating to the top 1 per cent of incomes) increased less rapidly than the others over the period 1959 to 1963: by 19 per cent, against 25–27 per cent for the rest (Table 2). After tax, however, the increase is the same as for the other groups (Table 6). Similarly, the proportion of incomes before tax taken by the top 1 per cent class fell over this period, from 8·4 to 7·9 per cent. (Table 3), whereas on a post-tax basis the share was unchanged, at 5·2 per cent (Table 7).

Thus, tax changes underline the ending of the movement towards equality, since their effect is to improve the relative position of the top income groups – a somewhat striking result, conflicting with what might have been expected from a tax system in which rates are steeply progressive.

The burden of taxation

Table 8 shows that between 1949 and 1957 the proportion of total tax collected from the top 5 per cent of incomes fell from 69·5 to just over 54 per cent, while that raised from the middle 11 per cent–70 per cent band increased correspondingly, from 20·5 to 36 per cent. This shift in the burden of taxation reflects the combined effects of three factors: changes in the tax rates, which were reduced during these years; the inflation of money incomes – so that equivalent real incomes are taxed at higher proportionate rates; and the redistribution of pre-tax income away from the highest income groups taxed at the highest rates, a development which Paish has called the 'loss of taxable capacity'. This loss of taxable capacity (shown by the figures in Table 3) was the main cause of the shift. Although tax rates on the highest incomes fell proportionately less than those on lower incomes, the percentages of pre-tax income taken in direct taxes (shown in Table 9 overleaf) fell for the top 5 per cent of incomes but rose or remained constant for the 6 per cent–70 per cent band.

Table 8 **Percentages of total income tax and surtax raised from specified groups of income-recipients**

Group of income recipients	1949	1957	1959	1960	1961	1962	1963
Top 1%	46·0	35·3	34·5	34·4	30·0	28·4	28·0
2%– 5%	23·6	18·9	20·1	19·7	19·9	18·5	19·3
6%–10%	8·6	9·0	10·2	10·0	10·0	10·8	11·0
11%–40%	16·2	24·9	24·8	25·4	27·6	29·7	29·8
41%–70%	4·4	11·2	9·7	9·7	11·4	11·8	11·3
Bottom 30%	1·3	0·7	0·6	0·8	1·0	1·0	0·6

Between 1957 and 1963 the tax burden continued to be lightened on the highest incomes. The proportion of total tax collected from the top 5 per cent of incomes fell from 54 to 47 per cent, but that from the 6 to 10 per cent band rose from 9 to 11 per cent and that from the 11 to 70 per cent band increased from 36 to 41 per cent (Table 8), the major part of these shifts occurring after 1960. How did this happen?

During these years, as we have seen, the distribution of income before tax was virtually unchanged. There was, therefore, no further significant loss of taxable capacity. The shift in the tax burden must, then, have been

Table 9 **Percentages of pre-tax income of specified groups of income-recipients taken in direct taxes**

Group of income-recipients	1949	1957	1959	1960	1961	1962	1963
Top 1%	48·8	45·5	43·1	46·1	41·5	39·7	39·1
2%–5%	22·4	18·4	18·3	19·7	20·0	19·9	19·0
6%–10%	10·9	10·7	11·3	11·6	11·5	12·6	12·5
11%–40%	5·5	7·1	6·8	7·5	8·2	8·8	8·4
41%–70%	2·7	5·2	4·5	5·1	5·4	5·9	5·5
Bottom 30%	1·2	0·7	0·7	0·9	1·1	1·1	0·6
All incomes	11·9	10·6	10·5	11·4	11·2	11·4	11·0

the result of the greater proportionate reduction after 1960 in tax rates on the highest incomes (Table 4). Indeed, as Table 9 shows, it was only for the top 1 per cent that there was a fall in the percentage of income taken in direct taxes over the period 1957 and 1963, a fall proportionately greater than that between 1949 and 1957. For all other ranges of income the reduction in tax rates has been offset by the inflation of money incomes, with a corresponding rise in the relative amounts taken by the tax collector.

Thus, although the burden of direct taxation has shifted over the whole period 1949 to 1963 the explanation of the shift has changed. Before 1957 it was due to loss of taxable capacity in the highest income groups; since then it has been due to changes in tax rates.

Reasons for check to greater equality

The trend towards the reduction of inequality in the distribution of personal income seems to have come to an end by 1957. Indeed if, as is sometimes suggested, certain 'tax avoidance' incomes and other claims on wealth outside personal income have increased over the last decade and are concentrated more among higher income-recipients, it is possible that the distribution of incomes on some wider definition may have moved towards greater inequality. This, however, is conjectural. In the context of personal income as defined in the national income accounts, a comparison of Tables 3 and 7 shows that the significant change has been the end of the trend towards equality in incomes before tax. Why has this occurred?

The reasons for the continued movement towards equality after the war were rising prices, continuously high demand and the virtual elimination of unemployment, all of which led to earned income rising faster than other forms of personal income. Lydall's view was that, so long as these trends were unchecked, the tendency towards equality would continue. There was certainly no failure of demand after 1957 – gross domestic product grew at a marginally faster rate 1957–63 than over the years 1949–57 – and employment was no less full. What, then, has happened? It is true that consumers' prices increased at a faster average rate in the years 1949 to 1957 than in the later period 1957 to 1963: at 3·9 per cent, against 2·0 per cent, a year. This may have been a contributing factor to the end of the movement towards equality but is unlikely to be the whole explanation. More important has been the change in the rates of growth of different forms of personal income.

Table 10 **Growth of forms of personal income**

	1938–49 (1938 = 100)	1949–57 (1949 = 100)	1957–63 (1957 = 100)
Wages	231	173	129
Salaries	237	190	157
Total employment income	240	179	140
Professional persons	189	129	136
Farmers	509	129	118
Sole traders	179	129	125
Total self-employment income	216	129	125
Rents, dividends, interest	104	142	172
Transfers	271	170	179

The first two columns, covering the periods during which reductions in inequality of personal income have been demonstrated by Paish and Lydall, show that the most rapidly growing sector of personal income was income from employment, growing faster than total self-employment income and incomes from rent, dividends and interest.

Since 1957 the pattern has changed. Growth of employment income has slowed down relatively to that of self-employment income and, within employment income, the rate of growth of wages has slowed down relatively to that of salaries. In self-employment income, that of professional persons has expanded most rapidly, faster, in fact, than wages. The most striking change, however, has been the accelerating rate of growth of rent, dividends and interest after the war, emerging as the most rapidly-growing sector of personal income since 1957.

Some light on the relative growth-rates of total wages and salaries is shed by the figures below, derived from the national income accounts, showing numbers of wage- and salary-earners, and average wages and salaries in manufacturing industry.

Between 1949 and 1957 the average wage in manufacturing increased by 73 per cent and average salary by only 54 per cent. Up to 1955, moreover, the number of wage-earners increased more than the number of salary-earners. Since 1957 average salaries have caught up, and increased at much the same rate as average wages; between 1957 and 1963 the increases in manufacturing industry were 35 per cent for salaries and 31 per cent for wages, rates of growth confirmed by the Ministry of Labour's indexes of salaries and average earnings (which include industries and services outside manufacturing). The number of wage-earners, however, has fallen since 1955, whereas the number of salary-earners has continued to rise, indeed by nearly one fifth since 1957. Thus, with the average salary increasing as fast as the average wage, the relatively greater rate of growth of *total* salaries than of wages since 1957 is due to the continued increase in the number of salary-earners. Table 11 shows also that the average salary is about 50 per cent greater than the average wage but, of course, salaries reach up into much higher income ranges than wages.

Table 11 **Wages and salaries in manufacturing industry**

		1949	1955	1957	1963
Wage-earners	(000)	5870	6340	6290	6150
Salary-earners	(000)	1170	1500	1600	1890
Average wage	(£)	290	444	503	659
Average salary	(£)	489	661	754	1020

It is not possible to obtain estimates of numbers or average incomes of those classified in the national income accounts as professional persons, but since these include doctors, dentists, lawyers and architects, average professional incomes are certainly very much higher than wages. Rent, dividends and interest, like salaries and professional incomes, are usually associated with higher incomes and it is, therefore, the more rapid growth of these three forms of personal income, particularly rent, dividends and interest, compared with that of wages, that has ended the trend towards equality in income.

Dr Lydall, writing of the years up to 1957, saw the trend to greater equality, though unlikely to continue as rapidly in the future as in the immediate past, as a long-term development which might be stopped or reversed only by the onset of a major slump. Professor Paish was more doubtful

It seems likely, however, that the process of redistribution would tend to slow down even if prices continued to rise. . . . Most of all it could be because investors and others . . . will increasingly seek out means for ensuring that their money incomes rise at least part of the way with them.

The more rapid growth of the incomes of professional people and of rent, dividends and interest since 1957 supports Paish's view. A particular instance of the latter is seen in the increased buying of equities by private individuals, either directly or through unit trusts specializing in high-income yields adding to income or in capital growth adding to wealth (which is more unequally distributed than income) and making for future capital gains. How far these tendencies will be offset by the capital gains tax or by changes in rates of income tax which, under a Labour government, may reverse recent trends and become more steeply progressive, it is impossible to say. The corporation tax introduced in April, 1965, is intended to give a strong inducement to companies to plough back more of their profits for expansion. It is possible, therefore, that the proportion of company income distributed as dividends – which has increased over the past decade – may decline. Nevertheless, the aggregate amount distributed as dividends can be expected to increase as total profits increase, so that personal income from dividends will continue to grow even if, possibly, less rapidly than in the past.

At the other end of the scale, the increases in pensions introduced in 1965 will raise some incomes in the lower ranges, but it is unlikely that this will bring about any fundamental change in the distribution of incomes, because relatively small amounts are involved and increases in pensions tend to lag behind increases in other incomes. Certainly, the present deflationary policies, the incomes freeze and the slowing down of the growth of the national product, following the stability of the income distribution since 1957, must make it doubtful whether the trend in the distribution of incomes for the immediate future is set in the direction of greater equality.

Editor's note

The tables given in Reading 6 cover the period 1949–63. This note brings two of his key tables up to date. Unfortunately these tables can only be extended to the year 1967, since the relevant information is no longer published in the National Income and Expenditure Blue Book. The decision to cease publication of this series – on grounds of 'the increasing amount of estimation required' (Blue Book, 1971, p. 101) – represents a serious reduction in the amount of information available about the distribution of income.[1]

The changes in the before tax distribution of income are summarized in Table 3a (which is in the same form as Table 3 in Reading 6). The extension of the period to 1967 does not affect Nicholson's conclusion that 'the most considerable change is that which took place between 1949 and 1957' (page 102).

1. The only official estimates available for years since 1967 are those published by the Inland Revenue, which are much less complete.

Table 3a **Percentage distribution of incomes before tax**

Group of income recipients	1949	1957	1963	1967
Top 1%	11·2	8·2	7·9	7·4
2%–5%	12·6	10·9	11·2	11·0
6%–10%	9·4	9·0	9·6	9·6
11%–40%	34·9	37·6	39·0	38·9
41%–70%	19·2	23·1	22·6	22·7
Bottom 30%	12·7	11·3	9·7	10·4

Sources: Figures for 1949–63 from Nicholson, Table 3.
Figures for 1967 supplied by the author.

Table 7a **Percentage distribution of incomes after tax**

Group of income recipients	1949	1957	1963	1967
Top 1%	6·4	5·0	5·2	4·9
2%–5%	11·3	9·9	10·5	9·9
6%–10%	9·4	9·1	9·5	9·5
11%–40%	37·0	38·5	39·5	39·2
41%–70%	21·3	24·0	23·5	24·5
Bottom 30%	14·6	13·4	11·8	12·0

Source: as Table 3a.

Table 7a provides corresponding information for the distribution of incomes after tax (in the same form as Table 7 in Reading 6).

The period 1963–7 saw a very slight reduction in inequality in post tax incomes, and again supports the view that the experience of the 1960s differed significantly from that of the 1950s.

At the end of his article, Nicholson suggested that government policies 'must make it doubtful whether the trend in the distribution of incomes for the immediate future is set in the direction of greater equality' (page 109). Nothing in the estimates for 1963–7 indicates that this judgement was seriously wrong.

References

BLUE BOOK (1971), *National Income and Expenditure Tables*, Central Statistical Office.
LYDALL, H. F. (1959), 'The long-term trend in the size distribution of income', *J. of the Royal Stat. Soc.*, series A, 122, part 1, pp. 1–46.
PAISH, F. W. (1957), 'The real incidence of personal taxation', *Lloyds Bank Rev.*, vol. 43, pp. 1–16.
TITMUSS, R.(1962), *Income Distribution and Social Change*, Allen & Unwin.

7 H. P. Miller

Income Distribution in the United States

Excerpts from H. P. Miller, *Income Distribution in the United States*, A 1960 Census Monograph, United States Government Printing Office, 1966, pp. 1–26.

Introduction

Few statistics reveal as much about the operation of an economy as do those on income distribution. Although the levels of living that are possible in any society are prescribed by the size of the national product, a given output can be distributed in many different ways. It can provide palaces for live kings and pyramids for dead ones, but hovels and hunger for the mass of mankind; or it can be widely distributed and provide reasonably uniform levels of living for all.

In view of the complex questions that income statistics are used to answer, it would be surprising indeed if the data were easy to collect or to interpret. The difficulties of measurement and intepretation are attested to by Kuznets (1955, p. 4) who, after plowing this field for a lifetime, has called measures of income distribution '. . . preliminary informed guesses.' and by Brady, who has referred to income statistics in general as '. . . deficient in both quantity and quality' (1951, p. 4).

These judgements, however, can be made about all statistics. The more one knows about a set of numbers the less likely he is to be entirely satisfied with them. Numbers at best provide a very thorny path to the truth. Thus, the income statistician may find himself in a position not too different from that of Stephen Crane's 'Wayfarer'.

The wayfarer,
Perceiving the pathway to truth,
Was struck with astonishment.
It was thickly grown with weeds.
'Ha', he said,
'I see that no one has passed here
In a long time.'
Later he saw that each weed
Was a singular knife.
'Well', he mumbled at last,
'Doubtless there are other roads.'

As the story unfolds, the numerous and serious shortcomings of income statistics will be discussed in some detail. It would be a mistake, however, to dwell on the limitations of the data, for although there are still many unanswered questions, much more is now known about income distribution than ever before. The primary purpose of this monograph is to summarize and synthesize the information. It has been collected from many sources, but principally from the results of the past three decennial censuses, the annual surveys conducted by the Bureau of the Census since 1945, and data published by the Office of Business Economics of the Department of Commerce. The available data permit us to answer questions that would have been regarded as impossible to answer only a generation ago. We can now quantify with some degree of certainty the annual changes in the distribution of income among families (using several different definitions of income and the family), changes in the composition of lower and upper income groups, and the amount and direction of income changes among occupations and industries. We can also shed light on a host of other important economic questions.

To begin with, we might examine the widely held opinion that incomes in the United States are gradually becoming more evenly distributed. This view is held by prominent economists and is shared by influential writers and editors. Burns (1951) stated that the '. . . transformation in the distribution of our national income . . . may already be counted as one of the great social revolutions of history.' Samuelson remarked in 1961 that there are studies which suggest that '. . . the American income pyramid is becoming less unequal.' Several major stories on this subject have appeared in the *New York Times*, and the editors of *Fortune* announced in 1953 that 'Though not a head has been raised aloft on a pikestaff, nor a railway station seized, the US has been for some time now in a revolution' (1953, p. 52).

What are the facts about trends in the inequality of income distribution in the United States? Few would question that real incomes have risen for most of the population; or that even those who have been left behind enjoy a far higher level of living than most people in other parts of the world. Despite the generally high levels of living, we remain concerned about income shares.

Has there been any narrowing of this gap between the rich and the poor? If we stick to the figures, the answers are clear, unambiguous and contrary to widely held beliefs. The statistics show no appreciable change in income shares for nearly twenty years. The heart of the story is told in Table 1, which was obtained by ranking families and unrelated individuals from lowest to highest according to income and cumulating the amount of income each received. The table shows the per cent (or share) of the total income paid out each year that went to each fifth of the families and individuals, and to the top 5 per cent. The share received by the top 5 per cent is large because their incomes were so much larger than those of others. In 1962, families and individuals in the top 5 per cent on the average received $17,200 or more, whereas those in the lowest 20 per cent made $2900 or less (about $55 a week).

During the depression of the thirties there was a distinct drop in the share of the income received by the upper income groups. In 1929, the last year of the prosperous twenties, the top 5 per cent received 30 per cent of the income. Their share, which dropped regularly during the depression, amounted to about one fourth of the income at the time we entered the Second World War. The decline continued during the war years and in 1944 their share dropped to 21 per cent. Since that time there has been no significant change in the per cent of income received by the top 5 per cent, and a similar trend applies to the top 20 per cent.

At the bottom of the income scale, the data show that in 1935–6 the lowest 20 per cent of the families and individuals received only 4 per cent of the income, and that in 1944 their share rose to 5 per cent, where it has

Table 1 **Per cent distribution of families and unrelated individuals, by family personal income received by each fifth and by the top 5 per cent, for selected years, 1929–1962**

Income rank	1962	1961	1960	1944	1941	1935–6	1929
Families and unrelated individuals							
Total	100	100	100	100	100	100	100
Lowest fifth	5	5	5	5	4	4	}13
Second fifth	11	11	11	11	10	9	
Middle fifth	16	16	16	16	15	14	14
Fourth fifth	23	23	23	22	22	21	19
Highest fifth	46	46	45	46	49	52	54
Top 5%	20	20	20	21	24	27	30
Families							
Total	100	100	100	100	100	100	na
Lowest fifth	6	6	6	6	5	4	na
Second fifth	12	12	12	12	10	9	na
Middle fifth	17	17	17	16	16	14	na
Fourth fifth	23	22	22	22	22	21	na
Highest fifth	43	43	43	44	48	52	na
Top 5%	18	18	18	20	24	27	na

na Not available.
Source: Data for families and individuals from U S Bureau of the Census (1960, p. 166); and (1964, p. 8). Data for families for 1960–62 computed from U S Bureau of the Census (1964, p. 6); and for 1935–6, 1941 and 1944 from Goldsmith *et al.* (1954, p. 9).

remained ever since. The stability of the shares received by each of the other quintiles is equally striking.

These figures hardly support the view held by many Americans that incomes in our society are becoming more evenly distributed. The changes that took place – ending about a quarter of a century ago – involved in large measure a redistribution of income among families in the top and middle brackets. Although the share received by the lowest income groups increased slightly during the war, since then it has not changed.[1]

Problems of interpretation

The stability of income shares shown in Table 1 does not necessarily imply a stability of economic welfare; it is conceivable that a proportional increase in everybody's real income means more to the poor than to the rich. How can we compare the utility of a loaf of bread to the man who is starving, with the utility of another Cadillac to the man who already has three?

1. For an entirely different view of trends in income distribution see Kolko (1962). Kolko concludes that 'A radically unequal distribution of income has been characteristic of the American social structure since at least 1910, and despite minor year-to-year fluctuations in the shares of the income tenths, no significant trend toward income equality has appeared' (p. 13). This conclusion is based on data for 1910 to 1937 prepared by the National Industrial Conference Board and for 1941 to 1959 by the Survey Research Center of the University of Michigan. Kolko states that the NICB data are the best material on income distribution by tenths for the period prior to 1941. This statement is very questionable. The NICB data were considered so poor by a panel of experts, including Goldsmith and Kuznets, that they were excluded from US Bureau of the Census (1960), even though they had appeared in the earlier version of that book, Historical Statistics of the United States, 1789–1945. The figures for 1929 and 1935–6 shown in Table 1 are thought to be much more reliable than those used by Kolko.

An examination of the figures used by Kolko shows that the share of income received by the highest tenth of income recipients dropped from 38 and 39 per cent in 1927 and 1929, to 34 per cent in 1937 and 1941, to 29 per cent in 1958. He dismisses the figures for 1921 and 1929 without further explanation as representing exceptional years. He then concludes that the difference between the prewar and postwar figures can be eliminated when the latter are corrected to allow for their exclusion of all forms of income in kind and the very substantial understatement of income by the wealthy.' The figures in Table 1 include many types of income in kind and they have also been adjusted for underreporting of income. They do not include various items that accrue primarily to the wealthy which Kolko thinks should be added, notably expense accounts and undistributed profits. Also excluded from the concept and not mentioned by Kolko are various types of fringe benefits such as life insurance, medical care, health insurance and pension plans, as well as government services, which have been increasing rapidly in recent years and are widely distributed throughout the population. A study published in 1954 by Goldsmith and her colleagues showed that incomes were more equally distributed in the postwar period than in 1929, even when allowance is made for undistributed corporate profits (Goldsmith, et al., 1954, p. 20). A more recent study shows that the addition of capital gains to the distribution increases the share received by the wealthiest 5 per cent by only a fraction of a percentage point (Liebenberg and Fitzwilliams, 1961, p. 14).

Exact comparisons cannot be made; yet many people believe that satisfying the most urgent and basic needs of the poor implies some leveling up in the comforts of life, even though income shares have remained constant.

To cite further and similar examples, it is likely that the extension of government services which provide better housing, more adequate medical care and improved educational facilities has been of more benefit to low-income families than to those with higher incomes. And the increase in paid vacations has surely brought a more equal distribution of leisure time – a good that is almost as precious as money. Furthermore, improved working conditions, including air conditioning, better lighting, mechanization of routine work, and the like, have undoubtedly benefited more manual workers than those in higher paid and more responsible positions.

When allowance is made for these and other factors, it may well be that some progress has been made during recent years in diminishing the inequality of levels of living. But we do not know how much allowance to make, and our judgments could be wrong. Moreover, most opinions regarding changes in inequality, including those held by professional economists, are based on statistical measures of income rather than on philosophic concepts. With all their limitations, the income figures may well serve as a first approximation of changes in welfare.

The picture presented in Table 1 is further complicated by taxes. The figures shown are for income before taxes. Since families in the higher income groups pay a large share of the taxes, their share would be smaller on an after-tax basis. It is smaller, but not by as much as one might suppose. In recent years the top 5 per cent received 20 per cent of the income before taxes, and about 18 per cent of the income after Federal individual income tax payments were deducted (Goldsmith, et al., 1954, p. 132; Survey of Current Business, 1964, p. 8). Since the graduated income tax falls more heavily on the upper income groups than do most other major tax measures, it is not surprising that their share of the income is decreased when individual income tax payments are deducted. This tax, however, accounts for only 37 per cent of the $124 billion collected in 1962 by Federal, State and local governments from all sources (US Bureau of the Census, 1964, p. 416). Many of the other taxes – the sales tax, for example – are paid disproportionately by the lower income groups. Taking into account all tax payments, the equalization of income as a result of taxation would be less than that shown for the Federal individual income tax alone.[2]

Still restricting our attention to the interpretation of results shown in

2. For figures showing taxes paid as a per cent of income by income class in 1958, see Tax Foundation (1960, p. 17). This source shows no variation in the per cent of income paid in Federal, State and local taxes for each income class below $15,000. In each class, about one fifth of the income was paid in taxes.

Table 1, numerous other problems come to mind – problems centering largely on the definition of the income-receiving unit, on the accounting period over which income is cumulated, on concepts of income, and on the accuracy of the underlying data.[3]

To begin with definitions, the income-receiving unit shown in Table 1 is the family or the unrelated individual. The family is defined as a group of two or more persons related by blood, marriage, or adoption and living together. The income of the family is the combined total received by all family members during the calendar year. An unrelated individual is defined as a person (other than an inmate of an institution) who is not living with relatives. These persons are called unattached individuals in statistics compiled by the Office of Business Economics (OBE). For all practical purposes the terms are interchangeable.

When these definitions are examined critically a host of problems emerge. Since the end of the Second World War, a very sharp increase has taken place in the number of older people who maintain their own households rather than share living quarters with children or other relatives. This type of living arrangement has been made possible, for the most part, by the small measure of financial independence provided by the Social Security System, and by the prosperous conditions of the postwar years.

For the income statistician, the increasing tendency for older people to continue to maintain their own households creates serious problems. Today there are proportionately far more unrelated individuals than there were in the forties. These groups typically have very low incomes; thus their inclusion in the distribution tends to increase its inequality, since it creates relatively large numbers of units with little or no income at the bottom of the distribution. Therefore, even though the definition of the income-receiving unit has remained constant over time, changes in living arrangements of the population may have produced variations in the statistics. The impact of this change is minimized considerably by showing figures for families alone rather than for families and individuals combined. Table 1 shows that trends in income distribution for families alone are almost identical with those for families and individuals combined. Other methods of reducing the impact of changes in living arrangements on the measure of income concentration are described near the end of this chapter.

Closely related to the definition of the income-receiving unit is the accounting period covered by the figures. Kuznets (1955, p. 3) has referred to the classification of families by their income in a single year as the major limitation of income statistics for purposes of measuring income inequality.

3. Only brief reference to the conceptual problems associated with the interpretation of statistics on income distribution is made here. For a more complete discussion see Brady (1951).

Family income is defined as the combined receipts of all members of a family during a calendar year. Since the family includes only those persons living together at the time of the survey, some obvious distortions may arise. For example, a widow who had been supported by her husband during the year preceding the survey would be tabulated as an unrelated individual without income if she happened to be living alone at the time of the survey. Newly married couples who had been living with and supported by their parents during the preceding year would also appear at the bottom of the distribution. Here, of course, there is a dual problem – a change in family status, plus the fact that income is counted for only a single year. For a young family, low income has a significance entirely different from that for a middle-aged family.

Turning now to the income concept itself, we find that it presents several important limitations that complicate interpretation. The figures in Table 1 represent money and non-money income; in this respect they are much more complete than the census figures, which relate only to cash receipts. Since it is not feasible in a census to try to collect information on imputed income, the data necessary for adjustment were not available. However, much of what is counted as non-money income in Table 1 is included, not because it provides a more realistic portrayal of the funds available for consumption or saving by the average family, but for the sake of consistency with the national income accounts (Office of Business Economics, 1953, p. 20).

Few would argue about adding the value of non-money food or housing received by farmers or farm laborers. These items, however, accounted for only a little more than $3 billion of a total of about $25 billion of non-money income included in the aggregate that underlies the distribution for 1960 shown in Table 1. About $11 billion of the total represents imputed interest (largely the value of free banking services received by the owners of checking accounts, and the estimated amount that policy holders would receive if insurance companies distributed their property income), and about $6 billion is imputed rental income assumed to have been received by nonfarm homeowners who served as their own landlords.[4]

Money income includes the items usually thought of as income: cash wages and salaries; net income (after expenses) from self-employment; and cash income from other sources such as interest, dividends, net rental income, Social Security and unemployment benefits, private pensions, public assistance and regular contributions for support from persons not living in the household.

Both the family personal income concept (used in Table 1) and the

4. Based on data of the Office of Business Economics. For a more complete description of the items included in family personal income see appendix A [not reprinted here].

money income concept exclude imputed income from paid vacations, fringe benefits, and from many other receipts not normally counted as income. These concepts also exclude capital gains and losses, which have become more important during recent years for the upper income groups. While income from this source is of prime importance in many individual cases, it does not have a major impact on the overall income curve because it represents only about 2·5 per cent of total family personal income. An attempt made in 1958 to adjust the distribution of family personal income to include capital gains and losses showed that there was little if any change in the share of the aggregate received by each of the four lowest quintiles, and that the share received by the top 5 per cent increased only slightly – from 19·9 per cent to 20·3 per cent (Liebenberg and Fitzwilliams, 1961, pp. 12–15).

Distribution by income levels, 1929–62

[. . .] Since the depression of the thirties the increase in the aggregate and average family income has been widespread throughout the population, resulting in a general movement of families up the income scale. There have, of course, been many exceptions. The aged, uneducated and unskilled have not moved ahead as fast as the others; but even for these groups the sharp edge of poverty has been blunted (Harrington, 1962).

The more typical picture, especially during the postwar years, has been one of gradually rising family incomes due not only to the full-time employment of chief breadwinners, but also to the rising tendency for families to send secondary workers into the labor market. These factors, combined with the increasing productivity of American industry, have caused a persistent drop in the number and proportion of families at the lower income levels, and a corresponding increase in the middle and upper levels. Although part of the rise is due to an inflation of dollar values, even after adjustments are made for price changes, there has been a very marked increase in real family income.

The extent of the increase can be seen most dramatically in a single statistic. In 1929, at the height of the prosperous twenties, 31 per cent of the families and individuals had incomes under $2000. Using the same dollar standard, adjusted for price changes, we find that thirty-two years later only 12 per cent of the families and individuals had incomes this low. This decrease clearly means that there has been a very sharp drop in the proportion of persons living at near-subsistence levels, and that for millions of people *absolute* want has been eliminated.

Numerous studies have been made of trends in the overall distribution of families by income levels, and the factors associated with these trends are reasonably well known. The main reason for summarizing the data here is to provide a background for the more detailed analysis that will follow. Moreover, the summary data permit a comparison of figures from two of the major sources of information on the subject – the Census and OBE estimates. Tables 2 and 3 show the OBE data in current and constant dollars, respectively.

One dramatic change shown by these figures is a precipitous drop in the

Table 2 **Families and unrelated individuals, by family personal income level, for selected years, 1935–62**

Family personal income level	1962	1961	1960	1959	1958	1957	1956	1955	1954
families and unrelated individuals:									
Number millions	57·9	57·3	56·1	55·3	54·6	53·7	52·9	52·2	51·2
Per cent	100·0	100·0	100·0	100·0	100·0	100·0	100·0	100·0	100·0
Under $2000	12·0	12·9	13·1	13·6	14·1	14·2	14·6	15·8	17·5
$2000 to $3999	18·3	19·4	19·8	20·7	22·2	22·1	23·1	25·4	27·0
$4000 to $5999	20·4	21·3	21·7	22·3	23·9	24·3	25·8	26·1	25·7
$6000 to $7499	14·1	14·1	14·1	14·1	13·9	14·1	13·6	13·3	12·3
$7500 to $9999	15·7	14·7	14·5	14·0	12·6	12·6	11·6	10·0	9·2
$10,000 to $14,999	12·3	11·1	10·6	9·6	8·5	8·0	7·2	5·9	5·2
$15,000 and over	7·2	6·5	6·2	5·7	4·8	4·7	4·1	3·5	3·1
Average (mean) income	$7262	$6930	$6819	$6615	$6284	$6238	$6007	$5640	$5356
Aggregate income billions	$420·4	$397·0	$382·3	$365·8	$343·3	$334·6	$317·4	$294·2	$274·0
Per cent	100·0	100·0	100·0	100·0	100·0	100·0	100·0	100·0	100·0
Under $2000	1·8	2·1	2·1	2·3	2·5	2·6	2·7	3·2	3·9
$2000 to $3999	7·7	8·5	8·9	9·5	10·8	10·8	11·8	13·9	15·4
$4000 to $5999	14·1	15·3	15·9	16·9	18·9	19·2	21·3	23·0	23·8
$6000 to $7499	13·0	13·6	13·9	14·4	14·8	15·1	15·2	15·8	15·3
$7500 to $9999	18·6	18·2	18·3	18·1	17·2	17·4	16·5	15·1	14·7
$10,000 to $14,999	20·2	19·2	18·6	17·3	16·3	15·5	14·4	12·5	11·6
$15,000 and over	24·6	23·1	22·3	21·5	19·5	19·4	18·1	16·5	15·3
Families:									
Number millions	46·9	46·2	45·4	44·8	44·1	43·7	43·4	42·7	41·8
Per cent	100·0	100·0	100·0	100·0	100·0	100·0	100·0	100·0	100·0
Under $2000	6·9	7·5	7·4	7·8	8·0	8·2	8·4	9·3	10·7
$2000 to $3999	14·4	15·6	16·0	16·9	18·7	18·6	19·9	22·6	24·7
$4000 to $5999	20·6	21·8	22·6	23·6	25·7	26·3	28·5	29·3	29·1
$6000 to $7499	16·0	16·2	16·3	16·5	16·4	16·6	16·0	15·7	14·6
$7500 to $9999	18·6	17·5	17·4	16·7	15·1	15·1	13·7	11·9	11·1
$10,000 to $14,999	14·8	13·5	12·8	11·6	10·3	9·7	8·6	7·0	6·3
$15,000 and over	8·7	7·9	7·5	6·9	5·8	5·5	4·9	4·2	3·5
Average (mean) income	$8151	$7797	$7667	$7435	$7065	$6992	$6706	$6303	$5994
Aggregate income billions	$382·2	$360·1	$347·8	$332·9	$311·7	$305·3	$290·7	$268·9	$250·3
Per cent	100·0	100·0	100·0	100·0	100·0	100·0	100·0	100·0	100·0
Under $2000	1·0	1·2	1·2	1·3	1·4	1·5	1·6	1·8	2·3
$2000 to $3999	5·4	6·2	6·5	7·1	8·3	8·3	9·3	11·3	12·7
$4000 to $5999	12·7	14·1	14·8	15·9	18·2	18·8	21·0	23·1	24·2
$6000 to $7499	13·2	14·0	14·3	14·9	15·5	15·8	16·0	16·7	16·3
$7500 to $9999	19·7	19·3	19·4	19·3	18·4	18·5	17·6	16·1	15·7
$10,000 to $14,999	21·7	20·6	20·0	18·5	17·5	16·6	15·4	13·5	12·5
$15,000 and over	26·3	24·6	23·8	23·0	20·7	20·5	19·1	17·5	16·3

Table 2 – *continued*

Family personal income level	1953	1952	1951	1950	1947	1946	1944	1941	1935–6
Families and unrelated individuals:									
Number millions	50·5	50·2	49·5	48·9	44·7	43·3	40·9	41·4	38·4
Per cent	100·0	100·0	100·0	100·0	100·0	100·0	100·0	100·0	100·0
Under $2000	16·9	17·8	18·7	23·2	24·9	26·4	30·5	58·9	77·7
$2000 to $3999	26·6	28·2	31·0	34·2	38·2	40·1	40·3	32·1	17·5
$4000 to $5999	26·3	27·3	26·4	24·0	20·6	19·5	17·3	} 6·8	} 3·3
$6000 to $7499	12·6	11·6	10·7	7·9	7·0	5·9	5·5		
$7500 to $9999	9·4	8·2	6·8	5·6	4·8	4·0	3·4	0·9	0·6
$10,000 to $14,499	5·2	4·1	3·8	3·1	2·7	2·5	1·7	} 1·3	} 0·9
$15,000 and over	3·0	2·8	2·6	2·0	1·8	1·6	1·3		
Average (mean) income	$5389	$5122	$4904	$4444	$4126	$3940	$3614	$2209	$1631
Aggregate income billions	$272·2	$257·2	$242·7	$217·3	$184·6	$170·7	$147·7	$91·4	$62·7
Per cent	100·0	100·0	100·0	100·0	100·0	100·0	100·0	100·0	100·0
Under $2000	3·7	4·0	4·4	6·1	7·2	8·0	10·0	27·9	45·4
$2000 to $3999	15·0	16·8	19·2	23·1	27·8	30·4	33·2	40·1	28·7
$4000 to $5999	24·2	26·2	26·4	26·3	24·0	23·8	23·0	} 15·5	} 10·3
$6000 to $7499	15·6	15·1	14·7	11·8	11·3	9·9	10·1		
$7500 to $9999	14·9	13·5	11·8	10·8	10·0	8·7	8·0	3·5	3·2
$10,000 to $14,499	11·6	9·4	9·3	8·4	7·7	7·5	5·7	} 13·0	} 12·4
$15,000 and over	15·0	15·0	14·2	13·5	12·0	11·7	10·0		
Families:									
Number millions	41·1	40·8	40·4	39·8	37·0	35·9	33·3	32·9	30·4
Per cent	100·0	100·0	100·0	100·0	100·0	100·0	100·0	100·0	100·0
Under $2000	9·9	10·7	11·3	15·6	17·3	18·5	22·0	53·2	74·1
$2000 to $3999	24·1	26·2	29·8	34·1	39·5	42·2	43·4	36·2	20·3
$4000 to $5999	29·8	31·3	30·3	27·9	23·9	22·7	20·3	} 8·0	} 3·8
$6000 to $7499	15·1	13·8	12·8	9·4	8·3	6·9	6·6		
$7500 to $9999	11·3	9·8	8·2	6·8	5·8	4·8	4·1	1·1	0·7
$10,000 to $14,499	6·3	4·9	4·6	3·8	3·2	2·9	2·1	} 1·5	} 1·1
$15,000 and over	3·5	3·3	3·0	2·4	2·0	2·0	1·5		
Average (mean) income	$6041	$5737	$5477	$4969	$4574	$4369	$4027	$2437	$1784
Aggregate income billions	$248·4	$233·9	$221·4	$197·7	$169·3	$156·7	$134·1	$80·2	$54·3
Per cent	100·0	100·0	100·0	100·0	100·0	100·0	100·0	100·0	100·0
Under $2000	2·1	2·4	2·7	4·1	5·0	5·6	7·0	24·2	41·5
$2000 to $3999	12·4	14·2	16·9	21·0	26·2	29·3	32·4	41·4	30·5
$4000 to $5999	24·5	27·0	27·3	27·5	25·2	25·0	24·4	} 16·7	} 10·9
$6000 to $7499	16·7	16·1	15·6	12·5	12·0	10·5	10·9		
$7500 to $9999	16·0	14·4	12·5	11·5	10·7	9·3	8·6	3·8	3·4
$10,000 to $14,499	12·4	10·1	10·0	9·0	8·3	8·0	6·2	} 13·9	} 13·7
$15,000 and over	15·9	15·8	15·0	14·4	12·6	12·3	10·5		

Source: Family data for 1955–62 from Fitzwilliams (1964, p. 6); and for 1935–6, 1941, 1944, 1946, 1947, and 1950–54 from US Bureau of the Census (1960, p. 164).

proportion of families and individuals with incomes under $40 a week (less than $2000 a year). During the depression of the 1930s about 3 out of every 4 families and individuals received incomes less than this; by 1941, the proportion had dropped to 3 out of 5, and by 1950, to 1 out of 4. In 1962 only 1 of each 8 were receiving incomes this low.

Another view of this same change may be had in terms of share of all incomes received by families and individuals with incomes below $2000 per year. During the thirties, this group received nearly half of all incomes, and its share fell to about 1 in 4 by the start of the Second World War, and to about 1 in 50 in 1962.

It is true that the change in the value of the dollar during the last thirty years makes it hard to extricate the real change from the apparent change, but the figures suggest strongly, as does other information to be dealt with later, that there has been an impressive decline in the proportion of families and individuals at the lowest income levels.

During the same period, equally impressive changes were taking place at the other end of the income scale among the top income groups. During the thirties, and even as recently as 1941, only 1 per cent of the families in these groups had incomes over $10,000. By 1950, the proportion had increased fivefold, and in 1962, nearly one fifth of the families and individuals were in this income class. In terms of aggregate income, this top class received only one eighth of the total in the prewar period, compared with 45 per cent in 1962.

Table 3 **Per cent distribution of families and unrelated individuals, by family personal income level in 1962 dollars, for selected years, 1929–62**

Family personal income level (1962 dollars)	1962	1961	1960	1959	1947	1941	1929
Families and unrelated individuals							
millions	58·6	57·3	56·1	55·3	44·7	41·4	36·1
Total	100	100	100	100	100	100	100
Under $2000	12	12	13	13	16	27	31
$2000 to $3999	19	19	19	20	28	29	39
$4000 to $5999	21	22	22	22	26	22	15
$6000 to $7999	18	18	18	18	14	12	7
$8000 to $9999	11	11	11	11	7	4	3
$10,000 to $14,999	12	11	11	10	6	}6	5
$15,000 and over	7	7	6	6	3		

Source: Fitzwilliams (1963, p. 15).

The figures in Table 3 on income distribution, adjusted for price changes, show that although some of the preceding analysis must be modified, the basic conclusions are substantially unchanged. Starting at the bottom, we find that even during the boom of the twenties about one third of the families and individuals had incomes under $2000. This proportion dropped to about one fourth (27 per cent) at the outbreak of the Second World War, but was only 12 per cent in 1962. Thus, in a third of a century, the proportion of families and individuals with real incomes under $2000 has been reduced by about two thirds. During the same period, there was also a significant bulge in the proportions in the middle and upper income levels. In 1962, for example, the $6000 to $10,000 income group contained nearly three tenths of the total, compared with only one tenth in the prewar period. The purchasing power of this middle income group rose proportionately. The top income class – $10,000 and over – has also had a four-fold rise since the depression.

The Census figures corresponding to the OBE figures previously discussed are presented in Table I–7 [not included here – Ed.]; but it is the comparison of both series at selected points in the distribution, shown in Table 4, that clearly portrays the similarity of the trends in these data. At the lowest quintile both series show a relatively large increase between 1950 and 1951, moderate gains during the next two years, and a drop during the 1954 recession. The years 1955 and 1956 show a relatively strong recovery in both series – stronger in Census than in OBE – followed by four years of slow-to-moderate growth. Similar patterns of change are also found at the middle and top quintiles.

Trends in income inequality

Starting with Pareto in the latter part of the nineteenth century, interest in income distribution centered largely on the construction of Lorenz curves and the measurement of inequality rather than on other aspects of the subject. The early emphasis on the measurement of inequality may have been due partly to the fact that the statistical evidence was based on tax return figures for Western Europe, which could provide reasonable measures of income concentration, even though the figures did not represent the entire population.

However, since tax returns lacked the demographic and sociological data now commonplace in household surveys, it was not possible to analyse many of the factors that affect income distribution. A further reason for the early emphasis on the measurement of inequality was the search for broad generalizations about the nature of the income curve. One such formulation, the 'Pareto Law', was discussed in much of the literature of the early 1900s.

During recent years emphasis has shifted from the measurement of inequality toward an analysis of various parts of the income curve and the causes that underlie changes in income distribution. During the past decade, for example, two congressional hearings were held on the low-income problem in the United States, and a good deal of research has gone into the measurement and analysis of the causes of poverty. Much other research has centered on measuring the financial returns from investments in education – a type of analysis first touched on in the twenties but not revived seriously until the sixties.

Figures showing trends in the inequality of income distribution between the outbreak of the First World War and the years immediately after the end of the Second World War are found in the work of Kuznets, using data from Federal individual income tax returns. The major findings with respect to trends in income inequality based on Kuznets' work are summarized in Table 5. The method used to prepare these data will be reported here only in brief, since it has been described elsewhere in detail (Kuznets, 1953).

Briefly – and at the risk of oversimplification – Kuznets' method involves the calculation, for each net income class shown annually in *Statistics of Income*, of the amount of net income per tax return and the population represented by the returns. Net income in this case is defined as the sum of wages and salaries, net income from self-employment, interest, dividends, rents and royalties; excluded are capital gains and deductions from income except for business losses. The population represented by the returns includes those for whom income is reported as well as those listed as dependents. Per capita income is computed for each income class and the classes are ranked in descending order of per capita income. The cumulative totals of population and income recorded on the returns are then converted to percentages of the total population and of the aggregate income received, and the share of income received by the top 1 per cent and the top 5 per cent of the population is estimated by interpolation.

Table 5 shows that there was no change in the share of income received by the top 1 per cent or the top 5 per cent of the population between 1913 and 1930. In 1914, at the outbreak of war in Europe, the top 1 per cent received between 13 and 14 per cent of the income. This range prevailed in all but two years during the twenties and showed some tendency to rise during the latter part of the period. There was a slight drop in income inequality during the thirties, a marked drop during the Second World War and relative stability throughout the early postwar years.

Trends in inequality of income distribution for recent years, based on data published by OBE and the Bureau of the Census, are shown in Table 6.[5] These figures show changes in income shares not only for the top income groups, as in the Kuznets series, but throughout the whole range of the distribution. Focusing first on the top income group during 1929–47, we

5. The figures shown in Table 6 are for families and unrelated individuals combined. OBE data for families alone are shown in Table 1 for selected years. Census data for families alone appear in US Bureau of the Census (1963, Table 1). The trends based on families alone are virtually identical with those based on families and unrelated individuals combined.

Table 4 Selected quintile values of bureau of the census and office of business economics distributions of families and unrelated individuals, by income level: 1947 to 1962

Year	Lower limit of second fifth						Lower limit of middle fifth						Lower limit of highest fifth					
	Census			OBE			Census			OBE			Census			OBE		
	Income $	Increase from preceding year		Income $	Increase from preceding year		Income $	Increase from preceding year		Income $	Increase from preceding year		Income $	Increase from preceding year		Income $	Increase from preceding year	
		Amount $	Per cent		Amount $	Per cent		Amount $	Per cent		Amount $	Per cent		Amount $	Per cent		Amount $	Per cent
1962	2032	121	6·3	2940	150	5·4	4235	224	5·6	4950	240	5·1	9020	415	4·8	9900	440	4·7
1961	1911	-7	-0·4	2790	20	0·7	4011	20	0·5	4710	50	1·1	8605	306	3·7	9460	190	2·0
1960	1918	75	4·1	2770	80	3·0	3991	158	4·1	4660	160	3·6	8299	419	5·3	9270	360	4·0
1959	1843	101	5·8	2690	80	3·1	3833	191	5·2	4500	210	4·9	7880	366	4·9	8910	460	5·4
1958	1742	58	3·4	2610	20	0·8	3642	81	2·3	4290	10	0·2	7514	381	5·3	8450	130	1·6
1957	1684	35	2·1	2590	50	2·0	3561	109	3·2	4280	110	2·6	7133	180	2·6	8320	360	4·5
1956	1649	172	11·6	2540	150	6·3	3452	266	8·3	4170	250	6·4	6953	446	6·9	7960	550	7·4
1955	1477	130	9·7	2390	190	8·6	3186	216	7·3	3920	220	5·9	6507	325	5·3	7410	310	4·4
1954	1347	-94	-6·5	2200	-60	-2·7	2970	-98	-3·2	3700	-70	-1·9	6182	49	0·8	7100	-60	-0·8
1953	1441	38	2·7	2260	90	4·1	3068	204	7·1	3770	160	4·4	6133	419	7·3	7160	400	5·9
1952	1403	12	0·9	2170	80	3·8	2864	86	3·1	3610	190	5·6	5714	224	4·1	6760	310	4·8
1951	1391	275	24·6	2090	280	15·5	2778	366	15·2	3420	400	13·2	5490	550	11·1	6450	600	10·3
1950	1116	53	5·0	1810	x	x	2412	171	7·6	3020	x	x	4940	283	6·1	5850	x	x
1949	1063	-97	-8·4	na	na	na	2241	-84	-3·6	na	na	na	4657	-62	-1·3	na	na	na
1948	1160	21	1·8	na	na	na	2325	115	5·2	na	na	na	4719	157	3·4	na	na	na
1947	1139	x	x	na	na	na	2210	x	x	na	na	na	4562	x	x	na	na	na

Minus sign denotes decrease.
na Not available.
x Not applicable.
Source: Census data derived from US Bureau of the Census (annual issues); OBE data from *Survey of Current Business* (1964); and US Bureau of the Census (1960).

can see that the OBE series shows much the same picture as the previously described Kuznets series. According to OBE the share of the aggregate income received by the top 5 per cent of families and individuals dropped progressively from 30 per cent in 1929 to 21 per cent in 1947; while for the same period the Kuznets series shows a drop from 26 per cent to 17 per cent in the share received by the top 5 per cent of the population.

Neither the Census nor the OBE data show any change during the post-war period in income shares at any point in the income distribution. According to OBE the poorest 20 per cent of the families may have received a very slight gain in the share of income during the war years; but since 1944 the share has been constant at about 5 per cent. The Census data confirm this finding. Similarly, the wealthiest 5 per cent of the families and individuals received a constant share (about 20 per cent) of the aggregate in each year during the post-war period. This finding is also confirmed by the Census data (about 18 per cent).

Even though all available evidence points to a stability in the overall income curve during the fifties, this stability may be more apparent than

Table 5 **Percentage share of total income received by the top 1 per cent and top 5 per cent of the population: 1913 to 1948** (total income is defined here as the sum of employee compensation, entrepreneurial income, rent, interest and dividends)

Year	Top 1%	Top 5%
1948	8·38	17·63
1947	8·49	17·41
1946	8·98	18·20
1945	8·81	17·39
1944	8·58	16·62
1943	9·38	17·75
1942	10·06	18·94
1941	11·39	21·89
1940	11·89	22·71
1939	11·80	23·45
1938	11·45	22·80
1937	12·84	23·80
1936	13·14	24·35
1935	12·05	23·73
1934	12·48	24·88
1933	12·48	25·34
1932	13·25	26·71
1931	13·31	26·27
1930	14·12	26·19

Table 5 – *continued*

Year	Top 1%	Top 5%
1929[1]	14·50	26·09
1929[2]	14·65	26·36
1928	14·94	26·78
1927	14·39	25·96
1926	13·93	25·25
1925	13·73	25·20
1924	12·91	24·29
1923	12·28	22·89
1922	13·38	24·79
1921	13·50	25·47
1920	12·34	22·07
1919[1]	12·96	23·13
1919[2]	12·84	22·91
1918	12·69	22·69
1917	14·16	24·60
1916	15·58	na
1915	14·32	na
1914	13·07	na
1913	14·98	na

na Not available.
1 Comparable with earlier years.
2 Comparable with later years.
Source: US Bureau of the Census (1960, p. 167).

real. According to one theory, there is a good possibility that the equalization of incomes during the Second World War and the years immediately preceding the outbreak of the war continued into the postwar period but was obscured by other statistical factors. Kuznets has summarized this theory as follows:

[. . .] even in the 1950s there may have been forces making for narrower income inequality, but their effects may have been offset by the greater fractionalization of consuming units at both ends of the age distribution of heads (1962, pp. 36–7).

In other words, the splitting up of family groups, made possible by the growing importance of Social Security payments, would tend to increase the inequality of income by creating a relatively large number of low-income families. Elsewhere, Kuznets has hypothesized that the increasing urbanization of the population has tended to increase inequality of income because, '. . . all other conditions being equal, the increasing weight of urban population means an increasing share for the more unequal of the two component distributions' (1955, p. 8).

Table 6 Distribution of family personal income and total money income received by each fifth and the top 5 per cent of families and unrelated individuals, for selected years, 1929–62

Year	Census (total money income)							OBE (family personal income)						
	Total	Lowest fifth	Second fifth	Middle fifth	Fourth fifth	Highest fifth	Top 5 %	Total	Lowest fifth	Second fifth	Middle fifth	Fourth fifth	Highest fifth	Top 5 %
1962	100·0	3·3	10·5	17·3	24·6	44·2	17·3	100·0	4·6	10·9	16·3	22·7	45·5	19·6
1961	100·0	3·3	10·0	17·0	24·5	45·2	18·2	100·0	4·6	10·9	16·3	22·7	45·5	19·6
1960	100·0	3·4	10·3	17·4	24·4	44·5	17·9	100·0	4·6	10·9	16·4	22·7	45·4	19·6
1959	100·0	3·4	10·4	17·6	24·3	44·3	17·6	100·0	4·6	10·9	16·3	22·6	45·6	20·0
1958	100·0	3·5	10·7	17·8	24·6	43·4	16·9	100·0	4·7	11·0	16·3	22·5	45·5	20·0
1957	100·0	3·5	10·8	18·0	24·7	43·1	16·8	100·0	4·7	11·1	16·3	22·4	45·5	20·2
1956	100·0	3·4	10·6	17·5	24·5	44·0	17·5	100·0	4·8	11·3	16·3	22·3	45·3	20·2
1955	100·0	3·3	10·6	17·4	24·6	44·2	18·0	100·0	4·8	11·3	16·4	22·3	45·2	20·3
1954	100·0	3·1	10·2	17·5	24·7	44·5	17·7	100·0	4·8	11·1	16·4	22·5	45·2	20·3
1953	100·0	3·2	10·8	17·5	24·6	43·9	17·6	100·0	4·9	11·3	16·6	22·5	45·7	19·9
1952	100·0	3·5	10·7	17·2	24·0	44·6	18·9	100·0	4·9	11·4	16·6	22·4	44·7	20·5
1951	100·0	3·5	11·2	17·5	24·3	43·6	17·6	100·0	5·0	11·3	16·5	22·3	44·9	20·7
1950	100·0	3·2	10·4	17·2	24·1	45·1	18·2	100·0	4·8	10·9	16·1	22·1	46·1	21·4
1949	100·0	3·3	10·5	17·1	24·1	45·0	17·9	na	na	na	na	na	na	na
1948	100·0	3·6	10·7	17·1	23·9	44·8	18·1	na	na	na	na	na	na	na
1947	100·0	3·6	10·6	16·7	23·5	45·6	18·8	100·0	5·0	11·0	16·0	22·0	46·0	20·9
1946	na	na	na	na	na	na	na	100·0	5·0	11·1	16·0	21·8	46·1	21·3
1944	na	na	na	na	na	na	na	100·0	4·9	10·9	16·2	22·2	45·8	20·7
1941	na	na	na	na	na	na	na	100·0	4·1	9·5	15·3	22·3	48·8	24·0
1935–6	na	na	na	na	na	na	na	100·0	4·1	9·2	14·1	20·9	51·7	26·5
1929	na	na	na	na	na	na	na	100·0	12·5		13·8	19·3	54·4	30·0

na Not available.
Source: OBE data for 1955–61 from US Bureau of the Census (1964); and for 1929–54 from US Bureau of the Census (1960), census data from US Bureau of the Census (1963).

These hypotheses were tested by constructing Lorenz curves for various demographic characteristics for each year in the postwar period, and ascertaining which groups, if any, have had appreciable changes in income distribution. A summary of selected characteristics based on these data is shown in Table 7; full details have been published elsewhere (US Bureau of the Census, 1963). These figures show rather clearly that stability in the overall income curve reflects in large measure stability in the component distributions. For example, during 1947–60, there was no change at all in the distribution of income groups among urban families; the top 5 per cent and the top 20 per cent received about the same share of the aggregate income in every year during the decade. Thus there is no evidence of an equalization in the distribution of urban incomes offset by an increase in the proportion of urban families; nor is there any evidence that urban incomes are more unequally distributed than rural incomes. In fact, for the money income figures shown in Table 7, the reverse is evidently true. But even when total income is used, farm incomes appear to be more unequally distributed than urban incomes.[6] The idea that farm incomes are more equally distributed than nonfarm incomes (which appears elsewhere in the literature on income distribution) is without solid foundation (Copeland, 1947).

Of course it could still be argued that the overall stability of income distribution for the urban population masks important changes which have taken place for various subgroups within that population. But this hypothesis – like the idea that farm incomes are more equally distributed than nonfarm incomes – does not appear to be supported by the facts. As shown in Table 7, income distribution within the urban population has not shifted even when that population is further classified by labor force status of wife, age of head, or size of family. During the postwar years, for example, among urban families where the wife was in the paid labor force, there was no change in the share of income received by the wealthiest fifth and the top 5 per cent. The same is true for urban families with the wife not in the paid labor force.

However, it should be noted that incomes are much more equally distributed among families where the wife is working than where she is not working; the sizable increase in the proportion of families with working wives has therefore tended to decrease income inequality during the past decade.

The figures in Table 7 also suggest that the stability of income distribution during these years can be explained without reference to the increased tendency for older people to live alone. The figures for families headed by persons aged 35 to 44 and 45 to 54 show the same stability in income shares that appears in the total. It is conceivable, but not very likely,

6. Based on Lorenz curves constructed for data for farm-operator families and nonfarm families shown in Liebenberg and Fitzwilliams (1961).

Table 7 Gini ratio and per cent of aggregate total money income received by the top 20 per cent and top 5 per cent of families, by selected characteristics: 1947 to 1960

Year and income rank	All families									Urban families				
	Place of residence				Labor force status of wife		Age of head			Labor force status of wife		Age of head		
	United States	Urban	Rural nonfarm	Rural farm	In paid labor force	Not in paid labor force	35 to 44 years	45 to 54 years	4-person families	In paid labor force	Not in paid labor force	35 to 44 years	45 to 54 years	4-person families
Top 20%														
1960	42	41	42	49	37	43	39	41	40	36	43	39	40	39
1959	41	41	41	49	36	42	38	41	38	36	42	38	40	38
1958	41	40	39	47	36	42	38	43	39	35	42	38	41	39
1957	41	40	39	47	36	41	39	42	40	35	41	38	41	39
1956	41	40	41	48	36	43	39	42	39	35	41	39	40	38
1955	42	40	41	49	36	43	38	43	38	35	42	37	42	37
1954	42	40	42	50	36	43	39	42	na	35	41	37	40	na
1953	41	40	40	51	36	41	39	40	na	35	40	37	39	na
1952	42	41	41	50	38	43	39	43	40	37	41	38	42	39
1951	42	40	41	50	36	43	40	43	40	36	41	37	41	38
1950	43	41	43	51	37	44	42	44	41	35	42	na	na	na
1949	43	41	42	51	37	44	40	44	41	37	41	39	41	40
1948	43	40	42	51	na	na	41	43	42	na	na	39	41	40
1947	43	41	41	54	na	na	42	42	41	na	na	40	40	40

Table 7 – continued

| Year and income rank | All families | | | | | | | | | Urban families | | | | |
| | Place of residence | | | | Labor force status of wife | | Age of head | | 4-person families | Labor force status of wife | | Age of head | | 4-person families |
	United States	Urban	Rural nonfarm	Rural farm	In paid labor force	Not in paid labor force	35 to 44 years	45 to 54 years		In paid labor force	Not in paid labor force	35 to 44 years	45 to 54 years	
Top 5%														
1960	17	17	16	20	13	19	16	16	16	13	20	16	16	16
1959	16	16	16	21	13	18	15	16	14	12	18	15	16	14
1958	16	16	15	19	12	17	15	18	15	12	18	15	18	15
1957	16	16	15	18	12	17	16	17	16	12	18	15	17	16
1956	16	16	16	18	12	18	16	17	16	12	18	16	16	15
1955	17	16	17	19	12	19	15	18	14	12	19	14	18	14
1954	16	16	17	20	13	18	15	17	na	12	17	14	16	na
1953	16	16	14	21	13	17	14	15	na	12	16	14	15	na
1952	18	18	16	23	15	19	15	19	17	15	18	15	19	17
1951	17	16	16	22	13	19	16	18	16	13	18	14	18	15
1950	17	16	18	23	13	19	20	[1]	17	12	19	na	na	na
1949	17	16	17	23	13	18	15	18	17	13	17	16	16	16
1948	17	16	17	25	na	na	17	17	17	na	na	15	[1]	16
1947	18	16	16	25	na	na	17	17	17	na	na	16	16	16

[1] Represents cases where the upper limit of the fifth or top 5 per cent is in the open-end interval.
na Not available.

Gini ratio

1960	0·369	0·350	0·360	0·456	0·294	0·378	0·325	0·357	0·330	0·285	0·363	0·315	0·334	0·318
1959	0·366	0·344	0·356	0·456	0·285	0·368	0·315	0·355	0·306	0·272	0·346	0·301	0·331	0·295
1958	0·354	0·335	0·329	0·434	0·281	0·357	0·311	0·368	0·311	0·275	0·339	0·304	0·344	0·303
1957	0·351	0·332	0·331	0·445	0·283	0·358	0·319	0·360	0·317	0·265	0·332	0·302	0·336	0·303
1956	0·355	0·335	0·351	0·448	0·280	0·367	0·319	0·367	0·321	0·266	0·336	0·307	0·327	0·295
1955	0·366	0·337	0·354	0·451	0·280	0·377	0·310	0·379	0·306	0·261	0·340	0·282	0·348	0·278
1954	0·373	0·337	0·372	0·477	0·289	0·374	0·329	0·361	na	0·269	0·340	0·295	0·324	na
1953	0·360	0·329	0·341	0·486	0·283	0·361	0·315	0·339	na	0·269	0·327	0·292	0·310	na
1952	0·374	0·347	0·353	0·478	0·312	0·362	0·318	0·379	0·326	0·295	0·335	0·297	0·340	0·302
1951	0·361	0·329	0·356	0·460	0·289	0·365	0·335	0·369	0·318	0·272	0·329	0·291	0·338	0·286
1950	0·375	0·342	0·380	0·476	0·300	0·386	0·364	0·380	0·342	0·273	0·350	na	na	na
1949	0·379	0·339	0·365	0·488	0·307	0·377	0·341	0·384	0·341	0·286	0·336	0·312	0·341	0·314
1948	0·369	0·333	0·358	0·476	na	na	0·343	0·371	0·346	na	na	0·304	0·335	0·314
1947	0·378	0·344	0·348	0·493	na	na	0·353	0·365	0·341	na	na	0·321	0·336	0·305

na Not available.
Source: US Bureau of the Census (1963).

that the income distribution among younger families has been affected by the splitting off of elderly persons. This hypothesis cannot be tested; there is no way to add elderly persons back to family groups they would have joined had they lacked sufficient income to maintain their own households. In general, however, the incomes of elderly people tend to be quite low; it is doubtful that the addition of their income to the family total would have caused a significant change.

All available evidence presented in this chapter points to stability in the distribution of family income during the fifties, following a period of rather rapid change during the Second World War.

The data presented in Table 7 show that the Lorenz curves for most of the major component parts of the overall income curve were quite stable during the fifties. These curves, however, constitute only one element in determining the shape of the overall curve. Also important are the changes in the relative weights assigned to the various components and in their mean incomes. By the use of a standardization procedure it can be shown that changes in the weights assigned to the component distributions had no major impact on the overall distribution; that is, the actual overall distributions did not vary significantly from the distributions that would have been obtained if there had been no change in population weights throughout the period.

Table 8 shows the actual income shares received by the top 5 per cent and the top 20 per cent of the families for 1947 to 1960, and shares obtained from standardization procedures applied to the data. Similar information is shown in this table for Gini Concentration Ratios. The standardized figures for type of family (column 2) were obtained in the following way. Per cent distributions were obtained from the Current Population Survey for each year for each of the following twelve groups:

Urban –
    Husband–wife families, wife in paid labor force
    Husband–wife families, wife not in paid labor force
    Families with other male head
    Families with female head
Rural nonfarm – Same as for urban
Rural farm – Same as for urban

These per cent distributions were weighted by the number of families in each group in March 1960, and the results were summed to obtain a new total and per cent distribution for the country as a whole. The difference between the original and the adjusted (or standardized) distribution is entirely due to changes in the weights assigned to the component parts of the overall total.

Table 8 **Actual and standardized Gini concentration ratios of and shares of aggregate total money income received by the top 20 per cent and top 5 per cent of families: 1947 to 1960**

Year and income rank	Actual	Standardized				
		Actual distributions with 1960 population weights			1960 distributions with actual population weights	
		Type of family	Age of head	Size of family	Type of family	Age of head
	(1)	(2)	(3)	(4)	(5)	(6)
Top 20%						
1960	42	42	42	42	42	42
1959	41	41	41	41	42	42
1958	41	41	41	41	42	42
1957	41	40	40	40	42	42
1956	41	41	41	41	42	42
1955	42	41	42	42	43	42
1954	42	41	42	na	43	42
1953	41	40	41	na	43	42
1952	42	42	42	42	43	42
1951	42	41	42	41	43	42
1950	43	42	na	na	43	42
1949	43	42	43	42	43	na
1948	43	na	42	42	na	43
1947	43	na	43	42	na	43
Top 5%						
1960	17	17	17	17	17	17
1959	16	16	16	16	17	17
1958	16	16	16	16	17	17
1957	16	16	16	16	17	17
1956	16	16	16	16	17	17
1955	17	17	17	17	17	17
1954	16	16	17	na	17	17
1953	16	15	16	na	18	17
1952	18	17	18	17	17	17
1951	17	16	17	16	18	17
1950	17	17	na	na	18	17
1949	17	16	17	17	18	na
1948	17	na	17	17	na	17
1947	18	na	17	17	na	17
Gini ratio						
1960	0·369	0·369	0·369	0·369	0·369	0·369
1959	0·366	0·360	0·363	0·365	0·370	0·367

Table 8 – *continued*

Year and income rank	Actual	Standardized				
		Actual distributions with 1960 population weights			1960 distributions with actual population weights	
		Type of family	Age of head	Size of family	Type of family	Age of head
	(1)	(2)	(3)	(4)	(5)	(6)
1958	0·354	0·348	0·351	0·349	0·375	0·373
1957	0·351	0·346	0·349	0·346	0·375	0·370
1956	0·355	0·353	0·362	0·355	0·375	0·372
1955	0·366	0·357	0·365	0·359	0·378	0·374
1954	0·373	0·363	0·371	na	0·381	0·372
1953	0·360	0·346	0·356	na	0·376	0·372
1952	0·374	0·359	0·365	0·363	0·377	0·373
1951	0·361	0·357	0·361	0·356	0·379	0·372
1950	0·375	0·366	na	na	0·380	na
1949	0·379	0·362	0·371	0·371	0·382	0·374
1948	0·369	na	0·363	0·360	na	0·378
1947	0·378	na	0·365	0·360	na	0·375

na Not available.
Source: Table 7. See text for explanation of computations.

A similar procedure using residence by age of head (in 10-year age groups) was applied to obtain the data in column 3; and it was again applied using residence and size of family (two to seven or more persons) for column 4. Table 8 shows that in no case were the results based on the standardized distributions significantly different from the actual distributions. In no year did the share received by the top 5 per cent or the top 20 per cent of the families in the standardized distribution differ from the original distribution by more than one percentage point. The differences in the concentration ratios were equally small.

The figures shown in columns 5 and 6 were prepared by using the 1960 percentage distributions for each group for each year and weighting the distributions by the actual number of families in the group. The results were then summed to obtain an adjusted (standardized) distribution for the country as a whole. In this case, the difference between the original and the standardized distribution for the country as a whole is entirely due to changes in the component distributions. Here again, the differences between the actual and the standardized distributions are not significant.

References

BRADY, D. S. (1951), 'Research on the size distribution of income', *Studies in Income and Wealth*, vol. 13, National Bureau of Economic Research.

BURNS, A. F. (1951), *Looking Forward*, 31st annual report, National Bureau of Economic Research.

COPELAND, M. A. (1947), 'The social and economic determinants of the distribution of income in the United States', *Amer. econ. Rev.*, vol. 37, pp. 56–75.

FITZWILLIAMS, J. M. (1963), 'Size distribution of income in 1962', *Surv. curr. Bus.*, p. 15.

FITZWILLIAMS, J. M. (1964), 'Size distribution of income in 1963', *Surv. curr. Bus.*, p. 6.

FORTUNE, (1953), 'The changing American market', editors of *Fortune*, p. 52.

GOLDSMITH, S. F. *et al.* (1954), 'Size distribution of income since the mid thirties' *Rev. Econ. Stats.*, vol. 36, p. 9.

HARRINGTON, M. (1962), *The Other America*, Macmillan, Penguin edn, 1963.

KOLKO, G. (1962), *Wealth and Power in America*, Praeger.

KUZNETS, S. (1953), *Share of Upper Income Groups in Income and Savings*, National Bureau of Economic Research.

KUZNETS, S. (1955), 'Economic growth and income inequality', *Amer. econ. Rev.*, vol. 45, p. 4.

KUZNETS, S. (1962), 'Income distribution and changes in consumption', *The Changing American Population*, Institute of Life Insurance.

LIEBENBERG, M., and FITZWILLIAMS, J. M. (1961), 'Size distribution of personal income, 1957–60', *Survey of Current Business*, May, p. 14.

OFFICE OF BUSINESS ECONOMICS (1953), *Income Distribution in the United States*, Government Printing Office.

SAMUELSON, P. (1961), *Economics*, fifth edition, McGraw-Hill.

SURVEY OF CURRENT BUSINESS (1964), 'Data for families and individuals', Government Printing Office.

TAX FOUNDATION (1960), *Allocation of the Tax Burden by Income Class*, Tax Foundation Inc.

US BUREAU OF THE CENSUS (1960), *Historical Statistics of the United States: Colonial Times to 1957*, Government Printing Office.

US BUREAU OF THE CENSUS (1963), *Trends in the Income of Families and Persons in the United States: 1947–60*, technical paper no. 8, by H. P. Miller, Table 1, Government Printing Office.

US BUREAU OF THE CENSUS (1964), *Statistical Abstract of the United States: 1964*, Government Printing Office.

US BUREAU OF THE CENSUS (annual), *Current Population Reports – Consumer Income*, Series Pr-60, Government Printing Office.

8 H. F. Lydall and J. B. Lansing

A Comparison of the Distribution of Personal Income and Wealth
in the United States and Great Britain

H. F. Lydall and J. B. Lansing, 'A comparison of the distribution of personal income
and wealth in the United States and Great Britain', *American Economic Review*,
vol. 49, 1959, pp. 43–67.

Comparisons, though sometimes odious, are nearly always illuminating.
The possibilities for making comparisons between the United States and
Great Britain have been extended in recent years by the development in
both countries of sample surveys of consumers, particularly the Savings
Survey in Great Britain and the Surveys of Consumer Finances in the
United States.[1] The substance of this paper will be devoted to two main
topics:

1. The level of income and its distribution amongst households in the two
   countries;
2. The ownership of capital by households, its distribution and the types of
   assets held.

The distribution of income

The main emphasis in the following discussion will be on the distribution
of money income before income tax, but an attempt will also be made to
compare the distributions of income after income tax. Comparisons of
these distributions are intended to supplement comparisons already available from the national accounts of total income and average income per
capita. There is also an extensive literature on the distribution of income
for each country considered separately, e.g. (Cartter, 1955; Miller, 1955).
The survey data have two great advantages, however: The methods used in
the British and American surveys are similar, and the data are in such a
form that they can be reorganized in a flexible manner to prepare comparable tabulations.

The ratio of real incomes per capita for the United States and Great

1. In Great Britain Savings Surveys were initiated by the Oxford University Institute
of Statistics and carried out, with the help of grants from the Nuffield Foundation, for
three years in succession, 1952–4. The survey was continued in 1955 by the government
but it has been in abeyance for the past three years. The methodology used is broadly
similar to that in the Surveys of Consumer Finances in the United States. Most of the
data reported here has been drawn from those two surveys. Reports on the results of
the Surveys of Consumer Finances are published annually in the *Federal Reserve
Bulletin* and reports on the British Savings Surveys have appeared in the *Bulletin* of
the Oxford Institute of Statistics and in Lydall (1955).

Britain can be approximated from the national accounts, but the exact ratio is impossible to calculate, since patterns of output and expenditure, and effective prices and qualities of individual goods differ between the two countries. In one very careful comparison of the United States and the United Kingdom for the year 1950 it was estimated that, in American prices, per capita gross national product (at market prices) was 1·6 times as high in the United States as in the United Kingdom, while in British prices the same ratio was a little over 2 (Gilbert and Kravis, 1954, Table 27). The ratio of per capita consumption in the two countries, on similar calculations lay between 1·5 and 2.[2]

Measured in local currency the per capita gross national product of the United States in 1953 (at market prices) was nearly $2300 and of the United Kingdom about £330. This means that the American economy produced for each American (man, woman and child) nearly $7 for every £1 available for each inhabitant of the United Kingdom. A similar relation obtained also between per capita personal income before tax in the two countries.

Since they are designed for purposes of economic analysis, the surveys work with *income per household* rather than income per head. In the year 1953 the average total money income of American spending units, as estimated by the Survey of Consumer Finances, was $4570; in Britain the survey estimate for the year 1953–4 was £477. This represents a ratio of $9·6 to every £1. In comparing this ratio to the ratio of $7 to £1 from the national accounts allowance must be made for a difference in the average number of persons per unit, which is 2·9 in the United States against 2·25 in Britain. If per capita incomes were equal, the larger American units would receive larger incomes in the ratio of 2·9 to 2·25. Thus, the expected ratio of mean income per spending unit based on data from the national accounts adjusted for size of unit is not $7 per £1 but $9 per £1. It is reassuring to find that this ratio closely approximates that of $9·6 per £1 obtained directly from the surveys.

2. The relative purchasing power of the pound and the dollar varies widely for different goods and services. In general, those goods whose production is capital-intensive are cheap in terms of dollars while labor-intensive goods and all services are dear. A shopper in America who takes $4 to £1 as his standard of comparison will find that cars, television sets, washing machines and the like are much cheaper than in England; clothes are about the same or a little cheaper; and food varies according to type, with meat and highly processed foods being generally cheaper, while fruit and vegetables are often more expensive. The extreme example of a costly American service is the man's haircut. There is local variation in both countries, but the purchasing power parity ratio in this case appears to vary between $10 and $15 to £1. All personal services are expensive in America since the American wage or salary earner gets about $8 for each £1 paid to his British counterpart. Indeed, on an hourly basis he gets more. Hence, such services as education, medical attention, hotel accommodation and public catering are generally relatively expensive in America and cheap in England.

The difference may be partly attributable to differences in coverage – the surveys do not cover institutions and other quasihouseholds – or in the definition of income – the British survey includes certain income in kind which is not included in the American survey.[3] It is interesting to note, however, that the median survey incomes for the two countries were $3780 and £420 respectively; and these stand in the ratio of exactly $9 to £1. In the comparisons of distributions of spending-unit income which will be made below we shall frequently work on the assumption that $9 of spending-unit income in America is equivalent to £1 of spending unit income in Britain.[4]

There are various ways in which distributions of income in two different countries, or at different times in the same country, can be compared. A convenient method for our purpose is to rank the sample of spending units in each country in order of total income and then to divide them into tenths. The position of the deciles in relation to one another will provide a basis for comparing the shapes and degrees of dispersion of the two income distributions. Table 1 shows the pretax income deciles of British and American spending units derived from the 1954 surveys. In order to compare the relative positions of the decile points in the two countries ratios between pairs of deciles are shown in column 3.

As already noted, the ratio of the fifth decile (or median) in the United States to the fifth decile in Great Britain is exactly $9 to £1. And, in fact, six out of nine ratios are either 8·9 or 9·0. This means that for about two thirds of the way – from around 30 per cent from the top of the distribution to 10 per cent from the bottom – the two distributions are almost identical in shape. But both at the top and at the bottom there are deviations, with the ratios rising above 9·0 at the top and falling at the bottom decile to less than 8·0. The implication of these deviations is that American incomes are more widely dispersed than British incomes at each end of the distribution,

3. There are two items: income in kind of farmers, and the imputed value of owner-occupied houses.

4. The ratio of spending-unit income is not identical with the ratio of income per earner, since American spending units contain more earners on the average than British spending units. This is mainly because more American spending units are married couples. A rough estimate of the ratio of income per earner can be obtained by dividing the aggregate of 'earned income' in each country by the number of occupied persons. On the basis of such a computation it appears that the ratio of wage and salary income per employee (both full and part-time) in non-agricultural employment in 1953 was $8·5 to £1. If an individual in Britain wishes to compare his income with the income received by a person doing a similar job in the United States he may convert his annual income in pounds at this 'rate of exchange' (or a slightly lower rate for more recent years). If he finds an appreciable difference between the figure arrived at in this way and the dollar income of his 'opposite number' he can conclude that the two jobs occupy different positions in the two income scales.

Table 1 **Distribution by deciles, income before tax, United States and Great Britain**

Deciles	Spending unit income before tax, 1954 surveys			Family or household income before tax, 1952 surveys		
	United States ($)	Great Britain (£)	Ratio of US to GB	United States Families ($)	Great Britain Households (£)	Ratio of US to GB
Top	7680	810	9·5	7590	980	7·7
Second	6000	650	9·2	5760	720	8·0
Third	5000	560	8·9	4850	600	8·1
Fourth	4400	490	9·0	4180	520	8·0
Fifth	3780	420	9·0	3530	460	7·7
Sixth	3150	355	8·9	3000	410	7·3
Seventh	2500	280	8·9	2450	350	7·0
Eighth	1800	200	9·0	1700	280	6·1
Ninth	1000	130	7·7	940	170	5·5

or in other words, the distribution of income is more unequal in the United States than in Great Britain.

Since some part of the difference between the two distributions might be attributable to the difference in the size of the population units measured in the two countries a comparison was made of the ratios of deciles of family income in America to household income in Britain. The 'family' in the American surveys consists of all related persons living in the same dwelling; and distributions of family income are compiled for each American survey. The 'household' in Britain is slightly wider than the family and normally includes all persons, whether related or not, who share common house-keeping arrangements. Household income in Britain was compiled only in the 1952 survey, but on that occasion it was defined so as to exclude un-related boarders. Hence for the 1952 surveys it is possible to make a comparison between the distributions of family and household income in the two countries on a very similar basis.[5] The results of this comparison are shown in the right-hand portion of Table 1.

The effect of changing from a spending-unit basis to a family (or household) basis is to make the distributions from the two countries conform much more closely in the region above the median but to deviate more obviously below this level. In other words, this comparison makes it less clear that the American distribution of income is more widely dispersed at

5. The only difference is that a few of the British households contain indoor domestic servants and friends living with the family. The average number of persons per American family in 1952 was 3·23, and the average number of persons per British household 3·06.

the top of the income scale; but it reinforces the view that there is a significant difference between the British and American distributions at the bottom.[6]

A further difference between the two countries is in the nature of their tax laws. For some purposes it may be more appropriate to compare the distribution after taxes than the distribution before taxes. No attempt has been made to estimate the incidence of all taxes, but in both countries the survey staff did prepare an estimate of the liability of each spending unit for the national income tax. In Britain this estimate also included the liability for social security contributions. The inclusion of this item makes the British system of income taxation appear less sharply progressive than it is in fact. Even apart from this difficulty these estimates are subject to error. The investigators ranked the spending units by income before income tax and estimated the share of total income going to the top tenth, the second tenth and so forth. The results are shown in the first two columns of Table 2. The units were then re-ordered by income after taxes, and the shares of income after taxes accruing to each tenth are shown in the last two columns of Table 2. In studying the data it should be kept in mind that sample surveys do not properly represent the very highest incomes.

It is generally believed that the income tax in Great Britain is more progressive than in the United States, and some support for this view may be found in the table. The difference of three points between the share of all income received by the top tenth before taxes and that after taxes in the United States is clearly smaller than the corresponding difference of four points in Great Britain. But the main conclusion which emerges from the table is that while it may make some difference whether one compares the income distributions before or after taxes, it does not make much difference. In the remainder of this article we shall be concerned only with income before taxes.

The method of dividing the total population into tenths (or some other fraction) is one way of overcoming the difficulty which arises from the fact that each country uses its own *numéraire* or currency as a basis for its measurements. Another is to make a direct estimate of the relation between the two *numéraires*. Since the shape of the distribution of income is broadly similar in the United States and Great Britain, it is not unreasonable to scale the two distributions in relation to one another by reference to some central tendency. For this purpose we may take the relation between the

6. It is difficult to arrive at definite conclusions about the degree of dispersion at the top of the income scale on the basis of survey data, since it is probable that there is a lower response rate at these levels than amongst middle and lower income groups. The British survey of 1954 was less successful in this respect than the 1952 survey and it is probable that the 1954 distribution gives slightly too little weight to the top income groups.

Table 2 Spending units ranked by tenths according to income before taxes and after estimated income tax liability,[a] 1952 surveys

Tenths of spending units after ranking by income before taxes	Per cent of total income taken by each tenth		Tenths of spending units after ranking by income after taxes	Per cent of income after taxes taken by each tenth	
	US	GB		US	GB
Top tenth	31	30	Top tenth	28	26
2nd tenth	15	14	2nd tenth	15	14
3rd tenth	12	12	3rd tenth	13	13
4th tenth	10	10	4th tenth	11	11
5th tenth	9	9	5th tenth	9	10
6th tenth	8	8	6th tenth	8	8
7th tenth	6	7	7th tenth	7	7
8th tenth	5	5	8th tenth	5	5
9th tenth	3	3	9th tenth	3	4
Bottom tenth	1	2	Bottom tenth	1	2
Total	100	100	Total	100	100

[a] The taxes covered were: in the United States, federal income tax; in Great Britain, income tax (levied only by the central government), surtax (which is a part of the income tax affecting the highest incomes) and national insurance contributions (which are broadly invariant with income but depend to some degree on sex, age and occupational status).

two medians, which, as we have seen, are in the ratio – for spending units – of $9 to £1. Then, if we translate each range of British incomes measured in pounds into its equivalent in dollars at this 'rate of exchange', we can compare directly the proportion of all incomes falling within comparable income ranges. This is done in Table 3.

By this approach we are able to see more clearly where the differences between the two income distributions lie. The most striking difference is between the percentages of spending units receiving a total income of less than £100 or $900. At the other end of the income scale we also find that there are more American spending units than British with incomes above £1000 or $9000 and above £2000 or $18,000. It should be noted, however, that whereas there are more American spending units than British below the level of £100 (or $900), there are more British than American in the next income class running up to £200 (or $1800). The unusually high frequency of British spending units in this second lowest income class – which actually produces a secondary mode in the distribution – results from the social security arrangements in Britain which give married old-age pensioners an income in this range.

The proportion of elderly couples is greater in Britain than in the United

Table 3 **Distribution of spending units by total income before tax in comparable ranges of income, United States and Great Britain, 1954 surveys**[a] (percentages of spending units)

Comparable ranges of total income		United States	Great Britain
(£)	($)		
Under 100	(900)	8·3	4·5
100	(900)	11·5	15·7
200	(1800)	12·7	12·2
300	(2700)	14·2	14·4
400	(3600)	14·3	15·2
500	(4500)	13·5	12·8
600	(5400)	7·7	9·4
700	(6300)	5·7	5·4
800	(7200)	5·2	5·2
1000	(9000)	4·3	3·5
500	(13,500)	1·1	0·9
2000	(18,000)	1·6	0·9
Total		100·0	100·0

[a] Percentages in this and subsequent tables do not always add to exactly 100 because of rounding.

States, as can be seen from Table 4. But if elderly married couples in Britain were not receiving a government retirement pension they would not necessarily drop into the next lower income group. Most of them would probably cease to exist as separate spending units, becoming attached to the relatives with whom they already live or with whom they would be obliged to live in such circumstances.

Does the evidence so far presented justify the conclusion that American incomes are more unequally distributed than British? It must be admitted that the differences exhibited at the upper end of the income scale are not strictly significant in the sampling sense, and that they could even be the result of some slight difference in response rate amongst upper income spending units in the two countries. But the difference in the proportion of spending units in the lowest income group in Table 3 is well beyond the bounds of sampling error, in the sense that it could not have occurred by chance from similar populations except in a very small proportion of samples drawn at random.[7] It should also be noted that the differences

7. If the samples had been single-stage random samples the standard error of the difference between these two percentages would have been 0·65 per cent. Although the actual standard error of the difference between the two percentages has not been computed, it is most unlikely to exceed twice this figure, i.e. 1·3 per cent. The actual difference, of 3·8 per cent, is nearly three times this figure. For tables of sampling errors of the Surveys of Consumer Finances see (Federal Reserve Bulletin, 1956).

between the distributions of spending unit income shown by the 1954 figures are not exceptional: similar differences occur in the survey figures for 1952, 1953 and 1955. Moreover, there is reason to believe that the American survey estimates of the proportion of low income spending units in these years were if anything slightly too low, since new methods of drawing the sample of addresses in the surveys of 1956 and 1957 have revealed the existence of some low income spending units who were previously overlooked.[8]

Table 4 Age distribution of the total population[a] United States and United Kingdom, 1954

Age	Number in millions		Percentages of total	
	US	UK	US	UK
Under 10	34·2	8·2	21·0	16·0
10–19	23·9	6·8	14·8	13·3
20–44	57·7	17·9	35·6	35·0
45–64	32·9	12·5	20·3	24·5
65 and over	13·7	5·7	8·3	11·2
Total	162·4	51·1	100·0	100·0

[a] Both distributions are midyear estimates of the total population, including armed forces overseas.
Sources: US Bureau of the Census (1956); UK *Annual Abstract of Statistics* (1956).

Account should also be taken of the influence of certain differences in definition of the basic unit in the two countries. In America the 'spending unit' was defined as 'all persons living in the same dwelling and related by blood, marriage, or adoption, who pool their incomes for their major expenses'. In practice, any person of 18 and over, or a married couple, was treated as a separate spending unit if he (or she or they) earned more than $15 a week and contributed less than half his income to the common housekeeping expenses of the family. The British unit was defined in slightly narrower terms: all persons of 18 or over, and married couples, were to be treated as separate units unless they had an income of less than £50 a year

8. In 1956 the Survey Research Center made a substantial improvement in its sampling procedures in the field. The most important change was that, instead of relying exclusively on its own *ad hoc* lists of addresses within selected blocks, in many towns and small cities the Center began to make use of city directories. The result has been a more complete listing than could have been obtained by relying exclusively upon either the interviewers' lists or the directories. The dwellings previously missed tended to be small and inconspicuous, and many of them were occupied by low income spending units. Hence, one result of the change in sampling method was to increase the proportion of spending units with less than $1000 in the 1956 Survey by about one percentage point. Since the British surveys make use of official lists for drawing addresses, there is unlikely to be a similar bias in the sample coverage in Britain.

and were living with their relations. No questions was asked about the pooling of incomes and no combinations of adults were made except in the case just mentioned. In both countries children of under 18 were grouped with their parents or guardians. (The British unit was called an 'income unit', but for convenience the basic unit for both countries is referred to as a spending unit in this article.)

If the British definition of the spending unit had been used in America it might have been laid down that all persons with $500 or more of separate income should be treated as separate spending units, irrespective of whether they pooled the greater part of their income with the rest of the family or not. To investigate this possibility a special analysis of the composition of the spending unit was made, which is summarized in Table 5. The number of persons who, on the British definition, would have been treated as separate spending units, but were in fact combined with others in the American survey, amounted to only 4 per 100 American spending units. This is the measure of the difference introduced by the difference of definition. It means also that, had the American spending units been grouped according to the British rule (and taking $500 as roughly equivalent to £50) the average size of the American spending unit would have fallen only from 2·90 to 2·79.

Table 5 **Composition of the spending unit in the United States and Great Britain, 1954 survey** (persons per 100 S Us)

	US	GB
Married couples (2 persons per S U)	143	115
Single male heads of S Us	10	16
Single female heads of S Us	18	26
Total primary adults	171	157
Secondary adults with less than £50 or $500	13	1
Secondary adults with $500 or more	4	—
Total secondary adults	17	1
Children under 18	102	67
Total persons	290	225

Although only 4 per cent of American spending units would be treated differently according to the British rules, the effect of dividing up these spending units into separate 'British' units would be to increase the number of low income spending units in America. From a special analysis of American spending units in the 1954 survey it appears that nearly half the 'secondary' adults with $500 or more of income, who would have been treated as separate spending units in Britain, had less than $1000 of income. Moreover, if they were separated off, the parent spending units – with whom they were originally combined – would lose part of their income and some of them would fall below the $1000 level. The net result of applying the British definition would therefore, be, that the proportion of spending units with less than $1000 would increase from 9·5 per cent to 11·6 per cent. It can be presumed that the proportion of spending units with less than $900 would rise from the 8·3 per cent shown in Table 2 to at least 10 per cent.

Finally, it should be taken into account that the British population contains far more single person spending units than the American population. As shown in Table 5, there are 42 unmarried heads of spending units per 100 spending units in Great Britain compared to 28 per 100 in the United States. Similarly, in Britain the proportion of spending units containing only a single individual is nearly twice as high as in the United States (Table 6). Since the incomes of single person spending units are on the average much lower than the incomes of multi-person spending units, which often include more than one income receiver, this difference in demographic structure would tend, *ceteris paribus*, to produce more low income spending units in Britain than in America. A study of the British figures reveals that almost all the spending units with less than £100 of income in the 1954 survey were single person units. Hence, if the proportion of all British spending units which were single persons had been as low as in America the effect would have been to reduce the proportion of under £100 spending units in the whole sample from 4·5 to less than 3 per cent.

In view of all this, there can be no doubt at all that there is a significant difference between the proportion of low income spending units in Britain and in the United States. The next task is to consider what features of the two countries are responsible for this difference.

Table 6 **Number of persons in the spending unit, United States and Great Britain, 1954 surveys** (percentages of total spending units)

Number of persons	United States	Great Britain
One	21	40
Two	29	26
Three	17	16
Four	16	10
Five	9	5
Six or more	8	3
Total	100	100
Mean number per S U	2·90	2·25

Reasons for the differences in the distribution of income

Differences in the distribution of income from one country to another may reflect differences in the allocation of the labor force to the major types of occupation. For example, since there is an international tendency for the mean income paid skilled workers to be larger than that paid to unskilled workers, differences in the proportion of manual workers of different levels of skill may lead to differences in the distribution of incomes between two countries. Even if two occupation groups have the same mean income, if the distributions of income for the two groups differ in dispersion the allocation of the labor force between them will influence the distribution of income in a country. It is also possible for differences to exist in the relative economic position of occupation groups from one country to another.

There is in fact a fundamental difference in the structure of the American and British populations in respect of the occupations of the people. The next to the bottom row of Table 7 shows the distributions of spending units by the occupation of the head, as derived from the surveys. A comparison based on census data would yield very similar results.

It should first be noted that, largely as a consequence of the difference in age structure, there is a larger proportion of retired and unoccupied heads of spending units in Britain than in the United States. Some part of this difference is also caused by the fact that more elderly Americans are living as dependents of their children and are consequently not treated as heads of spending units. On the other hand, more Americans are unoccupied because of unemployment. Amongst the occupied heads of spending units the most striking difference is in the much larger proportion of self-employed in America. A substantial part of this difference is due to the difference in the number of farmers in the two countries. In Britain only 1 per cent of spending unit heads are farmers, compared with 8 per cent in the United States. (In total the United States has about 4 million farmers, against about 350,000 in Great Britain.)[9] But it is clear that there are also proportionately more persons in the United States who have their own business or professional practice than in Britain.

These differences should be interpreted in the light of the distributions of income for spending units classified by the occupation of the head of the unit, shown in the columns of Table 7. The classifications used were, as far as possible, the same in both countries; but there may have been some differences in the treatment of marginal cases, especially in allocating occupations between the two white-collar classes or between the two categories

9. The figures refer to the number of persons whose major occupation is farming. In the United States part-time farming is not unusual, and it is also common for persons living in farm families to obtain income from activities other than farming. In addition there are in both countries many spare-time and hobby farmers.

Table 7 Distribution of spending units by occupation of the head in comparable ranges of income, United States and Great Britain, 1954 surveys (Percentages of spending units in each group)

Comparable ranges of income £	$	Managers and technical US	GB	Clerical and sales US	GB	Skilled manual US	GB	Unskilled manual US	GB	All self-employed US	GB	Farmers US	GB	Other self-employed US	Retired and unoccupied[a] US	GB
Under 100	(900)	0·3	0·1	1·1	0·1	1·1	—	10·3	2·2	10·8	3·9	20·7		2·3	29·6	18·6
100	(900)	2·0	2·2	4·5	15·4	4·2	3·5	19·8	12·8	14·3	7·0	21·6		8·1	29·3	49·0
200	(1800)	4·7	5·3	14·2	19·4	9·6	7·1	22·9	23·8	13·4	11·4	20·6		7·3	15·8	13·9
300	(2700)	6·0	5·0	18·7	16·9	15·5	18·9	20·2	19·9	13·5	10·1	15·5		11·7	10·9	7·2
400	(3600)	11·7	9·9	20·4	11·9	21·2	22·0	11·6	22·5	8·1	10·1	5·0		10·7	4·9	3·8
500	(4500)	19·6	11·9	14·3	14·3	20·6	20·8	7·9	7·8	7·6	8·5	2·9		11·5	4·4	2·1
600	(5400)	11·0	11·1	6·5	9·7	11·3	13·7	4·4	7·3	4·3	13·7	3·4		5·1	1·8	0·7
700	(6300)	13·5	13·0	5·4	6·2	6·4	6·2	1·6	3·7	3·9	7·2	1·5		6·0	1·1	0·6
800	(7200)	12·9	14·6	5·4	5·1	2·9	6·0	0·8	—	4·9	8·2	3·5		6·0	1·1	1·6
1000	(9000)	12·5	17·6	4·2	0·7		1·6	0·6	—	8·1	10·9	1·3		13·8	1·1	
1500	(13,500)	3·4	5·1	0·4	0·2		0·2	—	—	3·8	3·6	1·9		5·5	1·1 }	2·5 }
2000	(18,000)	2·4	4·2	0·3	0·1	0·1	—	—	—	7·4	5·4	2·1		11·9		
Total		100·0	100·0	100·0	100·0	100·0	100·0	100·0	100·0	100·0	100·0	100·0		100·0	100·0	100·0
% of all heads of spending units[b]		11	10	12	11	32	38	11	13	17	7[c]	8		9	16	21
No. of cases		410	426	391	342	887	817	273	249	555	242	227		328	449	387

[a] Includes housewives, students and unemployed.
[b] Spending units with heads whose occupation was not ascertained amounted to 1 per cent of the total for the US.
[c] Of the 7 per cent self-employed in Great Britain, 1 per cent were farmers and 6 per cent other self-employed.

of manual workers. In view of these difficulties in securing identical standards of classification we should not make too close a comparison of the distributions.

Considering the large proportion of units headed by retired and unoccupied persons in both countries, and especially in Great Britain, it is particularly important to compare the income distributions of these spending units, given in the last columns of Table 7. While the bulk of spending units of this sort in both countries lie in the bottom income classes, more American spending units are in the very lowest class. The reason for this difference is doubtless the existence of a more extensive social security system in Britain, which lifts most of the lowest income class of retired and unoccupied persons up to at least the second income class.[10]

Take next the distributions of income for the self-employed. Table 7 includes a comparison – in comparable ranges of income – of the distribution of all spending units headed by self-employed persons in Britain with three arrangements of American self-employed spending units: all combined, farmers only and the remainder. In the case of the aggregate groupings for the two countries, while the distribution at the upper end of the income scale is not dissimilar, the distribution at the lower end is quite different. There are more American self-employed in the low income groups than there are British. The reason for this is immediately apparent when we divide the American self-employed into farmers and nonfarmers. In Britain the number of farmers is so small as to make little difference to the total picture; and, in any case, they are distributed by income in much the same way as the other self-employed. In America, on the other hand, the income distribution of farmers is quite different from that of other self-employed. The latter are distributed broadly along the same lines as the British self-employed, with perhaps a greater tendency to reach high income levels; but American farmers are distributed quite differently, with a high concentration in the low income classes.

One important reason, then, for the differences between the British and American distributions of income is the low average income of the American farmer. In the 1954 Survey the average total income of American farm operator spending units was a little over $3000 compared with about $4700 for all other spending units. Part of this difference can be explained by the exclusion of nonmoney income from the American survey definition of income; but, even with due allowance for this, American farmer spending units would have on the average not more than about three quarters of the

10. Of the heads of spending units aged sixty-five and over in the 1954 surveys, 80 per cent were in receipt of government transfers in Britain, compared with only 58 per cent receiving either government or private transfers in America.

income of other spending units.[11] A large proportion of American farmers fall in the two bottom income classes in our distribution; and it is clear that it is they who contribute quite substantially to the 'extra' low income spending units in America compared with Britain.

In general, the distributions for the remaining occupations are remarkably similar; and in the case of spending units headed by skilled manual workers they are almost identical. Amongst the managers and technical, professional and administrative workers the distributions at the lower end of the scale are similar but they differ somewhat at the upper end. There are more British manager spending units with incomes between £1000 and £1500 than American manager spending units with incomes of $9000–$13,500. Some of this difference, however, may be caused by a different allocation in the two countries of marginal cases between the 'manager' group and the 'clerical and sales' group. In the latter group there are more American spending units with high incomes than there are in Britain.

The only remaining major difference to be found in any pair of distributions is between the distributions of spending units headed by unskilled manual workers. In this case a substantially larger proportion of American spending units are in the two lowest income classes.

Are there any special reasons why so many American farmers and unskilled workers should fall in the lowest income class? In the case of farmers it may be said that the tendency for farmers' incomes to fall below other incomes is worldwide, with only a few exceptions, of which postwar Britain is one. But the other exceptions include such newly developed countries as Australia and New Zealand (Bellerby, 1956). In the United States, farm income per worker has been lower than nonfarm income per worker for many years. Available statistics suggest that the farm worker was even worse off compared to the nonfarm worker in 1910 than in 1954 (Black, 1956, pp. 23–8). It is, therefore, not surprising that the farm labor force in the United States declined from 11·5 million in 1910 to 9·5 million in 1940, 7·5 million in 1950 and 6·6 million in 1955. What is not clear on the

11. An interesting sidelight on the relative positions of farmers in Britain and America is given by the fact that while the average American farmer has only three quarters of the average income of other American spending units, the British farmer has about twice the average income of other British spending units. American agriculture ranges from large mechanized farms using highly rationalized techniques to the numerous small low income farms which populate the Appalachian region. The rapid rate of investment in farming plus the improvements in agricultural technique in recent years have increased the productivity of one group of farmers while reducing others to a marginal or sub-marginal status. Thus many American farmers, especially in the southern Appalachians, belong to an impoverished and dying class. The British farmer on the other hand is, broadly speaking, just another businessman.

H. F. Lydall and J. B. Lansing 149

face of it is why, even in 1954 after fifteen years of industrial prosperity in America, so many farmers should have continued to accept such low incomes.

Part of the answer, we suggest, lies in another feature of the American scene, namely, the lack of homogeneity of the labor force. An analysis of spending units with less than $1000 income (in the 1954 survey) by both occupation and race reveals that more than a third of the low-income farmers were Negroes and more than a third of low income unskilled workers were either Negroes or other colored persons. This compares with a figure of 11 per cent of colored heads of spending units in the whole population. Negro farmers, almost all of whom are in the South, comprise about one sixth of all farmers, but half of them – according to the 1954 survey – have money incomes of less than $1000. In the case of the unskilled the situation is different. The concentration of colored workers in the low income class of the unskilled is mainly attributable to the fact that a quarter of all unskilled workers are colored. In addition, the proportion of colored unskilled in the lowest income class is slightly greater than the proportion of white unskilled.

It seems reasonable to conclude that one factor making for the existence of a fairly large proportion of low-income spending units in America is the racial heterogeneity of the population. Negroes and other colored people are often of low education, and frequently suffer from other disabilities when in competition with whites in the labor market. Hence they tend to crowd into low-paid occupations and to earn less than would be acceptable to white members of the community. The British population, on the other hand, is nearly homogeneous and does not contain significant groups of workers who can be paid at lower rates than the generally accepted minimum. It can be expected that the progress of integration and the increasing industrial and geographical mobility of the Negro population will sooner or later eliminate this factor in the creation of low income spending units in the United States. Similarly, the gradual extension of improved social security arrangements to cover all sections of the population will reduce the number of retired and unoccupied spending units falling in the lowest income class.

The distribution of capital

A reasonably complete picture of the economic situation of an economic unit, or group of economic units, requires a knowledge of their balance sheets as well as of their income distributions. Data on the total value of capital owned by spending units have been collected occasionally though not annually in the British and American surveys. In this paper, the comparisons of capital ownership will be based on the American survey of 1953 and the British survey of 1954. Since the pattern of capital ownership changes very slowly this discrepancy of one year is of no importance.

The aim of the surveys in this field was to discover for each spending unit the current value of its total net worth – that is, its assets minus its liabilities. So far as possible all assets and liabilities were covered; but some were excluded because of expected difficulties in obtaining full and accurate information about them.[12] Estimates by Goldsmith (1956, p. 107) suggest that the total value of the excluded items for the United States in 1949 was nearly a third of aggregate personal net worth.

Both surveys exhibit a tendency to underestimate the aggregate value of both assets and liabilities. There are no perfectly suitable outside benchmarks for comparison, but there seems little doubt that the amount of personal liquid assets revealed by each survey is only about two thirds of the aggregate stock in the hands of private households. The explanation of this understatement is probably twofold: first, that the surveys fail to secure the cooperation of a few wealthy people who hold a large proportion of all financial assets; and secondly, that some people who do cooperate with the surveys in most respects are reluctant to give complete data on their financial assets. These influences tend to produce a similar degree of understatement of holdings of corporate stock (and in Britain of government securities). In respect of non-financial assets – such as cars, houses, farms and businesses – there are fewer grounds for expecting understatements to occur. Assets of this sort are visible and identifiable, and people are, on the whole, less reluctant to talk about them (Kish and Lansing, 1954, pp. 520–38).

As a result of the downward bias on estimates of financial assets, the surveys underestimate the value of total assets, and to some extent of

12. Assets included owner-occupied homes, farms and unincorporated businesses (where an owner-occupied house formed part of a building used also as a farm or for other business purposes, value of house included with value of farm or business), other real estate, cars, liquid assets, marketable stocks or shares, loans made to persons. Liquid assets included deposits in savings banks, other banks, and such financial institutions as savings and loan associations in the United States and building societies and cooperative societies in Great Britain; holdings of fixed-value government bonds such as US savings bonds and GB defence bonds and savings certificates; also, in the United States, other federal government bonds. Marketable stocks or shares included: in Great Britain the value of all private and government bonds, except defence bonds and savings certificates; the estimated market value of 'private company' shares; and in the United States the value of privately held corporations, which was included with the value of unincorporated businesses. Excluded assets were currency, consumer durables other than houses and cars, the value of insurance policy and pension fund reserves, assets held by trust funds and, in the United States only, private, state and local, and foreign bonds.

Liabilities included mortgage debt, instalment debt, bank debt, debts to other institutions and persons except charge accounts with retailers.

liabilities, especially of instalment debt. This understatement is, of course, additional to the understatement which arises from the restricted coverage of assets mentioned above. So far as the available evidence permits us to judge, the tendency towards understatement of financial assets is very similar in Britain and the United States; and it seems probable that the aggregate understatement of net worth which results from this bias, as well as from the restricted coverage of assets, is of the same order of magnitude in both countries. The influence on the distributions of spending units by size of net worth is also likely to be similar. It seems legitimate, therefore, to use the comparisons of the survey distributions of net worth as broadly indicative of the relative distributions of total net worth in the two countries.

In the American survey of 1953 it was found that nearly 85 per cent of spending units had some positive net worth, 4 per cent had exactly nothing, and 11 per cent had debts which exceeded their assets (see Table 8). Had consumer durables other than cars and houses been included in the survey definition of net worth, there would not have been any spending units with exactly zero net worth, and it is doubtful whether there would have been any with negative net worth. In the British survey of 1954 – on the same basis – it was found that only 66 per cent of spending units had some positive net worth, 21 per cent had nothing and 13 per cent had liabilities exceeding their assets. These figures draw attention to the first great difference between the two countries – a difference which is fundamental to our understanding of the comparisons which follow. Property is much more widely distributed in America than in Britain. There are comparatively few Americans who own nothing: there are many Britons who own nothing, or next to nothing.

In order to compare the two distributions of net worth over their whole ranges it is necessary to decide on an appropriate 'rate of exchange' between pounds and dollars. We could have taken the same ratio as we used for the comparison of incomes – $9 to the £ – but in order to avoid special tabulations, and since the comparison of net worth is in any case less exact, we have taken the ratio of $10 to the £. (Mean net worth per spending unit was about $12,000 in the United States and £1100 in Britain – a ratio of nearly $11 to the £.) In Table 8 the two distributions are given in comparable ranges of net worth on this principle. From the detailed comparison of the distributions it will be seen that, even amongst those spending units with some positive net worth, the British distribution is more unequal than the American. Both at the bottom of the distribution and in the highest net worth group the percentage of British spending units exceeds the percentage of American spending units in comparable class intervals. At the same time, the percentage of American spending units in the range of net worth from $4000 to $20,000 is almost twice as great as the percentage of British spending units in the comparable range of net worth – £400 to £2000. Altogether nearly half of American spending units have $4000 or more, against only 30 per cent of British spending units with more than £400.

Table 8 **Distribution of spending units by comparable ranges of net worth, United States and Great Britain** (percentages of spending units)

Comparable ranges of net worth[b] (£)	($)	United States 1953[a]	Great Britain 1954
Negative		11	13
Zero		4	21
Under 50	(500)	10	14
50	(500)	6	6
100	(1000)	10	8
200	(2000)	11	8
400	(4000)	8	5
600	(6000)	11	5
1000	(10,000)	15	8
2000	(20,000)	10	7
5000	(50,000)	4	5
Total		100	100

[a] Some of the figures for individual groups in this column have been estimated by interpolation.

[b] In both distributions there were a certain number of cases in which, because one or more components were not ascertained, total net worth was not exactly known. In these cases values of net worth were assigned on the basis of the information available about the spending unit, such as its income, age and occupation and the assets actually reported. There were 9 per cent of spending units in the American survey which were given assigned values in this way and 8 per cent in the British survey.

The differences between the British and American distributions of net worth are further illustrated in Figure 1. The two Lorenz curves deviate very substantially from one another, a pattern in marked contrast to the relative similarity of the Lorenz curves of income. The estimation of Lorenz curves by survey methods is subject to rather large errors, both for the reasons referred to in the last section and because of sampling fluctuations; but the differences between the net-worth curves shown here are so large that it is impossible to believe that they do not reflect a real underlying difference between the two countries.

If there are more American spending units who have *something*, what sorts of assets do they have? The answer, which is most instructive, is given in Table 9. The wider distribution of assets amongst the American population is primarily a result of the more widespread ownership of physical

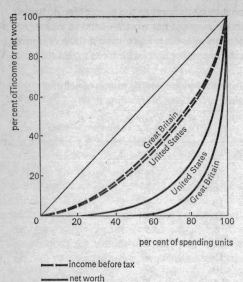

income before tax
net worth

Figure 1 Lorenz curves of income and net worth, United States and Great Britain

assets – homes, other real estate, farms, businesses and cars. In respect of financial assets, on the other hand, the difference between the two countries is much less. A slightly larger percentage of American spending units own some liquid assets and some corporate stock. A slightly larger proportion of American spending units own life insurance policies also.

Table 9 Percentages of spending units owning specified assets, United States and Great Britain, 1954 surveys

	United States	Great Britain
Physical assets		
Owner-occupied home	45	22
Other real estate	14[a]	4
Farm, business or professional practice	17[c]	7[c]
Car	66	11
Financial assets		
Any liquid assets	74	69
Corporate stock	10[a]	7[b]
Life insurance	75	69

[a] 1953 figure.

[b] Includes owners of any marketable stocks or bonds or shares in private companies.

[c] Excludes farms, businesses or professional practices owned by persons other than heads of spending units.

We turn now, as we did in the case of income, to consider the differences between the distributions of net worth within occupational groups. The main differences between occupations can be appreciated from the data presented in Tables 10 and 11. The first table, which gives the percentage of spending units in each occupation group who have some positive net worth, shows that the overall difference between the British and American patterns of property ownership is largely attributable to differences between the lower-paid occupations in the two countries. Property is more widely held in America than in Britain, not because the higher-paid occupations have more property in America, but because more manual workers, more clerical and sales workers, and more retired and unoccupied persons have property in America.

The primary reason for these differences is that more Americans in these occupation groups own their own homes and their own cars. For example, over 40 per cent of unskilled American heads of spending units own their own homes, compared with 16 per cent in Britain; 50 per cent own a car, compared with only 1 per cent in Britain. The differences in the proportions owning liquid assets are much less: 61 per cent in America against 47 per cent in Britain.

These figures suggest that in respect of property ownership there is more difference between the social classes in Britain than in the United States. A similar impression is given by the figures in the right-hand portion of Table 10, which show the average net worth of each occupation group expressed

Table 10 **Net worth in different occupation groups United States and Great Britain**

Occupation of head of spending unit	Percentage of spending units with positive net worth		Relative net worth[a]	
	US 1953	GB 1954	US 1953	GB 1954
Self-employed	94	94	254	392
Farmers	91	na	176	na
Others	97	na	328	na
Managers and technical	93	91	119	223
Clerical and sales	91	71	58	44
Skilled manual	84	65	44	28
Unskilled manual	64	45	25	23
Retired and unoccupied	81	58	124	157
All spending units	85	66	100	100

[a] Mean net worth of each group expressed as a percentage of the mean for all spending units in the population.

as a percentage of the average for all spending units in the same country. We see that the British self-employed are more above average in wealth than the American self-employed – though this is partly due to the position of American farmers, who are not as rich as other American self-employed. British spending units headed by managers and technical employees have net worth which is more than twice the all-British average, while American spending units in this group have net worth only slightly above the all-American average. At the other extreme, British manual worker spending units – especially skilled manual workers – are relatively badly off. The gap between them and the managers is very great, while in America it is only moderate. These figures tell the same story of more inequality in Britain, but from a slightly different point of view.

Another way of looking at the matter is to consider the composition of the aggregate personal balance sheet in Britain and America. For reasons already mentioned, the surveys are not very accurate instruments for measuring aggregate net worth or its components; but a broad interpretation of the survey data will help to throw some light on the pattern of capital ownership in the two countries. A percentage breakdown of aggregate net worth for all spending units and for four occupational groups is given in Table 11.

In this table the assets have been grouped, as previously, under two headings; physical assets and financial assets. Wherever possible liabilities have been offset against their related assets, so that only the net contribution of each asset to total net worth is taken into account. Thus mortgages on owner-occupied homes are deducted from the gross value of the dwellings concerned, and similarly with other property. It might have been useful to have deducted instalment debt on cars from car values; but the data were not available for Great Britain, and in any case some debt which is owed to banks and other institutions was originally incurred in order to finance car purchases. So all nonmortgage debt – called personal debt – has been offset against total financial assets.

The first thing to notice in the table is that net physical assets represent a much larger proportion of aggregate personal net worth in the United States than in Britain. A small part of the difference comes from owner-occupied homes and a similar amount from cars; but the biggest differences are in the proportions of capital represented by unincorporated businesses and farms and other real estate. It was to be expected that farms and businesses – especially farms – would bulk more largely in the United States than in Britain, since so many more American spending units own one or the other of these. We have also observed that more American spending units own other real estate. But the general significance of these facts now seems clearer: it is that more Americans have direct investments

Table 11 **Relative importance of net worth components in different occupational groups, United States and Great Britain**
(percentages of the total net worth of each group of spending units)

Net worth component	All spending units US 1953	GB 1954	Self-employed US 1953	GB 1954	Managers clerical and sales US 1953	GB 1954	Manual workers US 1953	GB 1954	Retired and unoccupied US 1953	GB 1954
Own home (net of mortgage debt)	31	27	14	9	39	35	61	54	35	24
Unincorporated business or farm (net of mortgage debt)[b]	28	19	59	66	8	1	1	2	—a	—a
Other real estate (net of mortgage debt)	13	6	10	4	13	6	11	6	24	8
Cars	6	2	4	3	9	4	12	3	2	1
Total physical assets (net of mortgage debt)	78	54	87	82	69	46	85	65	61	33
Liquid assets	14	23	10	11	20	28	18	37	13	24
Marketable stocks and bonds	9	23	3	7	12	27	2	2	26	42
Loans made	2	1	1	1	2	—a	1	—a	2	1
Less: personal debt[c]	−3	−1	−1	−1	−3	−1	−6	−4	−2	—a
Total financial assets (net of personal debt)	22	46	13	18	31	54	15	35	39	67
Net worth	100	100	100	100	100	100	100	100	100	100

a Less than half of one per cent.
b Includes owner-occupied homes forming part of a business or a farm.
c Nonmortgage debt, e.g. instalment debt, bank loans, loans from insurance companies.

in land. This land may include either their own homes, or farms, or other real estate.

There is, perhaps, nothing surprising in this. The continental United States contains nearly two billion acres of land; Great Britain only fifty-six million acres. Much of the United States was originally settled by homestead farmers, while the pattern of property ownership in Britain has evolved slowly from the opposite extreme of a feudal concentration in the hands of large landowners. Despite the movement in America from country to town and the broadening of property ownership in Britain in modern times, each country's past still leaves a strong imprint on its present structure.

An additional difference between the two countries arises from the difference in social philosophy with respect to public ownership of rental housing. In the United States there are only about half a million publicly owned housing units, amounting to about one per cent of all dwelling units. In Great Britain about one fifth of all households live in council houses.

The overall difference between British and American spending units in the arrangement of their assets is reflected in each of the occupational groups shown in Table 11. The difference is least marked – as might be expected – in the case of the self-employed; but even amongst this group an appreciably higher percentage of total assets is represented by other real estate in America than in Britain. The proportion of financial assets is smaller for each group in America than it is in Britain, and it is interesting to note that in every group British spending units keep a higher proportion of their total capital in liquid assets.

This bias towards liquidity is a marked feature of the British situation. The reasons may be partly the continuing overload of liquid assets from the war years and partly a tradition of putting savings into liquid rather than into other forms. The savings movement in Britain has a long and powerful tradition, and it has stimulated the accumulation over the years of very large sums in the various savings institutions and in special savings securities. The trend has been aided by the tax advantages offered to investors in many of these assets. It is possible also that the greater proportionate holding of liquid assets in Britain is a consequence of there being fewer alternative outlets for savings – especially into real estate and private business.

The ratio between aggregate net worth and aggregate income in the United States is not significantly different from the ratio between these two aggregates in Britain. It is not possible to explain the greater equality of distribution of net worth in America simply as the result of there being a greater total quantity of capital in America. Rather there is a tendency for each major type of asset to be more narrowly held in Britain. More American real estate is held directly by its occupiers or is distributed amongst a fairly wide group of small property owners; more British real estate is in the hands of large owners and companies. The same is true of financial assets. Not only do British spending units keep a larger proportion of their total capital in financial assets – which are potentially a more concentrated form of property than, say, owner-occupied homes and farms – but these financial assets themselves are more unequally distributed in Britain than in the United States. For example, the top tenth of owners of liquid assets hold about three quarters of the total in Britain compared with less than two thirds in the United States. In every respect the distribution of property is more widely spread in America than in Britain.

Conclusion

On the basis of comparisons of survey data from Britain and the United States it appears that pre-tax income per spending unit is, in general, very similarly distributed in the two countries. The only significant discrepancy is that the United States contains more relatively low income spending units. The reasons for this are the existence of a large population of low income farmers in America, the extensive program of social security in Great Britain, and the existence of a larger group of low income unskilled manual workers in the United States. An underlying cause seems to be the greater racial heterogeneity in America.

When we turn from a comparison of income distributions to a comparison of the distribution of capital, it is the British distribution which is more unequal than the American – and quite substantially so. More Americans directly own physical assets, such as their own homes, businesses, farms or other real estate. Even within the group of financial assets, the distribution is more unequal in Britain than in America.

In the modern world there are two opposite trends in the distribution of capital – both in Britain and in America. On the one side, in relation to producers' goods, there is great concentration of ownership in the hands of the big corporations which, in turn, are owned by a small fraction of the population. On the other side, there is a trend towards a greater diffusion of ownership of consumer durables. This latter trend, which is the result of a rising standard of living, is evidenced by the spread of owner-occupation of houses and by the growing importance of cars and other consumer durables. It may be that the process of concentration of producers' capital has still some way to go in the United States; but in Britain a spreading ownership of homes and cars will develop as the standard of living rises. It is possible, therefore, that the distributions of property in the two countries will gradually move closer together. This development is to be expected also on the general ground that countries with such similar income distributions are unlikely to retain permanently such large disparities in the distribution of property.

H. F. Lydall and J. B. Lansing 159

References

BELLERBY, J. R. (1956), *Agriculture and Industry; Relative Income*, Macmillan.

BLACK, J. D. (1956), 'Agriculture in the nation's economy', *Amer. econ. Rev.*, vol. 46, pp. 1–43.

CARTTER, A. M. (1955), *The Redistribution of Income in Postwar Britain*, Yale University Press.

FEDERAL RESERVE BULLETIN (1956), *Fed. Res. Bull.*, vol. 47, p. 700.

GILBERT, M., and KRAVIS, I. B. (1954), *An International Comparison of National Products and the Purchasing Power of Currencies*, OEEC.

GOLDSMITH, R. W. (1956), *A Study of Saving in the United States*, vol. 3, Princeton University Press.

KISH, L., and LANSING, J. B.. (1954), 'Response errors in estimating the value of homes', *J. Amer. stat. Assoc.*, vol. 49, pp. 520–38.

LYDALL, H. F. (1955), *British Incomes and Savings*, Blackwell.

MILLER, H. P. (1955), *Income of the American People*, Government Printing Office.

UK Annual Abstract of Statistics (1956), *Annual Abstract*, no. 93, HMSO.

US Bureau of the Census (1956), *Current Population Reports*, series P-25, no. 146, Government Printing Office.

Part Three
The Distribution of Earnings

For most people earnings are their major source of income. This section presents a number of extracts dealing with the theories which attempt to explain inequality in earnings.[1] How is it that a managing director can earn in a week what a labourer earns in a year? Are earnings differentials the result of education, ability, bargaining power or the hierarchical structure of our society?

The theories which have been put forward are of many different types. Mincer (Reading 9) describes the 'human capital' approach to the explanation of earnings. This approach is a modern development of the principle put forward by Adam Smith that

The wages of labour vary with the easiness, cheapness or the difficulty and expense of learning the business. . . . A man educated at the expense of much labour and time . . . may be compared to . . . expensive machines. The work which he learns to perform, it must be expected, over and above the usual wages of common labour, will replace to him the whole expense of his education, with at least the ordinary profits of an equally valuable capital.

In his article, Mincer begins by formalizing the relationship between earnings and years of training for a simple model where all individuals have identical abilities and equal opportunities to enter any occupation. This model is then extended to allow for unequal abilities and for differences among occupations in the lifetime profile of earnings. An early empirical test of the human capital theory was that made by Friedman and Kuznets as part of their study of the incomes of the professions and the principal findings are described in Reading 10. They estimated the percentage by which the average earnings of the professional worker would have to exceed the average earnings of the nonprofessional worker to compensate for the extra training required and reached the conclusion that 'the difference between incomes in the professions and in other pursuits is larger than can be explained by the free choice of occupations'. In other

1. At this point, the ground covered here overlaps with that in other volumes in the series: see McCormick and Owen Smith (1968) and Blaug (1968–9, vols. 1 and 2).

words, the human capital theory provides part but not all of the explanation.

A second explanation of earnings differentials is that they are related to natural abilities. The relationship between earnings and abilities has been discussed by a number of authors. Pigou found the relationship a puzzling one:

When ... a curve is plotted out for the heights of any large group of men, the resulting picture will not, as with incomes, have a humped and lop-sided appearance, but it will be a symmetrical curve shaped like a cocked-hat. ... Now, we should expect that, if, as there is reason to think, people's capacities are distributed on a plan of this kind, their incomes will be distributed in the same way. Why is not this explanation realised? (Pigou, 1948, p. 650).

Although Pigou's argument is clearly open to a number of objections, the supposed 'paradox' has generated a number of alternative explanations. Mincer, for example, shows in Reading 9 how differences in training introduces positive skewness (a 'lop-sided appearance' with the longer tail to the right). In Reading 11, Mayer not only puts forward a further explanation but also shows that there is little reason to assume that ability is in fact normally distributed. By combining unequal abilities with a hierarchical structure of responsibility, Mayer shows that a lognormal distribution of earnings can be generated from a normal distribution of abilities.[2] Even though his discussion of the distribution of abilities suggests that this particular result is of limited interest, the notion of a 'hierarchy' of earnings is an important one. This idea has been developed further by Simon (Reading 12), where he describes a simple theory of executive salaries based on the position occupied in the organizational hierarchy. He shows that this generates a distribution which approximates quite closely the upper tail of the earnings distribution.[3]

With the 'hierarchical' or 'organizational' theory of earnings differentials, we are moving away from a purely economic approach and the extract from Wootton (Reading 13) underlines the interaction between economic, political and social forces in determining the structure of earnings. The views expressed at the beginning of the extract are in fact close to the hierarchical hypothesis:

2. The normal distribution is symmetrical (Pigou's 'cocked-hat'), whereas the lognormal distribution is skewed and provides a reasonable fit to the middle ranges of earnings (see Lydall, 1968).

3. The generated distribution is of the Pareto form

$$f = A y^{-\mu}$$

where f is the number of people with earnings y, and A and μ are constants. The evidence given by Lydall (1968) suggests that the upper tail of the distribution is of approximately this form.

pay and prestige are closely linked; and (in spite of some exceptions) it is the rule that the high-prestige person should be also the highly paid person, and *vice versa* . . . [this] principle explains the importance attached to the rule that those who give orders should be paid more than those to whom orders are given.

The main part of the extract, however, is concerned with the mechanics of wage determination, drawing on Lady Wootton's experience on arbitration tribunals in Britain, and her emphasis on institutional aspects is a valuable antidote to other contributions.[4]

The final selection in this part focuses on the factors influencing the position of the lower paid workers in Britain. In Reading 14, Marquand examines the importance of different factors in leading to low pay, including the degree of unionization, the presence of Wages Councils and the change in employment. Although more recent information is now available from the New Earnings Surveys carried out by the government, her findings are still of considerable interest, and have major implications for minimum wage legislation and employment policy.

4. It is interesting to note, for example, that trade unions do not feature in the index to Lydall's major study of earnings (1968) – nor, for that matter, does Lady Wootton!

References

BLAUG, M. (ed.) (1968–9), *Economics of Education*, vols. 1 and 2, Penguin.
LYDALL, H. F. (1968), *The Structure of Earnings*, Oxford University Press.
MCCORMICK, B. J., and OWEN SMITH, E. (eds.) (1968), *The Labour Market*, Penguin, reprinted 1971.
PIGOU, A. C. (1948), *The Economics of Welfare*, 4th edn, Macmillan.

9 J. Mincer

Investment in Human Capital and Personal Income Distribution

J. Mincer, 'Investment in human capital and personal income distribution',
Journal of Political Economy, vol. 66, 1958, pp. 281–302.

Introduction

Economists have long theorized about the nature or causes of inequality in personal incomes. In contrast, the vigorous development of empirical research in the field of personal income distribution is of recent origin. Moreover, the emphasis of contemporary research has been almost completely shifted from the study of the causes of inequality to the study of the facts and of their consequences for various aspects of economic activity, particularly consumer behavior.

However, the facts of income inequality do not speak for themselves in statistical frequency distributions. The facts must be recognized in the statistical constructs and interpreted from them. Perhaps the most important conclusion to be drawn from research into the influence of income distribution on consumption is that the effects of inequality depend upon its causes.[1] Thus factors associated with observed inequality must be taken into account before the data can be put to any use.

Since income inequality is observable in terms of the shapes or parameters of statistical frequency distributions, theories of the determinants of personal income distribution, if they are to be operational, must predict features of the observable statistical constructs.

Probably the oldest theory of this type is the one that relates the distribution of income to the distribution of individual abilities.[2] A special form of this theory can be attributed to Galton, who claimed that 'natural abilities' follow the Gaussian normal law of error. This, it appeared to Galton, was a simple consequence of Quetelet's findings that various proportions of the human body are normally distributed. A seemingly natural corollary of this logic was the hypothesis of a normal distribution of incomes. Although the invention of intelligence quotients appeared to confirm conclusions derived by a *non sequitur*, the hypothesis of a normal

---

1. This is brought out in the distinction between the 'permanent' and the 'transitory' components of income as applied to the analysis of consumption in Friedman (1957).

2. A more detailed review of these theories can be found in Staehle (1943, pp. 77–87).

distribution of incomes was definitively shattered by Pareto's famous empirical 'law' of incomes.

For a long time this refutation of a logically weak hypothesis was considered to present a strange puzzle. Pigou (1932) termed it a paradox. How can one reconcile the normal distribution of abilities with a sharply skewed distribution of incomes? This became the central question around which thinking on the subject subsequently revolved.

One answer, of comparatively recent origin, is that the abilities relevant to earning power should not be identified with IQs. Indeed, relevant abilities are likely not to be normally distributed as IQs are, but to be distributed in a way resembling the distribution of income (Burt, 1943, pp. 95ff.; Roy 1950, pp. 489–505; Boissevain 1939, pp. 49–58). This amounts to saying that income distributions should not be deduced from psychological data on distributions of abilities but, conversely, that the latter, which are not observable, should be inferred from the former, which are. This reversal of independent and dependent variables may be of interest to psychologists, but income analysts are not left with much more than a tautology.

A more general and traditional answer, given by Pigou himself, is that income-determining factors other than ability intervene to distort the relation between ability and income. Thus, given a definition of the former independent of income, the relation between the two can be discerned only in subgroups homogeneous with respect to all other factors. Ability is relegated to a residual role, and the emphasis is shifted to other factors. Pigou pointed to the distribution of property as the most important of the other factors. This position resolves the paradox, but it is not a theory of income distribution until the other factors are built into models with predictive properties.

Curiously enough, the one factor consistently selected for such constructive purposes in the recent literature is 'chance', a concept as difficult to define as 'ability'. The earliest and basic version of the stochastic models is that of Gibrat (1931). Its logical construction is as follows: Start with some distribution of income, with mean M_0 and variance V_0, and let individual incomes be subjected to a random increase or decrease over time as a result of 'chance' or 'luck'. Let the variance of the annual changes in income in year t be v_t, and let those changes be uncorrelated with the levels of income on which they impinge. Then the variance of the income distribution at time $(t+n)$ will be

$$V_n = V_0 + \sum_{t=1}^{n} v_t.$$

With n increasing without bounds, any v_t becomes very small in comparison with $\sum_t v_t$, and similarly V_0 becomes small in comparison with V_n.

Under these conditions, probability theory guarantees that in time the distribution of income will approach normality, regardless of the form of the initial distribution.

Personal income distributions are not normally or symmetrically distributed, but the distribution of logarithms of income is rather symmetric and in a rough way approximates normality. The process of 'random shock' just described generates a lognormal distribution if applied to the logarithms of income rather than to income itself. Thus the proper assumption to be made is that the random shock consists of relative or percentage, rather than absolute, income changes, which are independent of income levels. This is Gibrat's 'law of proportionate effect'.

Kalecki (1945, pp. 161–70) has pointed out a serious defect in Gibrat's approach. The model implies that, as time goes by, aggregate income inequality increases because each subsequent random shock adds a term to the sum on the right side of the expression

$$V_n = V_0 + \sum_{t=1}^{n} v_t.$$

This, however, is empirically false.

Subsequent models correct this defect in either of two ways. One is to postulate a negative correlation between the size of the random shock and the level of income, to be interpreted as a decreasing likelihood of large negative changes with a decreasing level of income (Champernowne 1953, pp. 318–51). This restriction assures constancy of the variance of the distribution. Another way is to apply the random shock, without restriction, separately to age cohorts throughout their life histories (Rutherford, 1955, pp. 425–40). The income variance increases with time for each age cohort but, given a stable population, the aggregate variance remains unchanged.

Unless we assign specific interpretations to the 'chance' factor, it is difficult to see how the stochastic models increase our understanding of the processes underlying the formation of personal income distributions. If the 'chance' factor is to be understood as a net effect of all kinds of causes, this approach is an admission of defeat in the efforts to gain insight into systematic factors affecting the distribution of income. Moreover, the operational scope of the stochastic models has not kept pace with the increasing empirical knowledge about the multi-dimensional structure of the personal income distribution. With few exceptions (Rutherford, 1955), the sole purpose of the models is to rationalize a presumed mathematical form of the aggregate.

From the economist's point of view, perhaps the most unsatisfactory feature of the stochastic models, which they share with most other models of personal income distribution, is that they shed no light on the economics of the distribution process. Non-economic factors undoubtedly play an important role in the distribution of incomes. Yet, unless one denies the relevance of rational optimizing behavior to economic activity in general, it is difficult to see how the factor of individual choice can be disregarded in analysing personal income distribution, which can scarcely be independent of economic activity.

The starting point of an economic analysis of personal income distribution must be an exploration of the implications of the theory of rational choice. In a recent article Friedman (1953, pp. 277–90) has pointed out two ways in which individual choice can affect the personal income distribution. One, around which Friedman built his model, is related to differences in tastes for risk and hence to choices among alternatives differing in the probability distribution of income they promise. Friedman has shown that such a model is, no less than the others, capable of reproducing the more outstanding features of the aggregative distribution of income. The other, and more familiar, implication of rational choice is the formation of income differences that are required to compensate for various advantages and disadvantages attached to the receipt of the incomes. This principle, so eloquently stated by Adam Smith, has become a 'commonplace of economics' (Hicks, 1941, p. 3).

What follows is an attempt to cast one important aspect of this compensation principle into an operational model that provides insights into some features of the aggregative personal income distribution and into a number of decompositions of it which recent empirical research has made accessible. The aspect chosen concerns differences in training among members of the labor force.

A simple model

Assume that all individuals have identical abilities and equal opportunities to enter any occupation. Occupations differ, however, in the amount of training they require. Training takes time, and each additional year of it postpones the individual's earnings for another year, generally reducing the span of his earning life. For convenience, assume that a year of training reduces earning life by exactly one year.[3] If individuals with different

3. According to a recent study, the average length of working life in eight broad occupational groups is as follows

Occupation	Mean no. years in labor force	Occupation	Mean no. years in labor force
Professional and technical workers	40	Operatives and kindred workers	45
		Clerical and sales workers	47
Managers and officials	41	Non-farm laborers	51
Craftsmen and foremen	44	Service workers	52

amounts of training are to be compensated for the costs of training, the present values of life earnings must be equalized at the time a choice of occupation is made. If we add a provisional assumption that the flow of income receipts is steady during the working life, it is possible to estimate the extent of compensatory income differences due to differences in the cost of training.[4]

The cost of training depends upon the length of the training period in two ways. First and foremost is the deferral of earnings for the period of training; second is the cost of educational services and equipment, such as tuition and books, but not living expenses.

For simplicity, consider the case in which expenses for educational services are zero. Let

l = length of working life plus length of training, for all persons = length of working life of persons without training,

a_n = annual earnings of individuals with n years of training,

V_n = the present value of their life-earnings at start of training,

r = the rate at which future earnings are discounted,

t = 0, 1, 2, . . ., l—time, in years,

d = difference in the amount of training, in years, and

e = base of natural logarithms.

Then

$$V_n = a_n \sum_{t=n+1}^{l} \left(\frac{1}{1+r} \right)^t,$$

when the discounting process is discrete. And, more conveniently, when the process is continuous,

$$V_n = a_n \int_n^l (e^{-rt}) \, dt = \frac{a_n}{r} (e^{-rn} - e^{-rl}).$$

Similarly, the present value of life-earnings of individuals with $(n-d)$ years of training is

$$V_{n-d} = \frac{a_{n-d}}{r} (e^{-r(n-d)} - e^{-rl}).$$

Similar patterns were observed in 1930, 1940 and 1950. Commenting on the findings, the authors of the study observe 'In general men spend, on the average, fewer years in what may be termed the better jobs. The three occupations with the shortest working life are those in which greater training, education and experience are required. These are also the jobs which in general afford larger earnings. Clearly the men in the better jobs – as measured by earnings and education – spend a shorter period of their lives in the working force' (Jaffe and Carleton, 1954, p. 50).

4. With minor exceptions, the procedure is basically a generalization of the one used by Friedman and Kuznets (1945, pp. 142–51).

The ratio, $k_{n, n-d}$, of annual earnings of persons differing by d years of training is found by equating $V_n = V_{n-d}$

$$k_{n, n-d} = \frac{a_n}{a_{n-d}} = \frac{e^{-r(n-d)} - e^{-rl}}{e^{-rn} - e^{-rl}}$$
$$= \frac{e^{r(l+d-n)} - 1}{e^{r(l-n)} - 1}.$$

It is easily seen that $k_{n, n-d}$ is (a) larger than unity, (b) a positive function of r, and (c) a negative function of l. In other words, as would be expected, (a) people with more training command higher annual pay; (b) the difference between earnings of persons differing by d years of training is larger, the higher the rate at which future income is discounted, that is, the greater the sacrifice involved in the act of income postponement; (c) the difference is larger, the shorter the general span of working life, since the costs of training must be recouped over a *relatively* shorter period.

These conclusions are quite obvious. Less obvious is the finding that $k_{n, n-d}$ is a positive function of n (d fixed); that is, the relative income differences between, for example, persons with ten years and eight years of training are larger than those between individuals with four and two years of training, respectively. Hence the ratio of annual earnings of persons differing by a fixed amount of schooling (d) is at least as great as

$$k_{d, 0} = \frac{e^{rl} - 1}{e^{r(l-d)} - 1},$$

the ratio of earnings of persons with d years of training to those of persons with no training. However, since the change in $k_{n, n-d}$ with a change in n is negligible,[5] it can be, for all practical purposes, treated as a constant k.

This result can be summarized in the following statement: Annual earnings corresponding to various levels of training differing by the same amount (d) differ, not by an additive constant, but by a multiplicative factor (k).

This important conclusion remains basically unchanged when, in addition to the cost of income postponement, expenses of training are taken into account. The additional cost element naturally widens the compensatory differences in earnings particularly at the upper educational levels, where such costs are sizable.[6]

5. Assuming the values of r and l to be in a rather wide neighborhood of $0{\cdot}04$ and 50, respectively.

6. The percentage increase in relative income differences between persons with (n) and ($n-d$) years of training resulting from the introduction of schooling expenses can be measured by the ratio of annual schooling expenses to annual earnings in groups with ($n-d$) years of training. For example, if average earnings of high-school graduates

It is, of course, the purpose of the model to make the distribution of annual earnings a sole function of the distribution of training among members of the labor force. It follows from what we have just shown that this function is of a very simple form: given the distribution of training, the multiplicative constant k serves as a 'conversion factor' which translates it into a distribution of earnings. In order, therefore, to make statements about the theoretical distribution of earnings, we must first consider the distribution of training within the universe of this model.

Under the most stringent assumptions of identical abilities and equal access to training, the distribution of occupational choice, defined as choice of particular lengths of training, would become a matter of tastes, specifically those concerning the different activities in the different occupations and time preferences. It is not clear what form the distribution of training would assume in this conjectural state of affairs, even with the usual assumption of a symmetric, or normal, distribution of tastes.

Suppose, for the sake of argument, that the resulting distribution of training is symmetric. The point which this model brings home is that, even in that case, the annual distribution of earnings will depart from symmetry in the direction of positive skewness.

As we have seen, the annual earnings corresponding to various levels of training differing by the same length of time differ by a multiplicative factor k. Were this factor constant for all levels of training, a normal distribution of absolute time differences in training would reflect itself in a normal distribution of percentage differences in annual earnings, that is, in the familiar, positively skewed logarithmic-normal income distribution. Strictly speaking, the model implies that the factor k increases somewhat with the level of training, so that even the logarithms of income would be slightly skewed.

Formally, the existence of positive skewness introduced by compensatory income differences due to differences in training can be shown, and its extent can be estimated, in a rather simple way.

Let the quartile deviation in the symmetric distribution of training be d years, and let Y be the first quartile income, Q_1. It follows from the previous argument that the median, Q_2, equals Y times k^d and the third quartile, Q_3, equals Y times k^{2d}.

Hence Bowley's measure of skewness[7] is

---

are \$4000 and the annual expenses of a college education are \$1000, then to the compensatory income differences due to the deferral of income for 4 years (k^4-1) we must add $(1000/4000)$ (k^4-1) to compensate for the cost of tuition. This increases the differences by 25 per cent (see Mincer, 1957, ch. 2, note 2).

7. By the same procedure, a simple measure of relative dispersion is

$$\frac{Q_3 - Q_1}{Q_2} = \frac{k^{2d}-1}{k^d} = k^d - \frac{1}{k^d}.$$

$$Sk = \frac{(Q_3 - Q_2) - (Q_2 - Q_1)}{Q_3 - Q_1} = \frac{k^{2d} - 2k^d + 1}{k^{2d} - 1}$$

$$= \frac{(k^d - 1)^2}{k^{2d} - 1} = \frac{k^d - 1}{k^d + 1} > 0.$$

Since k is greater than 1, Sk must be positive.

If we now relax the assumption of identical abilities, a positive correlation between the amount of training and some ability traits is plausible. Given freedom of choice, persons with greater learning capacity are more likely than others to embark on prolonged training. Insofar as earnings are positively related to such qualities, aggregative skewness is augmented.

But whether or not the distribution of training depends on distributions of abilities,[8] the mere existence of dispersion in the amount of training implies that aggregative skewness is greater than it would be in its absence. In particular, even if it were true that abilities are distributed in a way which, *ceteris paribus*, implies a symmetric distribution of earnings, positive skewness would appear in that distribution as soon as choice of training was admitted into the model. Thus Pigou's paradox would persist even in the absence of the institutional factors that he invoked to explain it.

Extension of the model

Primarily for mathematical convenience, I have expressed differences in training in terms of definite time periods spent on formal schooling. However, the process of learning a trade or profession does not end with the completion of school. Experience on the job is often the most essential part of the learning process.

Just as formal training can be measured by the length of time spent at school, the other part of the training process – experience – can be introduced into the theoretical model in terms of the amount of time spent on the job. When this is done, 'intra-occupational' patterns of income variation, previously abstracted from, must emerge. By definition, the amount of formal training is the same for each member of an occupation. However, the productive efficiency or quality of performance on the job is a function of formal training plus experience, both measured in time units; hence it is a function of age. We are thus forced to relax another assumption, previously adopted for convenience, namely, that earnings are of the same size in each period of an individual's earning life.

Clearly, as more skill and experience are acquired with passage of time, earnings rise. In later years aging often brings about a deterioration of

8. Differences in abilities introduce additional dispersion into the income distribution. In particular, any degree of positive correlation between ability and differences in training magnifies the extent of 'interoccupational' income differences.

productive performance and hence a decline in earnings, particularly in jobs where physical effort or motor skill is involved. Thus, in general, the 'life-cycle' of earnings exhibits an inverted U-shaped pattern of growth and decline typical of many other growth curves.

We have already seen that differences in formal training result in compensatory differences in *levels* of earnings as between different 'occupations', the latter defined in terms of length of formal training. This compensatory principle must, of course, also remain valid when life-paths of earnings are sloped. An important new question arises: What specific assumption is to be made about differences between these slopes in the different occupations, since these in turn imply differences in the *dispersion* of earnings within the occupational groups?

Casual observation suggests that patterns of age-changes in productive performance differ among occupations as well as among individuals. The exploration of such differences is a well-established subject of study in developmental psychology. A survey of broad, rather tentative findings in this field indicates that (a) growth in productive performance is more pronounced and prolonged in jobs of higher levels of skill and complexity; (b) growth is less pronounced and decline sets in earlier in manual work than in other pursuits; and (c) the more capable and the more educated individuals tend to grow faster and longer than others in the performance of the same task (Mincer, 1957, ch. 2, note 1).

These findings suggest that experience influences productivity more strongly in jobs that normally require more training. The steeper growth of performance throughout the span of working life in occupations with higher levels of training implies that the growth of earnings is also greater.

These considerations point to the replacement of the previous assumption of horizontal life-paths of earnings with the assumption that the slopes of time-paths of earnings vary directly with the amount of formal training, that is, with 'occupational rank'.

Implications

In brief, we are lead to the following conclusion: Differences in training result in differences in levels of earnings among 'occupations' as well as in differences in slopes of life-paths of earnings among occupations. The differences are systematic: the higher the 'occupational rank', the higher the level of earnings and the steeper the life-path of earnings.

Two implications of basic importance for empirical investigation follow immediately from these findings.

1. Since, under our assumptions, intra-occupational differentials are a function of age only, the statement that life-paths of earnings are steeper for the

more highly trained groups of workers means that income differences between any two members of such a group differing in age are greater than income differences between their contemporaries in an occupational group requiring less training.

In itself, this conclusion does not necessarily imply a systematic difference in income dispersion within the two groups. It points to age distributions within the respective groups as another factor that must be considered. Clearly, if one group consists of members with very similar ages and in another there is a wide range of ages, there may be less income dispersion in the first group, even though its life-path of earnings may be steeper than that of the second group.

Observe, however, that such a phenomenon is in part ruled out by our previous assumptions. Membership in an occupational group was defined by the number of years of the individual's formal training, which is determined once for all by the calculus of occupational choice (the equalization of present values) *before* entry into the labor force. In other words, if we define 'vertical occupational mobility' as the movement from a group with, say, $n - d$ years of training to a group with n years of training, this is, by definition, impossible after the training period is over. If, in addition, secular occupational shifts are abstracted from, occupational distribution must be alike in all age groups after all training periods are over; *a fortiori*, age distributions must be alike in all occupational groups.[9] With this qualification, the direct translation of slopes of life-paths of earnings into patterns of income dispersion is achieved: dispersion must increase with 'occupational rank'.

2. Now consider income recipients classified into separate age groups. In our model, income differences within each age group are due to differences

9. Actually, the assumptions need not be so rigid, as a certain amount of dissimilarity in age distributions will not affect the systematic effects of differences in the steepness of life-paths on intra-group dispersion. Indeed, 1950 Census data indicate that the dissimilarity is rather small among broad occupational groups when comparisons are restricted to ages between 25 and 65:

Percentage distribution of ages by occupation, US male wage and salary earners, 1950

Occupation	Age groups				
	25–35	35–45	45–55	55–65	Total
Professional and managerial	30·6	31·1	23·8	14·5	100·0
Clerical and sales	35·8	28·0	21·8	14·4	100·0
Craftsmen and foremen	29·9	30·0	24·1	16·0	100·0
Operatives and service	33·8	29·8	21·6	14·8	100·0
Non-farm laborers	32·4	28·2	22·7	16·7	100·0

Source: *Occupational Characteristics* (Census Special Report P-E, no. 1B, Table 5, pp. 53–9).

in the occupational characteristics of its members. The income differences corresponding to those occupational categories, however, increase with age. Life-patterns of earnings are not parallel; their divergence becomes more pronounced with added years of experience, so that income dispersion increases as we move from younger to older age groups. Both statements can be made stronger by specifying that they apply not only to absolute but also to relative dispersion. The former follows directly from the model. If we now include in the assumption about the slopes of life-paths of earnings in various 'occupations' the observation that these slopes are negligible or even negative in occupations requiring little or no formal training, as in many manual jobs, then the two propositions must also apply to relative dispersion.

The argument underlying these propositions can be presented quite simply with the help of a geometric illustration. For convenience, divide the labor force into two broad groups of 'occupations', those requiring very little training, characterized by a practically flat life-pattern of earnings (ABU in Figure 1), and those requiring a considerable amount of training, with a pronounced positive slope of life path (CBT in Figure 1). First, we may note that absolute differences in earnings are small within untrained groups (life-path ABU), but they become pronounced in groups with higher levels of training (CBT). These differences (absolute dispersion) may be measured by the slopes of the paths or by the segments UL and TL, respectively. Income levels are represented by the heights US and TS, respectively. Clearly $UL/US < TL/TS$. That is, relative dispersion increases with 'occupational rank'. Second, the ratio TS/US increases with age: $TS/US > T'S'/U'S'$. That is, percentage differences and hence the relative dispersion

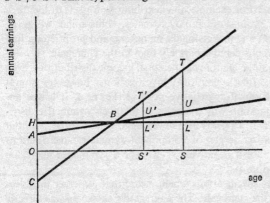

Figure 1 Hypothetical life-paths of earnings in occupations differing in the amount of training they require

of earnings increase as we move from a younger to an older 'occupation-mix'.

We may now return to the aggregative income distribution and explore the implications for the total of the hypothesis about patterns of income in component groups.

First, it is obvious that the addition of 'intra-occupational' differences to the 'inter-occupational' differences increases aggregate inequality. Moreover, 'inter-occupational' differences themselves must increase: The present value of a life flow of income of given size is smaller, the steeper the positive slope of the age-income relation. Hence the equalization of present values requires larger 'inter-occupational' differences in income than those derived on the assumption of horizontal income flows in all 'occupations'.

Finally, it can be shown that the conclusions about 'intra-occupational' patterns of income dispersion reinforce the implication of aggregative positive skewness reached on the basis of 'interoccupational' differences alone (in the simple model). This finding provides an answer to an important question frequently raised in discussions of personal income distribution.

Before invoking the distribution of property as a decisive explanation of positive income skewness, Pigou considered the possibility that positive skewness of the income distribution may arise from merging of a number of homogeneous, non-skewed sub-groups into a non-homogeneous, positively skewed total (Pigou, 1932, p. 246). Recently, H. P. Miller has offered evidence to suggest that 'the skewness of income distributions is largely due to merging several symmetrical distributions which differ primarily with respect to level and dispersion' (1955, pp. 55–71). He found that there is considerably more symmetry in component income distributions than in the aggregate. For example, the distributions for sets of the three broad occupational groups of employed males, 'blue-collar workers', 'white-collar workers', and professionals, managers, and proprietors, had less skewness when considered separately than in the aggregate.

Pigou's hunch about the anatomy of personal income distributions, even when confirmed by Miller's empirical investigations, however, cannot explain the phenomenon of aggregative positive skewness. It leaves unanswered the basic question why a merger of relatively symmetric distributions should result in a positively skewed aggregate. Clearly, without further specifications, a merger of component symmetric distributions could very well produce a negatively skewed or a symmetric aggregate (Mincer, 1957, ch. 2, note 4).

My model provides specifications which insure that a merger produces positive skewness in the aggregate. The aggregative skewness was already implied by the simple model. In that form, however, income dispersion within occupations was implicitly assumed to be zero. But if its existence is admitted, patterns of 'intra-occupational' dispersion might easily affect the aggregative, positive skewness previously derived. This would be the case, for example, if dispersion within less trained groups were systematically and considerably greater than that within more highly trained groups. Geometrically, this would mean shortening the right tail of the aggregative income distribution and extending the left tail – a change in the direction of negative skewness. However, this contingency is ruled out by my findings about component groups. In fact, I have derived patterns of 'intra-occupational' dispersion that are exactly the opposite of those given in the preceding extreme example. This positive relation between income levels and income dispersion in component groups reinforces the effect of intergroup ('interoccupational') skewness to produce an even greater positive skewness in the aggregate.[10]

10. For subsequent developments see Mincer (1970).

References

BOISSEVAIN, C. H. (1939), 'Distribution of abilities depending on two or more independent factors', *Metron*, vol. 13, pp. 49–58.

BURT, C. (1943), 'Ability and income', *Brit. J. educ. Psychol.*, vol. 13, pp. 95 ff.

CHAMPERNOWNE, D. G. (1953), 'A model of income distribution', *Econ. J.*, vol. 63, pp. 318–51.

FRIEDMAN, M. (1953), 'Choice, chance and the personal distribution of income', *J. Pol. Econ.*, vol. 61, pp. 277–90.

FRIEDMAN, M. (1957), *A Theory of the Consumption Function*, Princeton University Press.

FRIEDMAN, M., and KUZNETS, S. (1945), *Income from Independent Professional Practice*, National Bureau of Economic Research.

GIBRAT, R. (1931), *Les inégalités économiques*, Paris, Sirey.

HICKS, J. R. (1941), *The Theory of Wages*, P. Smith.

JAFFE, A. J., and CARLETON, R. O. (1954), *Occupational Mobility in the United States, 1930–60*, King's Crown Press.

KALECKI, M. (1945), 'On the Gibrat distribution', *Econometrica*, vol. 13, pp. 161–70.

MILLER, H. P. (1955), 'Elements of symmetry in the skewed income curve', *J. Amer. Stat. Assoc.*, March, pp. 55–71.

MINCER, J. (1957), 'A study of personal income distribution', unpublished Ph.D. dissertation, Columbia University.

MINCER, J. (1970), 'The distribution of labor incomes', *J. Econ. Lit.*, vol. 8, pp. 1–26.

PIGOU, A. C. (1932), *The Economics of Welfare*, Macmillan

ROY, A. D. (1950), 'The distribution of earnings and of individual output', *Econ. J.*, vol. 60, pp. 489–505.

RUTHERFORD, R. S. G. (1955), 'Income distributions: a new model', *Econometrica*, vol. 23, pp. 277–94.

STAEHLE, H. (1943), 'Ability, wages and income', *Rev. Econ. Stats.*, vol. 25, pp. 77–87.

10 M. Friedman and S. Kuznets

Incomes in the Professions

Excerpt from M. Friedman and S. Kuznets, *Income from Independent Professional Practice*, National Bureau of Economic Research, 1945, pp. 81–94.

[. . .] It is clear that the three million persons engaged in professional work are on the whole a fortunate group. Their earnings, though less equally distributed than those of nonprofessional workers, are between two and three times as large.

In small part this difference between the countrywide averages is illusory, reflecting differences in the location and age of the two groups of workers. Professional workers tend to be concentrated in the larger communities in which average incomes are relatively high. According to the National Resources Committee (1938) estimates for nonrelief families, over 40 per cent of professional families, but less than 30 per cent of other families, live in cities with populations over 100,000. Nonrelief families living in cities of this size received an average income in 1935–6 that was 56 per cent larger than that of nonrelief families living in small communities. A rough estimate suggests that if other workers were distributed by size of community as professional workers are, their average income would be raised slightly less than 7 per cent. Hence, professional workers apparently receive an average income between 85 and 180 per cent larger than that of nonprofessional workers living in communities of the same size.

It is more difficult to correct for the apparent concentration of professional workers in the younger age groups, which has presumably resulted from the rapid growth of professional activity in recent decades (Edwards, 1938, p. 26). The corresponding period of the professional career includes both the early years of low earnings and the intermediate years of average or better than average earnings. It is therefore not clear whether correction for the concentration of professional workers in the younger age groups would raise or lower the differential between the earnings of professional and nonprofessional workers. The net effect would probably be small.

These purely statistical factors therefore explain only a small part of the observed difference between the average incomes of professional and nonprofessional workers. There remains a difference of some 85 to 180 per cent between the average incomes of professional and nonprofessional workers in the same community and in the labor market the same number of years.

What factors account for this large difference? Why does it not lead young men to flock into the professions, thereby driving incomes in the professions down relatively to incomes in other pursuits?

One reason why this does not occur is that young men choosing their lifework take account of many factors other than expected earnings. They compare not monetary returns alone but, in Adam Smith's phrase, 'the whole of the advantages and disadvantages' of different occupations. The larger average earnings in the professions are balanced against the costs of the additional training that must be acquired. And purely pecuniary considerations are supplemented by many others – the character of the work in different occupations, the responsibilities involved, the possibilities of rendering service, their social standing, the hardships and pleasures attached to the work and so on.

The most objective of these additional factors is the longer period of training required of a professional man and the attendant extra investment. In most other fields, a man is ready to pursue his occupation at an early age. The professional man, as we saw in chapter 1, must undergo four to nine years of specialized training, at considerable expense and at the sacrifice of income that might otherwise have been earned. The professional man who goes into independent practice must in addition purchase capital equipment and in many cases provide for his maintenance during the initial years of practice.

In order that the 'whole of the advantages and disadvantages' may be the same as in other pursuits, pecuniary returns in the professions would have to be sufficiently high – relatively to the level that would be considered adequate on other grounds – to hold out reasonable prospects of recouping this extra investment.

When any expensive machine is erected, the extraordinary work to be performed by it before it is worn out, it must be expected, will replace the capital laid out upon it, with at least the ordinary profits. A man educated at the expense of much labor and time to any of those employments which require extraordinary dexterity and skill, may be compared to one of those expensive machines. The work which he learns to perform, it must be expected, over and above the usual wages of common labor, will replace to him the whole expense of his education, with at least the ordinary profits of an equally valuable capital. It must do this, too, in a reasonable time, regard being had to the very uncertain duration of human life, in the same manner as to the more certain duration of the machine (Smith, 1910, vol. 1, pp. 88–9).

The data available are so meagre and unsatisfactory that it is impossible to do more than make the roughest kind of guess about the percentage by which the average earnings of the professional worker would have to exceed the average earnings of the nonprofessional worker to compensate for the extra capital investment required. Our guess is that the difference would not have to be more than 70 per cent and might be a good deal lower. Interestingly enough, almost half of the 70 per cent is accounted for by the postponement of income involved in the choice of a professional career. The assumptions leading to the upper estimate of 70 per cent are presented in detail in the appendix to the next chapter (not included in this Reading). The more important are that the average period of training in the professions is seven years, the specific costs of professional training (tuition fees, books, special equipment, etc.) are $500 per year, the life expectancy of professional workers is three years longer than that of nonprofessional workers, and the average income of nonprofessional workers is equal to that of unskilled laborers, or approximately $750 per year. If the average income of nonprofessional workers is assumed equal to that of skilled laborers, or $1430 a year, the differential needed to make professional and nonprofessional pursuits equally attractive financially is reduced to 55 per cent.

On the basis of these figures, the actual difference between the incomes of professional and nonprofessional workers seems decidedly larger than the difference that would compensate for the extra capital investment required. The only other empirical study of this question of which we know, a study by J. R. Walsh (1935), reaches essentially the same conclusion. Walsh compares the present value of the life earnings of individuals with the cost of the special training they have had. The principal results are summarized in Table 1. The estimates of the present value of life earnings

Table 1 **Comparison between discounted and cost values of special training** (J. R. Walsh's estimates)

Rank of education (1)	Disc. value over elem. educ. (2)	Cost value of same (3)	Disc. value over H.S. educ. (4)	Cost value of same (5)	Disc. value over B.A. (6)	Cost value of same (7)
Men						
High school	7142	5000				
B.A.			35,009	6398		
M.A.			36,041	9848	1032	3450
Ph.D.			43,226	21,413	8217	15,015
B.B.A. or B.C.S.			57,631	12,963	22,622	6565
M.D.			37,690	22,143	2681	15,745
LL.B.*			67,784	16,447	32,775	10,049
LL.B.*			83,386	16,447	48,377	10,049
Engineers*			42,101	13,000	7092	6602
Engineers*			49,003	13,000	13,994	6602
Women						
B.A.			9030	6398		
M.A.					4631	2950

Reproduced from Walsh (1935, Table 5) with a few minor corrections.

  * Two estimates based on different sources.

in columns 2, 4, and 6 are based on scattered studies for years between 1926 and 1929, and are admittedly subject to wide margins of error. They were computed by determining the median earnings for different numbers of years of experience, adjusting these figures to allow for deaths and for the percentage of persons employed at each age so as to get the total amounts actually earned by the survivors, discounting the individual amounts at 4 per cent, and summing to obtain the present value of life earnings as of the middle of the first year of employment. The difference between the returns at a later and at an earlier stage of training were then compared with the corresponding difference in costs.

Columns 4 and 5, which compare the returns of training beyond high school with the corresponding costs, are of primary interest for an analysis of the professions as a whole. For every group the returns are considerably higher than the costs. Columns 6 and 7, which compare the returns of training beyond college with the corresponding costs, offer additional evidence on the adjustment among different levels of training. Even these comparisons show returns that exceed costs for six out of nine groups. And for one of the three groups for which the reverse is true, medicine (MD), the return computed by Walsh seems unduly low.[1]

Walsh's procedure is superior to ours in two important respects: first, it makes explicit allowance for difference among individuals in length of life; second, the income data purportedly are for individuals grouped by training rather than by the occupation they engage in. Counterbalancing these advantages are a number of defects that make correct interpretation of the results difficult.[2] On balance, it appears that correction of Walsh's figures

1. Walsh estimates the discounted value of median life earnings of M.D.s as $70,327 (1935, p. 267). Clark (1937, p. 70), on the other hand, estimates the discounted value of median life earnings of physicians for 1920–9 as $106,000 on the basis of one body of data, and as $116,000 on the basis of a second. He also gives an estimate for 1920–36 of $98,000. Both investigators use an interest rate of 4 per cent in discounting returns. Although the methods differ in other respects, the estimates for the other two occupations for which comparison is possible, law and engineering, give no reason to suppose that Clark's method has an upward bias relatively to Walsh's.

2. There are four defects in Walsh's procedure. (1) Walsh's cost figures include not only special expenditures for education but also living expenses and foregone income, income that would have been earned during the time devoted to additional training. These two items clearly duplicate each other; moreover, neither should be included for the present purpose. The foregone income included in the costs, say, of a college education is automatically counted in the returns to those with only a high school education. When the latter is subtracted from the returns to those with a college education, allowance is implicitly made for foregone income. Hence, including it in the cost figure involves duplication. (2) The use of median earnings makes the estimates of returns too low. The actuarial nature of the problem clearly requires arithmetic mean earnings, which are usually considerably higher than median earnings. (3) The present

for their defects would probably strengthen rather than weaken the conclusion suggested by Table 1; namely, that returns in the professions exceed returns in other pursuits by an amount considerably in excess of the extra costs involved, a conclusion independently supported by our earlier analysis.

Taking account of the extra costs as well as the extra returns of professional work weakens the pecuniary incentive to enter the professions, but apparently does not remove it. Extra costs can at most explain part of the difference between incomes of professional and nonprofessional workers. There must be other reasons why individuals do not flock into the professions in sufficient numbers to erase the rest of the difference.

It is hard to believe that one of these reasons is that a profession is considered a less desirable vocation than a nonprofessional pursuit. Professional men are everywhere held in high esteem and are ordinarily among the leaders of their communities. In addition, professional work is ordinarily regarded as more interesting than nonprofessional work, as socially more valuable, as giving greater play to individual aptitudes and initiative. These are necessarily qualitative judgments, and we could not easily test or prove them. Yet the balance seems so clear that we have no hesitation in discarding this possible explanation of the excess of pecuniary returns over pecuniary costs.

If this judgment is correct, the difference between incomes in the professions and in other pursuits is larger than can be explained by the free choice of occupations by young men. There is nothing surprising about this finding. It is clear that young men are, in fact, not equally free to choose a professional or nonprofessional career. There are two major reasons why this is so. First, the professions require a different level of ability than other pursuits; second, the economic and social stratification of the population leaves only limited segments really free to enter the professions.

---

value of returns and the accumulated costs refer to an age that differs from one level of training to the next since they are computed as of the middle of the first year of employment. To make the comparison valid they should refer to the same age for the different levels of training. The net effect of this defect is to inflate the difference between excess returns and excess costs at the later stages by accumulated interest on the difference between returns and costs at the earlier stage. The reason for this is that the difference between the present value of returns at the later and earlier stages is larger than it would be if the present values at both stages referred to the same age. The excess is equal to interest on the present value at the earlier stage for the intervening period. The difference between the costs at the later and earlier stages is affected in similar fashion. If the present value of returns equaled costs at the earlier stage, both sets of figures would be affected equally and the comparison between the excess returns and excess costs would be entirely valid. In fact, however, returns uniformly exceed costs at the earlier stages. (4) No allowance is made for differences among the groups in their distribution by location.

In some professions, such as medicine, dentistry, law and certified public accountancy, the need for special ability has been explicitly recognized by society. The practice of these professions is open solely to persons licensed by the state, and a license is granted only after the demonstration of a certain level of competence. Persons who cannot meet these standards are excluded from the professions. Some, recognizing their lack of aptitude or having it pointed out to them by their parents or teachers or friends, make no attempt to enter the professions; others are weeded out by the colleges and professional schools; still others, though as we saw in chapter 1 relatively few, by the licensure examinations. In professions not under state licensure the first two tendencies alone are operative, but these are enough to assure that on the whole persons who enter the professions have the special aptitudes required in higher degree than those who either decide not to enter the professions or are weeded out in the earlier stages. Persons who enter the professions might therefore earn more in other pursuits than persons who do not, though this would clearly not be universal, since special aptitude for one pursuit may not qualify a man for another. More important, earnings in the professions depend not on the total number of persons who would like to enter the professions, but on the number who have sufficient ability to do so.

The second factor that limits the number who are free to choose a professional career is the economic and social stratification of the population. It is not enough that a young man who wishes to enter the professions have sufficient ability; he must also be able to command funds to pay the expenses of training and to support himself during the training period. Because of the peculiar character of the capital investment in training, these funds cannot be obtained on the open market as a purely 'business loan', and hence are not freely available to all. 'The worker sells his work, but he himself remains his own property: those who bear the expenses of rearing and educating him receive but very little of the price that is paid for his services in later years' (Marshall, 1930, pp. 560–61). Consequently investment in training is not governed by the usual profit incentives. The non-economic values attached to a professional training might well lead an individual to invest in himself, his children, or his protégés even though he did not expect the added income to repay the cost; on the other hand, no investor in search of profit would invest in the education of strangers even though he expected that the return to the latter would greatly exceed the cost. The fact that the returns from capital investment in training and education seldom accrue to the person making it means that there is no reason to expect such investment to be pushed to the 'margin', i.e. to the point at which the accumulated cost, including interest, would equal the present value of expected future returns (Walsh, 1935, pp. 276–7).[3] If, relatively to the demand for professional services, there are few young men interested in entering the professions who can get the necessary funds, one would expect underinvestment; in the contrary case, overinvestment.

No hard and fast line divides occupations requiring a long period of specialized education from occupations requiring a short period. In Marshall's day the considerations set forth above may well have applied to all occupations requiring special training; and in no small degree they do even today.[4] But the widespread extension of free secondary education and the raising of the minimum age at which children may leave school mean that no considerable voluntary investment is likely to be required prior to entrance to college. The need for capital investment thus seriously impedes entry only into occupations requiring a college education. The professions bulk large in this group, though they do not exhaust it.

3. The argument may be put in a somewhat different fashion by using an analogy that at first blush may seem fantastic. Investment in professional training will not necessarily be pushed to the margin because earning power is seldom explicitly treated as an asset to be capitalized and sold to others by the issuance of 'stock'. An individual will rarely sell a fixed proportion of his future income to an investor (i.e. he will rarely sell 'stock' in himself), though he may borrow money, obligating himself to repay the principal and to pay interest at a rate that ordinarily cannot exceed a legally stipulated maximum (i.e. he may sell 'bonds'). Under such conditions, an investor who loaned money to a prospective professional man could at most get back his capital and the interest on it; he could never realize a 'capital gain'. But he could, and frequently would, suffer a 'capital loss', since, despite the average profitability of professional training, professional incomes differ greatly so that many individuals fare poorly and would be unable even to repay the principal. For this reason, it would be profitable for an investor to finance the professional training of individuals with no resources other than their expected future incomes only at a rate of interest that would be sufficiently high to provide for capital losses as well as for the usual interest charges. Such a rate of interest would probably exceed the expected return from investment in training even though the latter were well above the market rate of interest. On the other hand, if individuals sold 'stock' in themselves, i.e. obligated themselves to pay a fixed proportion of future earnings, investors could 'diversify' their holdings and balance capital appreciations against capital losses. The purchase of such 'stock' would be profitable so long as the expected return on investment in training exceeded the market rate of interest. Such investments would be similar to others involving a large element of risk, a type of investment usually financed by stocks rather than bonds.

4. See Fisher (1932, pp. 742–64). A report by the Educational Policies Commission (1940, p. 152) presents an impressive summary of evidence from a variety of studies on the role that the lack of funds plays in barring youths from high school and college. According to this report 'large numbers of youths are prevented from continuing their education through high school and into college, because of lack of ability to meet expenditures required. Many of these youths have superior ability. Where these superior youths are given financial aid permitting them to continue their education, they make superior records'.

Entry into a profession is likely to depend not only on deliberate comparison of alternative occupations and the possession of adequate financial resources, but also on educational facilities, the connections that a young man can exploit when he begins his career, his awareness of available opportunities and the like. These aspects of occupational determination are, in turn, likely to be related to a young man's social and national background, his geographic location, cultural environment, etc. These factors are far less important in the United States than in most countries, and far less important today than prior to the enormous development of higher educational opportunities supported by the state. The choice of occupation has probably never been so much restricted by social stratification in the United States, and it certainly is not today, as it was in England when, in 1848, John Stuart Mill was able to write

So complete, indeed, has hitherto been the separation, so strongly marked the line of demarcation, between the different grades of labourers, as to be almost equivalent to an hereditary distinction of caste; each employment being chiefly recruited from the children of those already employed in it, or in employments of the same rank with it in social estimation, or from the children of persons who, if originally of a lower rank, have succeeded in raising themselves by their exertions. The liberal professions are mostly supplied by the sons of either the professional, or the idle classes; the more highly skilled manual employments are filled up from the sons of skilled artisans, or the class of tradesmen who rank with them: the lower classes of skilled employments are in a similar case; and unskilled labourers, with occasional exceptions, remain from father to son in their pristine condition (1909, p. 393).

Despite the enormous decline in the importance of these factors, it is still true that they affect in no small measure the occupational opportunities open to a young man. For example, the child of a professional man is more likely to be cognizant of opportunities in the professions and better able to seize them than the child of an unskilled laborer, even though the professional man and the unskilled laborer have the same income and capital. The child of the professional man will have a background and associations that facilitate entry into the professions and make it seem natural; he will have contacts after he finishes his professional training that will ease his path.

The inference from this analysis is that professional workers constitute a 'noncompeting' group. The number and hence the incomes of professional workers are determined less by the relative attractiveness of professional and nonprofessional work than by the number of young men in the community who can finance their training, are cognizant of opportunities, and have the necessary ability, background and connections. Our data suggest that this group is sufficiently small to lead to underinvestment in professional training, i.e. that in the absence of financial and social limitations on entry, incomes in the professions would exceed incomes in other pursuits by less than they do now. The limitations of the data and the speculative character of our analysis necessarily make this conclusion tentative. Moreover, the conclusion relates solely to voluntary investment by prospective practitioners themselves, their parents or their direct benefactors. No allowance has been made for the investment by society in institutions of higher education and in professional schools. From the broad social standpoint of the efficient utilization of resources, investment of the latter type should also be taken into account.

At present, the limitations on the number of persons in a position to enter the professions must be considered the basic reason for the difference between extra returns and extra costs; more basic even than the difference in ability needed. A sizable number, perhaps a majority, of all young men are unable to enter the professions because they cannot make the necessary capital investment or for other reasons. If these hindrances were removed, the reservoir of persons unable to enter the professions could surely furnish many persons as able as those who now embark on professional careers. A higher level of ability among those who enter the professions may help to explain the current levels of remuneration; it could not maintain them if the other hindrances to entry were removed. At the same time, the higher level of specialized abilities among those who enter the professions and the insistence upon high qualifications for prospective professional men might well mean that, even if all other hindrances to entry were removed, earnings in the professions would still exceed earnings in other pursuits by more than enough to cover the extra pecuniary costs.

References

CLARK, H. F. (1937), *Life Earnings in Selected Occupations in the United States*, Harper.

EDUCATIONAL POLICIES COMMISSION (1940), *Education and Economic Well-Being in American Democracy*, National Education Association of United States and American Association of School Administrators.

EDWARDS, A. M. (1938), *Social-Economic Grouping of the Gainful Workers of the United States*, Government Printing Office.

FISHER, A. G. B. (1940), 'Education and relative wage rates', *Int. lab. Rev.*, vol. 25, pp. 742–64.

MARSHALL, A. (1930), *Principles of Economics*, eighth edition, Macmillan.

MILL, J. S. (1909), *Principles of Political Economy*, Longman.

NATIONAL RESOURCES COMMITTEE (1938), *Consumer Income in the United States*.

SMITH, A. (1910), *Wealth of Nations*, vol. 1, Everyman.

WALSH, J. R. (1935), 'Capital concept applied to man', *Q.J. Econ.*, vol. 49, pp. 255–85.

11 T. Mayer

The Distribution of Ability and Earnings

T. Mayer, 'The distribution of ability and earnings', *Review of Economics and Statistics*, vol. 42, 1960, pp. 189–95.

One of the standard problems in distribution theory has been to explain the skewness of the personal income distribution. In particular much has been written to explain the apparent contradiction between the allegedly normal distribution of abilities and the skewed distribution of income.[1] While this attempt to relate the distribution of earnings to the underlying distribution of ability is still with us (Roy, 1950a; 1950b; 1951), another approach has become popular in recent years. This new approach is not concerned with the distribution of abilities; instead it shows how 'chance' elements can generate a lognormal, a Pareto, or a similar income distribution.[2] This 'chance' approach has provided a new way of looking at the income distribution, but its proponents have paid too little attention to the economic meaning of the proportional shock mechanism (Mincer, 1958, p. 283). The present paper tries to combine parts of both of these approaches. It starts with the assumption of a normal distribution of ability and then shows how this leads to a lognormal distribution of earnings. This assumption of a normal ability distribution is only an expository device; as is shown in the Appendix there is little reason to assume that ability is in fact normally distributed.

The theory to be developed here deals only with earnings, i.e. wages and salaries. For property income the economic rationale of the multiplicative assumption used by the 'chance' theories presents no problem. If a man's

1. For a review of the literature see Staehle (1943, pp. 77–87). Champernowne (1953, 318–51); Rutherford (1955, pp. 277–94); Aitchison and Brown (1957, ch. 11), and (1954, pp. 88–107); Simon (1957, pp. 145–64); Solow (1951a, pp. 333–34), and Ph.D. dissertation (1951b). Friedman (1953, pp. 277–90), also uses chance elements, but does not relate them to a lognormal or to a Pareto distribution, and hence will not be discussed here.

2. Such chance effects can lead to a lognormal distribution if the size of an income increase, or the probability of its occurrence, is a function of the previous size of the variable. For example, if we take a group of people and in successive periods give \$1 to individuals selected at random, we will eventually approach a normal distribution. But if, instead of giving the fortunate individuals \$1 each, we give them, say, 1 per cent of their previous income we can get a lognormal distribution.

income increases so will his savings, at least in dollar terms, and hence, next year he will have a greater stock of income-bearing property.

The scale-of-operations effect

In analysing the relation between ability and earnings it is convenient to start with some definite assumption about the distribution of ability. Let us therefore make the popular assumption that ability is normally distributed. This assumption will be removed subsequently, and it will be shown that in the more general case whatever the distribution of ability, the distribution of earnings will have more positive skewness (or less negative skewness) than the distribution of ability. To show this a second assumption is needed; namely, that there is a correlation between a man's ability and his scale of operation.[3] This assumption need not hold strictly; as long as there is a *tendency* in this direction, the distribution of earnings will be more unequal than the distribution of abilities. Ability is defined here as the probability of completing a given task successfully. While this may not be the best definition for the psychologist, this definition has more relevance to the distribution of earnings than the usual measures such as I Q.

Given these assumptions, the distribution of earnings will be skewed because differences in ability are reinforced by differences in the scale of operation. Briefly, the greater a man's scale of operation, the greater is his gross output; hence, the greater is the *dollar value* of his superior ability. For example, if, because of differences in ability, one man completes 90 per cent of his tasks successfully and another completes only 80 per cent, and the total potential value of their output is $10, the difference in ability will lead to a $1 difference in earnings. But if the total potential value of their output is $1000, then the difference in ability is worth $100.

Symbolically, if N is the number of units in production, V the value of each unit, P the probability of completing each unit successfully, and I the cost of inputs, then the value of a man's output

$$W = N(VP - I).$$

Since V and I are constants, $VP - I$ has the same distribution (but on a

3. Unfortunately, this assumption conflicts with the previous assumption that ability and rank in the occupational hierarchy are correlated. The distribution of the number of subordinates controlled is L-shaped, and hence it cannot be closely correlated with a normal distribution. The best way to reconcile this conflict is as follows: if ability is normally distributed then any attempt to rank people according to ability into an L-shaped occupational distribution will leave some people redundant. We can then assume that these people work independently. (For a stimulating discussion of this point see Tuck (1954)). For the independent workers, ability is positively correlated with nonlabor inputs, and hence, as shown below, a scale-of-operations effect also applies to them.

different scale) as P.[4] But since N is correlated with P, the distribution of W will have more positive skewness (or less negative skewness) than P. For instance, in the special case where P is normally distributed, W will be positively skewed.[5]

This theory can be applied both to industrial work and to professional activities. To illustrate the latter, compare, for example, the earnings of two concert pianists of differing abilities. The abler pianist will have a higher income than his colleague for two multiplicative reasons; first, because people are willing to pay more for a ticket, and second, because he will play in a bigger hall. Similarly, the earnings of a very able lawyer exceed those of the average lawyer both because he wins more cases and because he is given the more important cases. Many other examples could be cited: outstanding doctors are likely to have rich patients, whose health, as measured by the market, is more important than the health of other people: outstanding architects are likely to work on bigger projects; the abler army officers are likely to have larger commands.

A more rigorous treatment can be achieved by applying the theory to industrial jobs, where inputs are primarily other people's labor. To do so it is convenient to add five more assumptions to the two previous ones. Hence, let us make a third assumption that a man can 'pass on' his ability to all his subordinates. For example, if a man with a 90 per cent chance of completing a certain job successfully hires men whose probability of completing the task successfully is only 80 per cent, the probability of the team completing the job successfully is 90 per cent.

Fourth, assume that the probability of completing a given task successfully is independent of a man's place in the work hierarchy. Assume, fifth, that a man can supervise a fixed number of subordinates, and sixth, that when he does so all his time is taken up with such supervision. In other words the 'working foreman' type of organization is excluded. Finally, assume that there are no nonlabor inputs. All of these assumptions will be weakened subsequently.[6]

To analyse the relation between W and P in greater detail, we can simplify

4. But if we exclude the possibility of negative Ws we have a truncated normal distribution and hence skewness.

5. The theory does not apply to completely routine jobs, i.e. jobs for which all people have the same P. If everyone has the same P everyone would maximize income by maximizing N (assuming $VP > I$). Under these conditions there is no determinate solution. This is not surprising. A theory based on differences in ability is of no use if everyone has the same ability. Similarly, if $I = 0$ everyone would operate at the highest feasible N.

6. The analysis of the immediately following pages cannot be applied to the whole labor force, otherwise there would be a conflict between the assumption of a normal ability distribution and the assumption of a positive correlation of N and P.

the above equation by choosing our units so that V (the value of each unit) equals unity, and N (the number of units) for a man working without subordinates, also equals one. We can then eliminate these two terms from the equation.[7] On the other hand, one additional variable has to be introduced; this is s, the number of subordinates a man can supervise. Hence the above equation can now be written as

$$W = sP.$$

An able man has the choice of working independently and producing P_2, where P_2 is his ability or hiring s less able men with an average ability of P_1. In the latter case his revenue is sP_2 (since he is able to 'pass on' his ability), his wage bill is sP_1, and his opportunity cost P_2. Thus if

$$sP_2 \geqslant sP_1 + P_2$$

he will set himself up as an entrepreneur, and competition among entrepreneurs will ensure that for the least able entrepreneur revenue and costs are just equal.[8] The earnings distribution generated by such a process consists of two parts. First, there are the employees with an ability measure of P_1, and since ability is, by assumption, normally distributed so is their W. For the entrepreneurs the distribution is skewed, since it is truncated at the marginal entrepreneur. When the distributions for employees and entrepreneurs are joined an additional reason for skewness is introduced, because, for entrepreneurs, differences in ability are multiplied by s. Hence, for these abler people differences in ability have a greater dollar value than differences for the less able people. The right side of the distribution is, so to speak, stretched out.

This procedure can be repeated for a third hierarchy level. The abler entrepreneurs then become 'second-stage' entrepreneurs, employing some of the previous entrepreneurs. The second-stage entrepreneur with ability P_3 hires first-stage entrepreneurs, paying each a wage equal to his previous profits $s(P_2 - P_1)$. If the second stage entrepreneur also hires s subordinates, his total wage bill is $s^2(P_2)$, and his opportunity cost as a second-stage entrepreneur is $s(P_3 - P_1)$. His revenue is, of course, $s^2 P_3$, and again for the marginal second-stage entrepreneur the two must be equal. The introduction of a third stage introduces additional skewness, and as more and more

7. This requires, however, that we measure P in dollars.

8. The marginal entrepreneur can be found if we know the ability distribution and the value of s. For him

$$sP_2 = sP_1 + P_2.$$

Transposing P_2, factoring, and dividing both sides by $(s-1)$ and P_1, we get

$$\frac{P_2}{P_1} = \frac{s}{s-1}.$$

stages are introduced the distribution of earnings approaches lognormality.[9]

Now to moderate the assumptions. The first assumption is the normal distribution of ability. As is shown in the Appendix there is little reason to assume that the distribution of ability is, in fact, normal when measured in the relevant way. If we therefore abandon the assumption of a normal ability distribution, and assume, instead, a positively skewed distribution, we have an additional factor making for inequality of earnings, but if the distribution of ability is negatively skewed this would make earnings more equal. Whatever the distribution of ability, due to the scale-of-operations effect earnings will have greater positive skewness than ability.

Assumptions two and three, the correlation between N and P, and the possibility of 'passing on' ability present a more serious problem. They cannot be abandoned without destroying the scale-of-operations effect. However, they can be relaxed. As long as there is a *tendency* for people with greater ability to hold higher places in the hierarchy, and as long as they can raise the ability of subordinates to *some* extent, the distribution of earnings will be more skewed than the distribution of ability. The greater the extent to which these two assumptions are true, the more skewed will be the distribution of income.

Assumption four, that the probability of completing a task successfully is the same at different levels of the hierarchy, though convenient for

9. To see this consider the table below. In the first column the Ps mark off equal intervals of ability, and the fs of the second column are, by assumption, normally distributed over this ability range. The third column measures the earnings associated with each level of P. For independent workers *net* earnings are simply equal to P, and for first-stage entrepreneurs they equal

$$s(P_2) - s(P_1) = s(P_2 - P_1).$$

Such an equation can, of course, be written for all levels of entrepreneurship. Since the Ps mark off equal distances on the ability scale, the differences between adjoining Ps are always equal and can be denoted by p. The final column shows the logarithms of earnings. Now the ps and the ss are the same for all P levels. Thus, ignoring the first term, as we increase the P level the logarithms of the Ws mark off equal distances on a logarithmic scale. Hence, if the fs are distributed normally when measured against the Ps on a natural number scale, they are distributed lognormally relative to earnings. Even the first case falls into line if we measure the ps from absolute zero (P_0). If so we can subtract this zero term from P_1 and multiply P_1 by s^0. The logarithm of the first term then has the same form as the other terms.

Ability	Frequency	Earnings	Logarithms of earnings
P_1	f_1	$W_1 = P_1$	$\log W_1 = \log P_1$
P_2	f_2	$W_2 = s^1(P_2 - P_1)$	$\log W_2 = 1 \log s + \log p$
P_3	f_3	$W_3 = s^2(P_3 - P_2)$	$\log W_3 = 2 \log s + \log p$
.	.	. .	. . . . . .
.	.	. .	. . . . . .
P_n	n	$W_n = {}^{n-1}(P_n - P_{n-1})$	$\log W_n = n-1 \log s + \log p$

expository purposes, can be relaxed somewhat. All that we have to assume is that the relation between the different Ps does not change as we move up the hierarchy, otherwise what is a normal distribution at one level of the hierarchy would be a different distribution at another. If the difference between the Ps decreases as we move up the ladder this would reduce the skewness of the earnings distribution, but if the difference increases it would tend to increase the skewness. It is likely that, at least in the early stages, the differences in the Ps increase as we move up the hierarchy, since the routine component of jobs, for which all Ps are equal, decreases. Finally, we may reach a stage at which decisions are so difficult to make that the 'pure guess' component becomes important – at this stage, the difference between the Ps decreases since all people are equally good at *pure* guessing.

Fifth, if it is assumed that there *are* 'working foremen', i.e. that the superior does spend some of his time on tasks other than directing subordinates, the distribution will tend to be less skewed, since now, for some part of a man's time, and hence for part of his earnings, the above-described principle does not apply.

The sixth assumption is that s (the number of subordinates) is the same at all levels of the hierarchy. If s is allowed to vary, then as we move up the hierarchy, instead of raising s to a higher power we would instead have to multiply it by a coefficient measuring the number of subordinates of the previous level supervised by one man.

Finally, there is the assumption that there are no nonlabor inputs. If these are introduced into the model they act as changes in s, since now the resources controlled at different levels of the hierarchy no longer increase at the same rate as before.

Thus, once we abandon the above assumptions the distributions or earnings need no longer be lognormal. The basic principle, however, is still valid. As long as there is *some* positive correlation between ability and place in the hierarchy, and as long as the superior's ability has *some* effect upon the subordinate's performance, the distribution of earnings will be more positively skewed than the distribution of ability.

Empirical tests

It remains to test the theory empirically. The main implication is that earnings have positively-skewed distribution unless ability itself is negatively skewed. While in fact the earnings distribution does have positive skewness this fact provides only a weak test of the theory, since there are also other theories explaining the same thing. Unfortunately, the predictions of the above theory cannot be made sufficiently specific to see if they fit the data better than other theories. There are three reasons for this. First, once we relax the special assumptions, the earnings distribution predicted by the theory need no longer be lognormal, and its detailed characteristics cannot be specified. For example, if we assume that the ability distribution has strong negative skewness, the earnings distribution predicted by the theory need no longer be positively skewed. Second, the earnings data available include transitory elements and hence do not provide a good test of the theory. Third, some of the skewness of the income distribution results from the merging of disparate elements of the population and is therefore unrelated to the theory to be tested (Miller, 1955, p. 29; Adams, 1958, pp. 390–98).

Fortunately there are two other implications of the theory which can be tested. First, if the scale-of-operations effect is important, then salaries should be a function of the scale of operation; and evidence suggests that the salaries of company presidents depend more on the company's size than on its profitability.[10]

Second, if the theory is correct we should find some recognition of the scale-of-operations effect in the extensive literature on job evaluation. Wage and salary administration theory has a close relation to earnings distribution theory since they are both dealing with essentially the same problem on different levels of aggregation and abstraction. Since a considerable amount of empirical work has been done on wage and salary administration this literature should be able to throw some light on the distribution of earnings. Thus, if it can be shown that the scale-of-operations effect has a parallel in wage and salary administration practice this can be taken as empirical verification of the theory. And such a parallel can be found in the concept of responsibility. As the quotations below show, responsibility is a major determinant of salaries (particularly on higher level jobs where the scale-of-operations effect is more important), and it is defined in a way which links it to the scale-of-operations effect.[11]

10. See Roberts (1956, pp. 270–94). Similarly, the salaries of divisional functional managers and chiefs tend to be correlated with volume of sales and other indications of size. See Howe (1956, p. 97). Roberts, incidentally, uses a scale-of-operations effect in his analysis. 'Company profit is the product of profit per unit and the number of units sold. Since a small firm sells relatively few units, even a substantial difference in profit per unit under two executives cannot yield a large difference in total company profit In the case of the large company the substantial number of units sold can convert even a modest difference in profit per unit into a large difference in total company profit' (Roberts, 1956, p. 292). In a general way the principle had been used earlier by Ely *et al*. (1924, p. 548) as one of the explanations of the accumulation of great fortunes even in competitive and semi-competitive businesses: '. . . even a relatively small difference in efficiency with which it is conducted may make a very large difference in the earnings of a gigantic business undertaking. It may be real economy for a corporation to pay $100,000 a year to the best man in sight rather than $50,000 to the second best man.'

11. See Hoge (1955, pp. 167–8), mentions three factors: knowledge, headwork and

Indeed, if it were not for the above theory it would be hard to explain why higher wages should be paid for more responsible work.[12] Looked at from the supply side it may seem that many people try to avoid responsibility, but on the other hand, the desire for power, and hence responsibility,

---

accountability. The last is defined as 'requirement of independent responsibility for what happens. Since results are measured finally in financial health and growth, accountability winds up sooner or later in terms of money (e.g. human relations accountability should eventually be related to the cost of labor turmoil, lost sales and the like)'. Another study (Benge, *et al.*, 1941), discussing the Factor Comparison Method, states . . . 'Comparison of responsibility among positions being evaluated is based on the comparative moral "accountability" placed on the incumbent of the position by his employer. *Consideration should be given to the probability of error or improvement and the possible consequences of such error or improvement. . . .* Ratings for higher grade jobs tend to group together at constantly widening intervals along the scale because *differences in difficulty and responsibility increase geometrically rather than arithmetically*' (1941, pp. 102, 106). Barbor (1949, pp. 25–7), suggests that the facts of a job description should be fitted into the following pattern: (1) responsibility of the job, (2) duties of the job, (3) all hazards. Responsibility is defined as '(*a*) kind and extent of supervision received . . . (*b*) supervision of a work program. The basic factors here are volume and complexity of work supervised. *Volume is normally reflected by number of employees supervised. . . . Complexity is normally reflected by the wage or salary levels of jobs supervised.* (*c̄*) opportunity for independent judgment . . . (*d*) *consequences of error, as measured in terms of likelihood of error being caught by subsequent review, and probable losses resulting from error stated in monetary or other measurements of value*'.

The General Foods Corporation Managerial Position Evaluation plan cited in Warren (1950, p. 274), states that 'normally responsibility is the predominant characteristic of executive positions unless decisions are particularly difficult and thus become the most important characteristic'. Responsibility is defined as follows 'Responsibility is being *Accountable* for something, both the negative accountability for *prevention of loss* and a positive accountability for *getting things done*. Accountability is measured by a position's opportunity ultimately to affect profit and loss. Failure to meet the *Accountability* requirements of a position will have *Consequences* the *Likelihood* and *Seriousness* of which indicate the relative importance of that position's responsibility' (1950, p. 273).

Finally, Burk (1950), describes the way the Atlantic Refining Company defines responsibility: 'Appraisal of the relative weights to be assigned to "responsibility for men", "responsibility for money", etc. was made on the basis of moral or accountable load placed on the incumbent of the position for direct loss or improvements in each heading . . .' (1950, p. 154).

12. It might seem that according to the scale-of-operations theory, job evaluation schemes should use only a single factor, the level of responsibility. But this is not so. In the abstract model used in this paper continuous functions are assumed and hence each s (number of subordinates) is correlated with a unique P; thus if we know s we can infer P. However, in individual companies there are only a discrete number of hierarchy levels, and hence there is no unique relation of s and P. Moreover, even if there were such a unique relation it would probably be worthwhile to use more than one factor in job evaluation. By looking at the same job in terms of both s and P the chance of error may well be reduced.

is a strong trait of western society. The solution is to be found on the demand side – responsible jobs pay more than others because an optimum allocation of manpower requires that they be filled with abler people, and the very fact that these people hold responsible jobs raises their productivity. Indeed, in a recently developed theory, Jaques (1956) treats the level of responsibility as the primary determinant of salary for non-routine jobs.[13] His approach was developed out of his attempt to analyse the existing salary structure of a large British company and hence can be treated as a piece of empirical evidence for the theory presented in this paper.[14]

Conclusion

To summarize, it has been shown that the psychologist's normal distribution of ability and the economist's skewed distribution of earnings are not in conflict. Due to the scale-of-operations effect, a normal distribution of ability leads to a skewed distribution of earnings; and given certain restrictive conditions it leads to a *lognormal* distribution of earnings. Moreover, as is shown in the Appendix, the normal distribution of abilities on psychological tests does not tell us how ability is distributed when measured in ways relevant to the distribution of earnings.

13. Responsibility is measured by Jaques primarily by length of time normally elapsing until a man's work is reviewed by his superiors, but at some points Jaques does bring in the volume of resources controlled: see, for instance, the quotation in the following footnote.

14. At a number of points Jaques's theory is very close to the theory developed in this paper. Thus he describes the attitudes within the British firm he is analysing as follows: [. . .] 'Jobs that carried the greater amounts of potential discretionary damage in them were the ones that the operators concerned considered should carry higher rates of pay. There thus emerged a possible correlation between the degree of responsibility carried (or level of work done) and the amount of damage-avoidance, that is to say, the amount of wastage the operator was relied upon to avoid through the use of his discretion. . . . The members of the firm were – without being aware of it – operating a systematic set of principles governing status and grading. [. . .] These unrecognized principles were threefold. First, status and payment were accorded for the level of work that a person was expected to do. . . . Second, the level of work allocated to a person could be defined solely in terms of the decisions that he was called upon to take. . . . Third, what they experienced as level of work was the span of time during which a member was authorized to make his own decisions without opportunity of reference to his manager . . . and in the case of manual work the direct calculation of the amount of damage that might be caused if inadequate discretion were exercised. . . . Moreover, status and payment appeared to be given for what might seem to be negative reasons – that is to say, they were given for the amount of damage or loss to company resources (including time) that a member was expected to avoid' (1956, pp. 69, 73–4).

Appendix

The distribution of ability

Although the results of psychological tests usually have a normal distribution we do not really know what *the* distribution of ability looks like. This is because there is at present really no such thing as *the* distribution of ability: the distribution depends upon the measuring rod used and cannot be defined independently of it. To illustrate, consider mathematical ability: we can test for it in several different ways, and the distribution obtained will depend upon the type of test used. For example, if the test consists of solving ten equally hard differential equations, then, for a typical segment of the population, the distribution has positive skewness, most people being concentrated at $X = 0$. Conversely, if the test consists of ten additions of two numbers each, the distribution has negative skewness, with most people scoring 100 per cent. And if we use a test consisting of questions of various degrees of difficulty then we may get a normal distribution.

More generally, we can rank questions according to difficulty, ranging from ones so simple that all but one man can answer them all, to ones so difficult that only the ablest man can answer a single one. If we make up a test consisting of only the first type of questions, we get a negatively skewed distribution (the one-man tail being on the left) while if we include only the second type of question, we get positive skewness (the one-man tail being on the right this time). If we include questions of intermediate difficulty, we get a different distribution, and we can, of course, choose our questions so that the resulting distribution will be normal. Hence the normal distribution on the usual psychological tests tells us something about how these tests are constructed, but it certainly does not tell us how ability in some absolute sense is distributed; by varying the ratio of easy and difficult questions we can get almost any distribution we like. Thus it is just as 'correct' to say that the distribution of ability has positive skewness, as it is to say that it is normally distributed, or has negative skewness.[15] For example,

15. Psychologists are aware that the normal distribution on psychological tests is connected with the way the tests are constructed. As Mann put it (1946, p. 302):
It has been argued that since intelligence has a biological basis the distribution of intelligence should conform to a normal curve. There are, however, some biological characters which do not conform to a normal curve and intelligence may be one of these. It should be remembered that the shape of any distribution is determined partly by units of measurement. Few test authors assume equality of units of measurement for their tests. In the Stanford–Binet Scale items were selected so as to ensure that the mental age of an age group equalled its chronological age. This scale does not pretend to

suppose that in a certain economy all tasks are easy. If we use the tasks of this economy as a measuring rod we would get one distribution of ability, but in another economy where most tasks are difficult we would obtain a quite different distribution.[16] Hence, even if the distribution of earnings mirrors the distribution of ability, we cannot specify what the distribution of earnings should look like.

Moreover, one should distinguish between gross and net output. Suppose for example, that by some coincidence the available tasks in the economy are such that when they are used to measure ability, ability is normally distributed. Even under these special conditions *net* output and earnings need not be normally distributed. For example, consider a simple economy with no division of labor and only a single industry. Gross output in this industry is, by assumption, normally distributed. But if each worker has to buy a fixed amount of inputs the least efficient workers may have a negative *net* product. If these workers with a negative product cease working (which would be the rational thing to do) the distribution of net earnings is no longer normal. It becomes a truncated normal curve and such a curve is skewed. Hence, even in this simple case where there is no scale-of-operations effect a normal distribution of abilities would lead to a skewed distribution of net output and hence earnings.[17]

---

measure in equal units; it is a scale showing the ability of the tested individual in comparison with other individuals in various age groups . . . Thorndike's distribution on the basis of equal units seems to dispose of this problem in favor of normalcy; but since his equal units were established by the use of normal curve functions he has merely demonstrated normality by assuming it in advance.

16. This implies that the normal distribution of many physical and personality traits is irrelevant for the purpose at hand. Height, for example, is measured 'objectively', and hence a six foot man is six inches taller than a five foot six inch man, both in a primitive and in a modern society. But a man who is twice as able as another man in a primitive society need not be twice as able in a modern society. Economic ability, in other words, cannot be determined by psychological factors alone but depends also on the type of economy.

17. This distinction between gross and net output can explain a phenomenon sometimes cited in discussions of the skewness of the income distribution. This is the skewed distribution of the number of scientific papers published per author in certain fields (Simon, 1957, p. 160). Let us assume, purely for the sake of the argument, and contrary to casual observation, that each author submits the same number of papers, say ten, and that due to the cost of other inputs (printing, etc.) the journals publish only the best 50 per cent of the papers. Assume further that the quality of the papers submitted is a unique function of the author's ability. In this case half the authors would publish ten papers and the other half none. By introducing a stochastic element into the relation between the author's ability and the quality of his papers we can, of course, get a more equal distribution. However, this example shows how a completely equal distribution of *gross* output (and hence 'ability'?) can lead to a very unequal distribution of *net* output.

References

ADAMS, F. G. (1958), 'The size of individual incomes: socioeconomic variables and chance variation', *Rev. Econ. Stats.*, vol. 40, pp. 390–98.

AITCHISON, J., and BROWN, J. A. C. (1954), 'On criteria for descriptions of income distribution', *Metroeconomica*, vol. 6, pp. 88–107.

AITCHISON, J., and BROWN, J. A. C. (1957), *The Lognormal Distribution*, Cambridge University Press.

BARBOR, A. W. (1949), *Principles of Salary and Wage Administration*, National Foreman's Institute.

BENGE, E. J., *et al.* (1941), *Manual of Job Evaluation*, National Foreman's Institute.

BURK, S. L. H. (1950), 'Case histories of wage and salary administration', in J. Dooker and V. Marquis (eds.), *Handbook of Wage and Salary Administration*, American Management Association.

CHAMPERNOWNE, D. G. (1953), 'A model of income distribution', *Econ. J.*, vol. 63, pp. 318–51.

ELY, R. T., *et al.* (1924), *Outlines of Economics*, fourth edition, Macmillan.

FRIEDMAN, M. (1953), 'Choice, chance and the personal distribution of income', *J. of Pol. Econ.*, vol. 61, pp. 277–90.

HOGE, R. H. (1955), 'Evaluating executive jobs', *Personnel J.*, vol. 34, pp. 167–8.

HOWE, R. J. (1956), 'Price tags for executives', *Harvard bus. Rev.*, vol. 34, p. 97.

JACQUES, E. (1956), *Measurement of Responsibility*.

MANN, C. W. (1946), in P. L. Harriman (ed.), *Encylopedia of Psychology*, New York.

MILLER, H. P. (1955), *Income of the American People*, Government Printing Office.

MINCER, J. (1958), 'Investment in human capital and personal income distribution', *J. Pol. Econ.*, vol. 66, p. 283.

ROBERTS, D. (1956), 'A general theory of executive compensation based on statistically tested propositions', *Q.J. Econ.*, vol. 70, pp. 270–94.

ROY, A. D. (1950a), 'The distribution of earnings and individual output', *Econ. J.*, vol. 60, pp. 489–505.

ROY, A. D. (1950b), 'A further note on the distribution of individual output', *Econ. J.*, vol. 60, pp. 831–6.

RUTHERFORD, R. S. G. (1955), 'Income distributions: a new model', *Econometrica*, vol. 23, pp. 277–94.

SIMON, H. A. (1957), 'On a class of skew frequency functions', reprinted in *Models of Man*, pp. 145–64.

SOLOW, R. (1951a), 'Some long-run aspects of the distribution of wage incomes', Abstract, *Econometrica*, vol. 19, pp. 333–4.

SOLOW, R. (1951b), *The Dynamics of Wage Income*, unpublished Ph.D. dissertation, Harvard University.

STAEHLE, H. (1943), 'Ability, wages and income', *Rev. Econ. Stats.*, vol. 25, pp. 77–87.

TUCK, R. H. (1954), *An Essay on the Economic Theory of Rank*, Oxford University Press.

WARREN, B. B. (1950), 'Evaluation of managerial position', in J. Dooker and V. Marquis (eds.), *Handbook of Wage and Salary Administration*, American Management Association.

12 H. Simon

The Compensation of Executives

H. Simon, 'The compensation of executives', *Sociometry*, vol. 20, 1957, pp. 32–5.

In a recent analysis of the available data on the compensation of business executives, Roberts (1956, pp. 270–94) has shown that the compensation of the highest paid official in a company is related to size of company and to virtually no other variables (in particular, not to profit) after the effect of size has been partialed out. Specifically, the relation that Professor Roberts finds in his data is a logarithmic one. Let C be total annual compensation of the highest paid official, S, annual dollar sales, and a and k constants. Then the observed relation is:

$$C = kS^a \qquad\qquad 1$$

or, on a logarithmic scale:

$$\log C = a \log S + k'. \qquad\qquad 2$$

Fitting the data to equation 2 by the method of least squares, we find a value of about 0·37 for a. The data are homoscedastic on the logarithmic scale.

Professor Roberts discusses the implications of these data for the theory of executive compensation and advances an explanation based on marginal productivity theory. In the present paper I should like to develop an alternative theory of a more sociological character. This explanation has the advantage that, unlike the one based on the marginal productivity theory, it predicts not only a positive relation between size of company and compensation, but also the logarithmic form of the function and the approximate value of the coefficient a.

Businesses, like all large-scale organizations, are roughly pyramidal in form, because of the hierarchical structure induced by the authority relation. Each executive has a certain number, n, of subordinates at the level immediately below him, and this number varies within only moderate limits in a given company, and even among a number of companies. At executive levels it is seldom less than three, and seldom more than ten, and usually lies within narrower bounds – particularly if we take averages over all executives in an organization at a given level.

There is a widely accepted attitude in industry that an appropriate differential in salary exists between an executive and his immediate subordinates, measured not in absolute terms but as a ratio. That is, an executive's salary 'should' be b times the salary of his immediate subordinates, no matter what his level.[1] Again, the value of b undoubtedly varies from situation to situation, but one can find figures quoted in the range of 1·25 to 2. While we would expect to encounter instances of larger or smaller ratios, averages can be expected to be relatively stable.

Now, consider an idealized organization in which each executive has exactly n immediate subordinates, and in which he receives a salary b times the salary of his immediate subordinates. Let S be the number of executives in the organization[2] and let L be the number of levels in the executive hierarchy. Then, we have the following relation between S and L

$$S = 1 + n + n^2 + ... + n^{L-1} = \frac{n^L - 1}{n - 1} \simeq \frac{n^L}{n - 1}. \qquad \qquad 3$$

Now suppose that executives at the first, or lowest, level are brought in at a salary of A. Again, if this lowest level represents recent college graduates, there is a good reason to suppose that there is a recruitment salary that does not vary widely from one position or one company to another. We then have the following equation to determine C, the salary of the top executive

$$C = Ab^{L-1} = Bb^L \qquad \qquad 4$$

Taking logarithms in **3**, we get

$$\log S = L \log n + \text{const.} \qquad \qquad 5$$

Similarly, from **4** we get

$$\text{Log}\, C = L \log b + \text{const.} \qquad \qquad 6$$

Eliminating L between **5** and **6**, we find

$$\log C = \frac{\log b}{\log n} \log S + \text{const.} \qquad \qquad 7$$

But equation **7** becomes identical with equation **2** if we take

$$a = \frac{\log b}{\log n}. \qquad \qquad 8$$

1. This 'rule of proportionality' receives prominent attention in most discussions of executive compensation, and its correctness as a norm is accepted more or less as a truism. See for example Patton (1951), and Koontz and O'Donnell (1955).

2. In the data we have available, the size of companies is measured by their dollar sales. We assume here an exact proportionality between dollar sales and total number of executives – which, of course, will hold only in an average sense. For this reason, we use the variable S indiscriminately to refer to both measures of company size.

We can test equation **8** further by seeing whether the observed value, 0·37, for *a* is consistent with reasonable values of *b* and *n*. Equation **8** defines *b* as a function of *n*, and vice versa, so that a whole set of possible pairs of values of the latter two variables will be compatible with a given value of *a*. We could have, for example, $n = 7, b = 2, n = 5, b = 1·75$, or $n = 3, b = 1·5$. All these pairs lie within the range we have postulated.[3]

There is one small additional piece of confirming evidence for our hypothesis. In 1936, General Motors made available data on the number of executives at various compensation levels. Davis (1941, p. 49) found that this distribution could be described by the equation

$$C' = mN^{-0·33},\qquad\qquad 9$$

where *N* is the number of executives receiving compensation *C'*, and where *m* is a constant.

Under our previous assumptions, the number of persons at *L'* levels from the top is

$$N(L') = n^{L'-1}.\qquad\qquad 10$$

From the proportionality assumption, the compensation, *C'* of persons at this level is

$$C'(L') = Mb^{1-L'}.\qquad\qquad 11$$

Taking logarithms, and eliminating *L'* between **10** and **11**, we get

$$\log C' = -\frac{\log b}{\log n}\log N + \text{const.},\qquad\qquad 12$$

which becomes identical with the logarithm of **9** if we set

$$\frac{\log b}{\log n} = a = 0·33.$$

This new estimate of *a* is not very different from that obtained from the regression of salaries on size of company.

Summary

In summary, I have proposed a theory of executive compensation that assumes that salaries are determined by requirements of internal 'consistency' of the salary scale with the formal organization and by norms of

3. It is worth observing that if we try to estimate *n* and *b* directly in a particular firm, we will find the notion of 'level' somewhat ambiguous, and will have difficulty distinguishing 'levels' from 'half-levels'. However, any errors we make in estimating *n* will lead to proportional errors in our estimates of *b*, so that the ratio of log *b* to log *n* will be only slightly affected. For this reason, the test of our theory does not depend in any critical way upon the definition of level we employ.

proportionality between salaries of executives and their subordinates. Three mechanisms are postulated: (*a*) economic determination, through competition, of the salaries at the lowest executive levels where new employees are hired from outside the organization; (*b*) social determination of a norm for the 'steepness' of organizational hierarchies (usually called the span of control); (*c*) social determination of a norm for the ratio of an executive's salary to the salaries of his immediate subordinates. Where these mechanisms operate, a relation will exist between the salaries of top executives and the sizes of their companies that matches very well with the observed relation. Moreover, if we take values that appear reasonable for the norms (*b*) and (*c*), we obtain a prediction of the slope of the relation between salary and company size that is in good quantitative agreement with the empirical data. Further, the same parameter values are obtained from data on the frequency distribution of executive salaries in a single company.

If the proposed theory is correct, it calls into question the usual economic explanation of compensation – that the executive is paid at a rate roughly equal to his marginal contribution to company profits. While the present theory is consistent with a positive correlation between compensation and ability, only an improbable coincidence would bring about equality between salaries determined by the mechanism described here and salaries determined by the marginal productivity mechanism. Hence, it would appear that the distribution of executive salaries is not unambiguously determined by economic forces, but is subject to modification through social processes that determine the relevant norms.

References

DAVIS, H. T. (1941), *The Theory of Econometrics*, Principia Press.
KOONTZ, H., and O'DONNELL, C. (1955), *Principles of Management*, McGraw-Hill.
PATTON, A. (1951), 'Current practices in executive compensation', *Harvard bus. Rev.*, vol. 29, no. 1, pp. 56–64.
ROBERTS, D. R. (1956), 'A general theory of executive compensation based on statistically tested propositions', *Q. J. Econ.*, vol. 70, pp. 270–94.

13 B. Wootton

Modern Methods of Wage Determination

Extract from B. Wootton, *The Social Foundations of Wages Policy*, Allen & Unwin, 1962, pp. 68–87.

Nearly all the features of the wage and salary structure sketched in the preceding chapter which are anomalies from the angle of economic theory become intelligible in a broader frame of reference. It is the social factors which are missed in the economists's interpretation; and what is anomalous to the economist may make perfectly good sense to the sociologist. In a hierarchical society such as ours, large issues of social status are involved in wage and salary scales. Pay and prestige are closely linked; and (in spite of some exceptions) it is the rule that the high-prestige person should be also the highly-paid person: and vice versa. Once this rule is admitted as a factor in its own right, it is remarkable how effectively it explains much that on a purely economic hypothesis, has to be explained away. On this principle the fact that the highest salary classes are monopolized by the first of the five social classes (professional, intermediate, skilled, partly skilled, unskilled) into which the Registrar-General classifies all occupations, is socially just as it should be; and the same principle explains the importance attached to the rule that those who give orders should be paid more than those to whom their orders are given. Where prestige depends on pay, one cannot be expected to obey, or even, perhaps, to respect, one's economic inferiors. Again, the positive relationship between monetary and non-monetary remuneration, which appears so persistently from top to bottom of our wage and salary structure and squares so badly with the economist's 'balance of net advantages', is just what one would expect in a society in which the dirty and disagreeable jobs are left to people whose pay is appropriate to their humble social position; nor is there anything to cause surprise in the fact that one may search in vain for signs of the supposed compensation of longer working hours by higher rates of wages.

. . The differentiation between the rates paid to men and to women in the same employment lends itself also to a comparable interpretation. The attitude of our society to women is highly ambivalent. On the one hand, a tradition of chivalry and a convention about their frailty make women objects of formal respect: conventionally well-mannered men do not sit when women are standing, or walk through doorways in front of their wives. On the other hand, in industry and in the world of affairs the assumption that women should normally occupy the humbler positions is still strongly entrenched. Rare indeed is the calling in which the proportion of women who attain the highest positions is comparable to the proportion of potential recruits of their sex to be found at lower levels. Those who do rise above these levels are nearly[1] always made aware of subtle differentiations or of tacit assumptions of masculine predominance. Indeed, an interesting parallel could be drawn, in the recent history of this country, between the position of women and that of the manual working classes. As members of two groups conspicuously ranked as socially inferior, both must have had many of the same experiences – including, on occasion, that of being (as it has been aptly called) 'elaborately treated as the equals' of more favoured social categories. Both also tend to be paid as befits their modest station. And both, in the present century, have succeeded in pushing themselves noticeably upwards, significantly improving their relative economic position in the process.

... It is of course easy to argue that high pay itself confers high prestige. That is no doubt true; but there is nothing in that to invalidate the converse proposition. Circular relationships are in fact everyday occurrences in social life: hens are constantly laying eggs and eggs growing into hens. In an acquisitive society those who enjoy large salaries are also, as a rule, accorded high social prestige; and the prestige of these callings in turn requires that their standard of pay should be correspondingly generous.

The broad similarity between the social and the wage hierarchy needs no elaborate demonstration. It could hardly be missed after even a most casual glance at the facts contained in the preceding chapter. Neither considerations of prestige, however, nor the laws of supply and demand can directly alter the size of anybody's wage-packet: prestige and economic calculation alike exist only in the minds of men. In order, therefore, fully to understand the forces that shape our wage structure, account must be taken of the human processes by which wage and salary rates are actually determined. Today these determinations are commonly the result of conscious and explicit decisions made, not by the phantoms that people the unimotivational fantasy world of the economics textbooks, but by men and women

1. Nearly, but not quite. In the course of my life I have myself had a hand in a good many jobs (paid and unpaid) in which members of both sexes were engaged. In perhaps two of these absolutely no discrimination on grounds of sex was detectable, and in one other the women appeared to suffer only a very slight disadvantage. These were, however, exceptions: as a rule the women were seriously handicapped chiefly by the tacit assumption that positions of higher responsibility would be (if with certain recognized exceptions) normally filled by men. For a fuller discussion of the bearing of the social position of women on the 'equal pay' issue, see (Wootton, 1946, pp. 114–15).

of real flesh and blood, whose business it is to fix wages in one or other of the ways described later in this chapter, and who must in so doing act according to their lights. Both the mental processes of these men and women and the social environment in which they move leave their mark upon the final picture. To the study of those processes and of that environment we may now turn.

Among the many social revolutions that have taken place in this country in the present century, not the least is the revolution in the institutional machinery for settling rates of wages and salaries. Today three main instruments are used for this purpose – collective bargaining, statutory regulation and quasi-judicial settlement by arbitration tribunals; and the part played by each is altogether different from what it was even fifty years ago.

At the beginning of the present century the practice of collective bargaining had already been established in some industries (as in engineering, iron and steel manufacture, and in textiles), often after a hard struggle on the part of the trade unions; but the unions were still fighting battles for recognition on many fronts; and, even where wage agreements were jointly made with employers, these were often only on a local basis even in such great industries as coal-mining. Comprehensive national bargaining was quite exceptional. Some idea of the change which has occurred in the prevailing mental climate may be gained by recalling that fifty years ago no trade union leader had ever been knighted or made a peer, and that even on the railways collective bargaining was not fully established until the second decade of this century. Comparisons of attitude are always dangerous when no precise measures are available, but it can safely be said that at the turn of the century employers were at best disposed to look upon the negotiation of wages with trade union representatives as an unwelcome concession to the growing power of the unions: fear and suspicion were the dominant themes in the conventional attitude to trade unionism. Today arrangements for collective bargaining are part of the ordinary constitutional machinery of industry, and few indeed are the manual jobs (other than those governed by statutory regulations or arbitration awards) for which a rate has not been jointly agreed (even if it is not universally observed) between employers' and workers' organizations. Miners, chemical and metal workers, engineers, shipbuilders, all branches of textile workers, leatherworkers, woodworkers, builders, paper workers and printers, brewers, transport workers on the roads and railways, in ships and aeroplanes, shop assistants and other distributive workers – all can now quote a recognized union rate for their jobs embodied in a formal collective agreement. Private domestic service and some fields of clerical employment must be almost the only remaining fields of substantial employment on which collective bargaining has made no perceptible impact. Meanwhile trade unions have become pillars of society, and governments of every political complexion go out of their way to stress the honourable place which these bodies occupy in the structure of the community. The entrance hall of the headquarters of the Trades Union Congress at Transport House, with its directory of titled or decorated names, epitomizes an astonishing social change.

Nor is it only in industry that collective bargaining has become respectable. Hardly less remarkable has been the spread of the practice amongst clerical and professional workers. The professional civil servants, the dental mechanics, the chief officers of local authority departments, the psychiatric social workers, the journalists, the remedial gymnasts, the hospital engineers – as well as doctors, actors, musicians and staffs engaged in broadcasting – all have their own professional organizations, every one of which is at least partly concerned in looking after the financial interests of its members. Even in the universities, where no formal arrangements for joint negotiation of salaries have yet been made, the Association of University Teachers and in extra-mural education the Tutors' Association act as collective spokesmen on orthodox trade union lines for the staffs from whom their membership is drawn.

These dramatic developments can hardly be dismissed without further inquiry, as just examples of the 'imperfect competition' described in the economics textbooks. Indeed, any attempt to explain trade union activity in terms of models based on monopolistic selling involves an important fallacy. For a trade union is not a monopolistic seller of labour: it is not a seller of labour at all, but a representative of individual sellers – which is something quite different. The manufacturer who enjoys a monopoly in the production of some article can weigh the probable rewards of a high-price-restricted-output policy against those of large output and low prices, choosing whichever he thinks will yield the highest return. Which of these two courses he decides to follow will affect the size of the resultant profit, but not its destination. If he is the sole owner of the business, he will obviously be the sole beneficiary (or sole loser) irrespective of whether a restrictive or an expansionist policy is pursued. Similarly, even if a monopolist is in fact a board of directors acting on behalf of a company, each shareholder's slice of the distributed profits (large or small) will be determined by the amount of his holding, and not by the type of price policy by which those profits were made. In the case of a union, however, this is not so. Even if we assume that a monopolistic labour market works in the same way as the market for any article the sale of which is monopolistically controlled, the parallel breaks down, when it comes to the distribution of the proceeds. Just as the model monopolist might in some circumstances anticipate a larger total profit from limited sales at high prices than from larger sales at low prices, so the union leaders might argue that the total wage bill would be greater if a small number of men are employed at a high wage rather than a larger number at lower rates. But the effect of these two policies upon the whole body of their members is entirely different. In the former case the whole benefit is appropriated by those individuals who are lucky enough to get employment: the rest get nothing. In the alternative case, whatever the size of the wage bill, a larger number will enjoy a share of it.

No simple analogy can, therefore, be drawn between the capitalist who prefers to hoard or to destroy goods rather than risk his spoiling his own market by selling them at possibly unfavourable prices, and the union which, by the same logic, might be expected to choose good wages for a few and unemployment for the rest in preference to lower rates all round. Unsold goods will cost a firm money, and any loss on that account must be deducted from the possible gain in keeping them off the market. Since both credit and debit items fall within the same business, that is a straightforward (if speculative) calculation; but the loss of income due to unemployment and the gain from higher wages accrue to *different* people. Furthermore, people and things are different in kind. A bag of coffee does not, presumably, care whether it is sold or whether, alternatively, it is burnt in order to keep up the price of the rest of the crop. An unemployed man is likely to take a different view of any policy that prices him out of the market.

Again, trade union leaders who negotiate collective contracts, unlike businessmen, are not out to make money for themselves. Their job is to get the best possible terms for their members. When contracts are made between agents on both sides – the union official on the one hand and the officer of the employers' association on the other – the relation of each party to his constituents is in principle the same; though even in this case the position of a representative acting for perhaps a score of firms is different from that of a union leader representing perhaps tens of thousands of workpeople. But when (as sometimes happens – more often perhaps in the United States than in this country) wage agreements are made between union officials on one side and the directors or owners of firms directly concerned on the other, the personal interest of the two parties in the outcome is of a quite different order. The one has to think of his own pocket, the other of the temper of the members to whom he will have to justify his action: the former is clearly much nearer than the latter to the ideal monopolist pictured by the economic theorists. The economic theory which postulates that the one part is simply concerned to minimize, and the other to maximize, the wage bill overlooks this distinction. An *individual* applicant for a post may say to himself, 'If I make my terms too stiff, I won't get the job.' To that, in collective negotiation, there is no true parallel.

The representative nature of collective contracts indeed distinguishes them in more ways than one from the bargains struck by individuals. The private individual has to convince an employer that he is worth the money that he is asking: the union has to persuade the employers or their representatives that the rate which it demands is appropriate for the job. Theoretically that can, of course, be done in strictly economic terms, on the lines of 'you can afford to pay what we are asking and you won't get the men you want until you do'. But in practice the argument is unlikely to stick at the economic level: the very fact of formal, representative discussion tends to push it on to a different plane. With the advent of collective bargaining, diplomatic negotiation takes the place of commercial haggling; and there are subtle differences between diplomacy and business. A case now has to be made, not just a bargain struck. That is why the role of the union, as not itself a seller, but as the spokesman of those who have labour to sell, becomes significant. Spokesmen and salesmen think in different patterns and use different language; and they may even come to different conclusions.

The formalization of discussion is thus itself a factor in the development of the handling of wage questions in ethical terms which is such a notable feature of our time and is discussed at length below (Chapter 5, not included here, Ed.) Although most collective bargaining takes place behind closed doors, in the more important cases progress reports are issued to the Press, and there is certainly much public interest in the outcome. If no agreement is reached, and the issue is referred to arbitration, hearings are sometimes held in public. A collective agreement demands a degree of social justification which a private bargain can ignore. Negotiators and diplomatists, despite their reputation for cynicism, are incurably ethical in their choice of arguments.

The trade union leader, moreover (whether elected or appointed), functions as the representative of a society which is organized for specific purposes under a democratic constitution. Like other representatives he is, therefore, necessarily concerned with what are essentially political issues – domestic issues affecting his own position *vis-à-vis* the membership, and external issues affecting the standing of the union in relation, not only to the employers, but also to any rival organizations catering for the same group of workers. Even if he is himself apprised of all the niceties of the economic situation, and reacts appropriately, his members cannot be expected to have attained an equal degree of sophistication. They look to the union to deliver the goods: to give them something tangible in return for their subscriptions and for the loyalty which is often a real force in the trade union world.

There are, moreover, but few unions whose membership is so completely homogeneous that no possibility arises of a conflict of interest within the membership between different grades or different geographical areas; whilst large national organizations covering many industries and occupations (the Transport and General Workers' Union is the outstanding example) consist of an extremely complex web of potentially divergent interests which have to be most delicately handled. Mishandling is not only damaging to the negotiating officers' comfort and prestige (though not to their pockets unless they actually get fired): it is damaging, no less, to the status of the union as an institution, and so enhances the risk of a breakaway. The modern union leader must shape his wage policy with due regard to the balance of interests within his own organization. In this country, where the Trades Union Congress keeps a tolerably firm hold upon empire-building activities by rival unions, the danger of actual disruption is indeed nothing like as menacing today as it was thirty or forty years ago. But the fact that it has not entirely disappeared is illustrated by the Engineering Officers (Telecommunications) Association's recent breakaway from the Post Office Engineering Union; or the relations between the Colliery Winders' Federation and the National Union of Mineworkers which were the subject of protracted negotiation ending in the absorption of the winders into the National Union of Mineworkers in 1951. The annual reports of the Trades Union Congress General Council regularly include accounts of inter-union disputes in which the Council has been called upon to intervene – as, to take a few examples from recent years, between the National Union of Printing, Bookbinding and Paper Workers and the National Union of General and Municipal Workers; or between the Confederation of Health Service Employees and the National Union of Public Employees; or between the latter and the Transport and General Workers' Union.

Professor Ross (1948) gives a number of examples of how these political issues affect the trade union leaders' attitudes in wage negotiations in the United States, where inter-union rivalry is still quite formidable; and in particular of how such issues may lead to decisions which by the standard of economic analysis must be judged quite irrational. Strikes, for instance, may be called when only the narrowest margin divides the parties, in gross defiance of the principles adduced by Professor Hicks to explain industrial disputes. Thus in the General Motors strike of 1945–6, 'the President's fact-finding board proposed a 19½ cent settlement in January; the company offered 17½ cents in February; and the parties finally settled for 18½ cents in March. Why', asks Professor Ross

was the extra penny so important to the Union? It will take the workers ten years to make up the loss of one month's pay, at the rate of a penny an hour. And why was the penny so important to the company? Again, in the bargaining process,

... the size of the wage adjustment (is) often more crucial than the amount of the wage which results. ... The trade union leader must achieve a 15 per cent increase for his group because most of the other locals affiliated with his international union have done so.

Equally irrational is the insistence of many unions on both sides of the Atlantic upon a uniform wage throughout their jurisdiction – a principle to which great importance is attached. By this policy unions throw away all the advantages known to the economist as the rewards of 'discriminating monopoly'. To quote Professor Ross again, 'There is little doubt that a union could achieve a higher average wage-rate, and a greater total wage income for its members, if it were to extract from each employer the most that he could be made to pay.' And why do unions constantly press for the area of the bargaining unit to be extended and for 'multi-union' and 'multi-employer' bargaining structures? 'The assumptions seems to be that the union's bargaining power varies directly with the size of the unit. ... A craft union representing only a minority of workers may have more bargaining power than a trades council representing all the workers. If the craft is indispensable and the workers are irreplaceable, the union can achieve the effect of a complete walk-out by withdrawing its own members (Ross, 1948, pp. 46, 48–9).

In this country Turner (1952) has recently traced in somewhat similar fashion the effect of internal political considerations upon the contemporary wage policy of a number of our own unions.

Turner's article deserves to be consulted at first hand, since it is too full of information to be readily summarized. Among the points which he makes, however, the following are of special interest in the present context. In recent years – indeed on and off ever since the First World War – there has been a persistent tendency in many industries for the wage differentials between skilled and unskilled workers to become narrower – largely as the result of the practice of awarding increases in the form of equal flat-rate additions to all grades. Alternatively, in other industries increases have taken the form of equal percentage advances all round. Both these methods contrast with the older practice of separate negotiation, usually on a local basis, for different classes of workers: they are in fact a characteristic of collective bargaining on a national scale. Indeed, it commonly happens that national agreements in the first instance simply result in the crystallization of existing differentials, both for locality and for skill. Some such arrangement, as Turner points out, is in fact practically a pre-condition of the establishment of national bargaining machinery involving separate groups of workers; for organizations which have previously looked after their own interests will only be induced to join with others, if by merging their separate identities they see a prospect of '*general* improvements in wages and conditions superior to those which the separate groups could achieve alone'. Amalgamations

in any case always involved lengthy and difficult inter-union negotiations and diplomatic interchanges. It was clearly advisable for their leaders to confirm them by some success, and equally politic for them to accept the existing relation *between* rates as the line from which to launch their campaign. Some minor standardization may have been envisaged on occasion, if only to facilitate central negotiation. But any great discussion of the relativities between the allied groups might not only have diverted their energies from the main ends of their cooperation but even endangered its continuance. . . . Certainly no united strategy could have been based on the assumption that disproportionate concessions might be given by one class of workers.

Once joint bargaining machinery has been established the

need of union negotiators to secure the widest possible consent of the workers they represent compels them so to formulate their claim as to avoid any appearance of discrimination against a substantial section of their constituents. . . . In such cases any settlement which appears to place the membership of one of the associated unions at a disadvantage as compared with the other groups puts a great strain upon the alliance and may lead to the withdrawal of the offended party.

When to these considerations we add the fact that an overall advance for everybody has the merit of simple convenience, it is easy to appreciate why it has become quite unusual for unions to ask for an increase in any form other than that of straight flat-rate or percentage additions for all the workers involved. What then determines the choice as between these two systems, between, that is, a method which reduces proportionate differences but stabilizes differentials measured in absolute amounts of money, and one which maintains relativities? Again Turner shows how the internal politics and structure of the unions concerned lead them to prefer one or other method. Individual unions show definite and consistent leanings to one side or the other, which reflect the balance of power between the different classes of worker included in their membership. Thus flat-rate claims tend to be preferred 'where the lower-paid sections of workers are powerfully organized, and particularly so in industries where the skilled and the unskilled belong to separate trade unions which negotiate jointly with employers'. The cotton textile workers are a case in point. Again the 'same sort of "balance of power" situation is also often seen within industrial unions where the lower grades of worker are strongly represented' – as in the National Union of Railwaymen. In some unions, too, constitutional forms, the block vote in particular, give a weight to the views of unskilled workers which if proportionate to their numbers does not nevertheless reflect what Turner calls 'the quality of their organization'. The constitutional structure of the unions in the building industry, for instance, favours the labourers whose 'attachment to both the industry and their unions is rather unstable'.

In those occupations, on the other hand, in which percentage, not flat rate, claims are the rule, as amongst the miners, the mule-spinners in the cotton industry, and the steel workers, three factors, as Turner reminds us, are important. First, none of the unions concerned has any rival to fear in its own field. Second, none of them has any membership outside its principal industrial interest. 'They organize occupations which are confined to the industries in which these unions operate.' Third, each of them operates a system of recruitment (either as the result of technical requirements, or thanks to rigid conventions which protect them from risk of dilution), in which vacancies in each grade are automatically filled from the ranks of those immediately below. These unions are thus relieved of the fear, which is a real factor in, say, the building or the engineering industry, that, if the skilled craftsman's rate is pushed too high, his job will be stolen by a professionally unqualified competitor.

Turner draws the moral that wage relativities are increasingly set 'by neither the accident of the labour market (a dubious term) nor the conscious will of those involved. They derive rather from the interplay of forces in the present structure of trades (*sic*) unionism, collective bargaining, and relations between people at work' (1952, pp. 244, 246, 259, 280). That structure, we may add, is itself the result of a history of struggles for power (both between the unions themselves and in their conflicts with employers) and of a thousand and one events in the lives of both individuals and institutions, which from the angle of economic theory must be judged wholly accidental. The appearance of two unions where only one grew before may be due to the clash of incompatible personalities: giant amalgamations may bear witness to the dominance of a single ambitious leader. The aristocratic attitude of one union, the political colour of another, the general intransigence of a third, reflect the interaction of individual personalities with the traditions and the economic and social environment of the organizations which they serve; and the resulting picture is as complex as the character of the men and women who moved across it. These complexities, unknown to the psychology of economic theory, are the familiar stuff of political life in any of its forms. They certainly leave their mark at the conference table where wage agreements are concluded.

The influence of the shape of trade union organization upon wage policy has, moreover, a potential importance in connection with the modern tendency, already mentioned, for more and more non-manual occupations to engage in collective bargaining. Now that collective bargaining has travelled far up the social scale, its influence upon our wage and salary structure has been revolutionized. The professions mentioned upon p. 206 include some that, as we have seen, rank among the most highly paid in the country. In consequence it is no longer true that trade union action or collective bargaining is primarily an instrument for levelling up the incomes of the lower-paid workers. Although his freedom of action may be restricted by sensitivity to public opinion, the trade union or professional representative in wage negotiation at *every* level has a duty to get the best bargain that he can for his members in all the circumstances of the moment (amongst which the prevailing mental climate must be included). And his concern is with his own members and nobody else: that is what he is paid for. Should he permit the interests of some other group to take priority over the claims of those whom he represents, he would, in fact, be open to just criticism for failure to fulfil the terms of his employment. It makes no difference that his own members may already have attained the £1000 or £2000 a year class: his vigour as their champion must not be tempered by any regard for egalitarian policies.

These developments really amount to a revolution within a revolution – both inside the trade union world, specifically so-called, and even more strikingly beyond its limits. At the end of the nineteenth century, the trade union movement consisted on the one hand of organizations catering for skilled craftsmen, and on the other hand of general labour unions. The professions and the blackcoats were hardly in the picture at all. While there were, without doubt, material differences in the rates earned by different groups within this field, all alike could fairly be said, on grounds of both income and social prestige, to fall within the category of the 'working-class'. To take a simple test, fifty years ago it would have been most un-likely that anybody holding the card of a union affiliated to the Trades Union Congress would have been found dining in the house of, say, an architect or other representative of the professional middle class. The Trade Union Congress could therefore fairly claim to speak for a group of which all the members had *something* substantial in common over and above the mere fact of working under a contract of employment. All trade unionists stood to benefit, though, in varying degrees, from egalitarian policies. This simple fact explains, no doubt, much both in the unions' own attitude and in the view of their activities taken by the members of other social classes.

Today, Equity representing the stage, the Medical Practitioners' Union representing doctors (though only a small minority of the whole profession), as well as the Association of Scientific Workers, with a membership drawn from all ranks of scientists, and the Association of Supervisory Staffs Executives and Technicians, representing managerial grades in engineering, are all affiliated to the Trades Union Congress. The Congress now has the benefit of advice from a Non-Manual Workers' Advisory Council (on which the National Federation of Professional Workers is in turn represented); and in 1950 its General Council was instructed to examine the constitution and general effectiveness of this body with a view to giving it 'greater freedom and encouragement to participate more widely in matters of concern to non-manual workers'. In consequence of this resolution the representation of non-manual unions on the advisory council was increased, and the number of delegates who attended its annual meeting was nearly doubled; though the number of resolutions moved at Congress primarily in the interests of the non-manual and higher-paid workers remains only a small proportion of the whole. (The Congress is in fact largely occupied with general topics, such as the development of hydro-electric power, the control of atomic weapons or the method of repayment of income tax credits.) At the 1951 Congress, however, a resolution was carried calling on the Minister of Health 'to take those steps which are urgently required to improve the working conditions of general practitioners'; and at the Margate Congress of 1952 the representatives of British Actors' Equity Association carried a demand for stricter quota legislation to protect British films and for discriminating tax relief in favour of British producers. These are indeed signs of the times.

The essence of the trade union attitude remains today as much as ever respect for the principle of the rate for the job; and the blackleg is still the man who accepts a post below the union rate. The difference between today and yesterday is that these principles are now applied at every level; and at every level the good trade unionist is expected (often to his own manifest disadvantage) to support them. Neither the significance of this revolution, which spells the end of the identification of trade unionism with the interests of the lower-paid manual working class, nor the possible range of its effects, is yet perhaps fully appreciated. Indeed it may not be fanciful to suggest that some link can be traced between these happenings and the somewhat similar changes that are noticeable in political life – particularly in the attitude of the Labour Party, which owes so much both of its income and of its ideology to the trade union world. Certainly the period which has seen the trade union umbrella extended to cover those who represent clerical and professional workers is also the period which has seen the gradual disappearance from Labour Party programmes of frankly egalitarian proposals. But to pursue this aspect of the matter further would not be relevant to the theme of the present study.

The traditional association of the Trades Union Congress with the manual workers (and with Labour politics) no doubt slows down the rate at which organizations of non-manual workers seek actual affiliation with the Congress. No such legacy, however, inhibits these bodies from copying the distinctive trade union practice of collective bargaining at more and more exalted levels. In consequence, this practice has been transformed, in little more than half a century, from a principal weapon of class struggle into a mechanism for the protection of vested interests that extends almost from top to bottom of the employed community.[2]

The machinery for statutory regulation of wages has often been described: only a broad outline need be repeated here. This machinery now (1954) covers agricultural workers, catering workers, and those engaged in over fifty miscellaneous trades covered by the Wages Councils Acts, including, since 1948, transport workers employed on vehicles used in the carriage of goods 'either wholly or partly for reward', who were previously covered by a separate Act. In addition, an Act of 1934 made provision for statutory effect to be given, subject to certain safeguards, to rates of wages agreed by employers' and workers' organizations in the weaving section of the cotton industry; while, in the event of complaint that the existing remuneration in any particular case is 'unfair', a statutory rate can be fixed for such workers engaged in the transport of goods by road as are not covered by the Wages Council Acts. The two last-named provisions are, however, little used to-day (no wage orders are now in force in the cotton industry) and they are neglected in the discussion that follows.

The basic machinery in all other cases follows an identical pattern with only minor variants. In each case a Wages Board or Council is established, appointed by the Minister of Labour (for agricultural workers the Minister of Agriculture) and consisting of equal numbers of representatives of employers and workers in the trade or industry concerned, together with a smaller number of 'impartial' or 'independent' members, one of whom is designated as chairman. All the members of these bodies are directly appointed by the Minister, who is however specifically required under the Wages Councils Acts to consult the appropriate organizations of workers and employers before choosing the representative members of the Councils. In practice this consultation means that the organizations are normally successful in getting their own nominees appointed; and there is in fact a considerable overlap of membership between different councils. The geographical as well as industrial range of these wage-fixing bodies varies considerably. Under the Wages Councils Acts there may be a single Council for the whole of Great Britain or one for England and Wales and another for Scotland; under the Catering Wages Act five separate Boards deal with

2. This statement must not be held necessarily to imply criticism. Vested interests are generally less dangerous when they are acknowledged; and frank discussion of their claims at least opens the door for justice to be done.

distinct sections of the industry. In agriculture, in addition to the Central Wages Boards for England and for Scotland, Committees are also established in every county. Originally, the initiative in fixing rates lay with these committees; but during the war this was transferred to the two Central Boards, though the Committees still have a legal right to make representation about proposed rates.

In all cases except that of agriculture, the rates proposed by wage-fixing bodies must be referred to the Minister before they come into effect. The Minister does not, however, enjoy any powers of amendment: he can only refer back proposals which he does not like, for reconsideration by the Councils concerned; and the Councils can (and do), if they are so minded, decline to modify their original proposals. Provision is also made for the establishment of committees to coordinate any two or more Wages Councils, and to recommend to those Councils how they should exercise their powers. Only one such coordinating committee has in fact been appointed, but the Councils are linked by a common secretariat based on the Ministry of Labour. Under the Catering Wages Act, a permanent Commission is established in addition to the Wages Boards; and this may inquire, with wide terms of reference, into the remuneration and conditions of workers covered by the Act, as well as into the means of meeting the requirements of the public, including visitors from overseas and the tourist traffic generally. This Commission has power to report directly to any Government department and the departments concerned are required to consider what the Commissioners have to say.

All these wage-fixing bodies, which together cover something like three million workers, and were responsible in 1953 for over one third of the total of wage advances granted throughout industry (*Ministry of Labour Gazette*, 1954, p. 3), have a duty to fix minimum rates of wages to which in due course force of law is given; and they mo_tly do fix elaborate scales for different grades of worker, including overtime and other special rates as well as in many cases piecework standards. How then do they set about the job? Parliament, which created them, has certainly given them very little guidance. The statutory formula varies a little from one case to another. Wages Councils under the Act of that name are simply instructed to 'fix' rates: the matter is left at that. The declared purpose of the Catering Wages Act is to make provision for regulating the 'remuneration and conditions of employment of catering and other workers and, in connection therewith, for their health and welfare and the general improvement and development of the industries in which they are employed'. The Wages Boards in this industry presumably, therefore, have a duty, in framing their wage policies, not to neglect the 'improvement and development of the industries' in which the workers concerned are engaged; but, apart from this not very specific instruction, their job, like that of Wage Councils, is simply defined as a matter of 'fixing' rates.

[. . .] Only in the regulation of agricultural wages has an explicit objective been prescribed. The Act of 1924, which first gave the power to fix statutory wages to county wage committees, laid down that each committee should fix such minimum rates in its own area as would 'so far as practicable secure for able-bodied men such wages as in the opinion of the committee are adequate to promote efficiency and to enable a man in an ordinary case to maintain himself and his family in accordance with such standard of comfort as may be reasonable in relation to the nature of his occupation'. This rubric certainly embodies a brave attempt to grapple with a problem which on other occasions has been consistently evaded. But it cannot, I think, have given much concrete help to the committees or to the Central Wages Boards which later took over their functions. At least in the attempt to answer one question it provokes a long string of others. In what circumstances must it be reckoned frankly 'impracticable' to award a wage that is adequate for efficiency? What is an 'ordinary case'? What size of family is supposed to be dependent upon this able-bodied worker in this 'ordinary case'? Six children? Two children? No children? And – most elusive (and question-begging) of all – what is a 'reasonable standard of comfort' and how is this related to the 'nature of a man's occupation'?

These are far from being frivolous questions. The agricultural wages formula puts into words the kind of considerations that must lurk at the back of the mind of everybody who has a hand in statutory wage determination: indeed, one of the many possible sets of practical answers to the questions which it raises is necessarily implied in every rate actually fixed. But the real difficulty lies in the fact that the range of possible answers is so large that the formula does nothing to ease what are in practice the critical problems of choice.

In these conditions some influence may perhaps be ascribed to the circumstances in which statutory wage authorities came into being and the fields in which they have been given power to operate. Parliament may not have disclosed just what these bodies were intended to do, but it must have had its reasons for inventing them, and for establishing them in some industries, and not in others: some guidance can presumably be derived from these. Certainly a broad hint was implied in the Act of 1909, which restricted the establishment of the first Wages Councils (or Trade Boards as they were then called) to industries in which the rate of wages was 'unduly low'. Such a requirement was indeed natural enough in an Act which followed directly upon a great public outcry against 'sweated labour'; and each Board must have felt bound to interpret it as a mandate for fixing statutory rates in the first instance somewhere above the then prevailing level. The Boards were, however, left to fend entirely for themselves in determining both how large an increase would be appropriate in any particular case; and how they ought to shape their policy as the years went by, and (thanks to their efforts) wages in their industries ceased to be 'unduly low'.

Nine years later the scope of statutory wage regulation was extended by a second Act, which, in place of the restriction of Trade Boards to industries having 'unduly low' wages, substituted a new formula, which, with only minor changes, is still in force today. In its modern version, as incorporated in the Wages Councils Act of 1945, this formula allows the Minister to make an order establishing a Wages Council in cases where he is of opinion that 'no adequate machinery exists for the effective regulation of the remuneration of the workers described in the order and that, having regard to the remuneration existing amongst those workers or any of them, it is expedient that such a council should be established'. Applications for a Wages Council can be addressed to the Minister by joint representative bodies in any industry on the ground that the existing machinery for collective bargaining is likely to cease to be adequate or to come to an end altogether. In such cases (as indeed sometimes also on his own initiative) the Minister appoints a Commission of Inquiry to advise him as to whether a Wages Council should be established. This Commission then reviews the bargaining machinery available in the industry concerned, and may make suggestions for improving this. Alternatively, should the Commissioners take a pessimistic view of the present and possible future state of such machinery, and also form the opinion that 'a reasonable standard of remuneration is not being or will not be maintained', they may draft a 'Wages Council recommendation' to which the Minister can, if he thinks fit, give statutory effect.

These provisions may reasonably be read to imply a radical change from the attitudes of 1909. The original purpose of statutory wage regulation was, avowedly, to raise wages where they were lower than (judged by some unspecified standard) they ought to have been. Today the ostensible object is to make good any gaps left in the voluntary arrangements for collective bargaining. Logically, such a transformation of Wages Councils into a kind of statutory substitute for spontaneous collective bargaining would seem to imply that the Councils should behave as nearly as possible as, in similar circumstances, voluntary negotiating bodies would have behaved; that they should envisage their role as that of bargaining instruments, rather than as the means of putting into effect high principles of social policy such as those to which the Agricultural Wages Act gave expression. Certainly the new formula reflects both the increased influence of the trade unions, who naturally have no wish to see their own functions transferred to statutory authorities, and the growing public acceptance of collective bargaining as the *normal* method of wage determination.

Actually, this change in terms of reference probably exaggerates any corresponding change in practical policy. The structure of Wages Councils (and of the earlier Trade Boards), with their representative members recruited from employers and workers in the industry affected by their decisions (in contrast to arbitration tribunals) encourages the view that they are more or less a sub-species of collective bargaining; and some points in their procedure facilitate this interpretation still further – as, for instance, the regulation which allows employers and workers' representatives to vote by sides, and not as individuals, the majority on each side determining the vote of that side as a whole. The role of the independent members can be harmonized with this interpretation if it is conceived as a matter of bridging gaps and effecting compromises between the parties directly concerned, rather than of importing *a priori* principles. Statutory wage-fixing boards all meet in private and are under no obligation to disclose to anybody the lines along which their minds travel: one may, however, conjecture that even the earlier Trade Boards may well have found that the formula 'unduly low' was most easily translated to mean 'lower than would have resulted from voluntary bargaining'. Nevertheless, the concept of inherently 'just' or 'reasonable' rates is not easily banished. Even today a Wages Council cannot be established under existing legislation *merely* because employers and workers have failed to develop the practice of collective bargaining. The law requires that regard should also be paid to the remuneration of the workers in the trades in which such Councils are proposed; and the Minister must ask himself, or the Commission of Inquiry must advise him, whether or not this remuneration is, and is likely to continue to be, 'reasonable'.

Statutory wage regulation operates, therefore, more or less in a vacuum: or perhaps one should say in a haze of vague suggestions, never explicitly formulated or reconciled with one another. The historical background of statutory wage regulation in this country suggests that its primary purpose was to secure 'living' or at least 'subsistence' wages. On the face of it a wage must surely be reckoned unduly low if it is too small to live upon. Any attempt to establish a criterion on these lines must, however, inevitably founder on the difficulties implicit in the agricultural wages formula. Apart from the problem of emptying out the large conventional element that enters into even the most severely scientific calculation of the cost of subsistence at physiologically minimum levels, there remains the insuperable difficulty that what is enough for one person is not enough for six, while bare subsistence for six is more than enough for one. The point is as obvious as it is important. The common way out of the difficulty is, of course, to calculate the subsistence wage in terms of an 'average family'. In an uncharted sea this formula may be as good a sailing direction as any other – so long as we recognize that its avowed destination is in fairyland. At any one moment the average family (usually reckoned at two adults and two or three children) is sure to be the exceptional family. According to the sample census returns of 1951, out of just under fourteen and a half million households in Great Britain, just under two million have two children, while just over a million more have three or four children. More than eight million have no children at all. In these conditions (family allowances at their present level notwithstanding) there can be no meaning in the concept of a 'living wage'. It is, therefore, perhaps not surprising that for more than thirty years the agricultural wages formula has stood alone: no attempt has been made to repeat or to improve upon it.

References

ROSS, A. M. (1948), *Trade Union Wage Policy*, University of California Institute of Industrial Relations.

TURNER, H. A. (1952), 'Trade unions, differentials and the levelling of wages', *The Manchester School of Economic and Social Studies*.

WOOTTON, B. (1946), *Royal Commission on Equal Pay*, Appendices 9 and 10 to *Minutes of Evidence Taken before the Royal Commission on Equal Pay*, H MSO.

14 J. Marquand

Which are the Lower Paid Workers?

J. Marquand, 'Which are the lower paid workers?', *British Journal of Industrial Relations*, vol. 5, 1967, pp. 359–74.

This paper is concerned with the problem of locating the main groups of low paid male workers whose pay may be too low to maintain an adequate standard of living, not because they have large families to support, but simply because their pay is very low indeed. An attempt is made to analyse some of the main economic characteristics of such groups.[1]

That such workers do exist, albeit in fairly small numbers when only men in full-time work are considered, is made apparent by the Ministry of Social Security (1967). This shows (Table II.1) that in the summer of 1966 there were 125,000 families with two or more children with the father in full-time work (more than 30 hours per week), with total resources less than the supplementary benefit level for such families. Of these 125,000 families, 55,000 had only two children (Table II.3). There were 65,000 families with the fathers in full-time work whose resources were less than £12·50p per week. The Report does not consider families with less than two children; hence it does not provide a complete estimate of the number of men in full-time work with incomes at this extremely low level. It does not provide a detailed analysis by industry or occupation of the fathers of families with resources below Supplementary Benefit level, other than to state that 'about 85,000 of the fathers whose families' resources did not meet requirements were manual workers, about 20,000 were employed otherwise than as manual workers and about 20,000 were self-employed' (p. 12, para. 30). They were distributed fairly evenly, in proportion to numbers employed, throughout industry with disproportionately heavy concentrations only in agriculture and among the self-employed (Table IV. 11, p. 39), but no attempt is made to distinguish among the various sections of manufacturing industry, where about 40 per cent both of the whole sample in the survey and of those with resources below requirements were found (p. 12, para. 29). Hence it may be concluded that recent evidence shows that there is a significant number of men in full-time employment, without particularly large families, whose incomes are such that their families' total

---

1. I am grateful to Mr E. Tipper for assistance in preparing the material for the statistical analysis.

resources are below the extremely modest Supplementary Benefit level.[2] When a higher level of income than the Supplementary Benefit level (except for very large families) is considered, it is found that net weekly resources in 8 per cent of families with the fathers in full-time work and where the mothers do not earn are below £14 (Table IV.6, p. 35).

To the extent that the problem of very low earnings relative to needs is a problem of large families, it is clearly inappropriate to attempt to remedy it by raising the earnings of whole groups of workers defined by occupation or by industry. However, the evidence above suggests that there is a problem of low pay, even for some relatively small families where the father is working full-time, and hence that it is worthwhile to try to identify those groups of workers who are particularly low paid.

The problem of women's pay will not be considered in this paper, partly because it is already unequivocally established that most women are low paid relative to most men, but mainly because the statistical information on the distribution of women's earnings in the Ministry of Labour distribution of earnings survey in October 1960 has two major faults: all workers who work for thirty hours a week or more are included, as are all women over the age of eighteen. Hence any groups of workers who are shown to have received particularly low pay may well include women who work less than a standard week, and girls aged eighteen to twenty-one who are paid on less than the adult scale.

Identification of groups of low paid workers

The most important source of information about the distribution of earnings by industry is the Ministry of Labour Distribution of Earnings Survey of 1960. Various objections have been raised to the use of this survey, particularly that it is out of date, that it records weekly earnings rather than hourly earnings, and that its coverage outside manufacturing industry is inadequate.[3] Since it is well established that the inter-industry earnings structure is extremely stable over long periods, the fact that the survey was conducted six years ago is unlikely to cause serious error. That the distribution of hourly earnings as well as weekly earnings is not recorded is unfortunate, and a rough attempt to examine the behaviour of hourly earnings in low paid industries is made later. The main industries omitted from the survey are agriculture, coal-mining, docks, railways, retail distribution and

2. For a family with two adults and two children, and with a rent allowance of approximately £2·50p per week, the net weekly resources associated with the Supplementary Benefit level are in the region of £11·50p to £12·50p per week, depending on the age of the children.

3. For a discussion of the deficiencies of the 1960 Survey, see Robinson (1967, pp. 2–7).

catering; and some attempt to relate such information as is readily available concerning earnings in these industries to the information available for other industries is made on pages 232–5.

The 1960 Distribution of Earnings Survey presents the information collected in two ways. In one set of tables are shown, by Minimum List Headings, the numbers of workers receiving less than £7 per week, £7 and less than £8 per week and so on. In the other set of tables are shown for each industry earnings at the lowest decile of manual workers, at the lower quartile, at the median, at the upper quartile and at the highest decile. For the purposes of inter-industry analysis, especially if picking an arbitrary pay level below which workers are considered to be low paid is to be avoided, the latter set of tables is the more suitable.

The first question which it was necessary to consider was the extent to which it was permissible simply to select those industries in which the workers who were 10 per cent or 25 per cent of the way up the earnings distribution were lowest paid relative to workers in the same position in other industries, and regard these industries as the industries with low paid workers. If the shape of the lower end of the earnings distribution were to differ significantly from industry to industry, no such simple selection of industries with low paid workers would be possible. By comparing the ranking of the 128 industries in the survey by the level of earnings at the lowest decile with the corresponding ranking at the lower quartile, a test of the similarity of shape of the earnings distribution was made. If the ranking were very similar, then the shapes of the earnings distributions could be considered to be similar, and conclusions could be based on the rankings of earnings at the lower quartile too and by extrapolation to points in between. It was found that all industries in the lowest quartile of industries when earnings at the lowest decile were ranked were also in the lowest quartile when earnings at the lower quartile were ranked, with the one exception of Marine Engineering (at the quartile boundary when earnings at the lowest decile were ranked, and in the second quartile when earnings at the lower quartile were ranked). Moreover, the only industry in the lowest quartile of industries which changed its ranking by as much as thirteen (one decile) between the ranking of earnings at the lowest decile and the ranking of earnings at the lower quartile was Woollens, etc. (ranking fourteenth from the bottom in the ranking of earnings at the lowest decile, and twenty-eighth from the bottom in the ranking of earnings at the lowest quartile). Hence it can be concluded confidently that those industries which have the lowest earnings at the lowest decile are indeed those industries where the lower end of the earnings distribution lies lowest.

In Table 1 are shown those industries which comprise the lowest quartile of industries, when industries are ranked according to the level of earnings

Table 1 Industries with lower paid workers

Minimum list heading	Weekly earnings, Oct. 1960 1/10 of adult male manual workers were earning not more than		Average hours worked, all male manual workers Oct. 1960	Estimated hourly earnings at lowest decile Oct. 1960	Employment (all male workers, manual and non-manual) June 1965	Wages Councils *
	s.	d.		s.	000s.	
422 Made-up textiles	164	1	46·3	3·54	9·4	*
445 Dresses, etc.	168	8	44·4	3·79	14·2	*
901 National government	168	11	45·0	3·75	366·5	
449 Other dress industries	171	8	45·4	3·78	8·6	*
415 Jute	172	6	47·8	3·60	8·9	*
444 Overalls, etc.	174	0	46·0	3·78	6·2	*
413 Cotton weaving, etc.	174	5	45·7	3·81	41·2	
412 Cotton spinning, etc.	175	2	47·3	3·70	40·1	
432 Leather goods	175	3	45·9	3·81	9·0	
446 Hats, etc.	176	8	43·5	4·06	4·0	*
421 Narrow fabrics	178	0	47·9	3·71	8·0	*
441 Weatherproof	178	6	46·6	3·83	7·0	*
885 Laundries	179	9	48·8	3·68	30·9	*
414 Woollens, etc.	179	11	50·1	3·59	84·2	
906 Local government	180	1	45·8	3·93	571·8	
888 Repair of footwear	180	3	45·6	3·95	10·5	*
239 Other drink industries	181	4	48·6	3·73	40·6	*
416 Rope, etc.	181	6	51·0	3·55	4·6	*
886 Dry cleaning, etc.	181	10	48·5	3·75	12·5	*
418 Lace	182	10	46·1	3·96	3·7	*
274 Paint, etc.	182	10	46·4	3·94	33·8	
493 Brushes, etc.	183	0	45·5	4·03	7·2	
887 Motor repairers, garages, etc.	183	1	46·1	3·97	349·5	
442 Men's, etc., outwear	183	11	44·0	4·18	31·0	*
342 Ordnance, etc.	184	6	45·0	4·10	20·0	
214 Bacon curing, etc.	184	7	48·5	3·80	42·0	
471 Timber	185	8	47·9	3·87	85·8	
102 Stone, etc., mining	186	1	52·5	3·85	26·7	
231 Brewing, etc.	187	4	48·0	3·90	78·0	
331 Agricultural machinery	188	0	45·5	4·13	38·5	
215 Milk products	188	11	50·4	3·74	23·9	
370·2 Marine engineering	189	2	47·1	4·01	48·8	
All manufacturing industries	208	0	47·4	4·39		
All industries covered	200	0	48·0	4·02		

	Median weekly earnings	
All manufacturing industries	297	2
All industries covered	283	4

Sources: *Ministry of Labour Gazette*, April 1961, March 1966

received by the worker at the lowest decile. For convenience, these industries will be referred to as low paid industries. The level of average hourly earnings at the lowest decile in each industry in October 1960 is also shown, and the average number of hours worked by *all* male workers covered by the Ministry of Labour hours inquiry in each industry in that month. On the heroic assumption that the number of hours worked by workers in the lowest earnings decile is the same as the average in each industry, it is possible to derive the average hourly earnings of workers at the lowest decile in each industry, and this series is shown. The number of males employed in each of these industries in June 1965 is also shown.

It may be noted that average weekly earnings of all men covered by the Ministry of Labour enquiries rose from 290s. 8d. in October 1960 to 406s. in October 1966, so that 160s. in October 1960 is very approximately equivalent to 223s. in October 1966, 180s. to 251s. and 200s. to 279s. The level of earnings in October 1960 approximately equivalent to £12 in October 1966 is 172s.

Workers with low hourly earnings

It has sometimes been argued that the information obtained from the 1960 Distribution of Earnings Survey is misleading because only weekly earnings are shown, whilst workers on low rates of pay often work extremely long hours in order to bring the level of their weekly earnings up to a tolerable minimum. There is also the possibility that workers with very low earnings work less than the average weekly hours worked in the industry. Hence we would not expect to find any very close association between average hourly earnings and average weekly earnings at the bottom of the earnings range, since those with very low weekly earnings would comprise three groups: those with very low hourly earnings who worked especially long hours, those with slightly higher hourly earnings who worked average hours, and those with low or average hourly earnings who worked less than average hours.

It may be misleading to assume that low paid workers in a given industry work the same hours as the average in the industry, precisely because it is within an industry at least as much as between industries that we might expect to find workers on low hourly rates of pay attempting to work long hours. However, for the purpose of comparing hours worked by low paid workers across industries, it is not necessary to assume that these workers work the average hours of all adult male manual workers in their industry, but only to make the slightly weaker assumption that the hours worked by low paid workers vary between industries in the same proportion as the hours worked by all adult male manual workers. When this assumption is made, an estimate of average hourly earnings by industry can be made, and the ranking of industries by average weekly earnings at the lowest decile compared with the ranking of industries by estimated average hourly earnings at the lowest decile.

It is found that all but seven of the thirty-two industries which are in the lowest quartile when industries are ranked by the level of average weekly earnings at the lowest decile are also in the lowest quartile when the industries are ranked by estimated average hourly earnings at the lowest decile. The seven industries with low weekly earnings, but not low hourly earnings, are Hats (average hours worked: 43·5); Brushes (45·5); Motor repairs and garages, etc. (46·1); Men's outerwear (44·0); Ordnance (45·0); Agricultural machinery (45·5); and Marine engineering (47·1). Conversely, the seven industries with low hourly earnings but not low weekly earnings were Grain milling (50·3); Biscuits (52·8); Lino, etc. (50·2); Polishes, etc. (51·5); Textile finishing (50·5) and Road haulage except BRS (56·1 and the lowest hourly earnings of all). Average hours worked in manufacturing industry in October 1960 were 47·4 and in all industries 48·0.

It would seem that there is a tendency for low hourly earnings and low weekly earnings to be found together. In general, workers with very low hourly rates of pay cannot be shown, by the rather inadequate statistics available, to be working particularly long hours. Only in the seven industries listed at the end of paragraph 12, and in the Rope industry, Woollens and Worsteds, and perhaps Jute, does very low hourly pay appear to be associated with long hours; in most manufacturing industries shown in Table 1, low hourly pay and short hours combine to yield low weekly earnings.

A related question on which the Ministry of Labour Survey can offer no illumination is that of how far the individuals receiving very low weekly earnings are working short hours because of ill health. The Ministry of Social Security (1967) found that 'the sample suggested that the earning powers of the fathers of 20,000 families out of the 125,000 families whose resources did not meet their requirement on the SB standard were limited by ill-health' (p. 12, para. 29). Since there is no reason to expect that fathers of families are not a representative sample of adult male workers where health is concerned, it would seem that ill health may be a main factor in low earnings for about one sixth of the workers involved, and there would appear to be no particular reason why these workers should not be distributed evenly by industry.

Characteristics of industries with low paid workers

Various characteristics are often ascribed to industries which are thought to be likely to have low pay. Basically, what is argued is that certain characteristics of an industry are likely to lead to low bargaining strength of the workers employed, and hence to low earnings. It is not easy to distinguish between characteristics which might be associated with low earnings for the industry as a whole, and characteristics which might be associated with low earnings for the lower paid workers in the industry but to the extent to which the lowest paid workers are found in the lowest paid industries it is unnecessary to draw this distinction.

Characteristics thought to be associated with low bargaining strength include:

1. A high proportion of women workers in the industry, since women are less readily unionized than men.

2. A high proportion of unskilled workers in an industry, since unskilled workers are in a more exposed position in the labour market than skilled workers, and are also, at least historically, less readily unionized.

3. Many small firms in the industry, rather than a few large ones, making a strong union more difficult to maintain.

4. A contracting industry, or at least one which is not expanding rapidly, since the demand for labour of all sorts is weaker than in an industry which is growing rapidly.

5. Particular institutional factors, especially:
a. Wages Councils, since these were set up where the bargaining position of the workers was weak. It is possible that Wages Councils, while perhaps ensuring that earnings in their industries are higher than they would otherwise have been, still make awards which lead to relatively low earnings in their industries.
b. Industries where the payments structure is such that workers are tied relatively closely to fixed scales, which are often fixed with regard to *wage rate* levels in competing industries which are tied much more loosely to earnings in those industries, rather than with regard to the *earnings* levels in those industries. Much of the public sector is in this position.

Tests of the relevance of each of these characteristics were carried out.

The proportion of women workers in industries with low paid (male) workers

The 128 industries in the Ministry of Labour Distribution of Earnings Survey were ranked according to the proportion of women employed and the ranking compared with that of earnings at the lowest decile. Out of the thirty-two industries in the lowest quartile of the earnings distribution, sixteen were in the highest quartile of the distribution by the proportion of women employed. If the relationship of the two distributions were random, we would expect to find eight industries in the lowest quartile of the earnings distribution and the highest quartile of the distribution by the proportion of women employed. In fact, there are sixteen. This suggests a strong tendency for industries employing many women to have particularly low rates of pay for the lower paid men employed in the industry. (There is also support for the converse proposition, that industries where the lower paid men are relatively high paid are not industries which employ many women.)

The proposition which is sometimes put forward, that industries with many women workers tend to be industries with low pay for male workers, is often supplemented with an example, 'like the textile and clothing industries'. Examination of all the industries with many women and with low paid men shows that only the example is valid; the situation is simply that all the industries with many women and with low paid men are textile and clothing industries, with the addition only of dry cleaning and laundering. In order of the proportion of women employed in the industry (highest proportion ranks 1), the industries with many women and with low paid male workers are:

Table 2 **Industries with many women workers and with low paid male workers**

	Ranking by proportion of women employed	Proportion of women
		%
445 Dresses, lingerie, infants' wear, etc.	1	88·5
444 Overalls, men's shirts, underwear, etc.	2	85·1
449 Dress industries n.e.s.	3	78·9
886 Dry cleaning	4	74·3
442 Men's and boys' tailored outerwear	5	73·9
441 Weatherproof outerwear	6	73·7
446 Hats, caps, millinery	9	66·6
885 Laundering	11	65·9
421 Narrow fabrics	12	65·5
412 Cotton spinning	13	65·1
432 Leather goods	14	64·3
413 Cotton weaving	17	61·0
416 Rope, twine, net	19	59·9
422 Made-up textiles	22	58·3
418 Lace	27	54·8
414 Woollens	29	54·2

The proportion of unskilled workers in industries with low paid workers

The 110 manufacturing industries in the Ministry of Labour Distribution of Earnings Survey were ranked according to the proportion of unskilled workers employed and the ranking compared with that of earnings at the lowest decile. Two effects might be expected to show up together when this comparison is made. Firstly, in industries where there is a high proportion of unskilled workers, earnings of the lowest decile of the distribution of earnings of *all* male manual workers will be a lower proportion of the distribution of the earnings of *unskilled* male manual workers than in industries where there are relatively few unskilled workers. Hence, if the shapes of the distributions are similar, the level of earnings at the top of the lowest decile should be lower in industries with many unskilled workers than in industries with few unskilled workers. Secondly, there may also be the effect that the presence of a high proportion of unskilled workers has an adverse effect upon the bargaining power of all workers in the industry.

When the rankings of earnings at the lowest decile boundary and the proportion of unskilled workers were compared, ten industries in the lowest quartile of the earnings distribution were in the quartile with the highest proportion of unskilled workers, and eight industries in the lowest quartile of the earnings distribution were in the quartile with the second highest proportion of unskilled workers. From the operation of the first mathematical effect alone it would be expected, subject to some random error, that all twenty-eight industries in the lowest quartile of the earnings distribution should be in the quartile of industries with most unskilled workers. If the second effect, that a high proportion of unskilled workers depresses the bargaining strength of workers in an industry, also operates, then it should reinforce the first effect. The observed relationship differs significantly from what the consideration of the two effects would lead us to expect.

Since the first of the effects leading us to expect a very close connection between low earnings and a high proportion of unskilled workers is an *a priori* consequence of the nature of the distributions being compared, and since this effect was not found to operate as strongly as expected, the simplest explanation of the results is that the second effect, the bargaining effect, operates to some extent in a reverse direction to that postulated above. Thus it would seem that unskilled workers are if anything organized more strongly than skilled workers. The usual explanation of this phenomenon is that where unskilled workers and skilled workers bargain together, unskilled workers are usually in the majority and have the dominant influence on union negotiating strategy.

Size of firm and level of pay

A rough test as to whether industries where smaller firms predominate have lower paid workers than other industries can be made using the Ministry of Labour statistics of employment by size of establishment by SIC Order for manufacturing industries for May 1964. Only firms with more than ten employees are included, so that there is no information from this source concerning the extent of employment in very small firms. However, it is possible to estimate for each SIC Order the proportion of employees in firms of more than ten employees who work in firms of 11–249 employees inclusive. When this is done, the orders with the highest proportions of employees in relatively small firms are found to be Leather (83·5 per cent of employees in relatively small firms); Timber (74·9 per cent); Clothing (68·5 per cent); Printing (53·6 per cent). Textiles ranks seven out of eighteen with 44·4 per cent of employees in relatively small firms. The manufacturing orders where low paid workers are concentrated are Clothing, Leather and Textiles. Thus there is some tendency for industries with low paid workers to be industries with relatively few large firms, but the test made was much too rough to allow any more specific conclusion to be drawn.

Rate of growth and level of pay

For all the 128 industries it was possible to calculate the percentage change in employment between June 1960 and June 1965. Of the 128 industries, sixty-eight expanded their employment during this period and fifty-nine contracted. Of the thirty-two low pay industries, thirteen expanded and nineteen contracted, but of the twenty-six low pay manufacturing industries included in these thirty-two industries, eight expanded and eighteen contracted. Of the six non-manufacturing industries, five expanded. Of the eight manufacturing industries and five non-manufacturing industries which expanded employment, only Bacon curing, Agricultural machinery, Timber, Dry cleaning and Motor repairing (none of them nearer than nineteenth to the bottom of the pay ranking) expanded by more than 3·5 per cent during the five year period, whilst employment in the 128 industries as a whole rose by more than 4 per cent. Hence it can be concluded with confidence that industries where the lower paid workers are relatively low paid are mostly industries where employment is contracting. Non-manufacturing industries may have low paid workers even if they are expanding. None of the eighteen industries with the lowest paid workers of all is expanding employment by as much as the average rate of expansion for all industries covered.

Whether the association between low pay and contraction of the industry can be ascribed to low bargaining strength on the part of the workers, or lack of demand for labour on the part of the employers, is purely a question of terminology. It is, however, relevant to mention one consequence of a labour market which functions in this way at its lower paid end. Where an industry is contracting, if this is associated with particularly low levels of pay, the contraction tends to take place through a falling off of recruitment and a failure to replace those who retire or leave through normal wastage. In the short run, this is satisfactory, but in the slightly longer run it leads to an ageing labour force in the industry, a need for recruitment of younger workers as the total labour force begins to decline more rapidly than is desired, and serious difficulty in recruiting these younger workers (e.g. in Coalmining). Even in a contracting industry it is desirable to maintain a balanced age structure in the labour force, so that quite apart from any considerations of social justice, the close association of low pay with contracting employment should not be viewed with equanimity.

Types of bargaining institutions and levels of pay

In Table 1, those industries where the lowest paid workers are relatively low paid which are covered wholly or partially by Wages Councils for bargaining purposes are indicated. In addition to these industries, National Government and Local Government manual workers fall into the category outlined on page 365, namely industries where the payments structure is such that workers are tied relatively closely to fixed scales.

The only industries in the twenty industries where the lowest decile of workers are lowest paid which do not fall under one of these two categories are Cotton weaving, Cotton spinning, Leather goods and Woollens, etc. For industries ranking more than twenty from the bottom of the earnings distribution, there are no special characteristics of the bargaining institutions which are particularly obvious.

Industries with large numbers of lower paid workers

So far, this article has been concerned only with those industries where the lower end of the earnings distribution lies relatively low. There may also be industries where average earnings are not especially low, and where earnings at the lowest decile are not especially low, but where large numbers of workers are employed, and hence relatively large numbers of workers may be found with pay so low as to be comparable with that of workers already considered.

In Table 3 are shown those industries in the Ministry of Labour Distribution of Earnings Survey with more than 2000 men earning less than £9 per week or with more than 5000 men earning less than £10 per week in October 1960. These earnings levels are roughly equivalent to £12 10s. and to £14 per week respectively in October 1966.

It would seem that the only industries included in the Ministry of Labour Survey with more than 5000 men earning less than £9 per week in October 1960 which are not included in the list of industries with very low pay at the lowest decile of the earnings distribution, shown in Table 1, are Construction and Shipbuilding, followed by Other machinery, Other metal

Table 3

Minimum list heading		No. of full-time men in October, 1960 earning:	
		Less than £9 per week	Less than £10 per week
906	Local government *	22,231	94,763
500	Construction	14,683	34,326
901	National government * –	11,081	23,127
370.1	Shipbuilding	5604	13,202
414	Woollens, etc. *	5577	10,428
413	Cotton weaving, etc. *	4715	6613
887	Motor repairs, etc. *	4602	10,733
339	Other machinery	3499	7635
412	Cotton spinning, etc. *	3432	6473
370.2	Marine engineering *	3353	7224
399	Other metal industries	2798	7805
703	Road haulage	2639	5858
702	Road passenger transport	2636	10,690
471	Timber *	2556	6129
423	Textile finishing	2273	5020
231	Brewing, etc.	2099	7770
383	Aircraft	2068	4826
101	Coalmining (day wage men)[1]	—	21,716
602	Electricity	465	7938
601	Gas	545	6609
311	Iron and steel	1899	5080

* indicates that the industry is listed as low paid in Table 1.

[1] From the *Ministry of Labour Gazette*, June 1961.

industries, Road haulage and Road passenger transport, with more than 2500 men in this category. Coalmining, with more than 20,000 men earning less than £10 per week in 1960, may also be added to the list of industries with low pay. Of these industries with large numbers of low paid workers, it may be noted that Shipbuilding and Coalmining are industries where employment is contracting and Road haulage contracting with very low average hourly earnings is covered by a Wages Council.

Industries not covered by the 1960 distribution of earnings survey

For *Coalmining*, there is a Ministry of Labour Survey of the Distribution of Earnings in October 1960 which is closely comparable with the information available for other industries. It shows that in October 1960, although no underground workers received less than £10 per week, 21,716 surface workers (25·30 per cent) received more than £9 but less than £10. These 25·30 per cent of surface workers comprise 5·56 per cent of all workers in the industry. Since the criterion for inclusion in the list in Table 1 is 10 per cent of workers receiving less than approximately £9 10s. 0d., it would seem that surface workers in coalmining, if they are considered separately from underground workers, probably rank somewhere at the upper end of the quartile of industries with lowest earnings for their lowest paid 10 per cent of workers.

For *Dock Workers*, there is a Ministry of Labour Survey of the distribution of earnings in November 1960, which shows that 2·30 per cent of dock workers had incomes of less than £10, and of these 1·35 per cent had incomes of less than £9. The level of earnings at the top of the lowest decile was somewhere between £11 and £12. Thus dock workers are not particularly low paid.

For *Agriculture*, until the Report of the National Board for Prices and Incomes (1967), only average earnings statistics were available. Before these could be evaluated, it was necessary to examine how far rankings of average earnings by industry correspond to rankings of earnings at the lowest decile. The 1960 Distribution of Earnings Survey gives median earnings, not average earnings, for the industries which it covers. It was found that of the thirty-two industries in the lowest quartile at the median earnings level, all but three were in the lowest quartile at the lowest decile earnings level. Hence rankings at the median can be taken as a good indicator of approximate rankings at the top of the lowest decile. Earnings distributions tend to be shaped so that average earnings are higher than median earnings. Hence if average earnings in Agriculture are compared with median earnings in other industries, it is probable that median earnings in Agriculture would rank lower than average earnings are found to do. From this it can be inferred that the lower end of the distribution of agricultural earnings lies lower than the position of average earnings in agriculture compared directly with median earnings in other industries would appear to suggest.

Average weekly earnings in Agriculture for the six months beginning October 1960 were 206s. 11d. At the top of the lowest quartile of industries, the median worker earned 257s. in October 1960, and the *lowest* earnings for the median worker were 207s. 7d. in National Government. Hence average earnings in agriculture were lower than the *lowest* median earnings in any industry covered by the Distribution of Earnings Survey, and it is legitimate to infer from this that lower paid workers in Agriculture in 1960 were almost certainly one of the lowest paid groups of workers of all.

The report of the National Board for Prices and Incomes (NBPI) on Agricultural pay considered the first nine months of 1966 and conducted an earnings enquiry. It was found that 'average weekly earnings in agriculture are below weekly earnings in any other industry for which figures are available, and average hourly earnings are well below those of any other industry. This suggests that there is a higher concentration of low paid workers in agriculture than elsewhere. Other figures support this conclusion About one third of male general farm workers earn less than £12 a week including overtime; and more than one third of adult male agricultural workers of all categories earn less than £13 a week. We have no up-to-date figures for other industries but if we assume that weekly earnings are distributed about the average in the same way as they were in 1960 . . . then no other industry has a similar proportion of low paid workers. The special position of agriculture is accentuated by the long hours worked' (National Board for Prices and Incomes, 1967a, para. 35).

For *Railways*, the relationship of average pay in October 1960 to median pay in other industries is again the most suitable source of information. In October 1960, average weekly earnings of non-workshop workers was 274s. and of workshop wages staff, 294s. This puts railway workers well above the quartile boundary. Median earnings in the lowest paid 25 per cent of industries were no higher than 257s.

For *Retail Distribution*, the sources of information are the Ministry of Labour pilot occupational earnings survey for May 1965, and the NBPI (1967b) Report. The former source shows that average weekly earnings for full-time men ranged from 299s. 2d. for workers employed in grocery, provision and other food shops with eleven to twenty-four employees, to 371s. 11d. for workers in multiples with more than 100 employees.

Applying an approximate correction to allow for the change in the general level of earnings between October 1960 and May 1966, the October 1960 equivalent of this range is from 215s. to 267s. Since the boundary of the lowest quartile in the distribution of median earnings by industry in October 1960 is at 257s., it appears rather probable that retail distribution is an industry in which the lower paid workers are low paid enough to fall within the lowest paid quartile of industries. This is supported by the findings of the NBPI (1967b, Table 14A). In October 1966 it was found that 7·6 per cent of adult male full-time workers in Retail Drapery had average weekly earnings of less than £12; 14·4 per cent had less than £13, and 29·5 per cent had less than £15. The 1966 equivalent of 190s. which is the quartile boundary by industry in Table 1 for the lowest paid decile of workers in each industry, is approximately 265s. per week. Hence pay in Retail Drapery would certainly appear to be so low that it should rank amongst the other industries listed in Table 1. It may also be noted that average hours worked in Retail Distribution are very short. For no category of male workers were average weekly hours worked in May 1966 more than 43·3. This implies that average hourly earnings for workers in retail distribution will lie considerably higher in the distribution of average hourly earnings by industry than do average weekly earnings in the weekly earnings distribution.

There appears to be no published information concerning earnings in *Catering*.

Conclusions

1. The problem of workers with resources insufficient for their needs (defined as Supplementary Benefit rates) is not simply a problem of large families, of fatherless families, or of ill health. There are some male workers in full-time employment in good health and with relatively small families whose earnings fall below this minimal level. Women workers have not been considered in this paper.

2. Those industries where the lowest paid tenth of workers have the lowest weekly earnings by comparison with other industries are shown in Table 1. There is no simple relationship, direct or inverse, between low weekly earnings and low hourly earnings. In ten industries, of which only Rope, Woollens and Worsteds, and Jute had low weekly earnings, very low hourly pay appeared to be associated with long hours; in most industries with low weekly earnings, it seemed that low hourly pay and short hours combined to yield low weekly earnings.

3. There was some tendency for industries with low weekly earnings for lower paid men to be industries with a high proportion of women employed. In particular, several textile and clothing industries, and Laundering and Dry-cleaning, have low earnings for low paid men and a large number of women employees.

4. There was no tendency for industries with low weekly earnings for lower paid men to be industries which employed a high proportion of unskilled men. Indeed, there was a slight tendency for industries with a high proportion of unskilled men to have slightly higher earnings relative to other industries than might have been expected.

5. There is a slight tendency for industries with low paid workers to be industries with relatively few large firms, but it was not possible to make any very precise test of this.

6. There is a very strong tendency for manufacturing industries whose lower paid workers are relatively low paid to be industries which are contracting, or at the most, expanding more slowly than the average. None of the eighteen industries with the lowest paid workers is expanding as fast as the average of all the industries in the survey. This is a relationship which may have serious consequences in the longer run.

7. Of the twenty industries with the lowest paid workers, fourteen are Wages Council industries, two are National Government and Local

Government, where workers are tied closely to fixed scales, and the others are Cotton weaving, Cotton spinning, Leather goods, and Woollens, etc.

8. Of major industries not covered by the 1960 Distribution of Earnings Survey, it is certain that lower paid workers in Agriculture are among the lowest paid, if not the lowest paid, of workers in any industry. Surface workers in coalmining (also closely tied to fixed scales) and workers in retail distribution are other groups of workers where substantial numbers of very low paid workers are found. No information was available for Catering although this is probably one of the lower paid industries.

9. There are several industries which do not rank as low paid when the distribution of earnings is examined, but which none the less have large numbers of low paid workers. Construction and Shipbuilding had more than 5000 men earning less than £9 per week in October 1960; Other machinery, Other metal industries, Road haulage and Road passenger transport had more than 2500 men in this category.

10. If the relative pay position of low paid workers is to be improved, a serious practical problem is the absence of detailed up-to-date information concerning the structure of pay in industries with very low paid workers. Whilst the information available may be adequate for the inter-industry comparisons made in this paper, much more detailed information, such as that collected specially by the NBPI (1967a and b) is needed if claims are to be considered in relation to the inter-industry and the intra-industry wage structure. However, the similarity of inter-industry earnings rankings at the median and at the lowest decile indicates that most industries with very low pay for their lowest paid workers have low pay for all their workers. Thus a settlement for all workers in the industry, leaving intra-industry differentials relatively undisturbed, would not make the better paid workers in the industry well paid by comparison with other industries. To the considerable extent that the industries listed in Table 1 are small industries, it is possible that generous settlements could be prevented from having serious repercussions on other industries, especially if attention is drawn to the *level* of earnings, rather than to the size of the increase.

11. A few of the industries listed in Table 1 – National Government, Woollens and Worsteds, Local Government, Motor repairers and garages, Timber and Brewing – employ as many as 50,000 workers. For these, as well as for the industries discussed on pages 232–5, it would be extremely unrealistic to expect that the relative position of low paid workers could be improved without very careful attention being paid to the intra-industry wage structure in order to minimize repercussions both within the industry, and between industries.

12. For the adequate formulation of such policies, fuller information is essential. But even the limited information available at present would seem to be sufficient to enable the spurious claim on behalf of low paid workers to be distinguished in most cases from the genuine one, and to provide a number of pointers to the places where the relative position of the lowest paid workers most needs to be improved.

References

MINISTRY OF SOCIAL SECURITY (1967), *Report on the Circumstances of Families*, July, HMSO.

NATIONAL BOARD FOR PRICES AND INCOMES (1967a), *Pay for Workers in Agriculture in England and Wales*, Report no. 25, January, cmnd 3199, HMSO.

NATIONAL BOARD FOR PRICES AND INCOMES (1967b), *Pay of Workers in the Retail Drapery, Outfitting and Footwear Trades*, Report no. 27, April, cmnd 3224, HMSO.

ROBINSON, D. (1967), 'Low paid workers and incomes policy', *Bull. Oxford Univ. Inst. Stats.*, February, pp. 1–29.

Part Four
The Distribution of Wealth

The readings to this point have been primarily concerned with the distribution of income, or the flow of resources received by a household over a certain period. This section focuses on the role of wealth, or the *stock* of assets which a household possesses: real assets such as consumer durables or houses and financial assets such as money in the bank, building society deposits or company shares. Wealth is important because it provides not only income (interest, dividends and rent) but also security, freedom of manoeuvre, and economic and political power. Moreover, wealth is very much more concentrated than income and has a major influence on the overall degree of inequality.

The first two articles in this section describe the evidence about wealth-holding in Britain (Reading 15) and the United States (Reading 16). This evidence is at best fragmentary, and Lydall and Tipping comment that 'the most striking aspect of this subject is the statistical darkness which surrounds it'. Both studies rely heavily on data from estate duty returns and these suffer from a number of serious shortcomings (in particular they omit a number of types of wealth and cover only part of the population). In view of this, extensive adjustment is required before the estate duty statistics can be used to throw light on the degree of inequality, and the information given by Lydall and Tipping for 1954 is the most recent at present available in Britain.[1] Their study shows quite clearly the high degree of concentration: the top 1 per cent owned 43 per cent of total personal wealth and top 10 per cent owned 79 per cent. These figures may be compared with shares of after tax *income* of $5\frac{1}{2}$ per cent and 25 per cent respectively. Lydall and Tipping also examine the trend in the concentration of capital over the course of the first half of this century, and note that there has been some reduction in inequality. At the same time, they point to an increasing tendency for the wealthy to distribute their property among their children well in advance of death (to avoid estate duty). This reduces the share of the top 1 per cent, but is likely to increase

1. The Inland Revenue publish statistics based on the estate duty returns, but these are not adjusted for missing wealth or for the population not covered by the returns.

the wealth of those just below them and indeed it can be seen from their Table VI (page 253) that the share of the next 9 per cent *increased* between 1911–13 and 1951–6.[2] The article by Lampman (Reading 16) reports a similar investigation for the United States. Like Lydall and Tipping, he finds a substantial degree of concentration, but it appears to be less marked than in Britain: in 1954 the top 1 per cent of American wealth-holders owned 24 per cent of total personal wealth (compared with 43 per cent in Britain). Contrary to popular belief, wealth is more unequally shared in Britain than in the United States. The same conclusion was reached by Lydall and Lansing (Reading 8).

The next two readings in this section examine the forces influencing the distribution of wealth in a capitalist society. In Reading 17, Meade describes how economic and demographic factors influence the accumulation of property, and this approach is further developed in the more mathematical analysis by Stiglitz (Reading 18). The readings indicate some of the equalizing and disequalizing tendencies that are likely to be at work. Meade, for example, argues that accumulation out of earned-income is likely to be an equalizing factor, but that the higher rate of profit on large wealth-holdings has the reverse effect. If a millionaire can earn 15 per cent (allowing for capital gains) on his capital, it is hard for the small saver with his money in the savings bank to stand any chance of catching him up. Accumulation is not, however, the only factor at work and we have to consider the transfer of wealth between generations. Even millionaires die, and the way in which their millions are passed on is of great significance. Meade gives particular attention to the way in which fortunes are consolidated through marriage, and the role of differences in fertility. Stiglitz introduces a further factor of great importance – customs about inheritance – and in section 8 of his paper demonstrates that primogeniture may preserve a substantial degree of inequality. If property is shared equally among children, then what Meade calls 'the general reshuffle generation by generation' tends to equalize inherited fortunes; if, however, all wealth is left to the eldest son, the inequality of wealth is perpetuated.

When we turn to the empirical evidence about the relative importance of different equalizing and disequalizing factors, it appears that very little is known about how wealth is in reality accumulated and about the pattern of transmission of wealth between generations. In Reading 19, Harbury provides one of the few sources on which we can draw in assessing the role of inheritance in the building up of large fortunes. His article, following an earlier work by Wedgwood (1929), is based on an investigation of the

2. In 1911–13, the share of those in the top 10 per cent but not in the top 1 per cent was 24·5 per cent; in 1951–6, it was 37·0 per cent.

wealth of the predecessors of more than 600 male wealth-holders dying in the second half of the 1950s. From his evidence, it is clear that inheritance is of major importance. Of those leaving more than £200,000 in 1956–7, two thirds had fathers who had left over £25,000 and the proportion of 'self-made men' (those whose fathers left less than £1000) was less than 20 per cent. Moreover, from a comparison of his results with those of Wedgwood for 1924–6, Harbury concludes that 'there was no very marked change in the relative importance of inheritance in the creation of the personal fortunes of the top wealth-leavers'.

Reference

WEDGWOOD, J. (1929), *The Economics of Inheritance*, Routledge & Kegan Paul.

15 H. F. Lydall and D. G. Tipping

The Distribution of Personal Wealth in Britain

H. F. Lydall and D. G. Tipping, 'The distribution of personal wealth in Britain',
Bulletin of the Oxford Institute of Economics and Statistics, vol. 23, 1961, pp. 83–104.

In the past twenty years the distribution of personal income in Britain has become significantly less unequal. According to estimates made by one of the present authors the proportion of real disposable income received by the top one per cent of the population fell from about $12\frac{1}{2}$ per cent in 1938 to about $6\frac{1}{2}$ per cent in 1957 (Lydall, 1959, p. 31). But the resources available to an individual depend not only on his income but also on his capital (including his ability to borrow). Accumulated wealth can be used – to a greater or less degree – in the same way as income to give command over current goods and services. At the present time the stock of personally owned capital (including debts owed to persons by the government and others) is equivalent to about four years' disposable income; and for those in the income class £2000 and over it is, on the average, probably as much as ten years' income. It is obvious, therefore, that people with appreciable amounts of capital (who are mostly but not exclusively in the upper income classes) are in a position to arrange their current expenditures without strict regard to their incomes. This freedom of manoeuvre is important not only to those who persistently overspend their incomes but also to that much larger class of persons who are able to use their capital to finance heavy temporary expenditures – such as on the education of their children – which may be of great long-term importance in maintaining their (or their children's) standard of living and status in society. Wealth gives power; indeed, it gives more power than income, because it is largely free of current commitment (and of current taxation).

For these reasons alone there is a case for paying some attention to the distribution of wealth. But there are two further reasons for an inquiry into this subject. The first is that, since 'capital' is the second of the great factors of production, the conditions governing its supply – one of which is the distribution of its ownership – are of fundamental importance.

The second additional reason for studying the distribution of capital is one that is peculiar to this country. All previous studies have shown that the distribution of personal wealth in Britain is extremely unequal (Daniels and Campion, 1936; Campion, 1939; Langley, 1950–51; Langley, 1954); and in a recent comparison (Lydall and Lansing, 1959, pp. 43–67) – based on survey data – it was found that the distribution of wealth was substantially more unequal in Britain than in the United States (and this despite the fact that the distribution of *income* in the two countries was rather similar, and if anything more unequal in the United States).

Despite the various attempts that have been made to discover the facts about the distribution of capital in Britain, the most striking aspect of this subject is the statistical darkness which surrounds it. In this respect Britain is no worse than most other countries (the main exceptions are the Scandinavian countries), but it is nevertheless remarkable that a subject which is of the importance indicated above has so far been kept so much of a mystery. One of the conclusions that will be drawn from the present study is that the available data are grossly inadequate for the purpose in hand.

The purpose of this paper is to see what can be done with existing data to throw light on the following questions: First, what is the current total value of net capital owned by persons in Britain? Secondly, how is this capital distributed? Thirdly, what are its major components, and how are they distributed? Fourthly, what is the degree of concentration of ownership of personal capital as a whole, and of its main components? Fifthly, what have been the trends in the degree of concentration of capital and in its composition over the past few decades? And finally, how is capital distributed between age groups?

But before we proceed to address ourselves to these questions we shall give a brief outline – in the following section – of the statistical sources and methods employed in this study. More complete details about the methods used are presented in the appendix.

Summary of sources and methods used

Information on the distribution of personal wealth can be obtained at present from two main sources: the estate duty statistics and unofficial sample surveys. The estate duty statistics relate only to the persons dying in a given year and must therefore be further 'processed' if they are to throw any light on the situation in the population as a whole. Sample surveys can be designed to be representative of the whole population, or of a specified part of it. Information about the distribution of personal net worth has been collected in two national sample surveys – the savings surveys of 1953 and 1954 – each of which was aimed to be representative of the non-institutional population of Great Britain. In this paper we shall make use of both these sources, drawing – in the case of the surveys – on the 1954 savings survey, which seems to have given a rather more complete picture than the preceding one (Hill, 1955, pp. 129–72; Lydall and Lansing, 1959).

Both these sources suffer from serious defects. The estate duty returns cover only estates with a net value exceeding £3000 (before 1954, £2000, and before 1946, £100); they exclude certain forms of property (e.g. immovable property situated abroad, certain government securities, property settled on a spouse and passing on the death of the spouse, discretionary trusts, the assets of pension funds, and estates of persons killed on active service); and they undervalue others, either *de jure*, as in the case of owner-occupied houses in the post-war years (until 1958), or *de facto*, because of 'kind-heartedness' by the official valuers (as for certain types of household goods) or because of outright evasion (particularly likely in the case of cash and valuables in the deceased's own possession). Moreover, as estate duties are assessed on the estates of individuals, it is not possible to discover from them the distribution of capital between families. Thus a growing tendency for owners of large properties to distribute their assets amongst the members of their families well in advance of death will affect the shape of the distribution of capital *between persons*, even though the distribution *between families* has remained unchanged.

In spite of these defects, the estate duty returns remain our major source of information and the corner-stone of this analysis. The data from the savings surveys suffer from other defects, which make them even less reliable – on their own – for the purpose in hand. The principal difficulty with unofficial surveys is the impossibility of ensuring complete and accurate response. The 1954 savings survey achieved a response rate of only 67 per cent amongst the 'income units' approached for interviews; and there was almost certainly a substantial amount of understatement of assets even by those who were 'successfully' interviewed. In the outcome, the estimates of the total amount of personal capital which can be derived from this survey appear to represent only about two thirds of the true amount. Nevertheless, the savings survey figures can be used to give some indication of the distribution of capital amongst persons with less than £2000 of net capital; and this is the purpose for which they have been employed here.

Savings survey estimates for the population are arrived at by multiplying the average net worth per income unit in the sample by the estimated total number of units in the population. Estimates from the estate duty returns cannot, of course, be obtained in this manner, as the persons who die in any given period are not a random sample of the population. The probability of death rises with age and differs between the sexes. But it is reasonable to assume that *within* each age-sex group death strikes more or less at random. Hence, if the estate duty returns are given for each age-sex group separately it is possible to 'blow-up' the sample by the reciprocal of the mortality rate within each group.[1] As a further refinement the mortality

1. This method was first applied by Bernard Mallet (without distinguishing sex) to figures specially assembled by the Inland Revenue for the years 1905 and 1906 (Mallett, 1908, pp. 65–84).

rates used in these calculations may be based on the mortality experience of persons in 'upper class' occupations only, on the assumption that persons with taxable estates belong predominantly to such classes. This adjustment was first made by Daniels and Campion (1936) in their estimates for the years 1911–13 and 1924–30, and was continued by Campion in his estimates for 1932–4 and 1936 (1939).

Table 1 **Estimates of aggregate personal capital from the estate returns for Great Britain**

Year	Persons with over £2000 net capital		
	No. (000)	Percentage of all persons 20 and over	Aggregate net capital owned (£ million)
1951	2920	8·4	30,310
1952	3260	9·3	31,510
1953	2890	8·3	27,540
1954	2980	8·5	30,400
1955	3080	8·8	29,620
1956	2930	8·3	31,150
1957	3470	9·8	33,750
1958	3870	10·9	38,100
Average 1951–6	3010	8·6	30,090

In this study we cover the years 1951–8, and the estate duty returns for each year have been inflated by reciprocals of the estimated specific (age-sex) mortality rates of persons in social classes I and II, as defined in the 1951 Census. The annual tables published by the Inland Revenue show the number of estates on which duty was first paid in each financial year and the net capital on which duty was *actually* paid in that year, the estates being classified by ranges of net capital value, by country (England and Wales together until 1957–8, and Scotland), by age (eight groups), and by sex. We have blown up the figures in each of these cells separately and aggregated the results to give estimates for Great Britain. As a rough approximation it can be assumed that the returns for each financial year relate to deaths occurring in the previous calendar year (e.g. returns for 1951–2 relate to 1951); but because the process of assessing estates for duty sometimes takes several years there are certain peculiarities in the figures, which mean that the estimates for a single year may not be entirely satisfactory. To overcome this difficulty we have averaged the results for the period 1951–6 to provide an estimate of the situation existing at the beginning of 1954, which happens also to be approximately the date of the 1954 survey. As will be seen, there was no obvious trend in aggregate capital values between 1951 and 1956, so that these years can conveniently be treated as a homogeneous group.

The estate duty returns form the basis of our estimates of the distribution of capital amongst those possessing over £2000. For those below this level we have used a variety of sources and techniques, which include (1) extrapolation of cumulative frequency curves, (2) evidence gleaned from the 1954 savings survey about the relative holdings of particular assets by those above and below this level, and (3) information about total assets of persons (e.g. life funds) available from independent sources. A detailed description of how these calculations were made is given in the appendix.

The results
Estimates from the estate duty returns

When the estate duty returns are blown up by the methods outlined in the previous section, and aggregated, we obtain estimates of the total net capital of persons with net capital above the exemption limit in Great Britain (no figures are available for Northern Ireland). The exemption limit was £2000 from 1951 to 1954 and £3000 thereafter. For the year 1954–5 the returns show the number and value of estates falling between £2000 and £3000, from which estimates of the numbers and values in this range for the succeeding years have been made. The resulting figures are given in Table 1.

With the exception of a rather surprising upward fluctuation in the numbers in 1952, followed by a downward fluctuation in the values in 1953, the figures for the years 1951–6 appear to relate to a very stable situation. In 1957 and 1958, however, there seems to have been an upward trend both in the numbers and in the values. It is difficult to isolate the reasons for this trend, since the big rise in equity prices began in 1954, and house prices also began rising about the same time. The explanation may be that there is a longer average time lag in assessment than we have assumed. In any case, however, it seems reasonable to take the years 1951–6 as a group and to assume that the average of these years is the best estimate available of the situation existing early in 1954.

Table 2 shows the average estimated number of persons in each range of net capital in 1951–6 and the same figures expressed as percentages of the total number of persons with over £2000. As can be seen from the last column, the percentage of persons in each capital range fluctuated from year to year within the period. Chi-squared tests for each year (of the original estate duty figures) show significant differences from the average of the period in all the years (one at the 5 per cent level and the remainder at the 1 per cent level). This could be due to real fluctuations in the distribution of wealth (as opposed to those arising from sampling errors); it could also arise from changes in the time-lag between death and valuation.

Table 2 **Distribution of persons with over £2000 net capital, Great Britain**

Net capital	Average no. (000)	1951–6 per cent	Range of percentages over the six years
£2000–	1788	59·4	58·5–61·2
£5000–	639	21·2	19·6–22·6
£10,000–	398	13·2	12·4–14·0
£25,000–	121	4·0	3·5–4·4
£50,000–	44	1·5	1·2–1·6
£100,000–	16	0·5	0·4–0·6
£250,000–	4	0·1	0·1–0·2
Total	3010	100·0	–

The overall distribution of capital

In order to estimate the distribution of capital amongst all persons it is necessary to make a decision about the scope of the population capable of owning capital. In most earlier studies (Daniels and Campion, 1936; Campion, 1939; Langley, 1950–51) it was assumed that this population included only persons aged twenty-five and over; but we have thought it more realistic to lower this limit to twenty and over. Starting from the average figures for 1951–6 derived from the estate duty returns, (1) we have added estimates of the distribution of capital amongst persons with less than £2000, (2) we have slightly rounded the distribution of persons above this level, and (3) we have increased somewhat the amount of capital estimated to be owned by them. Explanations of all this are given in the appendix. Table 3 gives our final estimates.

In broad outline these figures suggest that total personal net capital in early 1954 was about £40,000 million. Of this, nearly £31,000 million was owned by three million persons possessing over £2000 each; and the remaining £9000 million was owned by the other 32 million persons aged twenty and over. In the top capital group there are 20,000 persons with more than £100,000 each and an average holding of over £250,000; in the bottom group are sixteen million persons with less than £100 each and an average holding of less than £50.

In compiling these figures no adjustment has been made for capital which escapes assessment. The most important deficiencies in this respect arise from the exemption of pension funds, property settled in trust on a spouse (which is exempt from assessment when the spouse dies) and property in the hands of discretionary trusts (which may avoid assessment for an almost indefinite period). Pension funds at the end of 1953 amounted to about £2000 million; but no one knows how much property is held by

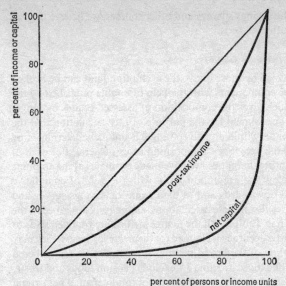

Figure 1 Lorenz curves of post-tax income and net capital, 1954

trusts. It is believed that property avoiding duty because of settlement in 1954 was about 10 per cent of the amount of net capital actually assessed. If this is so, an addition of about £3000 million should be made under this head; and, with a further allowance of perhaps £1000 million for discretionary trusts, the amount of personal net capital in 1954 might be estimated at about £46,000 million. It would not be unreasonable to assume that the whole of the trust capital belonged to those with over £2000, and about half the pension funds, giving them altogether about £36,000 million out of £46,000 million, or approximately 78 per cent of the total.

Our estimates of total capital are substantially higher than those made by Langley for 1951 (1954, pp. 1–13) and, more recently, by Morgan for 1954 (1960). Part of the difference is due to the large allowance made above (admittedly arbitrarily) for trusts. The difference from Langley's figures is also due to her use of general mortality rates instead of 'upper class' mortality rates. Professor Morgan's estimate of aggregate personal net capital in 1954, including pension funds but excluding trusts, comes to less than £36,000 million, compared with our figure – on the same basis – of £42,000 million. It is not possible to discover the exact reasons for this very wide difference; but it seems that Professor Morgan has made much smaller allowance for the capital holdings of those with less than £2000 than we have done, and a much larger allowance for liabilities. From such evidence

H. F. Lydall and D. G. Tipping 249

as we have, from the savings surveys and other sources, we believe that we are nearer to the truth than he is.[2]

The components of personal capital

Total net capital owned by those above the exemption limit can be broken down into its major components with the help of a table published by the Inland Revenue which gives the composition of assessed estates by ranges of value. It has to be assumed for the purpose of this calculation that the composition of capital (within any given range) is uniquely determined by its size, and not by the age or sex composition of its owners.[3] For each of these assets, and for total liabilities, we have made estimates of the amounts owned by those below the exemption limit, with the help of cumulative curves extrapolated downwards and of data from the savings survey and other sources. The results of these calculations – more fully described in the appendix – are given in Table 4. All the figures are heavily rounded so as to make it clear that little accuracy is claimed for them. Nevertheless, they may be useful as an outline of the broad picture. It must also be remembered that these figures – like those in Table 3 – exclude pension funds and trusts.

Very roughly, it seems that about a quarter of total personal net capital is invested in land, buildings and trade assets, or, if we add household goods about 30 per cent in physical assets. Of the remaining 70 per cent (approximately £28,000 million) one quarter consists of cash and bank deposits, one quarter of government and municipal securities, about 30 per cent is in stocks and shares, and the remainder is distributed over other assets.

Liquid assets owned by persons in 1954 consisted of £7500 million of cash and bank deposits, about £2000 million in building societies and co-operative societies, and £3000 million in national savings securities, making about £12,500 million in all, or about 30 per cent of total net capital.

It will be seen that nearly all stocks and shares in companies are estimated to belong to those with net capital of over £2000, as well as four fifths of government and municipal securities. People with less than £2000 keep most of their capital in cash, bank deposits (including savings banks), government securities (mostly national savings certificates), houses, and life insurance. In addition they probably have a large share in accumulated pension funds (perhaps as much as £1000 million out of £2000 million).

2. Professor Morgan himself admits that his estimates are too low when compared with other data arising from his study (1960, pp. 185–6).

3. Mr J. R. S. Revell, of the Cambridge Department of Applied Economics, has recently arranged for tabulations of each asset by age, sex and total capital range, from which he will be able to check the validity of this assumption.

Table 3 Estimated distribution of personal net capital in Great Britain, early 1954

Net capital (original ranges) (£)	No. of persons aged 20 or over (000)	Amount of net capital (£ million)
Under 100	16,000	685
100–	10,500	2800
500–	3,100	2365
1000–	2,400	3300
2000–	1,780	5930
5000–	640	4930
10,000–	400	6990
25,000–	120	4140
50,000–	40	3295
100,000–	20	5665
Total	35,000	40,100

Table 4 Estimated components of total personal capital in Great Britain, early 1954 (£ million)

	Held by persons with net capital of:		
	£2000 and under	Over £2000	Total
Cash and bank deposits	2900	4600	7500
Shares and deposits in building societies, cooperative societies, etc. and mortgages, bonds, bills, etc.	550	2700	3250
Government and municipal securities	1500	6000	7500
Stocks and shares in companies	200	8500	8700
Land, buildings and trade assets	3250	7750	11,000
Household goods	500	700	1200
Other property, income due, etc.	100	1100	1200
Life insurance funds	1550	1000	2550
Total assets	10,550	32,350	42,900
Total liabilities	1400	1400	2800
Total net capital	9150	30,950	40,100
Number of persons aged twenty and over	32,000,000	3,000,000	35,000,000

The concentration of ownership of capital

Personal wealth, as we have said, is very unequally distributed in this country. From the data assembled for this study it is possible to estimate – by interpolation – the proportions of total net capital (excluding pension

Table 5 **Concentration of ownership of various assets, Great Britain 1954**

	Percentages of total owned by:		
	Top 1%	Top 5%	Top 10%
Total personal net capital (excluding pension funds and trusts)	43	68	79
Cash and bank deposits	23	48	64
Government and municipal securities	42	71	83
Stocks and shares in companies	81	96	98
Land, buildings and trade assets	28	58	74
Net capital of person at lower limit (£)	15,000	3550	1700

funds and trusts) owned by various strata of the population. Table 5 gives figures for the top 1 per cent, top 5 per cent and top 10 per cent respectively of the adult population of Great Britain.

These estimates suggest that in 1954 the top 1 per cent of British adults owned 43 per cent of total net capital and the top 10 per cent 79 per cent. This distribution is very much more unequal than the distribution of income – either before or after tax. In 1954 the top 1 per cent of incomes (married couples and single adults) received about $5\frac{1}{2}$ per cent of 'allocated' income after tax, and, according to a rough estimate about 7 per cent of total income (Lydall, 1959, p. 31); and the top 10 per cent of incomes received about 25 per cent of allocated income after tax (1959, p. 14). Lorenz curves comparing the distribution of total net capital and of allocated income after tax are shown in Fig. 1.[4] The Gini coefficients of concentration are 0·34 for Income and 0·87 for Capital (1·00 being the maximum concentration possible).

Amongst the different types of asset, some are highly concentrated in the hands of the top strata of capital owners and others less so. As can be seen from Table 5, stocks and shares of companies are very highly concentrated, some 81 per cent being held by the top 1 per cent of persons and almost all by the top 10 per cent. Government and municipal securities are distributed very similarly to total capital; but cash and bank deposits, and land, buildings and trade assets, are somewhat more widely dispersed.

Trends in the concentration of capital

Estimates of the distribution of capital amongst persons aged twenty-five and over in England and Wales were made by Daniels and Campion for

4. These curves are not strictly comparable because they show the concentration of capital amongst *persons* aged twenty and over, and the concentration of income amongst *income units* (married couples and single persons with incomes above £50). But these differences in definition could not account for more than a very small part of the differences in degrees of concentration shown. Both sets of data have been cumulated from the lowest ranges upwards.

1911–13 and 1924–30 (1936), and by Campion for 1936 (1939). In order to continue this series we have computed estimates for persons aged twenty-five and over in England and Wales in 1951–6. By interpolation on double-logarithmic cumulated curves of (a) numbers of persons and (b) amounts of net capital, we have estimated the proportions of total net capital owned by various strata of the population, starting from the top. These figures, given in Table 6, suggest that in the period from 1911–13 to 1936 there was a slow but persistent tendency towards less inequality. But in the final period – from 1936 to 1951–6 – the distribution of capital appears to have altered much more radically.

In interpreting these figures we must again bear in mind, first, that they exclude pension funds and trusts; and secondly, that there has probably been an increasing tendency for large owners of property to distribute their property amongst their families well in advance of death.[5] This tendency has probably reinforced by an increasing tendency to take advantage of the Married Woman's Property Act, under which the proceeds of insurance policies on the life of the husband which have been made over absolutely to the wife are treated as separate estates. The effect of all this will be to reduce the apparent concentration of capital in the hands of the top 1 per cent of owners. But very little such property is likely to find its way into the hands of persons below the top 10 per cent of property owners, since the top 10 per cent in 1951–6 included everyone with more than £1700 of capital.

Table 6 **Changes in the percentages of personal net capital owned by various groups of the population, 1911–1956**
(England and Wales, persons aged twenty-five and over)

Stratum of the population	1911–13	1924–30	1936	1951–6
Top 1 %	65·5	59·5	56·0	42·0
Top 5 %	86·0	82·5	81·0	67·5
Top 10 %	90·0	89·5	88·0	79·0
Top 20 %	—	96·0	94·0	89·0

Sources: 1911–13 and 1924–30 from Daniels and Campion (1936).
1936 from Campion (1939).
1951–6: see text.

Thus it is almost certainly misleading to take account solely of the trend in the share of capital owned by the top 1 per cent of persons. If, however,

5. In order to escape assessment in the donor's estate, gifts *inter vivos* must have been made at least five years before death. Redistribution of capital through gifts will not alter the estimate of total personal capital, unless donors succeed in choosing donees with an average expectation of life above that for their age and sex group.

we make the assumption that redistribution within families affects only the distribution within the top 10 per cent of persons, but not beyond that range, it is possible to gauge the trend in the distribution of capital by measuring the share of total capital owned by the top 10 per cent of persons. We can see from Table 6 that this share declined only very slightly from 1911–13 to 1936; but from 1936 to 1951–6 it fell from 88 per cent to 79 per cent.

How far would these figures be altered if we could take into account the distribution of beneficial ownership of pension and trust funds? In our present state of ignorance it is impossible to give any reliable answer to this question. Campion (1939) guessed – with the help of the Inland Revenue – that settled property escaping assessment in 1936 was of the order of 5 per cent of property assessed. In 1954, as we have said, it seems probable that this proportion may have risen to about 10 per cent. Pension funds in 1936 were very small, perhaps only £400 million, but most of this would be owned by the top 10 per cent of property owners. In 1954 pension funds amounted to about £2000 million, of which, as we have suggested above, about half may have been owned by the top 10 per cent of owners. About discretionary trusts we know nothing. For the sake of example, however, let us assume that in 1936 the top 10 per cent of property owners in Great Britain owned £1000 millions of settled property, £300 million of pension funds and £300 million of discretionary trust funds, while in 1954 they owned £3000 million of settled property, £1000 million of pension funds and £1000 million of discretionary trust funds. (The remaining £100 million of pension funds in 1936 and £1000 million in 1954 are assumed to belong to the bottom 90 per cent of property owners.) With this combination of assumptions the proportion of total capital owned by the top 10 per cent of property owners shows a decline from 88·5 per cent in 1936 to 79·5 per cent in 1954, which is virtually the same as the decline shown in Table 6.[6]

We believe, therefore, that it is fairly safe to conclude that there has been *some* reduction in the inequality of wealth in the past twenty years. But the extent of this change should not be exaggerated; nor can it be known at all certainly unless the authorities are prepared to collect (and publish) much more information than exists at present about the capital owned by trusts and about the characteristics of their beneficiaries.

Comparison with the United States

In a recent study of the concentration of personal wealth in the United States Lampman (1959) has estimated that in 1954 the share of total

6. For the sake of this example the percentages given in Table 6 have been applied to estimates of total capital in Great Britain in these years in order to estimate the amounts owned by the top 10 per cent in each year.

personal net capital (excluding pension and trust funds) owned by the top 1 per cent of Americans aged twenty and over was about 24 per cent. If this is compared with our figure for Great Britain of 43 per cent (Table 5) it is obvious that the concentration of personal wealth in this country is much greater than in the United States (see also Lydall and Lansing, 1959). In the 1920s the difference between the two countries in this respect was even more striking. Lampman estimates that 32 per cent of personal net capital was owned by the top 1 per cent of American adults in 1922, and 36 per cent in 1929. In England and Wales, according to Daniels and Campion's figures (1936), the comparable figure for 1924–30 was at least 60 per cent (see Table 6).[7] It is probable that the concentration of personal wealth in

Table 7 **Estimated components of personal net capital in Great Britain, 1936 and 1954**

Components	Amount (£ million)		% of total net capital	
	1936	1954	1936	1954
Cash and bank deposits	2300	7500	11·5	18·7
Building societies, etc.	1900	3250	9·5	8·1
Government and municipal securities	4300	7500	21·5	18·7
Stocks and shares in companies	6450	8700	32·3	21·7
Land, building and trade assets	4250	11,000	21·2	27·4
Household goods	600	1200	3·0	3·0
Other property, etc.	800	1200	4·0	3·0
Life insurance funds	1200	2550	6·0	6·4
Total assets	21,800	42,900	109·0	107·0
Total liabilities	−1800	−2800	−9·0	−7·0
Total net capital	20,000	40,100	100·0	100·0

Britain has always been greater than in America. In 1890, according to G. K. Holmes and C. B. Spahr (quoted in [Lampman, 1958, p. 388]), the top 1 per cent of American families owned 51 per cent of total wealth; but Lampman believes that this must be an overestimate.

Changes in the composition of personal capital

In 1936 total personal net capital (excluding pension and trust funds) in Britain was estimated by Campion (1939) to be about £20,000 million. This can be broken down, by similar methods to those used by us for 1954, into its major components. Rough estimates for the two years are set side by side in Table 7.

7. The figures in Table 6 relate to persons aged twenty-five and over. If they were adjusted to a population aged twenty and over they would be slightly higher.

It is interesting to note, first, that over this period total personal capital approximately doubled, whereas personal disposable income increased nearly threefold and consumer prices increased nearly two and a half times. Thus the relative economic significance of accumulated capital declined. If, however, we include pension and trust funds in total personal capital, it is probable that it increased between 1936 and 1954 more than twofold – from about £21,000 million to about £46,000 million, or by about 120 per cent.

Within the total some assets have increased faster than others. Cash and bank deposits increased more than threefold and land, buildings and trade assets nearly as fast (the main influence in the latter case being the rate of increase in the value of buildings). Government and municipal securities almost doubled; but a great deal of this was caused by the expansion in holdings of national savings securities, which increased sixfold. Other British government securities rose much less rapidly, and personal holdings of municipal and foreign government securities – at market value – probably declined.

Total personal holdings of stocks and shares in companies (including private companies) increased between 1936 and 1954 by only about a third. (In the past few years, however, the rise in equity values will have changed this picture rather substantially.) Somewhat surprisingly, personal holdings of public company shares seem to have remained a fairly constant proportion (about half) of the total value of such securities quoted on the Stock Exchange.

As a result of the varying rates of increase of the different components of personal capital, the shares of total net capital represented by the different components have changed. Cash and bank deposits have increased their share substantially, as also land, buildings and trade assets. The share of company securities fell (up to 1954) quite sharply, and of government securities to a smaller extent. In general, there has been a shift in the proportions away from 'upper class' assets and towards 'popular' assets. This shift was partly the result of the overall redistribution of wealth, but it also occurred *within* wealth groups. As can be seen from Table 8, broadly the same sort of shift in the composition of assets occurred amongst both the top 10 per cent of wealth owners and amongst the bottom 90 per cent.

Distribution of wealth between age groups

It is a well-known fact that *average* wealth increases with age, so that a disproportionate share of total personal capital is owned by elderly people. To a large extent, of course, this is the consequence of a planned substitution of capital for earning power.

We have made some approximate estimates of the distribution of total

Table 8 **Distribution of assets among top 10 per cent and bottom 90 per cent of adults** (persons aged twenty and over in Great Britain)

Components	% of total net capital owned by			
	Top 10 %		Bottom 90 %	
	1936	1954	1936	1954
Cash and bank deposits	9·1	15·0	28·4	33·3
Building societies, etc.	9·1	8·6	12·2	6·2
Government and municipal securities	23·0	19·4	11·2	16·0
Stocks and shares in companies	36·3	26·6	4·1	2·5
Land, buildings and trade assets	20·7	25·3	25·4	35·8
Life insurance funds	3·9	3·4	21·1	17·9
All other assets, net of liabilities	−2·1	1·7	−2·4	−11·7
Total net capital	100·0	100·0	100·0	100·0

capital (excluding pension and trust funds) between age groups, and these are summarized in Table 9. It will be seen that the proportion of persons owning over £2000 of net capital shows a steady rise with age. Reflecting this, nearly half of total net capital is owned by persons aged fifty-five and over, who represent less than a third of the adult population. Average net capital per person rises from about £330 in the twenty to twenty-four age group to over £2000 in the group aged 75 and over. But a very large number of old people have little or no capital. According to the 1954 savings survey nearly half the income units in which the head was aged sixty-five or over owned less than £50 of net worth (not counting household goods and personal effects).

Table 9 **Estimated distribution of capital between age groups, Great Britain, 1954**

Age group	% in group owning over £2000	% of total net capital owned by age group	% of total population aged twenty and over in age group	Average net capital per person (£)
20–	1·6	2·6	9·1	330
25–	3·5	11·9	20·3	670
35–	6·1	15·9	20·3	900
45–	9·7	21·7	19·7	1260
55–	13·0	20·2	14·9	1550
65–	16·1	16·9	10·4	1860
75–	18·4	10·8	5·3	2310
Total	8·6	100·0	100·0	1140

Within age groups the greatest degree of concentration of wealth is amongst the youngest adults. Of those aged twenty to twenty-four less than 2 per cent have more than £2000; and the dispersion amongst these is very wide. Average net capital held by those with more than £2000 varies from nearly £16,000 per person for those aged twenty to twenty-four to less than £10,000 per person for those in the age groups forty-five to seventy-four. In the final age group (seventy-five and over) it rises to about £11,000. Amongst those with over £100,000 the average for the under 45s in 1951–6 was as high as £450,000, compared with less than £250,000 for those above this age. Presumably, this difference is largely the result of deliberate redistribution of very large fortunes by older people in anticipation of death. It thus gives some indication of the influence of the estate duty tax structure on the shape of the apparent distribution of wealth.

Summary and conclusions

The study of the distribution of wealth is important, first, because of the economic and social power which wealth confers (independently of income), and secondly, because of the influence which the distribution of wealth exerts on the supply of capital. In addition, there is a special reason for giving close attention to this problem in this country since the distribution of wealth in Britain is exceptionally unequal.

The data available for such a study are, however, very inadequate. For those with net capital of over £2000 (who represent about 10 per cent of all adults) there is a good deal of information from the estate duty returns. Although these are deficient in several respects, they can be used, in conjunction with estimated 'upper class' mortality rates, to obtain rough estimates of the distribution of capital amongst persons owning more than £2000. These estimates exclude property settled on spouses and capital owned by discretionary trusts and pension funds, as well as certain less important items. The values of some goods are also understated.

For the rest of the population the principal direct source is the savings surveys of 1953 and 1954, which attempted to obtain figures for total net worth (with certain exceptions) from a representative sample of the non-institutional population. These figures are also not entirely reliable, because of a downward bias in response; but they have been used, together with other information, to arrive at rough estimates of the amounts of capital owed by persons below the estate duty exemption limit.

The estate duty returns suggest that in the years 1951–6 the total value of personal net capital remained fairly stable. In 1957 and 1958, however, there were distinct increases in the value of property held by those above the exemption limit. In order to smooth out errors in the annual figures, we have averaged the estimates of numbers of persons and of total capital above £2000 for the years 1951–6 and treated these results as applying to the midpoint of the period, i.e. early 1954. This was also the date of the 1954 savings survey.

Our final estimates of the distribution of capital (excluding pension and trust funds) suggest that in early 1954 the total value of personal net capital in Great Britain was about £40,000 million. This is almost exactly double the amount estimated by Campion for 1936. If pension and trust funds were included, the total for 1954 might be of the order of £46,000 million, which would be more than twice the equivalent figure in 1936.

The concentration of ownership of capital is much greater than the concentration of income. Out of total real disposable income the top 1 per cent of income units received in 1954 only about 7 per cent; out of total personal net capital (excluding pension and trust funds) the top 1 per cent of persons aged twenty and over in 1954 owned 43 per cent.

Wealth is much more unequally distributed in Britain than in the United States. In 1954 the top 1 per cent of Americans aged twenty and over are estimated to have owned only about 24 per cent of total personal net capital.

Over the past twenty years there has been some reduction in the inequality of personal wealth in Britain. Capital owned by the top 1 per cent of persons aged twenty-five and over (in England and Wales) fell from 56 per cent of the total in 1936 to 42 per cent in 1951–6. Part of this fall, however, must be attributed to an increasing tendency to redistribute capital within families, in order to minimize death duties. But, since almost all of this redistribution is likely to take place within the top 10 per cent of persons, the tendency towards less inequality can be shown by the decline in the share of the top 10 per cent of persons, which fell from 88 per cent in 1936 to 79 per cent in 1951–6.

These changes in the distribution of wealth are reflected in changes in the composition of the total personal balance sheet. The proportions of liquid assets and physical property (especially owner-occupied houses) in the total have risen and the proportion of stocks and shares has declined (up to 1954). But similar changes have also occurred *within* similar layers of the population (in terms of their ranking by total capital).

Estimates of the distribution of capital between age groups confirm the well-known fact that average wealth increases with age. Within age groups the greatest degree of concentration is amongst the youngest. Much of this, however, probably reflects a redistribution of capital between age groups designed to avoid death duties.

Although our figures give some indication of the distribution of wealth in Britain in the 1950s, the most striking thing about them is their extreme roughness. The fact is that existing sources of data on personal wealth are quite inadequate for a serious study of the problem. Different investigators arrive at different conclusions, even in some cases about the orders of magnitude of the figures; and none can be sure which, if any, are the more reliable figures. In view of the extreme inequality of wealth distribution in Britain, and of the economic and social effects of this inequality, it is time that steps were taken in this country to collect better and more comprehensive statistics about the ownership of personal capital.

Appendix

Estimating methods employed

The blow-up of the estate duty returns

The estate duty data are taken from the annual *Reports of the Commissioners of Her Majesty's Inland Revenue* for the years ending March 31, 1952–9. For each year the Reports contain tables of numbers of estates first paying duty in that year and the amount of capital on which duty was actually paid, classified by country (England and Wales together, and Scotland), by age (eight significant groups and one for 'age not stated'), by sex, and by range of net capital value of estate (seven groups).

The data for each financial year can be assumed broadly to apply to the estates of persons dying in the preceding calendar year (i.e. it is assumed that there is an average time lag of three months in assessment); but some estates – especially the very largest – take several years to complete, and this causes some further difficulty. For example, in a period of rising values this extra time-lag is likely to produce an underestimate of the value of estates falling in each year. Fortunately, in the period 1951–6 the total number and value of estates subject to duty remained relatively stable, so that we considered it not inappropriate to average the (blown-up) figures for these years and regard the results as applying to early 1954.

In order to blow up the Inland Revenue data it is necessary to estimate suitable mortality rates for each age-sex-country class. For this purpose we started with general mortality rates for each age-sex-country class derived from the *Annual Abstract of Statistics*. But owners of property above £2000 are likely to have lower mortality rates than the general population. We assumed – following Daniels and Campion (1936) – that their mortality rates would correspond more closely to the average rates for Social Classes I and II, as defined in the Population Census. These classes cover so-called 'professional' and 'intermediate' occupations, married women being classified according to the occupation of their husbands. The total number of persons in these two classes in 1951 was almost twice as great as our estimate of the number of persons with estates above £2000, so that mortality rates based on their experience may be overestimates rather than underestimates of the rates appropriate to persons with over £2000 of capital.

'Social class' mortality rates can be calculated only for the years in which a Census is taken, and we have had to assume that the proportionate difference between general mortality rates and 'upper class' mortality rates remains constant during the years following each Census. Thus the procedure followed was to estimate 'upper class' mortality rates in 1951, to compare them with general mortality rates in the same year and to adjust the general mortality rates in subsequent years by the same proportions as were found to apply in 1951.

Social class mortality rates for England and Wales, based on the mean number of death registrations in the years 1949–53 and the Population Census for 1951, are given in Registrar General for England and Wales (1958). Separate figures are given for males, for married women, and for single women. But before using these figures we were obliged to make certain adjustments. The first adjustment arises from the fact that some people fail to record their occupation (or previous occupation) in the Census schedule. Similarly, such data are sometimes (but less frequently) omitted from the death registrations. It was necessary to make some assumption about the social class distribution of such people and – for want of any better – we decided to distribute them proportionately over the social classes in the Census and in the death registrations respectively.

Secondly, there is a tendency for the death registrations to give a somewhat more rosy view of the social class distribution of the deceased than the Census. In a special matching study of Census schedules and death registration statements for 10,000 deaths registered three weeks after the 1951 Census the General Register Office found significant discrepancies, and – in the case of males – a distinct upward bias in the recording of social class in the death registers. On the basis of this sample it would appear that the 'upper class' mortality rates for males given in Registrar General for England and Wales, (1958) are overestimated by 8·3 per cent. We have, therefore, adjusted our estimates of 'upper class' mortality rates for males to this extent.

Since information about the social class of widowed and divorced females is very poor, our calculations of female social class mortality rates have been based solely on the relation between general mortality rates and 'upper class' mortality rates for married and single women combined.

For Scotland the distribution of males by social class – as recorded in the 1951 Census – is given in (Census 1951, 1956); and the distribution of male deaths by social class – for the years 1949–53 – is given in Registrar General for Scotland (1956),. In each case, as for England and Wales, we distributed the 'unoccupied' proportionately amongst the social classes and, in the absence of a special matching study for Scotland, we assumed that there was the same net upward bias in recording the social class of male deaths in Scotland as in England and Wales. In this manner we arrived at estimates of 'upper class' mortality rates for males in Scotland in 1951.

No information has been published about the social class distribution of female deaths in Scotland, so we were obliged to estimate the 'upper class' mortality rates of Scottish females in 1951 indirectly. We first assumed that the ratio of 'upper class' male and of 'upper class' female mortality rates would be the same in Scotland as in England and Wales. But when we performed the same calculation for general mortality rates we found that it resulted in underestimates of the general mortality rates for females in Scotland. So we adjusted our provisional estimates of 'upper class' female mortality rates in Scotland by the ratio of the actual general mortality rates for females in Scotland to the 'calculated' general mortality rates. The resulting figures are obviously not very reliable; but such errors as they contain will have relatively little effect on the aggregate estimates of capital for Great Britain as a whole.

The outcome of all these calculations was a series of estimated ratios of 'upper class' mortality rates to general mortality rates in 1951. These are given in Table A.

It will be noted that the mortality rate of 'upper class' males aged twenty to twenty-four has a smaller proportionate deviation from the rest of the population than that of most of the higher male age groups. This may be because young 'upper class' males engage in various risky undertakings, including the driving of fast cars. It will also be noted that the Scottish figures show less consistency than those for England and Wales, which suggests that they are of less reliability.

With the help of this table we proceeded to estimate 'upper class' mor-

Table A **Estimated 'upper class' mortality rates as percentages of general mortality rates in 1951**

	Age groups						
	20–24	25–34	35–44	45–54	55–64	65–74	75 and over
England and Wales							
Males	96·4	75·5	74·2	80·6	83·7	87·5	91·8
Females	66·7	72·5	84·6	89·4	92·9	91·5	92·5
Scotland							
Males	87·9	76·6	81·2	80·3	85·8	95·4	95·6
Females	61·1	73·5	92·5	88·7	95·2	99·8	96·4

tality rates for each of the years 1951–8, by multiplying the general mortality rate for each age-sex-country class in each year by its corresponding 'correction factor', as given in the table. Next, we multiplied the figures published by the Inland Revenue of the numbers and values of estates paying duty by the reciprocals of these 'upper class' mortality rates, thus estimating the total numbers of persons owning capital above the exemption limit in Great Britain as a whole, and the amount of capital owned by them. For the purpose of these calculations we assumed

1. That estates covered by the heading 'age not stated' in the Inland Revenue tables could be distributed proportionately (within estate ranges) amongst the reported age groups,
2. That the reciprocals of the mortality rates for persons aged twenty to twenty-four could be applied to estates of persons aged 'under 25', and
3. That estates of persons aged seventy-five and over could be combined in a single class (no information being available for distinguishing 'upper class' mortality rates for persons aged eighty-five and over).

The number of persons with net capital between £2000 and £3000, and the total net capital value of their holdings for the years after 1954 (when the exemption limit was raised to £3000) had to be estimated on the basis of the proportions in that range in 1954, the only year for which such data were given.

Estimates for the whole population

The estimates of capital derived from the estate duty returns are deficient in several respects. In particular: (a) they exclude people owning net capital below £2000, (b) they undervalue certain assets, e.g. owner-occupied houses, and (c) they fail to cover some assets at all, e.g. settlements on spouses (on the death of the spouse), pension and trust funds, and other minor exemptions.

It is not possible, with existing information to allocate the items covered by (c) above; nor even to do more than guess at the aggregate size of some of them. We have, therefore, limited ourselves to estimating the distribution of capital amongst those below the exemption limit and to making certain adjustments to the estimates for those above that limit to take account of some of the undervaluation.

The first step in estimating the capital ownership of those owning less than £2000 was to cumulate the frequency distribution of persons in the seven ranges of value above this level. These figures were plotted on a double-logarithmic scale against the net capital values exceeded by each group, and a smooth curve was drawn through the points. This curve was then extrapolated so as to pass through the point corresponding to thirty-five million persons exceeding £10 (it being assumed that all persons aged twenty and over owned at least £10). From this curve we derived estimates of the number of persons in various class intervals below £2000. These intervals correspond to those used for analysing net worth in the savings surveys, and the mean values of net worth within these classes in the 1954 survey were assumed to be appropriate to the distribution of persons just obtained. By multiplying out the frequency by the mean of each class we then obtained estimates of the aggregate capital owned by each class below £2000. The total arrived at in this way was £8470 million which, when added to the estimated £30,090 million for those over £2000 gave a figure for the whole population of £38,560 million.

The next step was to check this calculation by carrying out a similar type of analysis for each main class of asset. For this purpose the capital owned by each group above £2000 was first divided into its components in the manner described in the text. Each of these components was then cumulated, and double-logarithmic curves were drawn showing the amount of each asset held by persons above each given level of total net capital.

In order to extrapolate these curves it was necessary to make an estimate of the total amount of each asset held by the whole adult population. In most cases such estimates were made by referring to savings survey data. But a difficulty arises because the savings surveys relate to 'income units', not to persons. Income units contain on the average about one-and-a-half persons aged twenty and over, so that one might expect them to hold on the average one-and-a-half times as much capital as individual persons. But the 1954 savings survey estimates of net worth are biased downwards by about one third. Consequently, as a very rough approximation, it was assumed that the division of the income unit population at the £2000 level of net worth corresponded to the division of the individual population at the same level of net capital. On this basis we used the proportionate division of each asset in the 1954 savings survey between income units above and below £2000 of net worth as a rough guide to the division of that asset between individuals above and below £2000 of net capital.

This rule was not followed universally. In the case of bank deposits, for example, it seemed probable that there was more downward bias amongst income units above £2000 of net worth than amongst those below that level; and an adjustment was made accordingly.

Special difficulties arose with two types of asset, namely house property and life insurance funds. Under an administrative concession, which was in force until 1958, the Inland Revenue valued owner-occupied houses at less than their market value (with vacant possession) in those cases where 'a near relative of the deceased, who was ordinarily resident with him, remained in the house and had no other place of residence available'. Such houses were valued at their pre-war value plus any increase in the value when sold *without* vacant possession. The importance of this concession in monetary terms is unknown; but it may have resulted in an undervaluation of owner-occupied houses in 1951 of about 25 per cent, gradually falling away over the next seven years. For 1954 we have assumed that the item 'house property and business premises' should be raised by about 10 per cent. Even when this is done, a comparison with the 1954 savings survey shows aggregate property values substantially larger than this. It is possible that the savings surveys tend to overestimate property values; but it is also possible that an even larger adjustment should be made to the Inland Revenue's figures.

The valuation of life insurances presents some curious problems. In principle, it might be expected that a blown-up sample of estates would yield an estimate for life insurance of the aggregate value of 'sums assured' by persons with capital above the exemption limit. According to published data the aggregate of sums assured early in 1954 was nearly £8000 million. But the estimate from the estate duty returns of the value of life insurance policies held by persons with more than £2000 of net capital in 1954 amounts to less than £900 million. It is impossible to believe that this is a correct measure of the total of sums assured by this group; and it seems that, for some reason, the value of life insurance policies recorded in the estate duty returns is understated.

One possible explanation of this phenomenon is that many life insurance policies are associated with mortgages on owner-occupied property (and with other loans to persons). When the owner of such a policy dies the policy matures and is used immediately to extinguish the debt. Only the balance of the value of the policy over the debt would thus be paid to the executors and only this sum would appear in the assets of the estate. In so far as this system operates, the value of both insurance policies and of liabilities would be undervalued in the estate returns. But it seems improbable that this feature accounts for the whole deficiency in the life insurance figures.

In view of these considerations it became necessary to make completely new estimates of the distribution of life insurance funds between capital ranges. Although these estimates are based on very inadequate material, they at least aim to distribute the life *fund*, which is what is required. We started with the savings survey estimates of life insurance *premiums* paid by different net worth groups of income units. We assumed that premiums paid by income units with less than £400 of net worth were in respect of 'industrial' assurances and the remainder in respect of 'ordinary' life assurances. We then assumed that, on the average, the ratio of premiums to accumulated funds would be constant within each of these groups. So the estimate of the aggregate premiums paid by each of these groups was multiplied by an appropriate factor so as to arrive at a total life fund (excluding pension schemes) of £2550 million. Of this, about £1000 million was found to be attributable to those with net worth of £2000 and over. This sum was distributed – very arbitrarily – amongst the various ranges above this level in proportion to the amounts of life insurance estimated for these ranges from the estate returns. The remainder was distributed amongst persons below £2000 by extrapolation of the over £2000 figures so as to arrive at the correct total.

When all these extrapolations and adjustments had been made – for each main asset and for total liabilities separately – the amounts estimated for each range of net capital were added up and compared with the estimates obtained by the original (global) extrapolation of the estate duty data. It was found that total net capital had been increased by about £1500 million (to £40,100 million). Most of this addition was due to the upward valuation of house property; a smaller amount came from the adjustment to the life insurance figures; and the rest was the result of estimating the distribution of each asset separately. We cannot say how reliable these final estimates are; we can only say that we have studied them in detail and from every angle, and that they represent the best that can be done with the existing – very limited – amount of information available.

References

CAMPION, H. (1939), *Public and Private Property in Great Britain*, Oxford University Press.

CENSUS (1956), *Scotland 1951, vol. 4, Occupations and Industries*, HMSO.

COMMISSIONERS OF HER MAJESTY'S INLAND REVENUE (annually), *Annual Reports*, HMSO.

DANIELS, G. W., and CAMPION, H. (1936), *Distribution of National Capital*, Manchester University Press.

HILL, T. P. (1955), '*Income savings and net worth – the savings surveys of 1952–4*', *Bull. Oxford Univ. Inst. Stat.*, vol. 17, pp. 129–72.

LAMPMAN, R. J. (1959), 'Changes in the share of wealth held by top wealth-holders, 1922–56', *Rev. Econ. Stat.*, vol. 41, pp. 379–92.

LANGLEY, K. M. (1950–51) 'The distribution of capital in private hands in 1936–8 and 1946–7', *Bull. Oxford Univ. Inst. Stat.*, vol. 12, 13, December, February.

LANGLEY, K. M. (1954), 'The distribution of private capital, 1950–51', *Bull. Oxford Univ. Inst. Stat.*, vol. 16, pp. 1–13.

LYDALL, H. F. (1959), 'The long-term trend in the size distribution of income', *J. Roy. stat. Soc.*, vol. 122, pp. 1–46.

LYDALL, H. F., and LANSING, J. B. (1959), 'A comparison of the distribution of personal income and wealth in the United States and Great Britain', *Amer. econ. Rev.*, vol. 49, pp. 43–67.

MALLETT, B. (1908), 'A method of estimating capital wealth from the estate duty statistics', *J. Roy. stat. Soc.*, vol. 71, pp. 65–84.

MORGAN, V. E. (1960), *The Structure of Property Ownership in Great Britain*, Oxford University Press.

REGISTRAR GENERAL FOR ENGLAND AND WALES (1958), *Decennial Supplement, England and Wales 1951; Occupational Mortality*, part 2, vol. 1, commentary, HMSO.

REGISTRAR GENERAL FOR SCOTLAND (1956), *Annual Report, 1955*, HMSO.

16. R. Lampman

The Share of Top Wealth-Holders in the United States

R. Lampman, 'Changes in the share of wealth held by top wealth-holders 1922–56', *Review of Economics and Statistics*, vol. 41, 1959, pp. 379–92.

This paper presents estimates derived from federal estate tax data of the numbers of top wealth-holders[1] and of the aggregate amounts of wealth held by them for selected years between 1922 and 1956. Changes in the concentration of wealth during that period are delineated by relating the numbers of top wealth-holders to the population and the amount of wealth held by the top group to independent estimates of the amount of wealth held by all persons.

The discussion is organized under the following headings:

1. History of Wealth Distribution Study;
2. Sources of Data and Methods of Estimation;
3. The Share of Top Wealth-holders in 1953;
4. A Comparison with Survey of Consumer Finances for 1953;
5. Historical Changes in Inequality;
6. Comparison with Wealth Distribution in England and Wales;
7. Summary.

History of wealth distribution study

Studies of wealth distribution in the United States are quite rare. Up to the close of the Second World War only ten scholars are known to have attempted nation-wide size distributions of personally held wealth.

Several important steps in the history of wealth distribution study taken after 1945 were prerequisite to any advance in understanding which may be contributed by the present study. One was the first demonstration in this country of the use of the estate multiplier method. This pioneering work was done by Horst Mendershausen. While earlier investigations had used estate tax data, none of them had used this method to estimate the distribution of wealth among living persons. Mendershausen's study, 'The pattern of estate tax wealth' (Goldsmith, 1956), is the platform from which

---

1. The term 'top wealth-holder' is here defined to mean a living person having wealth in an amount above the estate tax exemption.

this inquiry departs. A second step was the completion of a set of national balance sheet accounts for a limited number of bench-mark years. These accounts as published by Goldsmith (1956, vol. 3, part 1) show considerable detail by sectors of the economy and by type of property and make possible the calculation of the shares of several types of wealth held by the top wealth-holding groups. The balance sheet data for 1945, 1949 and 1953 were prepared for use in this study by Morris Mendelson of the National Bureau of Economic Research.

A third and highly significant post-war contribution to the study of wealth distribution was made by the Survey Research Center of the University of Michigan in the carrying out of the first nation-wide sample studies of assets and net worth held by spending units. These studies were part of the Survey of Consumer Finances for the years 1950 and 1953. They yield a broad picture of the distribution of the national total of most kinds of property and it is to be hoped that they will continue to be made and published at frequent intervals as the basic source of information on wealth distribution.

From the point of view of this study, the Survey of Consumer Finances has a special usefulness. It provides an independently arrived at set of estimates for 1953 against which our findings for 1953 can be checked for accuracy, and thus furnish us with a kind of anchor for the historical series.

Sources of data and methods of estimation

The principal source of data upon which this study is based is tabulations of federal estate tax returns. The federal estate tax has been in existence since 1916 and some information on returns filed has been published for most years. The minimum filing requirement, which is currently $60,000, has varied from $40,000 to $100,000 over the period. However, the necessary information concerning age and sex of decedents, cross-classified by type of property, is presented in such a way as to enable the derivation of a detailed representation of the distribution of wealth among living persons for relatively few years. For 1953 the Internal Revenue Service made available to the National Bureau of Economic Research the most complete tabulation of estate tax returns which has ever been prepared. In this tabulation the variables of gross estate size, age, sex and residence (by community-property state or non-community-property state) of decedents were cross-classified by type of property. For the year 1944 a similar breakdown, but without sex or residence information, had been prepared by the Internal Revenue Service and was the basis for the intensive study by Mendershausen referred to above. For 1948, 1949 and 1950 there is information by age and gross estate size which makes possible an estimate of aggregate gross estate without a breakdown by type of property. Similar but unpublished data for 1941 and 1946 were made available to Mendershausen. Data on economic estate by net estate size and age are available for 1922, 1924, 1941, 1944 and 1946. Finally, data on the sex of decedents by age and size of estate are available only for the years 1922, 1923, 1948, 1949, 1950 and 1953.

The method which was followed in dealing with estate tax returns is known as the estate multiplier method. This method calls for multiplying both the number of, and the property of, decedents in each age-sex group by the inverse of the mortality rate experienced by that age-sex group. This process yields an estimate of the number of living persons and the amount of estate in each age-sex group and in each estate size class. A simple hypothetical example will illustrate what is involved. Suppose that out of a population of 1000 men aged forty to fifty, two men died in the year with estates of between $100,000 and $200,000. Suppose further that it is known that 5 per cent of all the 1000 men aged forty to fifty died in the year. Then it may be assumed that the two men who died with $100,000–200,000 estates were 5 per cent of all the living men in the group with estates of this size. Hence, to estimate the number of living men in this estate size class we should multiply two by twenty (the inverse of 5 per cent) to get the answer of forty living men having $100,000–200,000 estates.

The leading disadvantage of thus deriving wealth estimates from estate tax returns arises from the fact that the 'sampling' is done by death rather than by a random draw of living persons. This means that a connection can be established between decedent wealth-holders and living wealth-holders only by use of a set of mortality rates which are assumed to reflect the mortality experience of the upper wealth-holding groups. The selection of mortality rates presents an opportunity for considerable error in the estimation of the number of living persons in each estate size, and, similarly, in the aggregate of wealth held by such persons. Other problems arise to the extent that decedents' reported estates may differ from the 'actual' estates of non-decedents in the same age-sex groups.

Space here does not allow a full exploration of these two difficulties. However, we have attempted to find the most appropriate set of multipliers for this purpose, and have examined in detail the peculiarities of the method of sampling by estate tax returns. We have estimated quantitative corrections in those instances in which by law or practice individual wealth items are included, excluded, or differently valued than an ideal definition of personal wealth would require. In the course of the inquiry two ideal definitions were improvised. 'Prime wealth' is used to connote the wealth to which a person has full title and over which he has power of disposal. 'Total wealth' is a broader concept; it includes prime wealth and also wealth in which a person may have an income interest but over which he may not have any present power of disposal. Examples of the latter are rights to personal trust funds or to equities in pension and retirement funds. Our rough estimates indicate that basic variant aggregate estimates (which are the blown-up estate tax data with only one correction, namely that for reduction of insurance face value to equity amounts) are not substantially different from an ideally arrived at estimate of prime wealth, but are considerably lower than the aggregate of total wealth.

Share of top wealth-holders in 1953

In 1953 there were 36,699 decedents for whom estate tax returns were filed. The aggregate gross estate reported on those returns was $7·4 billion. By use of the estate multiplier method it is estimated that the number of living persons in that year with $60,000 or more of gross estate was 1,658,795 and that their gross estates aggregated $309·2 billion. This number of persons comprised 1·04 per cent of the total population and 1·6 per cent of the adult population. They held about 30 per cent of the total of personal wealth on the basis of either the prime wealth or total wealth variant of personal wealth. See Figure 1 and Table 1. Table 1[2] needs some explanation. The data in columns 1–7 are derived from the national balance sheet accounts referred to above. These accounts record estimates of aggregate assets,

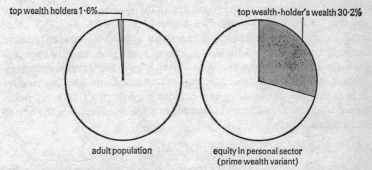

Figure 1   Share of personal sector equity (prime wealth variant) held by top wealth holders, 1953 (Source : Table 1, column 12)

liabilities and equities for sectors of the economy. Several of these sectors have been combined and adjusted to form a 'personal sector' which is conceptually adapted for comparison with the holdings of individual wealth-holders. As shown in Table 1 the personal sector is defined to

2. Similar tables have been drawn up for 1949, 1945, 1939, 1929 and 1922 but are not reproduced here.

include the following subsectors: 'household', 'farm business', and 'non-farm, noncorporate' and 'personal trust funds'. (We have excluded non-profit organizations entirely.)

Since the household subsector consolidates balance sheets of all households, the debts owed by one household to another are cancelled out. In other words, intra-household debt is excluded both as an asset and as a liability. Another difficulty arises in the treatment of households' equity in unincorporated business. Because the national balance sheets do not consolidate the household, farm business, and nonfarm business subsectors while the estate tax wealth data in effect do consolidate them[3] the balance sheet totals for most types of property are relatively over-stated. This means that we do not have strict comparability on a line-by-line basis, but it is believed that this is not a serious difficulty for most types of property. Double-counting of the equity in unincorporated business is avoided by showing it in the household sector but not adding it into the personal sector totals. Hence, this does not lead to any errors in the total gross and economic estate figures. Following the concepts discussed above, we refer to prime wealth and total wealth variants of personal wealth. Prime wealth differs from total wealth in that prime wealth excludes personal trust funds, annuities, and pension and retirement funds.

The top wealth-holders, i.e. those with estates of $60,000 or more, in 1953 held 30·2 per cent of the prime wealth in the personal sector, and 32·0 per cent of the total wealth. (See Table 1, columns 12 and 13.) These columns also show estimates of the share of each of several types of property held by top wealth-holders. These range from over 100 per cent for state and local bonds down to 9 per cent for life insurance reserves. Particular interest attaches to the corporate stock figure. Our estimate for 1953 is that the top wealth group held 82 per cent of all the stock in the personal sector. This matter is discussed in more detail below in the section on type of property.

Comparison with SCF findings, 1953

The broadest view obtainable of the wealth holdings picture in 1953 is that furnished by the Survey of Consumer Finances for that year. According to the survey the median net worth of the nation's fifty-four million spending units was $4100. 4 per cent of the nation's spending units had net worth of $50,000 or more. Eleven per cent had net worth of $25,000 or more. This upper 11 per cent held 56 per cent of total assets and 60 per cent of total

3. That is, estate tax wealth is not uniformly classified to show all assets held by unincorporated enterprises as 'equity in unincorporated business'. In some cases they are separately listed as real estate, cash, etc. The equity item is listed under the heading of miscellaneous in Table 1.

Table 1 Role of top wealth-holders in national balance sheet accounts, 1953ᵃ (dollar figures in billion)

	All sectors	Personal sector				Total, total wealth variant	Total, prime wealth variant	Top wealth-holders			Share of wealth held by top wealth-holders		
	Total wealthᵇ variant	House-hold	Personal trust funds	Farm business	Non-farm, noncorporate business			Basic variant	Prime wealth variant	Total wealth variantᶜ	Basic variant col.8/col.7	Prime wealth variant col.9/col.7	Total wealth variant col.10/col.6
	(1) ($)	(2) ($)	(3) ($)	(4) ($)	(5) ($)	(6) ($)	(7) ($)	(8) ($)	(9) ($)	(10) ($)	(11) (%)	(12) (%)	(13) (%)
Real Estate	765·1	317·9	2·0	78·8	45·9	444·6	442·6	70·1		71·7	15·8		16·1
Structures, Residential	294·9	270·6			14·5								
Nonresidential	260·3			14·7	17·3								
Land	209·9	49·3		64·1	14·1								
US Bonds	260·6	47·3	7·3		5·8	60·4	53·1	17·4		23·2	32·8		38·2
State and local bonds	33·9	7·8	8·2			16·0	7·8	10·8		17·3	ᵍ		ᵍ
Other bonds								2·8		5·4	100·0		88·5
Corporate bonds	56·0	2·8	3·3			6·1	2·8						
Stockᵈ	245·5	127·2	28·5			155·7	127·2	105·7		128·3	83·2		82·4
Cashᵉ	306·5	138·8	2·6	6·6	13·0	160·0	158·4	44·6		46·7	28·2		29·1
Monetary metals	27·4	0·2		0·2	0·2								
Currency and deposits	258·1	127·2		6·4	12·8								
Deposits in other financial institutions	20·9												

Table 1 – continued

	All sectors	Personal sector						Top wealth-holders			Share of wealth held by top wealth-holders		
	Total wealth variant[b] (1)	House-hold (2)	Personal trust funds (3)	Farm business (4)	Non-farm, noncorporate business[c] (5)	Total, total wealth variant (6)	Total, prime wealth variant (7)	Basic variant (8)	Prime wealth variant (9)	Total wealth variant[c] (10)	Basic variant col. 8 / col. 7 (11)	Prime wealth variant col. 9 / col. 7 (12)	Total wealth variant col. 10 / col. 6 (13)
Mortgages and notes	234·0	19·5	1·2		10·5	31·2	30·0	10·5		11·3	35·0		36·2
Receivables from business	106·7	0·6			6·3								
Receivables from households	31·1				4·2								
Loans on securities	4·9	1·1											
Mortgages, nonfarm	84·1	14·6											
Mortgages, farm	7·2	3·0											
Life insurance reserves	69·8	78·2				78·2	78·2	7·1		10·4	9·0		13·3
Pension and retirement Funds	56·7	63·5				63·5				3·8			5·9
Private	8·8	11·0											
Government	47·9	52·5											
Miscellaneous	611·0	332·5	0·9	39·2	35·6	220·8	219·9	39·6		40·3	18·0		18·2
Durable producer goods	134·7			17·2	19·5								
Durable consumer goods	122·7	128·8											
Inventories	106·8			18·9	16·1								
Equities, farm and nonfarm	187·4	(187·4)[f]						(20·0)					(10·9)
Equities, mutual financial organizations	16·1	16·1											
Other intangibles	43·3	0·2	0·9		3·1								

	1	2	3	4	5	6	7	8	9	10			
Gross estate	2639·3	1135·5	54·1	124·6	110·8	1237·6	1120·0	309·2	327·6	381·2	27·6	29·2	30·8
Total tangible		447·9	2·0	115·1	81·7	132·8	132·8	27·7	28·8	28·8	21·3		22·1
Total intangible		687·4	52·1	9·5	29·1								
Debts and mortgages	299·8	85·0		13·7	34·1								
Payables to banks	44·9	9·6		2·8	6·9								
Other payables to business	79·9	13·2		2·7	9·1								
Payables to households													
borrowing on securities	3·2	3·2											
Mortgages	91·2	58·8		7·8	15·1								
Other liabilities	80·6			0·4	3·0								
Economic estate	2339·3	1050·5	54·1	110·6	76·6	1104·8	987·0	281·5	298·8	352·4	28·5	30·2	32·0

a Source for columns 2–7, preliminary national balance sheet estimates for 1953 by National Bureau of Economic Research.

b Column 1 shows preliminary estimates for 1952. All-sector totals are not yet prepared for 1953.

c 80 per cent of each type of asset in personal trust fund wealth is allocated to the top wealth-holder group. This allocation was adopted after inspection of tabulations of fiduciary income tax returns, which suggest that 80 per cent of fiduciary income distributable to beneficiaries went to persons with estates worth $60,000 or more since it was from parcels of wealth of at least $60,000 in value. However, available data do not enable an identification of the share of each type of property (e.g. real estate and stock) in the personal trust fund aggregate allocable to the top wealth-holders. Lacking any better data, we have applied the 80 per cent ratio to each type of property. For pensions and retirement funds, 10 per cent of private and 5 per cent of government funds are so allocated, and 20 per cent of annuities are estimated to belong to the top wealth-holders. This column does not add to gross estate as shown. The gross estate figure of $381·2 billion is our best estimate.

d The original estate tax data for stock include shares in savings and loan associations. However, we have adjusted the top wealth-holder account in column 8 and 10 to exclude those shares from 'stock' and to include them in 'cash'. The assumption used for 1953 was that the top wealth-holders held 70 per cent of the $22·5 billion worth of shares in savings and loan associations held by 'individuals'. This assumption is based on the belief that such shares are less concentrated than corporate stock and corporate bonds.

e Including shares in savings and loan associations.

f Excluded from columns 6 and 7 but included in gross estate and economic estate in column 2.

g In excess of 100 per cent.

net worth. While this group held only 30 per cent of consumer capital goods, they held 80 per cent of business and investment assets (see Table 2).

Inspection of 1950 survey results suggests that the spending units having $60,000 or more of net worth were 3 per cent of all spending units in 1953. These spending units held 30 per cent of total assets and 32 per cent of total net worth.[4] These particular figures about the top 3 per cent are ones we

Table 2 **Proportion of net worth and components held within net worth groups, early 1953[a]**

Net worth	Spending units	1952 Money income before taxes	Consumer capital goods[b]	Business and investment assets[c]	Fixed value assets[d]	Total assets	Debt[e]	Net worth
	Per cent							
Negative ⎫	31	19	⎧ 1	(f)	(f)	(1)	6	(g)
0–$999 ⎭			⎩ 1	(f)	2	1	4	1
$1000–$4999	23	20	13	1	9	7	18	5
$5000–$24,999	35	37	55	19	37	36	51	34
$25,000 and over	11	24	30	80	52	56	21	60
All cases	100	100	100	100	100	100	100	100
	Billions of dollars							
Aggregation valuation	..	219	288	328	109	725	84	641

[a] Source: *Federal Reserve Bulletin* (1953, supplementary Table 5, p. 11).

[b] Includes automobiles and owner-occupied nonfarm houses.

[c] Includes owner-occupied farms, farm machinery, livestock, crops, interest in unincorporated business, and privately held corporations, real estate other than home or farm on which owner is living, and corporate stock.

[d] Includes liquid assets and loans made by spending units.

[e] Includes mortgages and other real estate debt, installment and other short-term debt.

[f] Less than one half of 1 per cent.

[g] Negative or less than one half of one per cent.

would like to compare with the estimates of the holdings of top wealth-holding individuals as made via the estate multiplier method.

First, however, it should be noted that there are some limitations to the 1953 Survey data as a representation of wealth-holdings. Not all types of property were included in the count. Insurance, consumer durables other than automobiles, currency, personal trust funds, annuities, pension reserves, bonds of corporations and of state, local and foreign governments were all omitted. Further, there appears to be some understatement of those assets which were included, with perhaps the largest understatement

4. It is of interest that the survey conclusions about this top group are based upon interviews with 124 spending units.

for liquid assets.[5] These exclusions and the difficulty of getting full representation of top wealth-holders and complete reporting of their holdings would lead one to suspect that the survey has probably understated the degree of inequality of wealth distribution on a prime wealth basis and more certainly on a total wealth basis.

Since all our estate tax data are for individuals, it is awkward to check them against the spending unit estimates of the Survey. This study shows that while the top wealth-holder group in 1953 made up 1·6 per cent of all adults they represented a minimum of 2·3 per cent of the families. More precisely, in 2·3 per cent of the families there was one or more person with $60,000 or more of gross estate. In some unknown number of other families the combined holdings of two or more persons will equal $60,000 or more. In the light of this the Survey's estimate that 3 per cent of the spending units have $60,000 or more of net worth seems altogether reasonable. Similarly, their estimate that this group had 30 per cent of total assets and 32 per cent of total net worth seems compatible with our findings that the top 1·6 per cent of adults held 30·2 per cent of total economic estate. To add another 0·7 per cent of all families would mean to add another 400,000 persons to the top wealth-holder group. If we impute $60,000 to each one of them this would add $24 billion or an extra two percentage points to the top group's share of total economic estate – 30·2 plus 2 equals 32·2 which is close to the survey's finding of 32 per cent of net worth. In spite of the fact that the survey figures tend to minimize the degree of inequality by exclusions of certain kinds of property, we find only slightly more inequality than is found by the survey. However, the principal conclusion is that the survey gives some confirmation to our estimates at one end of the historical series.

Historical changes in inequality[6]

Table 1 and unpublished companion tables enable a comparison of top wealth-holders and the personal sector for the years 1953, 1949, 1945, 1939,

5. Approximately 80 to 85 per cent of the full value of the included items is accounted for by the survey. Among the excluded items, personal trust funds, annuities and pension reserves, which together totalled about $100 billion, fall outside our definition of prime wealth. For a comparison of survey and national balance sheet aggregates, see Goldsmith (1956, p. 107). Further difficulties with survey data are discussed in the *Federal Reserve Bulletin* (1958, p. 1047).

6. So far as is known, this is the first attempt to relate estate tax data to national balance sheet aggregates. Several other students of wealth distribution have examined changes in concentration *within* the group of decedent estate tax wealth-holders. W. L Crum (1935) studied the returns for the period 1916–33 and concluded that 'with respect to curvature, as with respect to the coefficients of average inequality, a rough lagging correlation with the economic cycle is evident. Prosperity is followed by a much greater

1929, and 1922. In looking for trends over the decades the reader should remember that varying numbers of wealth-holders are involved in each year. These changes are due to changing exemption limits, changing prices and incomes, and changing population numbers. Figure 2 records the changing number of top wealth-holders and the changing population between 1922 and 1953.

Comparison over the years, at least as regards aggregate economic estate, is facilitated by Table 3. Here we have shown as much information as could be assembled for the years 1922–56. In some cases the results are the product of interpolation. The estimates shown for 1929, 1933, 1939 and 1954 and 1956 are particularly contrived, since the estate tax data for those years are not presented with age and estate size breakdowns and it has been necessary to use judgment in selecting devolution rates[7] for those years. The 1945 results are adjusted on the basis of 1944 findings, for which considerable basic data were available.

In columns 14–18 the proportion that estate tax wealth-holders are of the total population is shown with their share of total wealth. Thus, in 1922 0·47 per cent of the population held 29·2 per cent of the total equity of the personal sector. In 1949 0·80 per cent of the population held 22·7 per cent of the total equity. In 1953 1·04 per cent of the population held 28·5 per cent of the total equity. The whole set of figures suggests a downward drift in the degree of concentration of wealth, particularly from 1929 to 1945.

---

stretching into high total valuations of the few largest estates than is depression' (p. 10).

Working from a distribution of estate tax returns by net estate classes, Mendershausen was able to make some comparisons of inequality among living top wealth-holders for the 1920s and the 1940s. He concludes as follows:

... we find less inequality in the 1944 and 1946 distributions than in those for 1922 and 1924. This pertains of course to all returns for each of the several years, which, as has been noted before, extended over a changing range of wealth classes owing to changes in exemptions (p. 344). These exemptions were $50,000 in 1922 and 1924, and $60,000 in the 1940s.

The introduction of the marital deduction in 1948 makes the net estate data after that year noncomparable with that for earlier years. Hence, we cannot compare the inequality among top wealth-holders in the 1920s and 1940s with the 1950s. It is possible to compare the distribution of gross estate among the top wealth-holders in 1944 and 1953. We find virtually no difference in inequality in the two years. It should be emphasized that there is great difficulty in the way of presenting a meaningful comparison of the degree of inequality among estate-tax wealth-holders over the years. Because of the dollar exemption (which itself changes) and the changing level of asset prices and the general growth in the economy, the top wealth-holders constitute a varying proportion of the total population. To compare the inequality within a group whose limits are so arbitrary and whose relative importance is so variable is apt to raise more questions than it answers.

7. A devolution rate is an average estate multiplier for number of persons or amount of estate.

Table 3 Selected data relating top wealth-holders to population and estate tax wealth to national balance sheet aggregates for selected years, 1922–53

Year	Total assets, all sectors total wealth variant (1)	Total assets, personal sector total wealth variant (2)	Total equity, personal sector total wealth variant (3)	Total equity, personal sector prime wealth variant (4)	Total population (5)	Population aged 20 years and over (6)	Number of estate-tax wealth holders (basic variant) White mortality (7)	Adjusted mortality (8)
	Billions of dollars				Millions		Thousands	
1922	653·0	347·8	296·6	278·3	110·1	65·1	454[b]	517[b]
1924					114·1	68·0	495[b]	
1929	981·7	521·5	441·8	409·8	121·8	74·4	290[f]	330[f]
1933	733·1	387·9	329·1	300·7	125·7	78·8	402[f]	461[f]
1939	877·4	426·6	368·7	326·5	131·0	85·5	641[f]	758[f]
1941					133·4	87·8	529[b]	
1944					138·4	91·7	660[b]	782[b]
1945	1626·2	722·5	671·8	598·4	139·9	92·9	759[b,c]	914[b,c]
1946					141·4	93·9	859[b]	1045[b]
1947					144·1	95·5	967[b]	1014[b]
1948					146·6	97·0	938	1107
1949	2063·5	942·7	855·0	760·6	149·2	98·0	1003	1187
1950					151·7	99·2	1079	1269
1952	2639·3				157·0	101·4		
1953		1237·6	1104·8	987·2	159·6	103·4	1417	1659
1954		1340·9	1190·7	1060·2	161·2	105·4		1661
1955		1465·4	1292·0	1142·4	164·3	107·8	—	—
1956			1400·0[h]	1230·0[h]	167·2	110·0		2109

Table 3 – continued

Year	Top wealth-holders' aggregate economic estate				Top wealth-holders, aggregate gross estate	Top wealth-holders as per cent of		Wealth of top wealth-holders as per cent of wealth in personal sector		
	Basic variant		Prime wealth variant	Total wealth variant	Basic variant adjusted mortality	Total pop.	Adult pop.	Basic variant	Wealth prime variant	Total wealth variant
	White mortality	Adjusted mortality	Adjusted mortality[d]	Adjusted mortality[e]		$\frac{col.8}{col.5}$	$\frac{col.8}{col.6}$	$\frac{col.10}{col.4}$	$\frac{col.11}{col.4}$	$\frac{col.12}{col.3}$
	(9)	(10)	(11)	(12)	(13)	(14)	(15)	(16)	(17)	(18)
	Billions of dollars					Per cent				
1922	70·0[a,b]	81·3[a,b]	86·2	98·1	92·2[a]	0·47	0·79	29·2	30·7	32·7
1924	75·9[a,b]	86·6[b,a]								
1929	104·2[f]	119·1[f,a]	126·1[g]	146·2	138·4[a,f]	0·27	0·44	29·0	30·7	33·2
1933	60·6[f]	70·1[f]	72·1[g]	89·9		0·37	0·44	23·3	24·0	27·3
1939	81·0[f]	95·1[f,a]	100·8	126·3	109·3[f,a]	0·58	0·89	29·1	30·6	34·1
1941	65·1[i,b]									
1944	105·0[b]	124·7[b]				0·56	0·86			
1945	117·8[b,c]	139·6[b,c]	148·0[g]	183·6	153·6	0·65	0·98	23·2	24·7	27·4
1946	130·5[b]	152·2[a,b]				0·74	1·11			
1947						0·70	1·06			

1948	133·9[a]	159·4[a]		177[a]		0·75	1·14			26·0
1949	144·0[a]	171·4[a]		190·2[a]		0·80	1·26	22·7	24·6	
1950	162·9[a]	193·9[a]		216·2[a]		0·81	1·23			
1952			181·7[g]	223·9						
1953	235·2	281·5	298·8	309·2	352·4	1·04	1·60	28·5	30·2	32·0
1954		297·0[a,f]	314·8[g]	315·0	375·8	1·04	1·57	28·0	29·7	31·5
1955		—	—	—	—	—	—			
1956		406·6[a,f]	431·0[g]	432·6	510·0	1·26	1·90	33·0	35·0	36·3

[a] Includes a reduction of life insurance to equity value. For 1950 this correction was estimated to be $20 billion; for 1949, $19 billion; for 1948, $19 billion; for 1946, $15 billion; for 1939 and 1929, $7 billion; for 1924 and 1922, $5 billion.

[b] Multiplier process carried out for both sexes combined, hence these estimates are slightly high relative to those of 1948–53.

[c] Estimated from 1944 and 1946 findings.

[d] Relationship between basic variant and prime wealth variant estimated on basis of 1953 findings.

[e] Personal trust funds allocated to estate tax wealth-holders on this basis, 1953, 85 per cent of the total; 1949, 80 per cent; 1939, 75 per cent; 1933 and 1929 and 1922, 66 per cent.

[f] Estimates of wealth-holders and aggregate economic estate made by multiplying number of returns and economic estate on returns by selected devolution rates. The rates were selected by inspection of devolution rates in surrounding years and with reference to changing exemption limits.

[g] Basic variant adjusted to prime wealth variant on basis of 1953 relationship of basic to prime wealth.

[h] Estimated from 1953, 1954, and 1956 balance sheets.

[i] Apparently there was an abnormally old group of decedent wealth-holders in 1941.

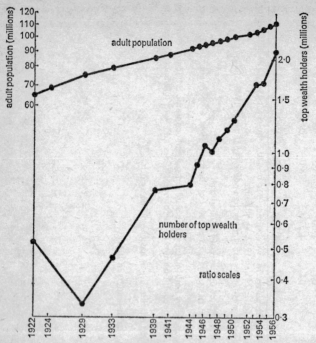

Figure 2 Top wealth holders and the adult population, selected years, 1922–53
(Source: Table 3)
Note: as it is defined in the text a 'top wealth-holder' is a living person having
wealth in an amount above estate tax exemption level. The sharp drop in number of
top wealth-holders in 1929 was due to the extraordinarily high estate tax exemption
of $100,000 effective in that year

1929 stands out as the peak year for inequality in this series with 0·27 per
cent of the population holding 29·0 per cent of the wealth. There is considerable variability in these relationship over short periods. The variability
may be due to sampling errors or other errors in the estate tax wealth estimates or to difficulties in the National Balance Sheet estimates or to a
combination of such errors. On the other hand, it is not altogether im-
plausible that the degree of inequality would have increased during the
1920s, returned to below the pre-1929 level in the 1930s, fallen still more
during the war and then increased from 1949 to 1956.

Table 4 summarizes, perhaps in a clearer way, what changes in inequality
are estimated.[8] It shows the same top per cent of population in 1953 as the
total group of estate tax wealth-holders were in some earlier years. Thus, in

8. This section has been much improved by the suggestions of Thor Hultgren.

Table 4 **Share of top groups of wealth-holders shown as per cent of total population in personal sector total equity (basic variant) selected years, 1922–53**

Per cent of population	1922	1929	1933	1939	1945	1949	1953	1954	1956
Per cent of wealth									
Top 0·27	—	29·0	—	—	16·9	—	18·0		
0·37	—	—	23·3	—	18·6	—	20·2		
0·47	29·2	—	—	—	20·2	—	22·0		
0·58	—	—	—	29·1	21·8	—	23·8		
0·65	—	—	—	—	23·2	—	24·8		
0·80	—	—	—	—	—	22·7	26·6		
1·04	—	—	—	—	—	—	28·5	28·0	
1·26	—	—	—	—	—	—	—	—	33·0
Top 0·50	29·8	32·4	25·2	28·0	20·9	19·3	22·7	22·5	25·0

Source: Table 3, columns 14 and 16. Percentages for top 0·5 per cent of population, shown in last row above are derived from Chart 3 by extension of lines from known points. The extensions were made by drawing lines parallel to that for 1953, except for 1945, for which detail is available for the top 0·65 per cent.

1922 the estate tax wealth-holders comprised 0·47 per cent of the total population and held 29·2 per cent of the wealth. In 1953 the top 0·47 per cent held 22·0 per cent of the wealth. This is shown graphically in Figure 3 which shows the upper right-hand section of a Lorenz curve.[9] The easiest way to see what changes are involved is to hold the per cent of population constant, which can be done with minimum guessing only for the top one half per cent of the population for the series of years. (See bottom row in Table 4.) This shows quite clearly that there were three periods with inequality declining in jumps from the 1920s to the 1930s, and then to the war and postwar periods.

The change in inequality over time is modified somewhat by considering the per cent that estate tax wealth-holders are of adults rather than of the total population. In 1920 persons over twenty years were 57·9 per cent of the total population; in 1930, 61·1; in 1940, 65·9; in 1950, 65·7 per cent; and in 1955, 63·8. In view of this striking change, and also because adulthood is relevant to wealth-holding status, we have shown the percentage that estate tax wealth-holders were out of the adult population in column 15 of Table 3. While the share of wealth held by the top 0·5 per cent of all persons fell

9. This chart should be read downward and to the left from the upper right-hand corner. The line of equality shows the relationship that would obtain if the top 1 per cent of the population held 1 per cent of the wealth. It will be noted that the farther a line is from the line of equality the more the inequality being represented. According to this chart the share of wealth held by the top one half per cent moved from 1929 to 1953 about one third of the distance toward absolute equality.

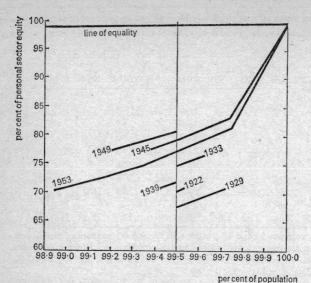

Figure 3 Upper sections of Lorenz curves showing share of personal sector (basic variant) held by upper percentiles of the total population for selected years, 1922–53 (Source: Table 3)

from 32·4 in 1929 to 22·7 per cent in 1953 (Table 4), the share held by the top 0·44 per cent of adults had a slightly larger percentage fall from 29·0 to 19·7 per cent (Table 5). The fact that there were more children, most of whom held zero wealth, per 100 of population in the 1920s than in 1953 means that the top 1 per cent of adults were a larger part of the total population in 1953 than in 1922. Further, it means that to include the top 1 per cent of adults in 1953 one has to count down to smaller estate sizes than in 1922. Presumably it is because of this that we find a greater loss of share on an adult than on an all-person basis. The share of the top 1 per cent of adults shows a greater fall over the years than does the share of wealth of the top one half per cent of all persons.[10] The top 1 per cent of adults held

10. A comment by P. F. Brundage to the author makes it clear that one may make a further step here to say that a statistical determinant of the degree of inequality of wealth-holding is the age-composition of the population. Increasing the percentage that adults are of the total population tends to decrease the degree of inequality, or to offset a rise in inequality. Similarly, increasing the percentage that older-aged adults are to the total population would tend toward a showing of decreasing inequality. The reasoning runs like this: there is, in general, a positive association between age and size of estate. Hence, up to a point, as a larger part of the population moves into older age groups, the per cent of the total population with no wealth or with small estates will fall and hence the degree of inequality will fall.

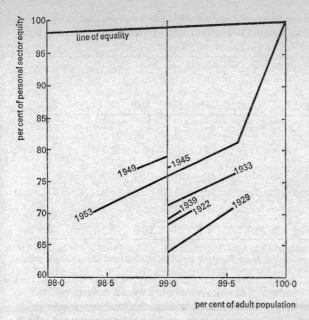

Figure 4 Sections of Lorenz curves showing share of personal sector equity (basic variant) held by upper percentiles of the adult population for selected years, 1922–53 (Source : Table 3)

31·6 per cent of wealth in 1922 and 23·6 per cent in 1953. (See Table 5, bottom row and Figure 4).

Evaluation of the finding that inequality among all persons and among all adults has fallen over the period 1922 to 1953 is aided by moving to the family as the wealth-holding unit. The nearest that estate tax data enable us to come to a family wealth distribution is a rough count of the number of families having at least one member with at least $60,000. This was established by subtracting the number of married women from the total of top wealth-holders. Thus, for 1953 the total of 1·6 million top wealth-holders less the 0·3 million married women yields the minimum estimate of 1·3 million families. The identical calculation for 1922 is 517,000 top wealth-holders less 45,000 married women, which yields the minimum estimate of 472,000 families.[11]

11. Married women were 9·7 per cent of decedent estate tax wealth-holders in 1953, but only 5·5 per cent in 1922. (5·3 and 6·0 per cent in 1923 and 1924.) In the estimate of living top wealth-holders married women are 18 per cent in 1953 and 8·5 per cent in 1922.

Table 5 **Share of top groups of wealth-holders (shown as per cent of total adult population) in personal sector total equity (basic variant), selected years 1922–1953**

% of population aged twenty years and over	1922	1929	1933	1939	1945	1949	1953	1954	1956
Top 0·44		29·0	23·3				18·7		
0·79	29·2						22·0		
0·89				29·1			22·9		
0·98					22·9		23·5		
1·26						22·7	25·9		
1·57							28·0		
1·60							28·5		
1·90							—		33·0
Top 1·00	31·6	36·3	28·3	30·6	22·8	20·8	23·6	23·6	26·0

Source: Table 3, columns 15 and 16. Percentages for top 1 per cent of adults, shown in last row above, are derived from Figure 4 by extension of lines from known points except for 1953.

Setting these numbers of families among top wealth-holders against the numbers of total adults less married women in the total population yields the finding that families among the top wealth-holder group were 1·4 per cent of all families in 1922[12] and 2·0 per cent of all families in 1953. Since the top wealth-holder groups in the two years held almost the same share of total equity (29·2 per cent and 28·5 per cent, respectively), it follows that the reduction in inequality is shown by the increase in the percentage of families.[13] By plotting these points on a Lorenz curve and projecting the

12. W. I. King estimated that in 1921 the top 2 per cent of property owners held 40·19 per cent of all wealth. The top 1·54 per cent held 37·25 per cent of wealth; the top 0·63 per cent held 28·14 per cent of wealth. This may be compared with our finding that in 1922 roughly the top 1·4 per cent of families held 29·2 per cent of wealth. Since some families include two or more property owners, it is probable that there would be more concentration among families than among property owners. Hence, it appears that King, by his entirely different methods, found a higher degree of inequality in wealth-holding than we do for the same period (King, 1927, p. 152).

It is also of interest that both G. K. Holmes and C. B. Spahr concluded that the top 1 per cent of families in 1890 owned 51 per cent of wealth (Holmes, 1893, pp. 589–600; Spahr, 1896). It is difficult to believe that wealth was actually that highly concentrated in 1890 in view of the 1921 and 1922 measures.

13. Using the Census definition of 'households' yields the even smaller change of from 1·9 per cent in 1922 to 2·3 per cent in 1953. However, this overlooks an important change in household size over the years. In the 1920s households included many more sub-families than was the case in any period since. (In 1910 23 per cent of persons were heads of households; in 1950, 29 per cent were heads of households. Glick (1957, p. 11). To get around this difficulty it seemed best to adopt the 'adults less married females' concept referred to above as the family measure.

lines a short distance we estimate that the top 2 per cent of families in the two years had 33 per cent of all wealth in 1922 and 29 per cent in 1953. It is apparent that a considerably greater amount of splitting of estates between spouses was being practised in 1953 than in 1922 since the percentage of adults who were top wealth-holders doubled while the percentage of families with a top wealth-holder increased only 40 per cent (see Table 6 and Figure 5.)

Table 6 **Selected data on top wealth-holders 1922 and 1953**

Year	Top wealth-holders' share of total personal equity	Top wealth-holders		
		As % all of persons	As % all of adults	As % all of families
1922	29·2	0·47	0·79	1·4
1953	28·5	1·04	1·68	2·0

It is concluded, then, that the decline in inequality shown on the basis of individuals tends to be an overstatement of the decline which would be found on a family basis.

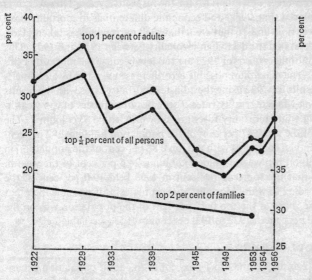

Figure 5 Share of personal sector wealth (equity, basic variant) held by top wealth-holders, selected years, 1922–53 (Source : Table 5, bottom row ; Table 4, bottom row, and Table 6)

Another way to test whether we have really found a decline in inequality or not is to enter a question about how much error there would have to be in the balance sheet estimates upon which all the percentage estimates of wealth-holdings are based in order to invalidate our finding of a decline. Suppose the balance sheet estimates of personal sector total equity are 10 per cent too high in 1953 and 10 per cent too low in 1922. Correction for this assumed error (in the direction unfavourable to the hypothesis that there was a decline in inequality) yields the result that instead of the top wealth-holders having 29·2 per cent of total equity in 1922 and 28·5 per cent in 1953, they would have 26 per cent in 1922 and 32 per cent in 1953. Plotting these points on Figure 4 will indicate that both points could very well lie on the same Lorenz curve and hence that no decline in inequality actually took place. In this writer's judgment there is little likelihood of an error of this size.

Interestingly, the conclusions about changes over the years are not affected by selection of one or another variant of wealth. The gap between prime wealth and total wealth as here defined changed very little in the thirty year period (see Table 3, columns 16, 17 and 18). A more significant difference may be involved in the choice of mortality rates. The findings shown in Table 6 are based on our adjusted mortality rates, calculated as constant percentages of white rates for the respective years. However, it is generally believed that social and economic differentials in mortality have narrowed over time and, to the extent that such narrowing has taken place, we have understated the decline in inequality between 1922 and 1953. This means the multipliers used for 1922 are too low because the mortality rates are too high. The maximum possible error here is suggested by a comparison of the results for 1922 using the adjusted mortality rates with the results for 1953 using white mortality rates. Estimates of numbers of top wealth-holders using white mortality rates are shown in Table 3, column 7. The 1922 result of the top 0·47 per cent of the population holding 29·2 per cent of the wealth then compares with the top 0·88 per cent of the population in 1953 (1·4 million top wealth-holders) holding 24·6 per cent of the wealth. This means that the top 0·47 per cent in 1953 held 19·0 per cent of the wealth, according to white mortality rate estimates. It is possible then that the fall in the share of the top 0·47 per cent of the population was on the order of 29·2 per cent in 1922 to 19·0 per cent in 1953 (see Table 7).[14]

Changes by type of property

Between 1922 and 1953 the top 1 per cent of the adult population experienced a decline in share of personal sector total equity and a decline in the

14. The relative fall of 10 percentage points is meant to be indicated here. The percentage for 1953 is believed to be substantially too low.

Table 7 **Share of personal sector total equity held by top 0·47 per cent of persons**

Year	Adjusted mortality rates	White mortality rates
1922	29·2	—
1953	22·5	19·0

share of most types of property (see Table 8). Notable exceptions are 'stock' and 'other bonds', which appear to have changed little in degree of concentration. All studies of stock ownership indicate that this asset is highly concentrated.[15]

However, the unreasonable variation of some of these series plus the greater than 100 per cent figures for state and local bonds, yield a less than convincing picture. It would seem appropriate to review the possible sources of error in the whole process of estimating wealth distribution. The irregularities referred to above could have arisen out of random errors in the sampling process.[16] For example, the stock figure in one year could be too high because of an unrepresentative age distribution of decedents with large stock holdings. Another possible cause is the selection of mortality rates; we could have the wrong measure of the differential mortality enjoyed by the rich, or, it could be that there are errors in the way property is valued or classified on the estate tax returns. On the other hand, it could be we are confronted with difficulties in the national balance sheet aggregates for the several types of property.[17] It is also possible that we have double-

15. Butters, Thompson and Bollinger (1949, chs 16, 17) give as their best estimate for 1949 (based on S R C data, tax return data, and their own field surveys) the following: The upper 3 per cent of spending units as ranked by income owned 75 per cent of marketable stock; the top 1 per cent, 65 per cent; the top one half of 1 per cent slightly over one half; and the top one tenth of 1 per cent, about 35 per cent of all the marketable stock owned by private investors. They indicate these percentages would be higher if the stock held by personal trust funds were allocated to individuals. As regards a ranking by size of stock-holdings, the 1 per cent of all spending units that owned $10,000 or more of stock accounted for at least two thirds of the total value of stock reported to the *Survey of Consumer Finances*, *Federal Reserve Bulletin* (1952, p. 985). For one measure of concentration of stock ownership by use of a total wealth ranking, see Goldsmith (1956, Table W-53). He estimated that in 1950 those spending units with $60,000 or more of net worth held 76 per cent of corporate stock. The reader is cautioned that rankings by income and wealth are not interchangeable.

16. The top wealth-holder group held substantially more market value in stocks in 1953 than in 1949. The aggregate gross estate of decedent top wealth-holders was 36·5 per cent in stock in 1949, but 40·5 per cent in stock in 1953.

17. It seems probable, for example, that balance sheet difficulties are responsible for the high state and local bonds percentage in 1929 and 1939.

Table 8 **Share of personal sector assets and liabilities, total wealth variant, held by top one per cent of adults, by type of property, 1922, 1929, 1939, 1945, 1949, 1953**[a]

Type of property	1922 (%)	1929	1939	1945	1949	1953
Real estate	18·0	17·3	13·7	11·1	10·5	12·5
US government bonds	45·0	100·0	91·0	32·5	35·8	31·8
State and local bonds	88·0	b	b	b	77·0	b
Other bonds	69·2	82·0	75·5	78·5	78·0	77·5
Corporate stock	61·5	65·6	69·0	61·7	64·9	76·0
Cash	—	—	—	17·0	18·9	24·5
Mortgages and notes	—	—	—	34·7	32·0	30·5
Cash, mortgages and notes	31·0	34·0	31·5	19·3	20·5	25·8
Pension and retirement funds	8·0	8·0	6·0	5·9	5·5	5·0
Insurance	35·3	27·0	17·4	17·3	15·0	11·5
Miscellaneous	23·2	29·0	19·0	21·4	15·0	15·5
Gross estate	32·3	37·7	32·7	25·8	22·4	25·3
Liabilities	23·8	29·0	26·5	27·0	19·0	20·0
Economic estate	33·9	38·8	33·8	25·7	22·8	27·4

[a] Source: Table 1 and companion unpublished tables, column 13. National balance sheet data used for 1922, 1929, and 1939 are from Goldsmith (1956); for 1945, 1949, and 1953, from preliminary unpublished tables by the National Bureau of Economic Research.

[b] In excess of 100 per cent. See text.

counted some of the assets in personal trust funds in making adjustments to move from the basic variant to the prime wealth to the total wealth variant of wealth held by top wealth-holders.

All of these considerations urge that the whole of Table 8 be used in evaluating any single figure in it, and that each individual item be treated with caution.

Comparison with England and Wales

In appraising a given degree of inequality in wealth distribution it is useful to have not only an historical perspective, but a comparison with other national economies. The only other nation for which similar studies have been made is Great Britain. British study of wealth distribution by use of the estate multiplier method goes back to the work of Bernard Mallet in 1908 and includes the later work of G. H. Daniels, H. Campion and T. Barna. More recently Allan M. Cartter, an American, and Kathleen M. Langley (1951) have used this method with British tax data. The British estate tax has had a low filing requirement of £100 and hence the estate multiplier method can give a much more nearly complete picture of wealth distribution for Britain than for this country.

Comparison of inequality in the United States and in England and Wales is made possible by our findings as set forth above and those of Langley, who related her own study of postwar distribution to studies by others of earlier periods. Except for the exclusion of life insurance the British data seem to be quite comparable to our own for the United States. Property in trust is treated in the same way in the two countries. Such a comparison yields the finding of much greater inequality in England and Wales.

A similar finding of greater inequality in England appears in a comparison of the 1953 parallel surveys of net worth conducted in the two countries.[18]

It would appear that the historical picture of decline in the degree of inequality of wealth distribution is similar in the two countries, at least for the period 1922 to 1946 (see Figure 6). However, throughout the whole period the inequality has been considerably greater in England and Wales than in the United States. Langley explains the British decline as follows:

The distribution of capital had gradually become more equal during these years. One per cent of the persons aged twenty-five and over in England and Wales owned 50 per cent of the total capital in 1946–7; in 1936–8 the percentage was 55; in 1924–30 1 per cent of the persons owned 60 per cent of the total capital; while in 1911–13, 1 per cent of the persons owned 70 per cent of the total capital. The scale of wealth had changed from that of 1911–13; there were more people in each of the groups over £100. Inequality had lessened by 1946–7 but capital was still unequally distributed. Ten per cent of the total number of persons aged twenty-five and over owned 80 per cent of the total capital in this period while 61 per cent of the adult population owned 5 per cent of the total capital in 1946–7 (1951, p. 47).

Summary

Thirty per cent of the assets and equities of the personal sector of the economy in 1953 are assignable to the top wealth-holders, i.e. persons with $60,000 or more of estate tax wealth, who were 1·6 per cent of the total adult population that year. The top group owned at least 80 per cent of the corporate stock held in the personal sector, virtually all of the state and local government bonds, nearly 90 per cent of corporate bonds, and

18. K. H. Straw (1956, Table 2, p. 4) supplies us with some clues as to why the difference in inequality may prevail. In Great Britain 16 per cent of the population is over sixty years of age, while the comparable figure for the United States is 12 per cent. In the United States, 9 per cent of the spending units are headed by farm operators while only 1 per cent of the British income units are so headed. In the United States half the spending units own their own homes, while in Britain only 27 per cent of the primary income units own their homes. Also see Lydall and Lansing (1959, pp. 43–67).

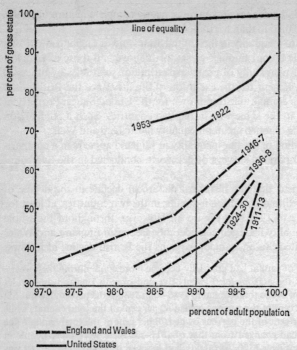

Figure 6 Upper section of Lorenz curves of the shares of personal sector gross estate held by top percentiles of adults, England and Wales and the United States, selected years, 1911–53 (Source: For England and Wales, Langley (1951); for United States, Table 3)

between 10 and 35 per cent of each other type of property held in the personal sector in that year. These relationships are quite close to those found by the Survey of Consumer Finances for the same year.

The top wealth-holder group, defined according to estate-tax requirements, has varied in number and per cent of the total population over the years. Also, their share of total wealth has varied. It appears, however, that the degree of inequality in wealth-holding increased from 1922 to 1929, fell to below the pre-1929 level in the 1930s, fell still more during the war and to 1949 and increased from 1949 to 1956. However, the degree of inequality was considerably lower in 1956 than in either 1929 or 1922.

To make a comparison of degrees of wealth concentration it is convenient to consider a constant percentage of the total adult population. The top 1 per cent of adults held 32 per cent of personal sector equity in 1922, 36 per cent in 1929, 31 per cent in 1939, and 24 per cent in 1953. It is probable that the decline in inequality among individual wealth-holders is greater than would be found if families were considered as the wealth-holding units, since it is apparent from the data that married women are an increasing part of the top wealth-holder group. Converting to a measure of 'adults less married women' suggests that half the percentage decline found for individuals between 1922 and 1953 would disappear on a family basis (Table 9).

Table 9 **Share of personal sector wealth (equity) held by top wealth-holders in 1922 and 1953**

Year	Top 1 % of adults	Top ½ % of all persons	Top 2 % of families[a]
1922	31·6	29·8	33·0
1953	23·6	22·7	29·0

[a] Families here defined as all adults less married females.

In these figures two types of error in estimation are likely to offset each other in some degree. On the one hand, the selection of mortality rates tend to understate the decline in inequality. On the other hand, the differences over time in completeness of reporting personal sector wealth and of estate tax wealth may tend to overstatement of the decline. It is difficult to imagine any combination of errors which would yield a result of increasing concentration over time. Interestingly, the conclusions about changes in concentration of wealth over the years are not affected by selection of one or another variant of wealth.

A leading exception to the general picture of declining concentration is corporate stock. This particular type of asset appears to have become no less concentrated in ownership over time.

Inequality of wealth distribution is considerably greater in Great Britain than in the United States, but a pattern of similar historical decline in inequality is observable in the two countries.

It helps to place these findings in perspective to compare them with Kuznets' findings (1953). He traced changes in the shares of the upper 1 and 5 per cent of persons in a per capita distribution from 1913 to 1948 and found that the top 5 per cent's share of basic variant income had a rather narrow range of movement during the period 1919–38, with no perceptible and sustained change. However, he found that 'From 1939 to 1944 it dropped from 23·7 to 16·8 per cent – almost 7 percentage points in five years; and in 1947 and 1948 its level was only slightly higher – 17·6 and 17·8 per cent respectively. During the last decade, then, the share of the top 5 per cent declined about a quarter' (Kuznets, 1953, p. 37). The fall for the top 1 per cent was from 12 per cent in 1939 and 1940 to about 8½ per cent in 1947 and 1948. In the disposable income variant the top 5 per cent's share fell by well over three tenths, from 27·1 to 17·9 per cent.

Our finding that the share of wealth held by the top 2 per cent of families fell from about 33 per cent to 29 per cent from 1922 to 1953, or by about one eighth, would seem to be not incompatible with Kuznets' findings[19] and with the general belief that there has been some lessening of economic inequality in the United States in recent decades. Wealth distribution appears to have changed less than income distribution during this period.

19. Kuznets' per capita distribution of income should not be confused with a per capita earner distribution. In the former family income is divided by number of family members to obtain an array of families (or individuals) by per capita income. Since our wealth-holder data are not calculated on a per capita basis we cannot make a direct comparison with Kuznets' findings on income. Our estimates of the distribution of wealth by families seems to be conceptually closest to Kuznets' per capita procedure.

References

BUTTERS, J. K., THOMPSON L. E., and BOLLINGER, D. L. (1949), *Effects of Taxation: Investments by Individuals*, Harvard University Graduate School of Business.

CRUM, W. L. (1935), *The Distribution of Wealth*, Harvard University Graduate School of Business.

Federal Reserve Bulletin (1952), *Survey of Consumer Finances*, p. 985.

Federal Reserve Bulletin (1953), *Survey of Consumer Finances*.

Federal Reserve Bulletin (1958), 'Difficulties of survey data', p. 1047.

GLICK, P. (1957), *American Families*, Wiley.

GOLDSMITH, R. W. (1956), *A Study of Saving in the United States*, vol. 3, Princeton University Press.

HOLMES, G. K. (1893), 'The concentration of wealth', *Pol. Sci. Q.*, vol. 8, pp. 589–600.

KING, W. I. (1927), 'Wealth distribution in the continental United States', *J. Amer. stat. Assoc.*, p. 152.

KUZNETS, S. (1953), *Shares of Upper Income Groups in Income and Savings*, National Bureau of Economic Research.

LANGLEY, K. M. (1951), 'The distribution of capital in private hands in 1936–8 and 1946–7', *Bull. Oxford Univ. Inst. Stats.*, p. 46, Table 15B.

LYDALL, H. F., and LANSING, J. B. (1959), 'A comparison of the distribution of personal income and wealth in the United States and Great Britain', *Amer. econ. Rev.*, vol. 49, pp. 43–67.

SPAHR, C. B. (1896), *The Present Distribution of Wealth in the United States*, Cromwell.

STRAW, K. H. (1956), 'Consumers' net worth, the 1953 savings survey', *Bull. Oxford Univ. Inst. Stat.*, Table 2, p. 4.

17 J. E. Meade

Factors Determining the Distribution of Property

Extract from J. E. Meade, *Efficiency, Equality and the Ownership of Property*, Allen &
Unwin, 1964, pp. 41–52.

Let us turn our attention therefore to the questions why in the sort of free-
enterprise or mixed economy with which we are familiar we end up with
such startling inequalities in the ownership of property, what changes in
our institutional or tax arrangements would be necessary substantially to
equalize ownership, and what disadvantages from the point of view of
efficiency these reforms could themselves have.

I shall consider these matters in three stages. First, I shall assume that we
are dealing simply with a number of adult citizens who have presumably
been born in the past but who do not marry or have children or die or even
grow old in the sense of experiencing diminished ability or vigour as time
passes. I shall at this first stage examine the effects upon property distribution as these citizens work, save, and accumulate property. I shall
assume that the State taxes neither income nor property and does not interfere in any way with this process of private capital accumulation.

At a second stage I shall introduce the demographic factors – births,
marriages, deaths – and will examine the way in which they are likely to
modify the pattern of ownership that would otherwise be developing.

At the third stage I will introduce the State. At this stage we shall be concerned with the ways in which economic and financial policies might be
devised to modify the economic and demographic factors in such a way as
to lead to a more equal distribution of property (not included here – Ed.).

For the first stage I will employ a method which has been pioneered for
another purpose by my colleague Dr L. Pasinetti (1962).[1]

1. Pasinetti assumes two classes of persons: workers who save a low proportion of
their income and capitalists who do no work but save a high proportion of their income.
Since workers save, they also accumulate property; and Pasinetti is concerned with the
distribution of property between workers and capitalists which will result from this
dual process of capital accumulation as time passes. His obiect is to consider the
ultimate steady-state ratio between savings and profits in order to use this relationship
for the theory of economic growth. In an article by myself (Meade, 1963) I criticized
some of Pasinetti's assumptions but suggested that the Pasinetti process, with certain
modifications of assumptions about the distribution of earning power and about pro-
pensities to save, might serve as a powerful instrument in analysing the forces affecting

Consider two personal properties a small one K_1 and a larger one K_2. Will the small property be growing at a smaller or a larger proportional rate of growth than the large property? If the small property is growing at a greater proportional rate (say, 5 per cent per annum) than the large property (say, 2 per cent per annum), then the ratio of K_1/K_2 will be becoming more nearly equal to unity. In this case *relative* inequality will be diminishing.[2] We are concerned then at this first stage of our enquiry with the factors which will determine the proportional rate of growth of different properties.

These proportional growth rates (which we will call k_1 and k_2) for our two properties may be expressed as

$$k_1 = \frac{S_1(E_1 + V_1 K_1)}{K_1} \quad \text{and} \quad k_2 = \frac{S_2(E_2 + V_2 K_2)}{K_2}$$

respectively, where E_1 and E_2 represent the earned incomes or wages of the two property owners and V_1 and V_2 represent the two rates of profit earned by the two owners on their properties K_1 and K_2. Thus $V_1 K_1$ and $V_2 K_2$ represent the unearned incomes of the two property owners and $E_1 + V_1 K_1$ and $E_2 + V_2 K_2$ their earned and unearned incomes. If S_1 and S_2 represent the proportions of these incomes which are saved and added to accumulated property, then $S_1(E_1 + V_1 K_1)$ and $S_2(E_2 + V_2 K_2)$ are the absolute annual increases in the two properties and these, expressed as a ratio of the two properties measure their proportionate rates of growth.

In these pages I can do little more than enumerate the various influences at work. Some of them, it will be seen, tend to make $k_1 > k_2$ (these are the equalizing tendencies, and some tend to make $k_2 > k_1$ (these are the disequalizing tendencies). There is undoubtedly at work a large element of these latter disequalizing tendencies – what Professor Myrdal has called the principle of Circular and Cumulative Causation – the 'to-him-that-hath-shall-be-given' principle. On the other hand, trees do not grow up to the skies, and there are some systematic equalizing tendencies. It is the balance between these equalizing and disequalizing factors which results in the end in a given unequal, but not indefinitely unequal, distribution of properties. Let us consider in turn the influences of E, V and S upon the rate of growth of property k.

1. The influence of earned incomes, E, must be an equalizing factor so far as two properties at the extreme ranges of the scale of properties are con-

---

the distribution of the ownership of property. It is this application of the Pasinetti process which is the subject of the present section of this book.

2. *Absolute* inequality (i.e. $K_2 - K_1$) might, of course, be increasing; but it is, I think *relative* inequality which should concern us most. That one property should be £10,000 greater than another may be of great importance when K_1 is £1000 and K_2 is £11,000 and of very little importance if K_1 is £100,000 and K_2 £110,000.

cerned. We can see the point this way. If K_1 were zero, citizen 1 would have only an earned income E_1. If he saved any part of this, his savings would be $S_1 E_1$ and his proportionate rate of accumulation of property would be

$$\frac{S_1 E_1}{0} = \infty.$$

Consider at the other extreme a multi-multi-multi-millionaire. Now earning power, E_1 may well be enhanced by the ownership of property, but not without limit. In the case of our multi-multi-multi-millionaire, E_2 will be negligible relatively to K_2. If E_2/K_2 were for practical purposes zero, k_2 would equal

$$\frac{S_2 V_2 K_2}{K_2} = S_2 V_2.$$

As between the extreme ranges then, we have $k_1 > k_2$ and there is bound to be equalization. This is perhaps the basic reason why our measure of relative inequality K_1/K_2 can never reach zero or infinity. In the intermediate ranges, all we can say is that the higher is E/K, the more rapid the rate of growth of property k, other things being equal. If earning power were equally distributed among our citizens (with $E_1 = E_2$), then this factor would be an equalizing one as between any two properties K_1 and K_2.

$$k_1 = S_1 \frac{E_1}{K_1} + S_1 V_1 \quad \text{and} \quad k_2 = S_2 \frac{E_2}{K_2} + S_2 V_2.$$

If $S_1 = S_2$, $E_1 = E_2$, and $V_1 = V_2$, then $k_1 > k_2$ if $K_1 < K_2$.

2. The factor V, on the other hand, is unquestionably disequalizing – at least in the United Kingdom where there is strong evidence that the rate of return on property is much lower for small properties than for large properties.[3] This is so even if one does not take into account capital gains; but, of course, capital gains should be included in the return on capital. Since the wealthy in the United Kingdom at least invest on tax grounds for capital gains rather than for income, the inclusion of capital gains in V_2 and V_1 would make the excess of V_2 over V_1 even more marked; and this is clearly an influence which will raise k_2 above k_1.[4] It is probable that there will be

3. It will be remembered that at this stage we are dealing with incomes before tax is deducted.

4. The influence of capital gains could be even more marked than is implied in the text. Suppose that property owners regard as their income only the income paid out on their property and save a fraction of this, but in addition automatically accumulate 100 per cent of any capital gain not paid out in dividend or rent or interest. Then the formula for k becomes

$$k = S \frac{E}{K} + SV + V'$$

little difference in the V which is relevant for all properties above a certain range. It is doubtful whether the multi-millionaire can get any higher yield than the millionaire on his property. But as between the really small properties and the large range of big properties, this influence is likely to be disequalizing and to be a factor enabling the whole range of large properties to grow more rapidly than the small.

3. Finally, what is the influence of S, the proportion of income saved, on k for different sizes of K? Economists have done a great deal of theoretical and statistical work on the factors determining the proportions of income saved and spent. These investigations are of basic importance not only for theories of employment and of growth (i.e. for the determination of the 'multiplier' and of the relationships between the rate of profit, the rate of growth, and the capital-output ratio) but also for the determination of the distribution among individuals of the ownership of property.

Let us consider only the implications of two possible features of a probable type of savings function.[5] Let us assume (a) that the proportion of income saved rises with a rise in real income, though not, of course, without limit, since less than 100 per cent of income will be saved however great is income, and (b) that the proportion of income saved out of any given income falls the larger is the property owned. This second assumption means that a man with £1000 a year all earned will save more than a man with £1000 a year which represents the interest on a property of £10,000. For the ability to save will be the same, but the need to accumulate some property will be higher in the first than in the second case.

If the savings function is of this general form, then as between two unequal properties ($K_2 > K_1$) owned by two persons with the same earning power ($E_1 = E_2$), we cannot, without more precise information, say which will be growing the more rapidly. The fact that a larger total income will be enjoyed by the man with the larger property will tend to raise the proportion of income which he can save; but, on the other hand, the fact that he already has a larger property will tend to reduce the proportion of income which he will save, and, in addition, the fact that E/K is low in his case will keep down the rate of growth of his property (see pp. 296-7 above).

But with the sort of savings function which we are assuming there are two other kinds of comparison which one can make with more definite results. If one compares two citizens with equal incomes but unequal properties, the small property of the man with the high earning power will be growing

---

where V is the paid-out rate of return on capital and V' is the rate of return from capital gains. An excess of V'_2 over V'_1 will have an even more marked effect than an equal excess of V_2 over V_1 in raising k_2 above k_1.

5. Strong evidence for the importance of these factors in the savings function is given in Stone (1964).

the more rapidly; he has the same ability to save but a greater need to accumulate; his savings will be greater and his existing property smaller. If one compares two citizens with the same property, but different incomes, the property of the man with the high income (i.e. the high earning power) will be growing the more rapidly; he has a higher ability to save and the same need to accumulate; his savings will be greater and his existing property the same. The result is, of course, that with our assumed savings function there will be exceptionally strong forces at work associating high properties with high earning power. This combination of forces will exaggerate the inequality in the distribution of total personal incomes.

Let us pass to the second stage of our examination of the factors determining the distribution of property, namely the demographic factors. Consider two citizens, man and wife, each with a property. The rate of growth of their properties is determined by the economic factors we have just considered – S, E, V and K. They have children. These children grow up and start to earn and to save – they acquire Es and Ss of their own. They start to accumulate properties of their own, at first at indefinitely high proportional rates of growth, since they start with no property. At some time both parents die and leave their properties to their children. The children at some time – it may be before or after their parents' deaths – choose spouses. And so two citizens and two properties 'join together in holy matrimony' and restart the same process of marriage, birth and death.

What we want to consider is whether the factors of marriage, birth and death will lead to a greater or a lesser degree of concentration of property ownership than would have occurred through the processes of capital accumulation which we examined at stage one in the absence of marriage, births and deaths. The answer depends upon two things: the degree of assortative mating and the degree of differential fertility.

Suppose that any man was equally likely to be married to any woman in our society. Suppose, that is to say, that there were no assortative mating. Then the cycle of birth, marriage and death would introduce an important equalizing factor into the system. Let us isolate for examination this basic demographic factor by assuming for the moment that every married couple reproduces itself by producing one son and one daughter and then leaves half the joint property of the parents to each child. Consider in this context the wealthiest family in the community, i.e. the family which has the highest joint property of husband and wife; they have a son and a daughter who, if they married each other, would perpetuate the same extreme concentration of wealth which they inherited from their parents; but brother and sister do not marry each other; the rich son must marry a wife with less inherited property than himself and the rich daughter a husband with less inherited property than herself; they in turn have children who are not so much enriched by inheritance as they themselves were. The general reshuffle generation by generation through marriage tends to equalize inherited fortunes. If there were no assortative mating, there would be a strong probability that a citizen whose inheritance was exceptionally high would marry someone with a smaller inheritance and that a citizen whose inheritance was exceptionally low would marry someone with a larger inheritance. But of course in fact marriage is strongly assortative. The rich are brought up in the same social milieu as the rich, and the poor in the same social milieu as the poor. The reshufflement of property ownership is very much less marked.

Differential fertility could clearly have an important influence on the distribution of property. If rich parents had fewer children than did poor parents, the large fortunes would become more and more concentrated in fewer and fewer hands. If the rich had more children than the poor, the large properties would fall in relative size as they become more and more widely dispersed and the smaller would grow in relative size as they become more and more concentrated on a smaller number of children. At first sight it might, therefore, appear as if differential fertility might work in either direction – equalizing property ownership if the rich were exceptionally fertile and disequalizing it if the rich were exceptionally infertile. And this would, of course, be so in the short run; and it would be so in the long run as well, if there were some forces at work which caused riches itself to lead to exceptionally high or exceptionally low fertility.

But consider another possible type of cause of differential fertility. Suppose (a) that every couple has at least one child, but (b) that there is some genetic factor at work which makes some couples more fertile than others and (c) that this genetic factor is in no way correlated positively or negatively with any other relevant genetic characteristic. We may happen to start with the infertile at the bottom end of the property scale; if so, the immediate effect will be to tend to equalize property ownership. But gradually as time passes the infertile will be found, through the process of concentrated inheritance, further and further up the property scale. In the end it will be the rich who are the infertile and the poor who are the fertile. The permanent influence of such a form of differential fertility will thus ultimately be disequalizing in its effect upon property ownership.

But sons and daughters are endowed not only with inherited property but also with earning power. Here we are confronted with the great problem of nature *versus* nurture. Earning power undoubtedly depends largely upon environmental factors. We have already observed the great importance of investment in education in raising earning power. In a society which (as we are assuming in this second stage of our inquiry) left everything including education to private market forces rich fathers could educate their sons much more readily than could poor fathers. The inheritance of a good education would be just like the inheritance of tangible wealth from rich parents.

But high earning power is not wholly due to education and other environmental factors; there can be no doubt that there are also some genetic factors at work in determining a person's ability to earn. In so far as this is the case, there may be a social mechanism at work analogous to, although not identical with, the mechanism which some scholars have suspected to be at work in the case of social class and intelligence.[6] Let us very briefly outline this mechanism in the case of social class and intelligence and then point the possible analogy with property and earning power.

Suppose that whatever quality it may be which is measured by an intelligence test is a quality which enables one to succeed in modern life, so that there is some tendency for the intelligent to move up, and the unintelligent to move down, the social scale. Then at any one time one would expect to find a positive correlation between intelligence and social class; the more intelligent citizens will tend to be found with greater frequency at the top of the social ladder. Suppose further that whatever is measured by an intelligence test is a quality which has at least *some* genetic element in its causation. One would in that case expect to find some positive correlation, but a less than perfect correlation, between the intelligence of parents and the intelligence of their children. The children of intelligent parents would tend to be intelligent but not as intelligent as their parents; the children of unintelligent parents would tend to be unintelligent but not as unintelligent as their parents. This 'regression towards the mean' is to be explained by the fact that an intelligent father, transmitting only one of each of his chromosome pairs to his son, will on the average transmit only one half of the genes which made him exceptionally intelligent. The son of such a father has a higher chance than the average of being exceptionally intelligent, but on the average is not likely to be as exceptionally intelligent as his father (Carter, 1962).

As the following figures show, this is the pattern which in fact one finds (Burt, 1967, pp. 3–25). Column 1 shows how intelligence is higher, the higher the citizen concerned stands on the social scale. Column 2 shows the 'regression towards the mean'. The most (least) intelligent parents have children with above-average (below-average) intelligence, but not so much above-average (below-average) as the parents. The genetic 'regression towards the mean' tends to equalize the distribution of intelligence between social classes; but social mobility upwards of those children whose intelligence

6. See Young and Gibson (1963, pp. 27–36).

Table 1 Mean IQs of parent and child according to class of parents

	Parent	Child
Higher professional	139·7	120·8
Lower professional	130·6	114·7
Clerical	115·9	107·8
Skilled	108·2	104·6
Semi-skilled	97·8	98·9
Unskilled	84·9	92·6
Average	100·0	100·0

happens by the luck of the genetic draw to be high relatively to the social class of their parents, and mobility downwards for those children whose intelligence happens to be low relatively to the social class of their parents, restores the original association between class and intelligence displayed in the parents' generation.

Such is the hypothesis. If we had the figures and could draw up a similar table for property ownership and earning ability, would we find the same kind of relationship? It is possible that by the mechanism of accumulation already described (that is to say, because high earning power makes it easier to accumulate property) there is some positive correlation between large properties and high earning power. But if earning power is to some extent genetically determined, one would expect to find rich parents with high earning power having children with above average earning power, but not so much above-average as themselves; and one would expect to find the poorest parents with the lowest earning power having children with below-average earning power but not so much below average as themselves. But

	Earning power of	
	Owners	Children of owners
Very large properties	?	?
Large properties	?	?
Medium properties	?	?
Small properties	?	?
Very small properties	?	?

the association between property ownership and earning power may nevertheless be restored in the next generation by the exceptionally rapid accumulation of property by those children who happen to be born with exceptionally high earning power relatively to their inherited property and by the exceptionally slow rate of accumulation by those children who happen to be born with exceptionally low earning power relatively to their inherited property.

All that one can say in the present unhappy state of almost complete ignorance about this important aspect of society is that in so far as earning power is a factor which leads to the accumulation of property, then any 'regression towards the mean' in the inheritance of earning power would in itself tend to equalize the distribution of the ownership of property.[7]

We have so far considered some of the economic and biological factors which may systematically work towards the equalization or the disequalization of the ownership of property. But there are, of course, for any individual enormously important elements of pure environmental luck. Was a man lucky or unlucky in the actual school to which he went as a child and in the actual teachers which he there encountered? Was he lucky or unlucky in the actual locality in which he sought work or took his business initiatives? Was he lucky or unlucky in the choice of the subject matter of his education and training? In the choice of industries in which he invested his first savings or initial inheritance? In the bright ideas which he tried to exploit? A lucky combination of an able man with the right idea in the right place at the right time can – as in the case of men such as Ford – lead to an explosive growth of an individual property. We must regard society from the point of view of property ownership as subject to a series of random strokes of good and bad luck, upsetting continuously the existing pattern of ownership. But at the same time there are at work the systematic economic forces of accumulation and the systematic biological and demographic forces of inheritance which are some of them tending to equalize and some of them to disequalize ownership. The striking inequalities which we observe in the real world are the result of the balance of these systematic forces working in a society subject to the random strokes of luck. That is all we can say until this most important field for research and inquiry has been cultivated much more extensively than has been the case up to the present.

7. The preceding paragraphs suggest that (i) low fertility and (ii) high ability to earn may both be factors which tend to raise people upon the social scale and the property ladder. These factors probably both have some genetic elements in their determination. Moreover, it is a well-known fact that men and women are likely to marry within their own class. Thus there may be a continuous process tending to mate the genes for ability with those for infertility and the genes for inability with those for fertility. The dysgenic aspect of such a social arrangement is obvious (cf. Fisher, pp. 22–32).

References

BURT, C. Sir (1961), 'Intelligence and social mobility', *Brit. J. Stat. Psychol.*, vol. 14, pp. 3–25.
CARTER, C. O. (1962), *Human Heredity*, Penguin.
FISHER, R. A. (1932), *The Social Selection of Human Fertility*, Clarendon Press.
MEADE, J. E. (1963), 'The rate of profit in a growing economy', *Econ. J.*, vol. 73, pp. 665–74.

PASINETTI, L. (1962), 'Rate of profit and income distribution in relation to the rate of economic growth', *Rev. econ. Stud.*, vol. 29, no. 4, pp. 267–79.

STONE, R. (1964), 'Private saving in Britain: past, present and future', The Manchester School.

YOUNG, M., and GIBSON J. (1963), 'In search of an explanation of social mobility', *Brit. J. Stat. Psychol.*, vol. 16, pp. 27–36.

18 J. E. Stiglitz

Distribution of Income and Wealth Among Individuals

J. E. Stiglitz, 'Distribution of income and wealth among individuals', *Econometrical*, vol. 37, 1969, pp. 382–97.

1 Introduction

Although the recent literature has abounded with alternative theories of distribution of income among factors of production, there have been few attempts to develop a theory of distribution of wealth and income among individuals.[1] The purpose of this study is to isolate some of the economic forces which in the long run tend to equalize wealth and some which tend to make it less evenly distributed. In particular, we examine the implications for distribution of alternative assumptions about the form of the consumption function, the heterogeneity of labor skills, inheritance policies, and the response of the reproduction rate to different levels of income.

We begin by considering a simple model of accumulation, with a linear savings function, a constant reproduction rate, homogeneous labor, and equal division of wealth among one's heirs. In such an economy, if the balanced growth path is stable, all wealth and income is asymptotically evenly distributed, with the possible exception, in the case of negative savings at zero income, of a group with zero wealth. In the process of accumulation, there may, however, be a period during which wealth becomes less evenly distributed. We then show that the basic conclusions are unaltered under a variety of alternative savings assumptions, where savings is a function of wealth or of the distribution of income, or where savings is a nonlinear concave function of income, and that variable rates of reproduction make no difference at least to the asymptotic results. The effects of alternative taxes on the speed of equalization are investigated in Section 4 and in Section 5 we consider a simple example to see the order of magnitudes of time that are involved in the equalization process.

In the remaining sections of the paper, we investigate the 'forces for

1. Notable exceptions to this are the work of Champernowne (1953) and Mandelbrot (1961), but their work suffers from the deficiency that the distribution of income is determined by a stochastic process, the character of which seems to have little to do with economic processes themselves. They seem to have little to say about, for instance, the relationship of the distribution of income among factors to the distribution of income among individuals.

inequality': heterogeneity of labor force, class savings behavior, and alternative inheritance policies.

2 The basic model

In this section (and throughout the paper), it will be convenient to think of society as divided into a number of groups; all the members of any one group have the same wealth but groups differ in their *per capita* wealth holdings.

We assume that labor is homogeneous (all workers receive the same wage). Thus, all the members of any one group have the same income as well as the same wealth. Each factor is paid its marginal product. We assume a concave, constant returns to scale production function[2]; if y is output per man and k is the aggregate capital–labor ratio, then

$$y = f(k), \qquad f'(k) > 0, \qquad f'' < 0. \tag{2.1}$$

If w is the wage rate, and r the interest rate,[3]

$$r = f'(k), \qquad w = f(k) - kf'(k). \tag{2.2}$$

If y_i is the income *per capita* of group i, and c_i is the capital per man, then

$$y_i = w + rc_i. \tag{2.3}$$

Savings *per capita* is assumed to be a linear function of income *per capita*. Hence if s_i is the *per capita* savings of group i, m the (constant) marginal propensity to save, and b the per capita savings at zero income, then

$$s_i = my_i + b. \tag{2.4}$$

Reproduction occurs at a constant rate n, there is no intermarriage between income groups, and wealth is divided equally among one's offspring. These assumptions ensure that the proportion of the population in each group, a_i, remains constant.

We can now write down the basic equation of *per capita* wealth accumulation for group i:

$$\frac{\dot{c_i}}{c_i} = \frac{s_i}{c_i} - n = \frac{b + mw}{c_i} + mr - n. \tag{2.5}$$

2. Satisfying the Inada derivative conditions.

3. For most of the analysis, all we require is that the interest rate be a declining function of the capital–labor ratio and that the wage rate be an increasing function of the capital–labor ratio.

Moreover, if we let K_i be the total wealth holdings of group i, and define

$$k_i = \frac{K_i}{L} = a_i c_i, \qquad\qquad 2.6$$

it is clear that

$$k = \sum k_i = \sum a_i c_i. \qquad\qquad 2.7$$

Then the differential equation for aggregate capital accumulation is

$$\dot{k} = \sum \dot{k}_i = \sum a_i \dot{c}_i = b + mw + mrk - nk. \qquad\qquad 2.8$$

Observe that *the aggregate capital accumulation behavior is independent of the distribution of wealth*. This is an essential result of the linearity assumption.

In analysing this model, we shall first discuss the aggregate balanced growth paths and their stability. We shall then discuss the conditions under which a given group is in equilibrium, i.e. has unchanging *per capita* wealth. Next, we will consider short and long run movements in the wealth distribution. Finally, we will investigate what these results imply for movements in the distribution of income.

Aggregate balanced growth paths

If the economy is in balanced growth, $\dot{k} = 0$, i.e.

$$my = nk - b. \qquad\qquad 2.9$$

In the case of $b = 0$, a strictly proportional savings function, this is simply the 'Solow' equilibrium. If $b > 0$, there is a unique value for which $my = nk$, i.e. a unique aggregate balanced growth path. If, on the other hand, $b < 0$ (at a zero income a negative amount is saved), then there will in general exist two balanced growth paths.[4]

If there is only one balanced growth path, it is globally stable, since for capital–labor ratios greater than that of the balanced growth path, savings *per capita* is less than that required to maintain the same capital–output ratio with population growing at the rate n. The converse follows for capital–labor ratios less than that of the balanced growth path.

On the other hand, if there are two balanced growth paths (Figure 1), the lower one will be locally unstable and the upper will be locally stable. Differentiating the capital accumulation equation **2.8** with respect to k and evaluating it at $\dot{k} = 0$, we obtain

$$\frac{\partial \dot{k}}{\partial k} = mr - n. \qquad\qquad 2.10$$

4. These results are contingent on the concavity of the production function and on the production function satisfying the Inada conditions.

The balanced growth path is stable or unstable as $\partial \dot{k}/\partial k$ is less than or greater than zero. The slope of the my curve is mr, and n is the slope of the $nk-b$ curve. Since my is concave, it is clear that the lower intersection must have $mr > n$ and the upper intersection must have $mr < n$.[5]

Thus, to the left of the lower equilibrium, savings per man is less than that required to sustain that capital–labor ratio, and hence the capital–labor ratio falls (continually).[6] Above the lower equilibrium, but below the upper equilibrium (between k^* and k^{**} on Figure 1) the reverse situation holds, so that the economy has an expanding capital–labor ratio. Finally, above the upper equilibrium (k^{**}), the economy has a declining capital–labor ratio.

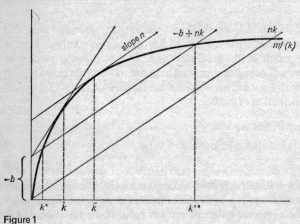

Figure 1

Equilibrium for wealth–income groups

Having analysed the aggregate properties of the model, we turn now to investigate the behavior of the separate wealth–income groups.

It should be clear that for any given aggregate capital–labor ratio k, there can exist at most only one group, with *per capita* wealth c^*, which is in equilibrium, i.e. only one group whose *per capita* wealth is neither increasing nor decreasing. We require $\dot{c}_i/c_i = 0$ or

5. In the singular case of a tangency between the my curve and the $nk-b$ curve, where the upper and lower equilibria merge together, we have a stable-unstable equilibrium: stable with respect to upward deviations, unstable with respect to downward deviations. In this equilibrium, $mr = n$, the rate of profit is equal to the rate of growth divided by the marginal propensity to save.

6. What happens when $k = 0$ is a question which we shall postpone for the moment. Negative k is possible only if there exist foreign countries from whom one can borrow. For a long run savings function it may well be argued on the basis of econometric evidence that b is zero; we prefer, however, to keep the analysis as general as possible.

$$c^* = \frac{b+mw\,(k)}{n-mr\,(k)}.$$ **2.11**

(Observe that c^* is a function of k.)

If we define (see Figure 1)

$$w(\hat{k}) = f(\hat{k}) - \hat{k}f'(\hat{k}) = -\frac{b}{m}$$ **2.12**

and

$$r(\tilde{k}) = f'(\tilde{k}) = \frac{n}{m},$$ **2.13**

then, because of concavity of $f(k)$, $k^* < \hat{k} < \tilde{k} < k^{**}$, and if

$k < k^*,$	$my+b-nk < 0,$	$mr-n > 0,$	$mw+b < 0;$
$k^* < k < \hat{k},$	$my+b-nk > 0,$	$mr-n > 0,$	$mw+b < 0;$
$\hat{k} < k < \tilde{k},$	$my+b-nk > 0,$	$mr-n > 0,$	$mw+b > 0;$ **2.14**
$\tilde{k} < k < k^{**},$	$my+b-nk > 0,$	$mr-n < 0,$	$mw+b > 0;$
$k^{**} < k,$	$my+b-nk < 0,$	$mr-n < 0,$	$mw+b > 0.$

It immediately follows that for any given k, there is a unique wealth-income group in equilibrium, and that $c^* > 0$ if $k < \hat{k}$ or if $k > \tilde{k}$, but $c^* < 0$ if $\hat{k} < k < \tilde{k}$.

It should be observed, however, that in the first case, with $k < \hat{k}$, groups with *per capita* wealth less than c^* have decreasing *per capita* wealth, while if $k > \tilde{k}$, groups with *per capita* wealth less than c^* have increasing *per capita* wealth. (The converse is true for those with *per capita* wealth greater than c^*.) In the intermediate case, all groups with wealth greater than c^*, and in particular, all groups with positive wealth holdings, have increasing *per capita* wealth.

Movements in distribution of wealth

We examine now how the distribution of wealth changes over time. Without loss of generality, we consider the case of two income groups. We wish to know whether c_1 is growing faster or slower than c_2, given that $c_1 < c_2$. If it is growing faster, then the ownership of wealth (at least in a relative sense) is becoming more 'equalitarian', if it is growing slower, it is becoming less 'equalitarian'. But

$$\frac{\dot{c}_1}{c_1} - \frac{\dot{c}_2}{c_2} = (b+mw)\left(\frac{1}{c_1} - \frac{1}{c_2}\right).$$ **2.15**

Hence, if $b+mw > 0$, the ownership of wealth becomes (relatively) more equalitarian, while if $b+mw < 0$, it becomes 'worse'. If $b = -mw$, there is no change in the (relative) ownership of property. Hence, to the left of $\hat{k}$ the ownership of capital is becoming more uneven; to the right it is becoming more even.

The economic reasoning behind this result should be clear. If $b+mw$ is equal to zero, increasing *per capita* wealth by a given percentage increases savings (mrc_i) by the same percentage, but it also increases the savings required to sustain that *per capita* wealth (nc_i) by the same percentage, so that whatever c_i happens to be, there it remains. If $b+mw$ is positive, increasing *per capita* wealth by a given percentage increases (*per capita*) savings by a smaller percentage, while the savings required to sustain that *per capita* wealth ratio goes up in proportion to c_i, and conversely for $b+mw$ less than zero.

Thus if the economy asymptotically converges to the upper equilibrium in the long run, there must be an equalitarian distribution of wealth, since at the upper equilibrium the wealth per man of the poorer groups grows faster than that of the richer groups. Indeed, if the economy is in balanced growth we can rewrite equation **2.15** as

$$\frac{\dot{c}_i}{c_i} - \frac{\dot{c}_j}{c_j} = (n-mr)k\left(\frac{1}{c_i} - \frac{1}{c_j}\right). \qquad 2.16$$

Since the condition for stability for aggregate equilibrium is $n-mr > 0$, we have the general proposition that, *if the economy is at a stable equilibrium, the distribution of wealth must eventually be equalitarian.*[7]

But at the lower equilibrium, those groups with initial *per capita* wealth less than the equilibrium will grow continually poorer, while those groups with initial *per capita* wealth greater than the equilibrium will grow continually richer. This follows from

$$\dot{c}_i = mw+b+mrk^*+m(c_i-k^*)r-nk^*-n(c_i-k^*)$$

$$= (c_i-k^*)(mr-n) \lessgtr 0 \qquad \text{as} \quad c_i \lessgtr k^*.$$

(And of course, those with more initial *per capita* wealth have a faster rate of growth of *per capita* wealth.)[8]

7. Thus, the fact that poor individuals have a lower average propensity to save than that of rich individuals does not necessarily mean that over time the distribution of wealth will become more disparate. See Friedman (1957), especially chapter 4.

8. If there is a lower bound on the amount of capital that one can hold (an upper bound on indebtedness), then we must modify our savings functions. Assume that the lower bound is zero. Then

$$s_i = b+mw+mrc_i \quad (c_i > 0),$$
$$s_i = 0, \qquad\qquad\quad (c_i = 0).$$

We assume that there are two groups, a 'poor' group with zero wealth and with a of the population, and a 'rich' group with $1-a$ of the population and all the capital.

Thus it should be clear that although the fact that each of the individual groups is in equilibrium implies that the aggregate is in equilibrium, the converse is not true. The aggregate can be in equilibrium while the distribution of wealth is changing.

We are finally ready to fully describe movements of the distribution of wealth in our economy.

1. There exist in general two balanced growth paths,[9] along which the capital–labor ratio, output–capital ratio, wage rate, etc. are all constant.

2. The one corresponding to the higher capital–labor ratio is stable both with respect to the aggregate (locally) and with respect to the component income classes (globally). If the overall capital–labor ratio is increased or decreased (provided it does not fall below k^*), the economy returns to the balanced growth path, and if individual income classes are perturbed, the economy eventually returns to the equalitarian state.

3. The one corresponding to the lower capital–labor ratio is unstable, both with respect to the aggregate and with respect to the component income classes. If the aggregate k is decreased, it continues to decrease (forever); if it is increased, it continues to increase until it arrives at the upper equilibrium. If individual income classes are perturbed from the equal distribution position in such a way that the aggregate capital–labor ratio remains constant, the classes with *per capita* wealth greater than the overall capital–labor ratio continually increase their *per capita* wealth. The converse is true for those with less wealth than the 'average'.

4. If the economy is initially within the region between k^* and $\hat{k}$, then the overall capital–labor ratio is increasing and the economy eventually arrives

---

Then

$$\dot{k} = (1-a)(b+mw)+(mr-n)k$$
$$= (1-a)b+mf(k)(1-a\alpha(k))-nk = \Psi(k)$$

where $y = w+rk = f(k)$ and $\alpha(k) = w/f(k)$. Then $\Psi'(k) = mf'+kf''am-n$. Hence, for $k > \tilde{k}, \Psi'(k) < 0$, and thus there can exist at most one equilibrium with $k > \tilde{k}$.

But since $\Psi''(k) = mf''(1+a)+f'''kma$, which depends on the third derivative of $f(k)$, there may exist more than one solution with $k < \tilde{k}$.

If the elasticity of substitution equals one, then there will exist at most two solutions, since the capital accumulation equation is identical to that examined earlier, with m replaced by $m(1-a\alpha)$.

We can extend these results to the case where the lower limit of *per capita* wealth is not zero, but e. Then, in the balanced growth path, we can show that

$$k = ae+\left(\frac{(1-a)(b+mw)}{n-mr}\right).$$

We can show, as above, that there can exist at most one solution to this equation for $k > \tilde{k}$.

9. There will be one if $b \geqslant 0$. If the Inada condition is not satisfied and the production function is not concave, then, of course, there may exist more or fewer equilibria.

in a state with completely equal distribution of income and wealth; but until the overall capital–labor ratio becomes equal to $\hat{k}$, the relative distribution of wealth becomes more uneven.[10]

5. For all capital–labor ratios greater than $\hat{k}$, the distribution of wealth becomes (relatively) more even, eventually reaching complete equality.

Movements in the distribution of income

The adaptation of these results to movements in the distribution of income is straightforward. If the elasticity of substitution of the production function[11] is equal to one, then the analysis carries over exactly. If the elasticity of substitution is less than one, for instance, then

1. in the region $\hat{k} < k < k^{**}$, the decreasing share of capital and the equalization of its ownership both serve to equalize the distribution of income;

2. in the region $k > k^{**}$ the increasing share of capital and the equalization of its ownership offset each other; eventually, of course, the equalization tendencies dominate;

3. in the region $k^* < k < \hat{k}$, the decreasing share of capital and the increasing spread in the ownership of capital offset each other; eventually, the economy moves into the region $\hat{k} < k < k^{**}$;

4. in the region $k < k^*$, the increasing share of capital and the increasing spread in its ownership both serve to make the distribution of income more unequal.

The case of elasticity of substitution greater than unity may be analysed similarly.[12]

3 Alternative savings and reproduction assumptions

The question naturally arises as to what extent the results obtained in the previous section depend on the particular assumptions made there. In this section, we show that the basic presumption for equalization obtains under a wide variety of specifications of savings and reproduction behavior.

10. Perhaps one should not draw morals about the real world from such simple models. If the distribution of wealth appears in the short run to be becoming more uneven, do not lose hope in the capitalist system. Eventually (which may be a long time), the economy may lead to an equalitarian state, by its own accord.

11. It should be noted that none of the results thus far has depended on the shape (except that f is concave and satisfies the Inada conditions) of the production function.

12. So far we have assumed that there is no technological change. Hence, in the long run, all incomes (in steady state paths) are constant. If there is technological change, in the case of nonproportional linear savings hypothesis, we must make some adjustments in the analysis. But the basic qualitative results will, of course, be unaffected by Harrod neutral technical change.

Nonlinear savings functions

Let savings *per capita* of the ith group be a nonlinear function of income *per capita* of the ith group, $s(y_i)$. Then, for any given aggregate capital–labor ratio, k, there may be any number of income classes which are in equilibrium, i.e. for which $s(y_i) = nc_i$. But if the savings function is convex or concave there can be at most two groups, since

$$\frac{d^2[s(y_i) - nc_i]}{dc_i^2} = s''r \lessgtr 0 \qquad \text{as} \quad s'' \lessgtr 0. \qquad \text{3.1}$$

But while aggregate savings behavior is independent of the distribution of income when the savings function is linear, it is not when the savings function is nonlinear. In general there will be any number of balanced growth paths, i.e. capital–labor ratios for which

$$s[w(k) + r(k)c_i] = nc_i \qquad \text{3.2}$$

where $k = \sum a_i c_i$. But if the savings function is concave, and the proportion of the population in each of the income groups is fixed, then there can be at most three balanced growth paths. Two will have only one class present and one will have two classes present.[13]

The two one-class equilibria have exactly the same stability properties as in the linear case, and nothing more need be said about it here. The two-class equilibrium has, as one might expect, properties of both the lower and upper equilibrium one-class economies; if part or the entire lower class is disturbed, so that their wealth *per capita* is less than that in equilibrium, they become increasingly poorer and if they become slightly richer (in *per capita* wealth terms) than in equilibrium, they become increasingly richer, until they 'merge' with the upper class. Of course, we have been assuming

13. The one class cases require $c_i = k$. Hence we require $s(w + rk) = nk$. But since $s(k)$ is a concave function of k, and nk is a linear function of k, there can be at most two solutions.

In the two-class case, let a per cent of the population be in the lower equilibrium and $(1-a)$ in the higher. Let $\bar{k} = ac_1(k) + (1-a)c_2(k)$ where $c_1(k)$, $c_2(k)$ are the solutions to equation 3.2 for given k. Then

$$\frac{dc_i}{dk} = \frac{-s'(c_i - k)f''}{s'r - n}$$

For the lower class, $c_i < k$, if the savings function is concave, $s'r > n$. The converse holds for the upper equilibrium. Hence

$$\frac{dc_i}{dk} < 0 \qquad \text{and} \qquad \frac{d\bar{k}}{dk} < 0.$$

There exists at most one k for which $\bar{k} = k$. As in the linear case, there is of course one further possibility existing (provided that at 'very large incomes' savings becomes approximately proportional to income) – the poor could reduce their capital to a lower bound of say zero while the rich become increasingly richer.

throughout this process that as individuals shift their class membership the aggregate capital–labor ratio changes in the appropriate way. As a larger proportion of the population join the upper class, the aggregate capital–labor ratio must rise. But as it rises, it leads all the other members of the lower class out of equilibrium, and since the lower equilibrium is unstable, there is no mechanism for them to reach equilibrium. It is unlikely then that any two-class equilibrium situation could ever be maintained for long.

Hence, in this model as in the linear model first examined, if the balanced growth path is stable, there is a tendency in the long run for the equalization of wealth and income – with the possible exception of a group (in an underdeveloped economy perhaps almost the entire economy) whose wealth is at some lower bound (zero, or the upper bound on indebtedness).

Savings as a function of wealth and income

Recent investigations into savings function have indicated that savings may be a function of wealth as well as income, e.g. $s = b + my + zc >$ so

$$\frac{\dot{c}_i}{c_i} = \frac{(b+mw)}{c_i} + mr + z - n. \qquad 3.3$$

The analysis proceeds exactly as in Section 2 of this paper, and **3.3** is identical to **2.5** with n replaced by $n-z$. If z is positive, then it is as if the rate of population growth is smaller than it actually is, so that the equilibrium capital–labor ratio is higher, r is lower, w is higher, etc. The more reasonable assumption is to make z negative, indicating that the more wealth one has, for any given income, the less one saves (as for instance some of the life cycle stories suggest); then it is as if n is higher, i.e. the equilibrium capital–labor ratio will be lower, wages will be lower, and the profit rate will be higher.

An alternative formulation of savings behavior is the following: individuals have a desired wealth–income ratio, given by q^*. If the wealth–income ratio is less than the desired, they accumulate. If it is greater than the desired, they decumulate. We may write the adjustment process as

$$\dot{c} = h(c^* - c), \qquad 3.4$$

where

$$c^* = q^*y = q^*(w + rc). \qquad 3.5$$

Substituting, we have

$$\dot{c} = h[q^*(w+rc) - c] = hq^*w + (q^*rh - h)c. \qquad 3.6$$

Since $k = \sum ac_i$,

$$k = hq^*w + (rq^*h - h)k = hq^*y - hk. \qquad 3.7$$

There is a unique balanced growth path, with $q^* = y/k$, and it is stable. Moreover, for any given aggregate capital–labor ratio, there is at most one c for which $\dot{c} = 0$:

$$c = \frac{q^* w}{1 - rq^*}. \qquad 3.8$$

This is meaningful only if $r(k) < 1/q^*$, i.e. for very low capital–labor ratios there exists no positive c for which $\dot{c} = 0$. In all cases, however, the poor accumulate capital faster than the rich, since

$$\frac{\dot{c}_1}{c_1} - \frac{\dot{c}_2}{c_2} = hq^* w \left(\frac{1}{c_1} - \frac{1}{c_2} \right), \qquad 3.9$$

and eventually all wealth is evenly distributed.

Classical savings function

Another savings hypothesis which has been strongly advocated, particularly in Cambridge, is the classical or Kaldorian (1956) savings function where different proportions of profits and wage income are saved. Again, because of the linearity assumption, the behavior of the economy as a whole is unaffected by the distribution of wealth and income. Except when $s_w = 0$, asymptotically, all wealth is evenly distributed:

$$\frac{\dot{c}_i}{c_i} - \frac{\dot{c}_j}{c_j} = (s_w w) \left(\frac{1}{c_i} - \frac{1}{c_j} \right),$$

where s_w is the savings propensity out of wages. In the singular case where $s_w = 0$, there is no tendency for equalization. Indeed, in balanced growth, since the aggregate capital–labor ratio is fixed, increases in wealth by one group must come at the expense of others.

Variable rates of reproduction

In this subsection, we assume that the rate of reproduction of the ith group is a function of its *per capita* income $n_i = n(y_i)$. For simplicity, we shall revert to the linear savings assumption. It is clear that different groups will in general have different rates of reproduction and the group with the highest rate of reproduction 'dominates' the entire population. All groups except the dominant one asymptotically 'disappear'. Assume there are only two groups – the rich and the poor. If the rich reproduce more quickly than the poor, then although it is true that 'the poor have ye always among you', in a relative sense they disappear. On the other hand, even if the rich reproduce more slowly than the poor, so that they become an infinitesimal part of the population, they may still have more than an infinitesimal part of the wealth of the total economy. To see this, if K_r is the capital of the rich and K_p that of the poor, and a is the proportion of the rich (asymptotically $a = 0$), then

$$\frac{d \ln(K_r/K_p)}{dt} = \frac{\dot{a}}{a(1-a)} + \frac{\dot{c}_r}{c_r} - \frac{\dot{c}_p}{c_p} = (mw+b)\left(\frac{1}{c_r} - \frac{1}{c_p}\right) + (n_r - n_p).$$

By assumption, $n_r < n_p$. If the economy is in an unstable equilibrium, $b+mw$ is negative so the wealth of the rich may be growing faster than that of the poor. But if the economy is in a stable equilibrium,

$$\frac{d \ln(K_r/K_p)}{dt} < 0$$

so that asymptotically, the rich are infinitesimal not only in numbers but also in total wealth holdings, relative to the total economy.

4 Taxation and equalization

Taxes for redistribution do more than just redistribute income today – they increase the rate at which wealth is equalized. To see this, consider the effects of a proportional income tax, in which all the proceeds are divided equally among the citizens.

If group i's income before tax is $y_i = w + rc_i$, its after tax income is

$$y_i' = (w+rc_i)(1-t) + t(w+rk)$$

and hence the *per capita* wealth accumulation behavior of the economy remains unchanged. The relative movements in *per capita* wealth of two groups are given by

$$g_c = \frac{\dot{c}_i}{c_i} - \frac{\dot{c}_j}{c_j} = (b+mw)\left(\frac{1}{c_i} - \frac{1}{c_j}\right) + mrtk\left(\frac{1}{c_i} - \frac{1}{c_j}\right), \qquad 4.1$$

and the change in the speed of equalization from the no-tax situation is

$$\Delta g_c = mrtk\left(\frac{1}{c_i} - \frac{1}{c_j}\right). \qquad 4.2$$

Again, we observe that for 'high' k, the poor increase their *per capita* wealth relative to the rich, until incomes and wealth are completely equalized, while for 'low' k the rich grow richer relative to the poor. But note the two effects of the income tax:

First, the critical k which determines whether there is wealth equalization or not is lower, since now the condition is not $b+mw = 0$, but $b + mw + mrtk = 0$. In fact, at a tax rate greater than $1 - (n/mr)$, even at the lower balanced growth path equalization of wealth will occur.

Second, the rate at which equalization occurs is increased (or, if the distribution becomes more uneven, it does so at a slower rate than in the absence of the tax).

Similarly, the effects of progressive income taxes, profits taxes, and wealth taxes may be analysed. It can be shown that for taxes of the same revenue the redistributive effects of either a profits tax or a progressive income tax are greater than those of the proportional income tax.

5 The speed of equalization: an example

In this section we shall work through an example to give the rough orders of magnitudes of the time involved. We take the Cobb-Douglas production function, $y = k^a$. If $b = 0$, the differential equation for the aggregate capital–labor ratio is

$$\dot{k} = mk^a - nk.$$

This can easily be solved explicitly for $k(t)$:

$$k(t) = \left\{ \left(k(0)^{1-a} - \frac{m}{n} \right) e^{(a-1)nt} + \frac{m}{n} \right\}^{1/(1-a)}$$

so that

$$\lim_{t \to \infty} k(t) = \left(\frac{m}{n} \right)^{1/(1-a)} = k^*.$$

If we use as our definition of distance from equilibrium $V(k) = [k(t) - k^*]^2$, then the rate of change of $V(k)$ is given by

$$\frac{d \ln V(k)}{dt} = -2 \frac{k(mk^{a-1} - n)}{\{[k(0)^{1-a} - m/n] e^{(a-1)nt} + m/n\}^{1/(1-a)} - (m/n)^{1/(1-a)}}.$$

On the other hand, the differential equation for *per capita* wealth of group i is

$$\dot{c}_i = mw + (mr - n)c_i = mk(t)^a(1-a) + (mk(t)^{a-1} - n)c_i$$

so

$$c(t) = e^{-\int_0^t (n - ma \, k(v)^{a-1}) dv} \left[c(0) + \int_0^t mk(\tau)^a(1-a) e^{\int_0^\tau (n - m \, k(v)^{a-1}) dv} d\tau \right].$$

If the economy is in aggregate equilibrium, this takes on the simple form

$$c_i(t) = [c_i(0) - k^*] e^{(mr-n)t} + k^*$$

or

$$c_i(t) = [c_i(0) - k^*] e^{(a-1)nt} + k^*.$$

If we use as our measure of inequality of wealth the variance

$$V(c) = \sum_i a_i[c_i(t) - k]^2,$$

we can immediately calculate the speed of equalization when the economy is in aggregate equilibrium:

$$\frac{d \ln V(c)}{dt} = 2(a-1)n.$$

It should be noted that the speed of equalization depends only on the rate of growth and the share of labor, and in fact is proportional to each.

To get an idea of the numerical values, let us assume that $a = 0.25$, $n = 0.01$, and $m = 0.2$. Then the 'half-life of wealth inequality' is 46·2 years, i.e. in 46·2 years, the variance in wealth is reduced in half. If, on the other hand, $k = 0.8k^*$, so $V(k) = 0.04k^*$, it takes 46·4 years for $V(k)$ to be reduced in half (i.e. for $k = 0.8586k^*$). We have already noted that the speed of equalization is very sensitive to n and a. If, for instance, the rate of growth increases from one per cent to two per cent, the 'half-life' is reduced from 46·2 to 23·1 years.

Above, we have identified some strong long-term forces leading the economy to equalization of wealth and income. There are, on the other hand, several forces tending to preserve inequality in wealth and income. The forces that we shall focus on in particular are (a) heterogeneity of the labor force, (b) 'class' type savings behavior, and (c) alternative inheritance policies.

6 Heterogeneous labour force

In this section we assume that some labor is more productive than other labor and receives accordingly a higher wage. We further assume that different kinds of labor are related to each other in a 'pure labor augmenting way' so the ratio of the wage of any two groups is constant, and there is no intermarriage between groups. We revert to the assumption of a constant rate of growth of population and a linear savings function.

If p_i is the number of efficiency units incorporated in each member of group i, it is easy to show that in equilibrium c_i, *per capita* wealth of the ith group, is a linear function of p_i:

$$c_i = \frac{b + mp_i w}{n - rm}.$$

Thus, for any given distribution of productivities, we can derive the resulting asymptotic distribution of wealth. If $g(p)$ is the density function of p, then the density function of c is

$$\frac{n - rm}{mw} g\left(\frac{c(n-rm) - b}{mw}\right).$$

If productivities are normally distributed, wealth will be normally distributed; if productivities are lognormally distributed, wealth will also be distributed lognormally (but a three parameter lognormal function).

Further insight into this economy may be had if we assume that the economy has only two classes – an efficient class with $p = 1$ and an inefficient class with $p < 1$. The economy is on a stable balanced growth path; thus $n - mr > 0$ and $b + mw > 0$. Then, if p is sufficiently small, i.e. $p \leqslant -b/mw$, all of the capital will be owned by one class. In fact, if $p < -b/mw$, the poorer class actually goes into debt to the richer class, and there exists an equilibrium *per capita* debt of the poorer class. The rich save enough to lend to the poor and sustain the capital–labor ratio.

If $p < -b/mw$, but a constraint is imposed on borrowing (say, no borrowing is allowed at all), then we have a two-class economy in which the poor consume everything and the rich (the capitalists) consume a proportion of their income. Denoting the efficient group by a subscript one,

$$k = a_1 \dot{c}_1 = a(mw + mrc_1 - nc_1 + b).$$

In balanced growth $k = 0$, so

$$r = \frac{n - [a(b+mw)/k]}{m} = \frac{n}{m} - \frac{ab}{mk} - \frac{aw}{k}.$$

If aw/k, the wage income of the rich divided by the *total* capital stock, is small and $b = 0$, we see that $r \approx n/m$, *the rate of profit is equal* (approximately) *to the rate of growth divided by the propensity to save* (of the 'rich'), exactly the result of the Cambridge theory of distribution (Pasinetti, 1962).

7 Class savings behavior

The presence of different classes in the economy with different savings behavior may also give rise to disparities in the distribution of wealth. Consider a two-class economy: a capitalist class which does not work and saves s_j of its profits, and a workers class which derives its income from wages plus return on the capital previously saved and saves s_i of its income (regardless of the source). Models with this savings behavior have been investigated by Pasinetti (1962), Meade (1963), Samuelson and Modigliani (1966), and Stiglitz (1967). Because of the linear savings assumption, the aggregate capital accumulation behavior is independent of the distribution of wealth. Thus, there is at most one two-class balanced growth path, (i.e. a balanced growth path with both capitalists and workers present). Along this balanced growth path, $r = n/s_j$. It is easy to see that distribution of wealth among the capitalists is an historic accident, and, as in the Kaldorian case with savings out of wages equal to zero, increases in the capital of one capitalist occur at the expense of other capitalists. All 'workers', on the other hand, have the same wealth and income asymptotically, since for any group,[14]

$$\dot{c} = s_i w + s_i r k_w + s_i r(c - k_w) - n k_w - n(c - k_w) \qquad \textbf{7.1}$$
$$= (s_i r - n)(c - k_w),$$

where k_w is the capital per man owned by workers. Since $s_i < s_j$, $s_i r - n < 0$, so that if any labor group has *per capita* wealth greater than the average, k_w, its *per capita* wealth declines. The converse holds for any labor group with less *per capita* wealth than the average.

There also exists a unique balanced growth path with only workers present (the 'dual regime' of Samuelson and Modigliani, 1966, pp. 269–302). But this case is identical to that investigated above in Section 2 with $b = 0$, for which we have already shown that asymptotically all wealth is evenly distributed.

8 Primogeniture

So far in this paper we have considered only cases where wealth was divided equally among one's children. Without going into a detailed exposition of alternative inheritance programs, let us consider the case perhaps most contrary to that which has been discussed thus far, that of primogeniture (all wealth being left to the first born son). To carry through the analysis we shall need to introduce some further simplifications, and shift the analysis to discrete time.

We consider a period in which the population doubles itself. Each 'family' has exactly two sons and two daughters. For simplicity, we shall say that children are born at the end of the period. Everybody lives for only one period, parents dying after giving birth to their quadruplets. We shall examine only equilibrium paths. Then, at the beginning of any period one half of the population has zero capital. Of the remainder, one half are born to fathers who were first born, one half to fathers who were not. $(1/2)(1/2)$ of the population has $b + mw$ wealth *per capita*. Of the remainder, one half are born to fathers who were first born and one half to fathers who were not, so $(1/2)(1/2)(1/2)$ of the population has $b + mw + (1 + mr) \times (b + mw)$ wealth *per capita*. And so on.

If we number our groups from the poorest to the richest, then the ith group has $(1/2)^{i+1}$ of the population (where the 0th group has zero wealth) and has a *per capita* wealth of

$$\frac{(b + mw)[(1 + mr)^i - 1]}{(1 + mr) - 1} = \frac{b + mw}{mr}[(1 + mr)^i - 1] \quad (i = 1, \ldots, n).$$

14. Since in balanced growth, $\dot{k}_w = s_i w + s_i r k_w - n k_w = 0$.

If we compare any two groups, their ratio of *per capita* wealth is

$$\frac{(1+mr)^i-1}{(1+mr)^j-1}.$$

For large i this yields the distribution function of an asymptotically Pareto form:

$$g(c > c^*) \approx \gamma c^{* \ -\ln 2/\ln(1+mr)},$$

where $\ln\gamma = \ln\frac{1}{2}[1-(\ln(b+mw/mr)/\ln(1+mr))]$ and where $g(c > c^*)$ is the proportion of the population with *per capita* wealth greater than c^*. To see this, note the proportion of the population in the ith group is always equal to the proportion in all groups whose index is greater than i. For large i, $(1+mr)^i-1$ is approximately $(1+mr)^i$, so the proportion of the population whose wealth is greater than $(1+mr)^i(b+mw)/mr$ is $1/2^{i+1}$, and the result is immediate. If $mr = 0.6$ (recall that r is the rate of return over a generation, e.g. if the rate per year is 0.05, a generation is thirty years, then $r \approx 4.48$), then the exponent of c is 1.48, an empirically reasonable value.[15]

9 Other sources of inequality

Among the more important sources of inequality not discussed here are the following:

1. Life cycle savings. If individuals save over their life time in a manner suggested by the life cycle hypothesis, the age distribution will be one of the prime determinants of the wealth distribution. There is some evidence to support this (see, e.g. Lampman, 1962).

2. Stochastic elements. Throughout the above discussion, we have made the assumption, conventional in growth theory, that there is no randomness in the rate of return on capital, in the rate of reproduction, etc. We have already noted that the theories of income inequality of Champernowne (1953) and Mandlebrot (1961) are based primarily on stochastic models. Champernowne and Mandlebrot have shown, for instance, that if: (i) $c(t)$ is a Markovian sequence in discrete time, (ii) for large c, $\log c(t+1) - \log c(t)$ is a random variable independent of $c(t)$, (iii) for large c, $E[c(t+1)-c(t))]$ for given $c(t)$ is negative, and (iv) for small c, the transition probabilities are such that not all $c(t)$ can become zero, then c (for

15. To derive the aggregate capital–labor ratio of the economy, k, observe that k is simply a weighted sum of c_i, where the weights are proportions in the population. If $\frac{1}{2}(1+mr)$ is less than unity, the infinite sum converges to $k = b+mw/(1-mr)$. If we rewrite this equation as $b+my = k$ and observe that $n = \Delta L/L = 1$ in our discrete model, we obtain exactly the Solow growth equation – aggregate equilibrium is unaffected.

large c) would have the Pareto distribution. They unfortunately have not provided any economic justification for these assumptions. A slight modification of our model can, however, provide us with an economic motivation for them. If, for instance, we assumed that the rate of return on capital is a random variable, uncorrelated with the amount of wealth an individual owned (at least for large c) but with an average value equal to the marginal product of capital, then (in the discrete time analogue of our model of Section 2), all the Champernowne conditions are satisfied, provided only that the economy has a sufficiently large[16] capital–labor ratio.

16. In the terminology of Section 2, provided $k > \tilde{k}$.

References

CHAMPERNOWNE, D. G. (1953), 'A model of income distribution', *Econ. J.*, vol. 63, pp. 318–51 (1953).

FRIEDMAN, M. (1957), *A Theory of the Consumption Function*, National Bureau of Economic Research, Princeton University Press.

KALDOR, N. (1956), 'Alternative theories of distribution', *Rev. econ. Stud.*, vol. 23, pp. 83–100.

LAMPMAN, R. J. (1962), *The Share of Top Wealth-Holders in National Wealth*, National Bureau of Economic Research, Princeton University Press.

MANDELBROT, B. (1961), 'Stable Paretian random functions and the multiplicative variation of income,' *Econometrica*, vol. 29, pp. 517–43.

MEADE, J. E. (1963), 'The rate of profit in a growing economy', *Econ. J.*, vol. 73, pp. 667–74.

PASINETTI, L. L. (1962), 'Rate of profit and income distribution in relation to the rate of economic growth', *Rev. econ. Stud.*, vol. 29, pp. 267–79.

SAMUELSON, P. A., and MODIGLIANI (1966), F., 'The Pasinetti paradox', *Rev. econ. Stud.*, vol. 33, October, pp. 269–302.

STIGLITZ, J. E. (1967), 'A two-sector two class model of economic growth', *Rev. econ. Stud.*, vol. 34, pp. 227–38.

19 C. D. Harbury

Inheritance and the Distribution of Personal Wealth in Britain

C. D. Harbury, 'Inheritance and the distribution of personal wealth in Britain',
Economic Journal, vol. 72, 1962, pp. 845–68.

The main work by economists on the distribution of personal wealth
follows a tradition going back to Mallett and Strutt. It is based largely on
a technique for estimating the size distributions of wealth among the living
by inflating the statistics of estates left by decedents in a particular year
with a multiplier incorporating the mortality rates applicable to the
deceased property owners. The most striking feature of the results of these
calculations for Britain is the extreme inequality of wealth distribution
among persons, whether by comparison with the distribution of income in
this country or with the distribution of capital in the United States
(Lydall and Lansing, 1959).

Recent studies using this technique (Langley, 1954; Revell, 1960;
Lydall and Tipping, 1961) have indicated some reduction in the degree of
inequality in the past few decades. But there is more than a suggestion that
the result is merely statistical, reflecting at least in part the tendency
induced by high rates of estate duty for parents to part with more of their
property in advance of death, effectively reducing the concentration in the
distribution of capital between persons, while leaving untouched the
distribution between families.[1] It is therefore of some interest to inquire
further into the inter-generation mobility of capital within families to see
what light can be thrown on the importance of inheritance as a factor in
the building up of large fortunes. For this purpose a study has been made
of the wealth of the predecessors of more than 600 of the top male wealth-
holders dying in the second half of the 1950s.[2] The study has yielded cross-
section data, an analysis of which is being published separately, but the

1. It is a likely explanation, for example, of the fact that the proportion of the total
number of large and medium-sized estates left by the older age groups in England and
Wales since 1926 has not risen as rapidly as the proportion of total deaths in the same
age groups over the period (see Revell, 1960, p. 8). A shift of top wealth to younger age
groups has also been observed in the United States. See Lampman (1962, p. 240).

2. The study was made possible by a grant of financial assistance from the Houblon–
Norman Fund of the Bank of England, for which the author wishes to express his
gratitude. Sincere thanks are also due to several officials at the Probate Registry,
Estate Duty Office and General Registry Office for assistance generously provided for
the inquiry.

purpose of the present paper is to extend it rather as part of a time series by attempting to obtain comparability with a somewhat similar study made for the 1920s by Wedgwood (1929). In this way it is possible to learn something of the relative importance of inheritance in the creation of personal fortunes for two generations, of the twenties and fifties of this century.

The present sample of decedents was drawn from the register of men whose wills were probated in 1956 and 1957. The names of such persons are listed alphabetically in the Calendars of the Probate Registry together (after some delay) with the gross value of estate for which probate or letters of administration have been granted.[3] So little is known about the characteristics of large wealth-holders in Britain that it was felt that no partial sampling procedure could be very satisfactory, hence the names of all men leaving property to the gross value of £100,000 and over were extracted from the Calendars of 1956 and 1957. This procedure yielded 590 names, quite as many as could be investigated with the resources available, but it was considered that it was also desirable to have some information about the inheritance factor in slightly smaller estates. A random sample, approximately 8 per cent was therefore drawn of ninety-five further names of men leaving between £50,000 and £100,000 in two years.[4] No size distribution of the quarter million estates printed in the Calendars is published, but two independent checks indicate that the sample is in fact likely to be close to 8 per cent.[5]

Before proceeding further it is important to explain that the estate values used throughout the study were the gross values of estates as admitted for probate. These values are well known to be deficient in a number of respects, associated in the main with techniques of estate-duty avoidance, and are discussed below. They are additionally deficient, moreover, by comparison with the estate valuations used by the Inland Revenue authorities, which

3. The term *probated* is henceforth used loosely here, for convenience, to cover intestacies where no will was in fact proved but a grant of administration was made.

4. It was done alphabetically, the first four or five names in each initial letter or volume being selected to give the required number.

5. One method was to use the ratio of the number of estates of £50,000 to £100,000 to the number of estates of £100,000 or over in the Inland Revenue Report for the financial year 1956–7 (cmnd. 341) in order to estimate the total number of estates in the lower size group from the known number probated of the larger size. The ratio of 1·94 yields a probable total of 1180 smaller estates, of which ninety-five represents 8·1 per cent. A check was provided by a size distribution of probate registry estates estimated by J. R. S. Revell, which was kindly made available to me. Based on the first entry in each size group on every tenth page of the calendar for 1954, the ratio of the two size groups of estates in the sample was of the order of 2. Although three years earlier the numbers involved are not very different, and it may be taken as further confirmation that the sample is near to 8 per cent.

include, in addition to the so-called 'free estate' for which probate is necessary for disposal, other non-free property consisting largely of certain settled property upon which duty is payable, joint property and gifts *inter vivos*.

The trouble about using the Inland Revenue valuations is that, although aggregates are published annually, no information about named individuals is ever released. Approximations to such values for individuals, however, can be made by grossing up at estimated duty rates from the totals of duty paid, which is shown on grants of representation issued since 1934 and which can be inspected at Somerset House. There are, however, two reasons why such values were not used for the main purposes of this study. The first is simply that details of the total duty paid are not available before 1934. Hence, it would be impossible to use comparable valuations for the fathers' estates, except for the small minority who died subsequent to that year. It follows also that, from the viewpoint of this paper, the results would not be comparable with those of Wedgwood, also working before 1934. A second reason for not using the grossed-up estate values is that they, too, are deficient, and in some cases in a manner which the gross probate values are not, since certain types of property are chargeable at less than average rates of duty. Notable here are the 45 per cent abatements of tax on agricultural property, industrial plant and machinery. There are also a number of other types of property which are not aggregable so that lower rates of duty apply. Nevertheless, the grossed-up values of the estates of all individuals in the sample have been calculated in order to act as some check on the gross probate values used here. In fact, the aggregates of the two sets of values for all estates are not far apart – the value calculated from the duty paid being in total about 93% of the gross probate valuation. In certain individual cases there are a small number of quite large differences, but in the majority the estimated value is within 10% of the gross probate value, and is more often below it. One further reason for this discrepancy stems from the fact that the taxable value of an estate is a *net* value after deduction of funeral expenses and debts due from the estate. Since the net value of estates is, in contrast, shown on grants of administration throughout the period covered by the study, it might have been thought more suitable to employ those values. Unfortunately, net values given by the Probate Registry before May 1, 1947, were restricted to personal property, so that their use in earlier cases would have excluded real estate and, in order to maintain consistency between the valuations of different generations, gross values were used throughout.[6] Net and gross values, moreover, do not differ as a rule by

6. Estates passing before 1898 excluded realty from even the gross valuation. But it is possible to make some corrections in these cases. See below, p. 338–9.

very large amounts. Exceptionally, a very big gross estate may have a small net value, and doubt must remain as to whether the figure used was reasonable. But there seem grounds for thinking that in at least a number of these cases the gross figure represents a better indication of the deceased's former (live) net worth – with large debts covered by non-dutiable assets therefore excluded from the Inland Revenue net valuation. (Can a beggar incur debts of, e.g. £100,000?)

The use of gross valuations and the exclusion, therefore, of the bulk of dutiable settled property is the principal reason for the divergence between the number of estates included here and those enumerated in the annual reports of the Commissioners of HM Inland Revenue.[7] A comparison of the average number of estates found in the Calendars for the two years 1956 and 1957 with the Inland Revenue Report for the financial year 1956–7, as in Table 1, shows the order of magnitude of the difference. There are roughly ninety more estates in the Inland Revenue Report of £100,000 and over than in the Probate Calendars, with a corresponding deficiency in total capital value of £23·6 million. The last figure represents 26 per cent deficiency – and is almost exactly the same percentage as the proportion of settled to total property in estates of £100,000 and over in the Inland Revenue statistics.[8] While this undoubtedly means that the sample is subject to bias, which is later discussed, it should be noticed also that the distributions of estates in the two series are not dissimilar in shape. It is to be hoped, therefore, that at least some of those estates which are of net taxable value of over £100,000, but with gross probate value of less than that, will still be caught in the £50,000–£100,000 net.

In addition to the matters discussed above, it is hardly necessary to point out that the probate valuation of a man's property is only a rough guide to his net worth while still alive. The reasons are well known. They apply

7. Another reason arises from the fact that the probate valuations entered on the Calendars are those originally made for the purpose of the Inland Revenue affidavit. When any alteration is made the affidavit is resworn, but since 1946 the revised valuations have only rarely been entered in the Calendars. A spot check of original and resworn values for earlier years was made in order to have some indication of the importance of this factor. It must be said that amendments were not particularly common. Where they occurred they rarely affected the value of an estate by more than 2 or 3 percentage points, though in a small number of cases among the largest estates it was more. In addition to this the Estate Duty Office kindly produced figures of original and resworn values for seventeen estates actually included in the 1956–7 sample. Since information about named individuals is restricted, the data were supplied for three groups of five or six estates. For those in the two smallest size classes of £50,000–£100,000 and £100,000 to £200,000, the resworn totals were 3·7 and 3·8 % higher. For the largest size group, however (£200,000 and over), the resworn aggregate of the six estates grouped together was 19·6 % above the original figure.

8. Additional breakdown kindly made available by the Estate Duty Office.

Table 1 **Numbers and total capital values of estates of males, England and Wales 1956–7** (cumulative)

Range of capital value of estate (£) (1)	Nos. probated, average of years 1956 and 1957 (2)	Nos. reported by H M Inland Revenue, year 1956–7 (3)	Capital value, £ million Gross probate value (4)	Capital value, £ million Net taxable value (5)
2,000,000 and over	2	2	10·6	12·8
1,000,000 ,,	4	6	13·3	18·3
800,000 ,,	5	6	14·1	19·2
600,000 ,,	10	14	17·2	24·7
500,000 ,,	14	25	19·1	28·4
400,000 ,,	22	35	23·1	33·3
300,000 ,,	38	54	28·6	39·0
250,000 ,,	50	71	31·9	43·5
200,000 ,,	78	112	38·0	53·0
150,000 ,,	121	185	48·8	67·1
100,000 ,,	285	378	67·6	91·2

more or less equally to the use of Inland Revenue valuation, however, and are regularly acknowledged by those who work with estate multipliers. Generally speaking, they arise out of estate-duty avoidance practices,[9] but include also difficulties stemming, for instance, from the fact that life-assurance policies have maturity values in excess of their surrender values during an assured's lifetime, and annuities ceasing on the death of an annuitant have then no value whatsoever. The principal causes of under-valuation involve so-called discretionary trusts, settled property subject to the surviving spouse duty exemption and immovable foreign property. There are also, of course, gifts made *inter vivos* more than five years before death, though most modern authorities are in disagreement with the view expressed by the late Lord Stamp that they cause estimates of the distribution of personal wealth by the estate multiplier method to be too low. There is additionally some undervaluation, especially among large estates, arising from the fact that tax-payers have the power to affect the form and value of certain types of property, so to speak on their deathbeds. Some of these involve complicated legal devices, applying perhaps most

9. Not to mention evasion by under-reporting. I have not been able to find any estimate of evasion in this country. In France before the war Michel (1933) used a factor of 1·5 to raise the value of private property reported as passing at death in order to allow for fraud. But he puts most of this down to the existence of bearer bonds. It is hard to believe that the extent of under-reporting of this nature in Britain is of anything like this order of magnitude if only because legal avoidance is relatively simple. In fact, it may well be that under-reporting is of greatest importance among the smallest estates (see e.g. Lampman, 1962, p. 66).

C. D. Harbury 327

easily to company shareholdings.[10] It is undeniably unfortunate that the data are deficient in these ways, but they are the best that are available and, as will be shown, can still yield results of considerable interest. And it should also not be inferred that any piece of property is necessarily excluded from probate valuation merely because it is not dutiable, for such is not the case.[11] It is, however, necessary to bear in mind these limitations, and an attempt is made to assess their general effect on the results later on. The nature of the sample of men included in the inquiry having been outlined, it is necessary to describe briefly the process by which the estates of their predecessors were traced. There are, basically, only two stages in the operation, first to find a father's name and second his date of death. For the 58 Peers, 45 Landed Gentry and 28 Knights Bachelor the first was not a difficult task, and there were additionally 63 persons who, while not coming strictly into any of these categories, appeared in one or another of the standard directories.[12] For such persons the father's name was nearly always given, and, in rather more than half the total, so was the father's date of death. For these it was a speedy task to find the probate of the father's will, usually within a year or two of death. For the others a general search of the Probate Calendars extending in some cases over about ninety years had to be undertaken. The same was, of course, also true of the four to five hundred other sons who did not feature in any of the standard reference works. The procedure in their case was considerably more lengthy. From the date of their death given in the Probate Calendar, it was possible to trace a death entry in the General Register Office at Somerset House. Now a man's death certificate does not give his father's name, but it does show his (reported) age at death. From this it is possible to calculate his approximate date of birth[13] and to search in the Register of

10. It is, for instance, generally preferable not to die in control of a private company, since the shares will then be valued on the basis of the balance sheet assets including goodwill, instead of at their hypothetical open market value. See also, Wheatcroft (1959) for what are there called the 'Strip Trick,' the 'In and Out Trick' and the 'Repeating Trick'.

11. For example, where the deceased was killed on active war service, and chattels of national or historic interest bequeathed to the State. Some settled land *is* also included in probate valuations.

12. *Kelly's Handbook of the Titled, Landed and Official Classes* and *Who's Who* were the main sources, but many local and specialized biographical dictionaries and directories were also employed.

13. Approximate for two reasons: (1) since births are registered by quarters, and (2) because the age at death is not entirely reliable, but is the age at death reported by the person registering it. It is known that this mis-states true age as compared with Census age (Census of Population, England and Wales, 1951, 1958, ch. 2) by more than one year in about 3% of all cases. For the sample of top property owners the error turned out to be less important, and largely one of overestimation of the true age of the deceased.

Births for the father's name. In the majority of cases a search of eight to twelve volumes in the Birth Register brought to light a single unambiguous entry, and armed with father's name (and also occupation and mother's maiden name to assist in the identification of wills) the search for the father's estate could proceed in the manner previously described, by searching in the annual Probate Calendars between the year previous to that of the son's birth and the present day. In some cases two or three possible birth entries were found, and the search carried out for the same number of possible fathers' wills. The entire operation was an exceedingly lengthy one, but was quite successful. It was, however, felt that there might be a strong bias relating to the inheritance element in the cases which were not traced,[14] and the utmost importance was therefore attached to achieving the highest possible degree of success. For this reason the entire search was carried out three times, and additional methods were employed in the cases which had by then yielded no result. These were of two principal kinds – those where no birth entry was identifiable (either because the sons' names were too common or because none could be found at all) and those where the fathers' names were known but no estates could be traced for them. In such cases a variety of methods were used. One was to refer to obituary notices in local newspapers, though it was surprising how seldom one existed which gave much help.[15]

Sons' wills were about as useful. But one with a very common name referred to his exact date of birth, and several mentioned a father, or more commonly a brother or sister, the birth registration of whom provided the necessary check. Again, where the son was known to be the director of an identifiable company, the files at Bush House occasionally threw up a father. The most important supplementary information in the more difficult cases, however, was obtained as a result of letters sent very largely to relatives, solicitors and executors but also, in a small number of cases, to churchyard superintendents, local public librarians and others.

Considerably more than 400 letters were in fact despatched, involving 226 cases where a father's estate had not been positively traced, all but 33 of which were eventually discovered largely as a result. The response rate was at least 75 per cent, this being the proportion of replies actually received to letters sent, but if allowance is made for the fact that over 10 per cent of those sent to relatives (mainly widows) were returned R T S (removed, or deceased) the rate rises to well over 80 per cent. It is, moreover, remarkable that of 429 letters sent and 310 replies received, only 9 directly objected to the nature

14. For an *ex post* justification see below, p. 337.

15. Some were even later found to be wrong on the crucial point, though marriage certificates were sometimes traced from obituaries, even when no father's name was directly mentioned.

or purposes of the inquiry, while 169 provided information concerning the date of father's death, accompanied in many cases with other helpful details, such as potted family histories, the estates of other relatives, loans of copies of wills and newspaper cuttings. A further 89 offered some help, while not being able to provide the date of father's death.

The final achievement was that predecessors' estates were traced (or known to have been too small to have been probated) with virtual certainty in 618 cases. In addition, a further 17 estates were found and analysed separately, since they did not command quite the same degree of confidence. It must also be mentioned that in 9 cases other kinsfolk than fathers were taken, where it was definitely known that an inheritance came in that line.[16] In assessing the proportion of the total sample that the figure of 618 represents, however, it should be pointed out that, of the original 685 estates, 8 were first eliminated because they were known to have predeceased their fathers, a further 25 were excluded as foreign (having been born or having died abroad) and whose fathers' estates were not traceable from this country, 2 more had died before 1950 and were rejected on that account, and 1 estate entered erroneously in the Calendar as £130,000 subsequently transpired to be of only £13,000. Of the 649 remaining, which might be considered as the maximum number which could have been found there were only 14 complete failures. In 7 of these, moreover, it had not been found possible to trace a single birth entry in the Registers at Somerset House, and there is a strong suspicion that 4 or 5 were born abroad and should really be excluded as foreign.[17] The failure rate, therefore, should be regarded as being certainly no higher than 31 out of 649 (or 4·8 per cent), or if the less-reliable predecessors and the additional suspect foreigners are excluded as low as 14 out of 644 or 2·2 per cent.

The study undertaken by Wedgwood for 1924–6 is adequately described in the original, and only the general outline is repeated here, mainly to stress differences from the present one.[18] Briefly, the early study comprised also two samples, one consisting of 99 English estates of gross probate

16. 4 grandfathers, 3 cousins, 1 brother and 1 uncle. In addition to these, in a further 18 cases the estate of a relative which was significantly larger than the father's was discovered, but these were not included in the analysis used for the present paper.

17. The failures included Charles Atkins of Caterham, Thomas Barron of Catforth, David Cameron of Sutton, Arthur Chadwick of Blackpool, Ronald Percy Gaze of London and Exning, Samuel Krohnberg of London, Morduch Lush of London, Alec Andrew Penney of Hornsea, Thomas William Austin Philpot of Bromley, Harry Taylor of Congleton, Arthur Percival Tiley of Alsager, Hugh Vivian of Swansea and Henry Thomas Walker of Morecambe and Heysham. Any information relating to the antecedents of any of these persons would be very gratefully received.

18. The author benefited greatly from discussions he was able to have with Mr Wedgwood.

value over £200,000 passing in 1924–5 and the second of 140 estates of between £10,000 and £200,000 recorded during six weeks in January and February 1926 (for brevity, both are referred to here as 1924–6 throughout). Both samples excluded foreigners, and the principal differences between the data and that used in the present study relate to the following:[19]

1. Sample size.
2. Sources. The samples for the early inquiry were drawn from estates listed in *The Times*, and not the primary Probate Calendars.
3. Success rates.
4. Probate valuations. Differences arise in two main ways: from the method used to estimate realty prior to 1898 and from the changing relative importance of settlements to total property.
5. The treatment of women's estates.

The biasing influences of different sources, success rates and probate valuations will be discussed below in conjunction with the results. It may simply be stated here that, as far as differences in sample size are concerned, the three-fold greater number in 1956–7 does produce some rather smoother curves, but it is not of great significance for the analysis of this paper.[20] It is also convenient to dispose at this stage of the difference arising from the fact that women were included in the 1924–6 study, whereas the present one is confined to men. The reason for the latter decision is probably more easily understood when it is pointed out that Wedgwood was eventually forced to exclude about half of the total number of women's estates[21]

19. Wedgwood also attempted in a number of cases to estimate the proportions of predecessors' estates bequeathed to individual inheritors in question, though it is clear that he did not regard these results with as much confidence as others. A similar attempt was made in the present study, but it was soon felt that it would not be of much value unless a great deal of time could be spared investigating matters of detail not readily available about family circumstances. For instance, in a large number of cases the inheritor received a share of the residue of an estate which was only deducible if one knew for certain the number of surviving brothers and sisters also sharing in the residue, as well as the number (and ages) of other surviving beneficiaries receiving legacies and annuities. There are also a mass of other complications arising, for example, out of marriage settlements mentioned but not valued, requirements to bring unspecified advancements into hotchpot and valuation problems, particularly of real estate and shares in family businesses, whether bequeathed to the inheritor in question or not. No use is therefore made in the present paper of the information relating to the proportion of predecessors' estates bequeathed to successors. Moreover, the entire study is concerned with the relationship between the estates left by fathers and sons alone, and no allowance is made for the fact that many sons may have benefited from more than a single will. There is, therefore, little justification in trying to relate sons' inheritances to a very doubtfully calculated version of the size of a particular inheritance.

20. The same is not true of the cross-section analysis to be published separately of the 1956–7 data, which simply could not yield significant results on a smaller scale.

21. In the second sample. The first was simpler and contained only six women.

because either their husbands' or their own maiden names were not stated. The channels and importance of inheritance among women, moreover, are quite different from among men,[22] and there is good reason for keeping them apart. Fortunately Wedgwood kept the data which he collected relating to women's estates separate from his totals in almost every instance, and it is not difficult to arrange his material to exclude them.

Subject to qualifications to be discussed, it is now convenient to set the results of the two studies alongside. This is done in Table 2. It should first be noted that, for purposes of comparison, the two Wedgwood samples have been included in the same table, as have those of the latest inquiry. But it should not be forgotten that, in the former case, the basis for the figures of estates of over £200,000 is very much more reliable, while in the latter case the division comes at £100,000. The same groupings by size of sons' estate have been attained by arrangement of the 1956–7 data. For estates in the range £50,000–£200,000 this cannot be so simply done because

Table 2 **Fathers' and sons' estates 1924–6 and 1956–7**

Size of sons' estate	Size of fathers' estate Cumulative percentages £000									All	Sample size
	Over 1000	Over 500	Over 250	Over 100	Over 50	Over 25	Over 10	Over 5	Over 1		
1924–6											
500 and over	16	37	53	53	58	63	63	68	79	100	19
300–500	5	18	27	45	55	64	64	73	77	100	22
200–300	5	10	17	45	57	67	71	78	86	100	42
50–200	n.a.	n.a.	n.a.	21	50	63	67	71	79	100	24
25–50	,,	,,	,,	4	21	42	54	67	75	100	24
10–25	,,	,,	,,	3	8	26	42	55	74	100	38
200 and over	7	18	28	47	57	65	67	75	82	100	83
1956–7											
500 and over	12	23	31	42	54	69	77	77	81	100	26
300–500	2	10	27	42	51	59	63	66	78	100	41
200–300	1	6	18	32	50	64	71	72	85	100	72
100–200	1	3	9	27	41	57	67	72	83	100	391
50,000–100	0	0	0	9	31	44	56	61	75	100	88
50,000–200	0	2	4	18	36	50	61	67	79	100	479

22. Dutiable settled property is, for instance, normally a much higher proportion of the total for women than for men, especially in the case of largest estates. The source of this information is the distribution of settled property by estate size and by sex of decedent for 1957–8 and 1958–9, made available by the Inland Revenue to the Department of Applied Economics at Cambridge, and shown to me by the courtesy of Mr J. R. S. Revell.

of the difference in sample size just referred to. The 1956–7 data for estimates of £50,000–£100,000 and £100,000–£200,000 have therefore been
shown separately, but the numbers in these two classes have also been
combined in such a way as to provide approximate comparability with
those for 1924–6 (see below).

The implications of the tables may most clearly be seen by constructing
Pareto-type charts from the data. These are cumulative percentage curves,
allowing one to read the percentage of the total number of sons who had
fathers who left estates in excess of varying amounts. Broadly speaking,
the further to the right (and the more ⌐-shaped) a curve is, the greater is
the importance of inheritance in the compiling of personal fortunes; since
a purely random relationship between the estates of fathers and sons would
be of L-shape lying very close to the two axes.[23]

The largest grouping with broad coverage common to both studies is
that of sons leaving £200,000 and over[24] (see Figure 1). Although the curve
relating to the 1956–7 data is set somewhat more to the left and below that
for 1924–6 the two curves do not, on the whole, diverge very markedly,
and actually intersect in three places. Indeed, perhaps the most striking
single feature of Figure 1 is the fact that very close to two thirds of each
generation of sons had fathers who left over £25,000.[25] As far as successors
with richer predecessors are concerned, however, there are distinctly larger
proportions in the generation of the 1920s. The difference is proportionately
more the higher the level of fathers' estate. For sons with fathers leaving
over a quarter of a million pounds, for instance, this was 28 per cent
for the earlier generation against 23 per cent for the later one. But the
numbers in the cells (especially for the 1924–6 data) here become progressively smaller and the percentages less reliable. For those sons with more
moderately well-off fathers, on the other hand, the differences between the
proportions are slight. And for the successors in this class whom we might

23. Randomness is used to mean that the distribution of fathers' estates in the samples
here discussed is the same as for any hundred randomly selected males dying in 1956–7.
See below, p. 341.

24. This class of sons' estates is in fact a very wide one, and it was thought proper to
test the effect of reweighting the numbers in each sub-group according to the size distribution of the probate values of estates in the 1924–6 inquiry and according to that of
the net capital values of estates liable to death duties as reported by the Commissioners
of HM Inland Revenue for the same years. The difference in the results from each of
such reweightings is barely perceptible, and they have not therefore been reproduced
here.

25. The curves cross at roughly £20,000. The difference between the proportions at
£25,000 is statistically significant, but in view of the intersection just below it this is not
a very helpful piece of information. Significance tests were not in fact generally relied
upon in view of the approximate nature of the valuations, and the existence of intersections.

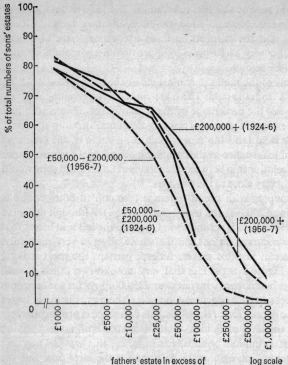

Figure 1

call 'self-made men' (whose fathers left less than £1000), there is virtually no difference between the two generations – under 20 per cent of those dying at each date.

No great service would be provided by reproducing here sets of curves corresponding to estates of the three sub-groups among the top echelons of rich successors. For the wealthiest group of all, those sons leaving £500,000 and over, there is a clear contrast marked by a single intersection affecting almost exactly 60 per cent of the two generations of sons and corresponding to a level of predecessors' estate of approximately £35,000. For those sons with richer fathers, the proportions are greater for the earlier generation, while the opposite is true for those with more moderately rich fathers. The other two sub-groups show on the whole higher proportions of sons with rich fathers in the case of the generation of the 1920s, but there are further intersections and it would hardly be sensible to emphasize the detail.

The second set of curves in Figure 1 relates to estates in the size class £50,000–£200,000. In the case of the 1956–7 data it will be remembered that this group includes estates sampled from the Probate Calendars in very different proportions. Specifically, the £50,000–£100,000 class represents approximately an 8 per cent sample, while all estates between £100,000 and £200,000 are included. In principle, therefore, the numbers in the smaller class should be grossed up by a coefficient of $12\frac{1}{2}$ before combining with the larger. However, this procedure would approximate a random sample of the group as a whole and would only be relevant if the 1924–6 sample data were similarly representative. Unfortunately, no breakdown of the results for the twenty-four estates in this size class found in the earlier study is available, but it would appear from the list of names of successors that they were drawn approximately equally from these two sub-groups.[26] It has therefore been considered appropriate to weight in similar fashion the numbers in each of these two size classes in the 1956–7 data before combining them.

In view of the relatively small size of the samples and the uncertainty arising from the aggregation problem, more caution is needed in making a comparison between the two generations than with the previous groups. But it is legitimate to observe subject to later qualification that the curve relating to the successors of 1956–7 show rather lower proportions of fathers who left estates greater than £1000. The difference is, however, only between 18 and 21 per cent in the case of predecessors' estates in excess of £100,000, and it should be added that the curve relating to 1924–6 is truncated above this amount due to the absence of further breakdown of the data.

In any assessment of the evidence put forward in the previous section it is necessary, in the first place, to make some estimate of the influence of differences in the two sets of data mentioned earlier. In the second place, some attempt should be made to indicate the extent to which changes in the price level, and the increase in the total numbers of persons leaving fortunes of various sizes, may have affected the measures of the importance of inherited wealth employed.

The three main differences in the nature of the data in the two studies relate to sources, success rates and probate valuations.

1. *Sources.* Wedgwood's samples, it may be remembered, were drawn from *The Times* lists of wills, whereas the names of successors for the 1956–7 study were taken directly from the Calendars of the Probate Registry. The

26. Wedgwood (1929, appendix to chapter 6). Estate values listed there, however do not take account of the additions in the case of excluded realty (see below, p. 339), and the estimate in the text above can therefore only be approximate.

latter contain for each year close on a quarter of a million names in alphabetical order and, though there were rather fewer in the 1920s, it would have been an enormously lengthy task to determine whether the early sample was biased. It was decided, however, that some information on this matter was desirable, and the 1956–7 sample of estates of £100,000 and over was checked against the lists of wills reported in *The Times*. It was then discovered that roughly 90 per cent of the total of those wills had been reported in the newspaper.

An attempt is made to assess the nature of bias arising from this in Table 3, which indicates the proportions of the total numbers of estates which had increased more than sixfold between the death of father and son for those cases not reported in *The Times* (NRT), and for all estates in the study. The procedure is, of course, only approximate, but it does suggest that we might eliminate this influence as an important source of bias in the largest two classes of sons' estates. In the £500,000 and over class, because only one estate is involved; and in the £300,000–£500,000 group because although a few more estates are included, the number is still small and the difference between the two distributions is insubstantial. For the two smaller groups, £100,000–£200,000 and £200,000–£300,000, on the other hand, there is a distinct bias – *The Times* lists of wills under-representing the 'self-made' men at the expense of those with inherited fortunes. One may well suspect the same to be true for decedents leaving less than £100,000, but in view of the smaller size of this sample and the much larger absolute numbers of persons involved, it was not felt to be a very reasonable test. An attempt to correct the results obtained in the present inquiry was, however, made by excluding all cases not reported in *The Times*, but this is

Table 3 **Ratio of** $\dfrac{\text{Son's estate}}{\text{Father's estate}}$ **1956–7**

Size of sons' estate	% of total no. of sons' estates where ratio $\dfrac{\text{Sons' estate}}{\text{Fathers' estate}} > 6$			Total nos. of sons' estates		
(£)	NRT	TAC	All	NRT	TAC	All
	(1)	(2)	(3)	(4)	(5)	(6)
500,000 and over	100	75	54	1	8	26
300,000–500,000	50	90	51	4	10	41
200,000–300,000	83	78	46	6	18	72
100,000–200,000	53	60	41	53	120	391
50,000–100,000	—	70	43	—	37	88

NRT = Not reported in *The Times*.
TAC = Traced after correspondence.

most conveniently dealt with after considering the next potential source of bias.

2. *Success rates.* As was pointed out earlier, the success rate in the present study was something over 95 per cent, while in the 1924–6 inquiry it may be estimated as about 89 per cent for the first sample of estates (over £200,000) and 83 per cent for the second.[27] It is highly likely that the higher success rate implies a relatively larger number of small predecessors' estates, which are the most difficult to trace, and consequently gives rise to a similar kind of bias to that encountered in the previous paragraph. It is a good deal more difficult, however, than with cases not reported in *The Times* to estimate the extent of this bias. Some indirect evidence on this point is again suggested in Table 3, col. 2 of which shows data relating to the 193 fathers' estates which were traced after correspondence (TAC) with relatives and other associates of the deceased successors. Compared with the entire sample, there is a marked and consistent tendency for the proportion of the total numbers of sons' estates which had increased more than six-fold between the death of father and son to be higher in the case of those predecessors' estates traced after correspondence. And on this occasion the bias is not confined to the lower ranges of sons' estates. It is not suggested, of course, that the figures in Table 3 indicate the extent of the bias. A number of parental estates in the 1924–6 inquiry were also traced as a result of a direct approach to the personal representatives of the deceased, though the proportion of the total was then about 14 per cent, while it was more than double this in the present study.

A possible way of estimating the influence of this type of bias, however, is to reduce artificially the success rate for the 1956–7 data, to achieve approximately the same rate as in 1924–6, by the expedient of excluding that proportion of the estates found after correspondence which produces this. Such a new set of *adjusted* data for the 1956–7 generation is displayed in Table 4. The adjustments take account of both tendencies to bias so far discussed. The figures are obtained after excluding, in the first place, all estates which were not reported in *The Times*. And, in the second place, the equivalent of sixty estates,[28] were deducted from the residuals, in order to secure success rates of approximately 89 per cent and 83 per cent for estates above and below the £200,000 division.

The results of this operation may be illustrated by observing the effect upon the Pareto-type curves for the two broad groups of sons' estates pre-

27. It was actually about 76 per cent for the whole sample. The figure of 83 per cent relates to the twenty-nine male successors with estates in the range of £50,000 to £200,000.

28. The procedure did not, of course, involve exclusion of particular estates, but the reduction of all cells in the table in the same proportion.

viously examined (see Figure 2). In the larger of the two classes, the adjusted 1956–7 curve lies above that relating to 1924–6 for a significant portion of its length, indicating that the proportion of sons who had predecessors with estates ranging from £1000 to £50,000 was larger for the generation of the 1950s. For successors with father's estates in excess of £50,000 the earlier generation has the higher proportions, but the difference between

Table 4 **Fathers' and sons' estates (adjusted values) 1956–7**

Size of sons' estate £000	Size of fathers' estate Cumulative percentages £000									All	Sample size
	Over 1000	Over 500	Over 250	Over 100	Over 50	Over 25	Over 10	Over 5	Over 1		
500 and over	14	25	33	46	60	76	85	85	88	100	22
300–500	0	9	29	46	55	64	69	72	84	100	34
200–300	2	6	21	37	56	73	78	78	88	100	60
100–200	1	4	10	31	44	62	71	77	87	100	297
50–100	0	0	0	10	34	50	61	66	79	100	75
200 and over	3	11	25	42	57	71	77	78	87	100	116
50–200	1	2	5	21	39	56	66	72	83	100	372

the two sets of sons is reduced. Moreover, in all three sub-groups of sons' estates over £200,000 the effect of the adjustment is to raise the 1956–7 curve, placing it higher and/or closer to that for 1924–6. Figure 2 shows also the adjusted data for successors' estates in the class £50,000–£200,000, combined as previously. The extent to which the curve for 1956–7 is raised is a little less than in the other instances, but it should be remembered that, for reasons given, no allowance has been made in the case of estates of £50,000–£100,000 for those cases not reported in *The Times*.

3. *Probate valuations*. Although the basis of valuation of estates was the same for both the 1924–6 and the 1956–7 data, there are two reasons for suspecting that the relationship between probate value and some ideal concept of 'true net worth' may not have remained constant. The first reason is a relatively minor one. The gross value of an estate, it has been stated, includes both personality and realty. But in fact this is not true for estates probated before 1898, when only personality was included. For predecessors' estates passing prior to this date it is necessary to use alternative estimates of real property, and these were obtained by capitalizing the gross annual values of properties listed in the Return of Landowners compiled by the Local Government Boards in the 1870s.[29] The most important implication that this has for the present discussion arises from the fact that the estimates of realty obtained in this way include settled land, which

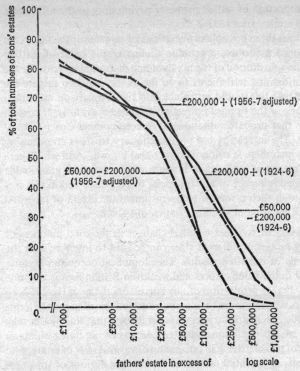

Figure 2

is largely excluded from the later estates valued as for probate. Furthermore, as one would expect, over half the total number of fathers in the earlier study died before 1898, as against 15 per cent in the present one. Consequently the values of predecessors' estates in the 1956-7 sample are likely to underestimate realty in a larger number of cases than in 1924-6. As with the previously noted sources of bias, therefore, the importance of inherited property is probably relatively underestimated in the present study. This suggestion is strengthened when it is added that a significantly higher proportion of land holdings of persons whose estates were probated before 1898 were found in the early inquiry than in the later one.

The second reason for questioning the constant basis of probate valuation, is that, as has been observed by Revell, there has been a declining

29. It is hardly necessary to discuss the deficiencies of these volumes, which do not affect the issue here and which are in any case well known. Wherever possible, the corrections contained in J. Bateman (1883) have been incorporated.

trend in the proportion of settled property paying duty to the total gross capital value of estates since 1897–8.[30]

Revell mentions three possible explanations of this trend: the fall in the price of gilt-edged securities, a genuine decline in the habit of settling property and the substitution of the tax-avoiding discretionary trust for the taxable straightforward settlement. In so far as the first two factors are concerned, the bias this would introduce into the comparison attempted here would work in the opposite direction to those previously discussed, since it implies that probate valuations have been coming closer to total true net worth. The increasing use of discretionary trusts is an offsetting factor, about which there is still not a great deal known. And while there is virtually no means of verifying it, it seems on the face of it improbable that the combined influence of all tendencies to bias discussed in this section can operate in such a way as to overestimate the extent of inherited property in the 1956–7 inquiry relative to that of 1924–6.[31]

It is next necessary to consider whether changes in the total numbers of persons leaving estates of different sizes can be said to interfere with the previous analysis of inherited wealth. This complication occurs because the rising trend in the value of personal wealth in Britain means that one would expect a higher proportion of any successors dying in the 1950s to have had fathers who left more than certain amounts fixed in money terms than in the 1920s. There are various ways, in theory, that this matter may be put to the test. The technique adopted consists of obtaining estimates of the numbers of persons dying in possession of various sizes of estate, who might be considered potential fathers of the two generations of sons here discussed. From these and a knowledge of the total number of deaths occurring each year, one can further estimate the proportions of sons who would have had fathers with more than given amounts if the wealth relationship between fathers and sons were purely random. This can be done for the two generations of successors, and the difference between the proportions in the two probability distributions of fathers' estates can be said to indicate the influence of changing total numbers of wealthy fathers.

Ideally one should work with weighted average distributions of fathers' estates. But although this could be done for the generation of 1956–7, it would be a lengthy procedure, since the range of predecessors' deaths extends over seventy-seven years. Moreover, the distribution of fathers' deaths is not even known for the 1924–6 generation, and in view of this

30. Revell (1961).

31. There is very much less doubt that the probate valuations for the *sons* of 1956–7 are greater underestimates of true net worth than for those of 1924–6, but this is not the point at issue.

and the existence of other deficiencies in the data, an approximation was made on the assumption that the distribution of fathers' estates in the median years of death of fathers in the two generations was representative of predecessors' estates in general. Table 5 shows the stages in the estimation procedure.

Table 5

Range of capital value of estates		Nos. of estates		Expected distribution of predecessors' estates (%)		Increase in percentages of expected predecessors' estates	
		1896	1916	1896	1916	1896–1916	1896–1919/22
(£)		(1)	(2)	(3)	(4)	(5)	(6)
1,000,000 and over		5	8	0·00	0·00	0·00	0·01
500,000	,,	25	24	0·00	0·00	0·00	0·01
250,000	,,	66	96	0·01	0·01	0·00	0·01
100,000	,,	252	352	0·04	0·05	0·01	0·02
50,000	,,	647	847	0·10	0·13	0·03	0·05
25,000	,,	1395	1894	0·21	0·29	0 08	0·14
10,000	,,	3419	4845	0·51	0·75	0·24	0·42
5000	,,	5800*	9116	0·86	1·40	0·54	0·90
1000	,,	16,391	27,668	2·44	4·26	1·82	3·21

* Estimated.

The median year of death of the fathers of the 1956–7 sample was 1916,[32] while the median intergeneration span of the first inquiry was given as $29\frac{1}{2}$–30 years (Wedgwood, 1929, p. 131). The total numbers of estates in 1896 and 1916 are therefore set out in columns 1 and 2 of the table, classified according to net capital values as in the Reports of the Commissioners of HM Inland Revenue. The numbers in each row are then expressed as percentages of the total numbers of deaths in the two years, representing very approximately the number of predecessors' estates of varying sizes over £1000 with which any random hundred successors might expect to be associated. It would clearly be dangerous to place too much reliance upon the absolute amounts in columns 3 and 4 for several reasons.[33,34] But it

32. This was also one of two modes as well.

33. In addition to the more obvious reasons, the following should be noted. No allowance was made for the fact that there is a discrepancy between numbers in any estate class valued for probate and for Inland Revenue duties. (A factor of 0·87 for the earlier sample and 0·75 for the later one is indicated by known information about the larger estates. But it would certainly not be as high as this for all estates over £1000.) Male and female estates are not separated in the returns for the early years. Size classes in the official returns are varied from time to time, and some estimation by interpolation of series plotted on double logarithmic graph paper was necessary.

34. The use of indices of association (see Glass, 1954) was eschewed, partly because of this, but also since the restriction of the data in this study to *élite* groups of second generation persons greatly limits their appropriateness.

is a good deal more reasonable to take the differences over time in these probability distributions as indicative of the extent to which changing total numbers of persons dying in particular capital classes may explain the results discussed in previous sections. The increases in the percentages of probable predecessors leaving various amounts of wealth between 1896 and 1916 are therefore shown in column 5. The latter year was a wartime one,[35] and a similar calculation was also made to show the trend between 1896 and the average of the years 1919–22. No claim to great precision can, of course, be made for these calculations, but they do indicate very roughly the influence of a general trend of growing riches. Referring back to Tables 2 and 3 (or Figure 2), it is convenient, in the first place, to draw a dividing line at something below £5000. At higher levels than this the increase in the total numbers of persons leaving estates of £10,000 and over is insufficient to make more than a marginal difference to the results; and this is still probably true down at least to £5000. Below the dividing line, on the other hand, the increase in numbers of persons with estates of £1000 and over is large enough to be taken note of. In particular, in so far as the successors of the fifties were observed to have had higher proportions of fathers leaving estates in excess of £1000 than those of the twenties, it can be held to supply a significant (if perhaps minor) part of the explanation.

Finally, it must be emphasized that the relationship between the estates of fathers and sons has so far been dealt with in purely money terms. It is hard to exaggerate the difficulties involved in trying to make allowance for changing price levels in so heterogeneous a collection of data over a period extending over more than a hundred years. Even were a suitable index to exist, the absence of information of the date of death and amount of estate in individual cases for predecessors in the earlier inquiry would, in any case, prevent a proper adjustment.

In point of fact, the matter is not quite so serious as might first be thought. The impact of price movements in raising the total numbers of estates of various sizes has already been dealt with. And the behaviour of the price level was not so very different throughout the two periods. By the time the great inflation of the recent past had got going the vast majority of the fathers of the 1956–7 generation of sons were already dead.

Nevertheless, it was felt that some, albeit rough, test of the influence of changing prices should be carried out, so as to make the real values of both fathers' and sons' estates in the two generations more comparable.

In view of the varied nature of the asset structure of different estates

35. Prices were hardly, however, untypically low. The consumer price index was above the average of the eighteen years either side of the median, the period discussed below.

and the absence of an appropriate price index, it was decided to fall back on the price index of consumer goods. Indeed, it may be argued that the purchasing power of the inheritance is the more relevant matter for standardization, and over the long period involved most[36] price-level trends may be roughly judged from it. Using Jefferys' and Walters' Consumer Goods and Services Price Index, the money values of estates of fathers and sons may be inflated so as to attain comparability with the estates of sons of the 1956–7 generation. The range of fathers' estates were increased by coefficients of 4·3 and 3·3. The former figure is the average price relative (based on the 1956–7 average) of eighteen years either side of the median year of death of the predecessors of the first generation; and the latter the average of the same number of years either side of the median year of death of the second generation of fathers.[37]

A similar correction on the basis of the price relative of 2·3 for the values of successors' estates in 1924–6 and 1956–7 could not be so simply applied, largely since the most recent probate valuations are particularly open to suspicion of underestimation, and to that extent less in need of relative deflation. The argument is most forceful with regard to estates in the highest size classes, where also the absolute numbers of decedents in the two sets of years are not greatly different.[38] It may be said, however, that the doubt concerning the 1956–7 probate valuations operates to a lesser extent the smaller the estate, and it may be thought to be unimportant for the lowest of the size classes of successors' estates of the generation of the fifties. If one is satisfied with a coefficient of 2 instead of 2·3,[39] then the 1924–6 generation of sons leaving £25,000–£50,000 should be directly

36. Not, of course, all, notably fixed-interest securities. It is scarcely useful to enter here into a lengthy discussion on the choice of deflater. It is possible to argue, too, that one should also deflate the estates of fathers and sons with the rate of interest in order to value them, not so much in terms of their purchasing power over current goods and services, but in terms of the annual income they are capable of yielding to their holders. While this aspect should not be overlooked, it should be recognized that such a procedure involves making assumptions concerning interpersonal valuations of present in terms of future income for different generations. And, in so far as the long-run rise in the rate of interest over the period here discussed may reflect a general feeling of increasing uncertainty and rising rate of time preference, such deflation would, moreover, be inappropriate.

37. Eighteen years was chosen on the basis of the known distribution of the number of predecessors' deaths each year in the present study. It just included all years in which there were at least ten fathers' deaths, and contained approximately 70 per cent of the total. It also corresponds roughly to the length of a generation.

38. The top seventy-nine estates left in 1924–7 and 1956–9 were, for instance, in the same size bracket – £300,000 and over (average of each set of three years). There were actually more millionaires and semi-millionaires in the earlier period than in the later.

39. There is also some evidence that, for the period 1938–57, the retail price index may overstate the extent of the price rise for high-income households. See Lydall (1959).

compared with the 1956–7 generation leaving £50,000–£100,000. Similarly, the £50,000–£200,000 size class of successors of the twenties should be set alongside a group of successors of the fifties leaving more than £100,000. For the reasons stated, however, it seems inappropriate to extend the upper limit here to £400,000, and in the absence of more reliable information it appears reasonable to take the same cut-off at £200,000 for both generations.

These two comparisons have therefore been made for the purposes of illustration in Figure 3, using the same Pareto-type curves, and employing the coefficients referred to above to inflate also the predecessors' estates for both studies. Any point on one of the curves now indicates the percentage of the total number of sons in a particular estate class who had fathers leaving property valued at 1956–7 prices in excess of amounts shown on the horizontal scale. The results cannot be considered as providing anything

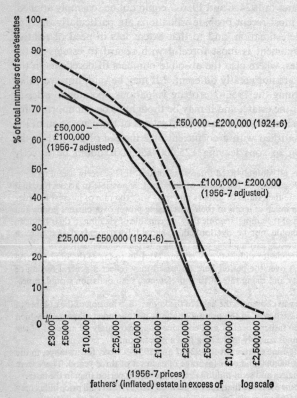

Figure 3

but rough estimates, and depend on the particular assumptions made above. They will certainly stand in need of modification if and when more light is thrown on the relationship between recent probate valuations and the elusive concept of the true net worth of the individual before death. But in the present state of knowledge it can hardly be said that the subject is worthy of more refined or extended treatment – a view which is supported by Figure 3, which sets out the situation as it affects the two groups of broadly comparable successors. Measured now in something approaching real terms, there appears very little consistent difference between the two generations in the proportions of sons having fathers leaving various amounts of capital.

Having regard to all the evidence presented here, it seems fair to conclude that there was no very marked change in the relative importance of inheritance in the creation of the personal fortunes of the top wealth-leavers of the generations of the mid-twenties and the mid-fifties of this century. For either, the chance of leaving an estate valued at over £100,000, or even over £50,000, was outstandingly enhanced if one's father had been at least moderately well off. Some statistical evidence of a decline in the proportions of rich successors having fathers who left estates in the very top-wealth ranges was noted, but this was reduced when adjustments were made to allow for sampling bias in the early study, and any remaining significance is naturally diminished by the suspicion that the incentive for tax avoidance has been growing most strongly for the highest levels of estate. Moreover, correction for changing price levels failed to alter the overall pattern of the results, and it was not found possible to lay much in the way of explanation at the door of the general increase in the value of personal wealth.

This conclusion is perhaps surprising to a reader of the Preface to the Penguin edition of *The Economics of Inheritance*, when Wedgwood wrote (as early as 1938) of the change in the relative importance of inheritance since 1924–6

... I should expect to see the proportion of inherited wealth reduced, because war, unsettled economic conditions, and especially inflation, combined with the relatively high rates of Estate Duty during the past twenty years, must reduce the economic influence of inheritance (1929, p. 8)[40].

Now it is possible that Wedgwood overlooked the influence of declining family size, but this view is otherwise consistent with the results presented

40. Subsequent evidence, moreover, suggests that the chief incidence of higher rates of estate duty may fall on the main beneficiary under a will (see Fijalkowski-Bereday (1950)). It should be noted, though, that Lampman makes reference to a Yale PhD dissertation which comes to precisely the opposite conclusion (1962, p. 238, fn. 12).

here only if the sample of decedents is thought to be very unrepresentative. Is it, perhaps, really too soon for the self-made men to have died in sufficient numbers to exert a strong enough influence? Or are the extreme tax-avoiders (leaving less than £50,000) and rich spendthrifts more typically those who have accumulated their own fortunes than was the case in the 1920s, when tax rates were lower?[41] Or is the explanation largely that steady accumulation of inheritances at compound interest is still so much the easiest way of amassing a substantial estate?[42] The need for answers to such questions should provide the stimulus for further research. It is only pertinent to add that the restriction of the wealth relationship studied here to father–son for all but a very small number of cases must, certainly reduce the importance of inheritance which has appeared. Wealth tends often to run in families.[43] The first Baron Dulverton (formerly Sir Gilbert Wills) died in 1956, leaving over £4 million, and was therefore included in the sample. His father left £3 million, but eight other members of the Wills family dying since 1900 left over £2 million. An extreme case, no doubt, but there were persons dying in possession of substantial estates in the 1956–7 study, of whom it is virtually certain that they inherited (unknown) large sums from other relatives.

41. Though still 20–40 per cent on £2,000,000 and over, and 14–20 per cent on £100,000.

42. At 3 per cent and a thirty-year inter-generation span, an estate which is taxed at or below 50 per cent stands a very good chance of maintaining or increasing its size. See Tait (1960). It may be added that, for example, the yield on Consols was certainly higher for the second generation, though the growth rate of GNP was greater for the first. See Paige *et al.* (1961).

43. It does not, of course, necessarily stay with all the members. It need hardly be added that the results of the present study do not provide much information about the prospect of retaining wealth (even in retrospect) for members of rich families. Such a study would be supplementary to this one, but would require a different approach.

References

BATEMAN, J. (1883), *The Great Landowners of Great Britain and Ireland*, Harrison.

Census of Population, England and Wales, 1951 (1958), *General Report*, ch. 2, HMSO.

FIJALKOWSKI–BEREDAY, G. Z. (1950), 'The equalizing effects of the death duties', *Oxford econ. Papers*, vol. 2, pp. 176–96.

GLASS, D. V. (ed.) (1954), *Social Mobility in Britain*, Routledge & Kegan Paul.

JEFFERYS, J. B., and WALTERS, D. (1956), 'National income and expenditure of the United Kingdom, 1870–1952', in *International Association for Research in Income and Wealth*, series 5, Bowes & Bowes.

LAMPMAN, R. J. (1962), *The Share of Top Wealth – Holders in National Wealth 1922–56*, Princeton University Press.

LANGLEY, K. M. (1954), 'The distribution of private capital 1950–51', *Bull. Oxford Univ. Inst. Stat.*, vol. 16, pp. 1–13.

LYDALL, H. F. (1959), 'The long term trend in the size distribution of income', *J. Roy. Stat. Soc.* vol. 112, pp. 1–46.

LYDALL, H. F., and LANSING, J. B. (1959), 'A comparison of the distribution of personal income and wealth in the United States and Great Britain', *Amer. econ. Rev.*, vol. 49, pp. 43–67.

LYDALL, H. F., and TIPPING, D. G. (1961), 'The distribution of personal wealth in Britain', *Bull. Oxford Univ. Inst. Stat.*

MICHEL, E. (1933), 'Dette hypothécaire', *Journal de la Société de Statistique de Paris.*

PAIGE, D. C. *et al.* (1961), 'Economic growth; the last hundred years', *National Institute econ. Res.*, no. 16, pp. 24–50.

REVELL, J. R. S. (1960), 'An analysis of personal holders of wealth', British Association, Section F.

REVELL, J. R. S. (1961), 'Settled property and death duties', *The British Tax. Rev.*

TAIT, A. A. (1960), 'Death duties in Britain', *Pub. Fin.*, vol. 15, pp. 344–65.

WEDGWOOD, J. (1929), 'A sample investigation of the fortunes of parents and children', in *The Economics of Inheritance*, Routledge & Kegan Paul, Penguin edition, 1939.

WHEATCROFT, G. S. A. (1959), 'Feather bedding death further deliberated', *Brit. Tax. Rev.*

Part Five
Poverty in Britain and the United States

In both Britain and the United States the mid-1960s saw a re-awakening of public interest in the problems of poverty. In Britain this was in large part stimulated by the publication of Abel-Smith and Townsend's *The Poor and the Poorest* and Reading 20 contains an extract from this study. As the authors described in their introduction, it was then widely believed that poverty had been 'abolished'. They showed, however, that in 1960 two million persons had incomes below the basic national assistance scale (which could be taken as representing the 'official' definition of a minimum standard of living), and that a further five and a half million were living at less than 40 per cent above the basic scale. Moreover, their study brought to light for the first time the extent of poverty among families with children. As they said, 'it has been generally assumed that such poverty as exists is found overwhelmingly among the aged', whereas they showed that in fact nearly a third of those in poverty were children. Since the publication of the report in 1965, its findings have been confirmed by a series of government surveys and these are described in the Note following Reading 20.

The second reading contains an extract from the Council of Economic Advisers' Report for 1964 which analysed the extent and causes of poverty in the United States and marked the beginning of President Johnson's War on Poverty. According to the definition adopted by the Council, one fifth of all families in the United States were living in poverty in 1962. More recent figures give a lower figure (nearer one tenth in 1969), suggesting that the downward trend in the incidence of poverty indicated by Table 3 of the Report has been continued. It is important to note, however, that the poverty standard used by the Council is not adjusted for rising standards of living (it is fixed in terms of constant purchasing power). As described in the Manpower Report of the President 1970,

The poverty index makes no allowance for an improvement in living standards, like that enjoyed by the population as a whole during the past decade ... Whereas in 1959 the poverty threshold represented about 48 per cent of the average income of all four-person families, in 1968 it represented only 36 per cent.

The American approach is quite different in this respect from that followed in Britain. The standard applied by Abel-Smith and Townsend in *The Poor and the Poorest* provided a higher real level of living in 1960 than in 1953–4 (although the increase was slightly less than the general level of living in the United Kingdom).

The Council of Economic Advisers' Report paid particular attention to the composition of the poor. As it says

to mount an attack on poverty we must know how to select our targets. Are the poor concentrated in any single geographical area? Are they confined to a few easily identifiable groups in society?

The answer given is that they are not: 'the poor are to be found among all major groups in the population and in all parts of the country'. At the same time there are substantial concentrations of poverty among certain groups. One of the groups with the highest concentration of poverty is non-white families. Although they account for only a quarter of those

Table 1 **Median income of white and non-white men**

	Ratio of non-white to white income as %
1948	54
1949	48
1950	55
1951	55
1952	55
1953	55
1954	50
1955	53
1956	52
1957	53
1958	50
1959	47
1960	53
1961	52
1962	49
1963	52
1964	57
1965	54
1966	55
1967	59
1968	61
1969	59

Source: US Bureau of the Census, *Current Population Reports*, Series P-60.

below the poverty line, the proportion of non-white families in poverty is nearly three times the corresponding percentage for white families. It is widely believed that the relative position of non-white families has improved. However, the study by Batchelder (1964) for the 1950s showed that, while the *New York Times* was expressing the view that 'the economic situation of the Negro again shows striking progress', the gap between the income of Negro and white men had in fact increased. From Table 1 it can be seen that the ratio of non-white to white income was lower at the beginning of the 1960s than a decade earlier. By the late 1960s, the relative position of Negro men had improved, but this largely reflected a fall in unemployment and cannot necessarily be expected to persist. Thurow (1969) has pointed out that 'as the economy moves toward full employment, non-white income rises more than proportionately, but the equalization does not continue once unemployment stops falling'.

The last reading is concerned with this problem of racial discrimination and in it Baran and Sweezy provide an analysis of the 'social forces and institutional mechanisms which have forced Negroes to play the part of permanent immigrants'. Of particular importance is their emphasis on the economic benefits derived by those practising discrimination. This view contrasts sharply with that put forward by Becker (1971), who argues that whites with a 'taste for discrimination' are willing to forgo income in order not to have contact with non-whites.

References

BATCHELDER, A. B. (1964), 'Decline in the relative income of Negro men', *Q. J. Econ.*, vol. 78, pp. 525–48.
BECKER, G. (1971), *The Economics of Discrimination*, second edition, University of Chicago Press.
THUROW, L. (1969), *Poverty and Discrimination*, Brookings Institution.

20 B. Abel-Smith and P. Townsend

The Poor and the Poorest

Extract from B. Abel-Smith and P. Townsend, *The Poor and the Poorest*, G. Bell & Sons, 1965, pp. 9–12 and 57–67; and editor's note.

Two assumptions have governed much economic thinking in Britain since the war. The first is that we have 'abolished' poverty. The second is that we are a much more equal society: that the differences between the living standards of rich and poor are much smaller than they used to be.

These assumptions are of great practical as well as theoretical importance. They form the background to much of the discussion of social and economic policy. But are they true? The findings of the survey carried out in 1950 in York by Rowntree and Lavers (1951) were encouraging. They seemed to confirm expert as well as popular supposition. The absence of mass unemployment, the steady increase in the employment of married women, the post-war improvements in the social services and the increase in real wages all seemed to point unequivocally to the virtual elimination of poverty, at least as it had been understood in the 1930s.

Second, the authors of a number of studies of income distribution have found a levelling of incomes since 1938 Seers (1951); Cartter (1955); Paish (1957, p. 1); Lydall (1959, p. 1). Indeed, many recent writers have concluded not only that there is less inequality of income in post-war as compared with pre-war Britain, but that the process of levelling continued during the 1950s.[1] The data produced by economists seemed merely to confirm what had been implied by the maintenance after the war of high rates of taxation, by the competition for labour in a society with relatively full employment and by the general increase in the number of persons with professional, managerial and technical skills. Both assumptions seemed to be strongly founded.

The direct evidence is nonetheless ambiguous, to say the least. Since 1945 the Rowntree–Lavers survey has been the only one conducted explicitly to find the incidence of poverty.[2] This survey was extremely

1. 'A study of the period 1938–57 reveals a continuous trend towards greater equality in the distribution of allocated personal income . . . For the future, unless there is a catastrophic slump, the trend towards equality is likely to continue, though probably not as fast as in the past twenty years' (Lydall, p. 34).

2. The Social Science Department of the University of Liverpool has recently been carrying out a study in that city.

limited in conception and the report left many questions unanswered.[3] The studies of the distribution of income are also far from being conclusive. This is largely because the data provided by the Board of Inland Revenue, on which they are based, have become of less value as the years have passed, as Professor Richard Titmuss has shown in a recent analysis (1962, p. 168).[4] Not only do the statistical data comprise a haphazard mixture of individuals and tax units, but they are based on a narrow definition of income which omits certain important categories – particularly the different forms of capital appreciation (a major source, if not *the* major source, of the wealth of the rich in the nineteen fifties and sixties). The statistics also omit many forms of indirect income, mainly benefits in kind, which have been of growing importance in contributing to the living standards enjoyed by many sections of the population. (These are usually called 'fringe' benefits – an epithet which may have misled a number of otherwise discerning economists.) The incomes described by the Board of Inland Revenue in the early 1960s represent a smaller proportion of real incomes than the incomes described in the pre-war reports.

What changes, however, have taken place in the resources of the richest 5 per cent or 1 per cent of the population and of the poorest 20 per cent? Information about the rich is sparse. It has always been difficult to make scientific calculations of their true wealth and recent developments in tax laws and in tax avoidance techniques have not made these calculations any easier. The loss, or partial loss, of estates by some wealthy traditionalists may be more than balanced by the acquisitions of a new class of property speculators. Very little is known about the composition of the wealthiest 5 per cent and the figures published by the Board of Inland Revenue of their taxable income may be serious underestimates of their real income, even according to the Board's definition of income. We need to develop better ways of measuring 'net accretion of economic power' in the financial year.[5] Until a really intelligent analysis of Inland Revenue information is

3. For example, it is unlikely that the working-class districts of the city of York – the area chosen for the survey – contained a representative number of the nation's low-income families. Indeed the authors themselves virtually admit this. '. . . We may safely assume that from the standpoint of the earnings of the workers, York holds a position not far from the median, among the towns of Great Britain . . . There are no large industries . . . where wages are exceptionally low' (1957, p. 6). The report is short and does not give an adequate account of methods of sampling and obtaining income data. For a discussion of these and other criticisms, see Political and Economic Planning (1952).

4. The statistics are increasingly presenting a 'delusive picture of the economic and social structure of society'.

5. The phrase was used in a memorandum of dissent by a minority of the Royal Commission on Taxation. The minority pointed out the narrowness of the Board's definition of income. 'In fact no concept of income can be really equitable that stops

produced and until a major empirical study of the rich is carried out by sociologists or economists, or both, assertions about changes in the income of the wealthiest minority will be limited to little more than crude aggregate estimates and speculations about the meaning of certain forms of conspicuous consumption – such as investments in houses and yachts in the Bahamas or, to take a very different example, investment in charitable foundations at home.

Equally, there is very little hard information about changes in the economic condition of the poor. Some statistical information is given by the Ministry of Pensions and the National Assistance Board about the numbers and kinds of persons receiving income security benefits.[6] However, it is difficult to relate the statistics of people receiving different benefits and we know far too little about those receiving no benefits or reduced benefits. It is even more difficult to relate this information to the statistics on wages and incomes issued by the Ministry of Labour and the Board of Inland Revenue. Economists generally have refrained from attempting to do so.

The concluding statements of those who have studied income distribution are usually reached by comparing the incomes of the very rich and those around the median in society. For example, Mr H. F. Lydall's statistical tables cover the first, fifth, tenth, twentieth and fiftieth percentiles. As Mr J. Utting pointed out during a professional discussion of Mr Lydall's paper, it 'deals wholly with the top 50 per cent of the income distribution – and the main part of it is concerned with the top 20 per cent. I am equally interested to see what has happened to the bottom 50 per cent, who are of major importance from the point of view of social policy, although their impact upon many aspects of the national economy is very much less than that of people at the top'. In reply, Mr Lydall said, 'I accept this criticism in principle and agree that much more thought is needed about this matter. But the real difficulty is the lack of data on the lower incomes, especially for pre-war. . . . The true situation can only be revealed by means of sample surveys in which the lowest income groups are covered equally with others (1959, p. 42).'

But how telling are these criticisms? It would of course be possible to give a long historical account of the various economic and social changes in Britain since the war. Even though there are considerable difficulties in measuring these changes in precise quantitative terms there is no doubt

---

short of the comprehensive definition which embraces all receipts which increase an individual's command over the use of society's scarce resources – in other words, his "net accretion of economic power between two points of time"' (1955, p. 8).

6. For example, the number of weekly allowances currently paid by the National Assistance Board was 1,694,000 in June 1953 and 1,793,000 in June 1960.

that the purchasing power of manual workers and of social security beneficiaries has increased substantially. There is also no doubt that during the
past twenty years the number of persons holding the traditionally better-
paid professional, managerial and skilled manual occupations has continued to increase relative to those in the semi-skilled and unskilled manual
occupations – at least according to the traditional definition of 'skill'.
Given the pattern of wage- and salary-levels that has existed in this country,
the number and proportion of incomes in the middle ranges have tended
to increase as a consequence. But beyond statements such as these it is
difficult to go. The precise nature of changes in income distribution are
obscure. Moreover, every generation tends to exaggerate its achievements.
Those living in post-war Britain were particularly anxious to show that
they had broken decisively with the past. Everyone wanted to erase the
bitter memories of the thirties. By the 1950s, both major political parties
had a vested interest in making the creation of the 'Welfare State' seem a
greater change than it actually was. Both wanted to gain political credit
for introducing it, and the Labour Party in particular wanted to gain or
sustain electoral popularity because of its legislative programme of 1945–51.
It was difficult for its members to tolerate criticism of its achievements or
even talk about them without exaggeration. The Conservative Party had
a two-fold motive – first to gain the credit for the original inspiration of the
Welfare State but secondly to show that it had become unnecessarily
extravagant. Middle-class anxieties about the 'burden' of taxation could
be legitimated by the belief that welfare had become excessive. Certain
types of information could be interpreted according to these various
attitudes.

There are many features of social belief and value which deserve fuller
explanation than we can attempt here. In particular the general assumption
that economic and social progress has been sharper and faster than it has
actually been is a sociological phenomenon of the first importance which
it would be instructive to analyse. Our point is, first, that society has tended
to make a rather sweeping interpretation of such evidence as there is about
the reduction of poverty and the increase of equality since the war and,
secondly, this evidence is a lot weaker than many social scientists have
supposed. Basically, its weakness derives from conceptual rather than
technical inadequacy, particularly in the sense that the measures of need
and of income that have been used are more appropriate to a static than
to a dynamic society.

A fresh approach is therefore called for. As a first step the income and
expenditure surveys carried out by government and outside bodies, usually
University departments, are likely to prove to be the most promising
source for revising or obtaining information about developments in the

post-war years and currently. The reports of these are tantalizingly silent on the two assumptions described at the beginning of this paper. They tell little about social conditions. They do not contain analyses of the circumstances of the poorest households in the sample in relation to conventional definitions of subsistence. Nor do they compare such households with wealthy or average households of similar or different composition. In fairness to those carrying out such surveys, they were not intended to do so. But the data could nevertheless be re-analysed in this way.

This was the starting point of the present inquiry. Our object was to secure evidence about poverty and inequality. Rather than seek immediately to launch a time-consuming and expensive survey we felt that every effort should first be made to explore existing information. The basic data collected by interviewers in previous national studies should be available for the kind of analysis in which we were interested. In the event we found it would be possible to study the data collected by the Ministry of Labour in two sample surveys of the United Kingdom, the first carried out in 1953-4 and the second in 1960.[8] This paper describes the results of this study.

[. . .] The limited object of the work upon which this report is based was to find out from data collected in government income and expenditure surveys in two post-war years as much as possible about the levels of living and the social characteristics of the poorest section of the population in the United Kingdom. In the process we have defined and used a national assistance standard of living, have re-applied a subsistence standard adopted in an earlier study of poverty (by Rowntree and Lavers in 1951), and have given some account of the extent to which households range in income and expenditure from the average for their type. In this chapter we will first of all discuss whether the evidence for 1953-4 and 1960 allows us to draw conclusions about changes in living conditions between the two years. We will then discuss briefly some of the implications of this report for future research, for government information services and for government action.

Changes between 1953-4 and 1960

Chapters 3 and 4 describe the proportions of the population found in 1953-4 and 1960 to have low levels of living, defined as less than 140 per cent of the basic national assistance scale plus rent and/or other housing costs. It is a tenable view that the basic assistance scale, with the addition of *actual* housing expenditure and a modest margin for special needs and disregards, represent the officially defined minimum level of living at a

8. A preliminary account of the results of analysing the data for the first year are to be found in Townsend (1962). A similar type of analysis for 1960 is reported by Wedderburn (1962).

particular time. The data for 1953–4 were calculated from expenditure and the data for 1960 from income. We set out below the results for the two years and *discuss in detail how closely they can be compared*. The matter is complex, not only because expenditure is taken into account in the one year and income in the other but also for the methodological reasons advanced in chapter 2. It is worth reviewing carefully because the data represent the best available information about the living standards of poor households in the post-war years.

Table 1 shows the percentages and numbers of the total population recorded as having low levels of living in the two years. The crude figures *suggest* a large increase in both the proportion and number of persons with low levels of living. Under 140 per cent of the basic national assistance scale were 10·1 per cent of the survey households in 1953–4 and 17·9 per cent in 1960. The percentage of persons in these households was 7·8 per cent in 1953–4 and 14·2 per cent in 1960. The largest increase took place at the lower levels and it was at these lower levels that the increase in household size was at its greatest. Under the basic assistance rates, the proportion of households increased from 2·1 to 4·7 per cent and the proportion of persons from 1·2 to 3·8 per cent. The estimated total of persons in households with low levels of living increased from nearly 4 million to nearly $7\frac{1}{2}$ million. The estimated total of persons in households living below the basic assistance scale increased from about 600,000 to about 2 million.

In considering these increases let us first review the comparability of the samples for the two years. Both under-represented the sick and aged (and

Table 1 **Percentage of households and persons and number of persons with low levels of living, 1953–4 and 1960**

Total expenditure (1953–4) or income (1960) as percentage of basic NA scale plus rent/housing	Percentage of households		Percentage of persons		Estimated persons in United Kingdom (thousands)	
	1953–4	1960	1953–4	1960	1953–4	1960
Under 80	0·5	1·3	0·3	0·9	152	471
80–89	0·6	1·0	0·2	0·9	101	471
90–99	1·0	2·4	0·7	2·0	354	1048
100–109	1·9	4·7	1·4	2·8	709	1467
110–119	1·7	3·1	1·4	2·4	709	1257
120–129	2·0	2·7	1·8	2·5	911	1310
130–139	2·4	2·8	2·0	2·7	1012	1414
140 and over	89·9	82·1	92·2	85·8	46,663	44,945
Total	100·0	100·0	100·0	100·0	50,611	52,383

therefore national assistance recipients). But, as shown earlier, the under-representation was greater in 1953–4 than in 1960. The crude figures suggest that the proportion of the population living at less than 40 per cent above the basic assistance scale increased from 7·8 to 14·2 per cent. We calculate that a quarter to a third of the difference can be explained by the difference in the extent to which the two samples represented the United Kingdom population of the two years.

Expenditure and income

Second, was any of the recorded increase in the proportion of households with low levels of living due to adopting an expenditure basis for the analysis of the 1953–4 data and an income basis for the 1960 data? In general it has already been shown that expenditure tends to be overstated and income understated in inquiries of this kind, particularly among low income households. Thus one would expect to find too few persons recorded as having low levels of living in 1953 and too many in 1960. Moreover, the aged, who were heavily represented among the poorer households, tend to be dissavers. Again, one would expect expenditure figures recorded over a three week period to be less widely dispersed than income figures, even possibly than '*normal*' income figures. Thus there would be a higher proportion of households recorded as having *temporary* low income in 1960 than a *more permanently* low expenditure in 1953–4.

Ideally we would have wished to examine for 1960 the relationship between expenditure and 'normal' income for each individual household in the sample. In practice we could only examine this relationship for a sub-sample of 152. In addition we were able to take into account a special analysis of the 60 households in the sample of that year with an income of under 60s, which had been produced by the Ministry. On the basis of the results from this sub-sample we were able to make broad estimates for the whole sample. These are compared with the income figures and with the 1953–4 expenditure figures in Table 2. Instead of 17·9 per cent of households, and 14·2 per cent of persons, living below or just above the national assistance standard it emerges that there would have been 15·9 per cent and 12·4 per cent respectively if current expenditure instead of normal income had been taken as the criterion. Instead of nearly 7½ million persons being in poverty or on its margins there would have been about 6½ millions. The basis for the expenditure figures given for 1960 in the table is explained in Appendix 4 [not included here – Ed.].

Although the 1960 expenditure estimates must be treated with caution since they are based on a small sub-sample of households investigated in the 1960 survey (percentages are therefore placed in brackets), two broad conclusions can be drawn from the table. First, the expenditure data con-

Table 2 **Percentage of households and persons with low expenditure, 1953–4 and 1960, and low income, 1960**

Total income/ expenditure as percentage of national assistance scale plus rent/ housing	1953–4			1960		
	House- holds	Persons	Estimated nos. of persons in the UK (000)	House- holds	Persons	Estimated nos. of persons in the UK (000)
Income						
Under 100	—	—	—	4·7	3·8	1990
100 but under 140	—	—	—	13·3	10·4	5448
140 and over	—	—	—	82·1	85·8	44,945
Total	—	—	—	100	100	52,383
N =	—	—	—	3540	10,765	—
Expenditure						
Under 100	2·1	1·2	607	(5·8)	(4·3)	2250
100 but under 140	8·0	6·6	3341	(10·1)	(8·1)	4243
140 and over	89·9	92·2	46,663	(84·1)	(87·6)	45,890
Total	100	100	50,611	100	100	52,383
N =	3225	10,270	—	212*	418*	—

* Sub-sample of 152 households plus data for 60 households with income of under £3. See Appendix 4 for further details.

firm the income data in showing an increase between 1953–4 and 1960 in the numbers and proportion of the population living below or just above the national assistance 'standard'. Second, the evidence suggests a marked increase in the proportion living *below* the basic national assistance rates. Although the overall percentage living in poverty or on the margins of poverty is lower according to the expenditure than according to the income criterion, the percentage *below* the scale rate is higher.

Table 2 also suggests that possibly a third of the increase between 1953 and 1960 in numbers of persons at low levels of living is due to our having taken an income basis for measurement in the second but not the first of these years. It is disappointing that the Ministry has not yet published information about this important matter, showing the distribution around the average and the disparity between income and expenditure for each household type.

Reasons for more people living at low levels of living
Part of the increase in the proportion of households with low levels of living seems however to be genuine. The most obvious reason for this is that the proportion of the aged (and particularly the proportion of the very aged) in the population increased between the two years. Between 1953 and 1960, the proportion of the population of the United Kingdom who were aged 65 and over increased from 11·1 to 11·7 per cent. We

Table 3 Percentage of households of different size with low levels of living, 1953–4 and 1960

No. of persons in household	1953–4 (low expenditure)	1960 (low income)
1	38·6	52·1
2	9·6	18·2
3	4·9	7·5
4	4·6	6·4
5	5·4	10·0
6+	11·5	25·2
All sizes	10·1	17·9

found that over two thirds of the households with low expenditure in the 1953–4 survey had retired heads. A second reason is the increase in the proportion of large families in the population.

In Table 3 we show the percentage of households of different size recorded as having low levels of living in the two years.

Among households of every size the proportion with low levels of living increased. The proportion of two-person households nearly doubled. The proportional increase was smaller for households of three or four persons and smallest for one-person households where the proportion with low expenditure was already nearly 39 per cent in 1953–4. The largest increase was among the very large households with six or more persons. There were 11½ per cent of such households with low levels of living in 1953–4 and 25 per cent in 1960.

The age distribution of persons in households with low levels of living is shown in Table 4.

Table 4 Age distribution of persons with low levels of living 1953–4 and 1960

Household expenditure (1953–4) or income (1960) as percentage of basic national assistance scale plus rent/housing	Year	Age			All ages
		Over 16	5–15	Under 5	
Under 100	1953–4	83·1	10·5	6·4	100·0
	1960	66·9	21·1	12·0	100·0
100–119	1953–4	68·3	23·2	8·5	100·0
	1960	79·7	14·6	5·7	100·0
120–139	1953–4	69·1	19·6	11·3	100·0
	1960	62·2	25·3	12·5	100·0
All under 140	1953–4	70·9	19·5	9·6	100·0
	1960	69·9	20·2	9·9	100·0

In general there was a modest increase in the proportion of children in the sampled households with low levels of living from 29·1 to 30·1 per cent. This concealed bigger changes at the different levels. There was in fact a fall in the proportion of children at and just above the assistance level from 31·7 to 20·3 per cent. This was more than balanced partly by an increase in the proportion of children at the higher level but also, and perhaps more importantly, by a greater increase in the proportion of children in households under the assistance level – from 16·9 to 33·1 per cent. Too much weight should not however be placed upon these figures in view of the small numbers involved in many of these categories.

Between 1953 and 1960, the proportion of children increased by about 0·5 per cent in both the total population and in the samples. The proportion of children in households with low levels of living increased by 1 per cent. These modest changes conceal much larger changes in family size. While the total population increased by 3·5 per cent between the two years, the number of families with four dependent children increased by about 20 per cent, with five children by about 26 per cent and with six or more children by 45 per cent.[9] Moreover, the economic position of large families was relatively worse in 1960 than in 1953. While we have shown that the general level of incomes of the country increased by just over 50 per cent in money terms, the family allowance for the second child remained at 8s. in both years, while the family allowance for a third or subsequent children increased from 8s to 10s. – an increase of only 25 per cent. No doubt the failure of family allowances to keep pace with the living standards of the community contributed to the higher proportion of households found to have low levels of living in 1960 than in 1953–4. But in view of the fact that only 14 per cent of low income households were found in 1960 consisting of a man, woman and three or more children, the changing size and economic position of the family can only have accounted for an increase of 3 or 4 per cent in the proportion of households with low levels of living.

A third reason for the recorded increase in the proportion of the population with low levels of living was the increase in the proportion dependent for long periods on sickness benefits. This is partly due to the relative increase in the proportion of the population aged between 55 and 65 and also to the relative increase in the proportions of men in this age-group who are chronically sick.[10]

9. Calculated from statistics on family allowances given in the Ministry of Pensions and National Insurance Reports for 1953 and 1960.

10. Between 1951 and 1960 'there was . . . an appreciable rise of chronic sickness among men in their late fifties, and a very substantial one, amounting to 30 per cent, in men in their early sixties'. The proportion of insured men aged 61–63 who were

In addition to the increases in the proportions of the aged, of large families and of the chronic sick, we cannot exclude the possibility that although *average* earnings increased by about 50 per cent, the lowest earnings increased by less than 50 per cent.

Definitions of poverty

What implications does this analysis hold for the future? First, much more thought needs to be given to concepts of poverty. The subsistence standards used by earlier writers on poverty seem at first sight to lend themselves to comparisons over time. This approach allows a basket of food-stuffs and other goods to be defined as necessary to provide subsistence. The cost of purchasing these goods can be calculated for different years and the number of households with insufficient income to purchase the goods can be ascertained. Although the principle seems easy to state, there are problems of applying it in practice. For example, the goods on the market at the later period may not be the same as at the earlier period. The cumbrous garments which convention required women to wear at the beginning of this century were unlikely to be found on the market in the 1930s let alone today. Electricity has replaced oil lamps and candles. Even food habits have changed. These are among the problems which face those who attempt to apply the same poverty line at different periods. Again, the choice of goods that are selected initially cannot be defended in narrowly 'physical' or 'nutritional' terms. In laying down what articles of clothing and items of food are necessary for physical efficiency those in charge of the surveys have been unable to prevent judgments about what is conventional or customary from creeping into their lists and definitions.

There are further kinds of difficulties. There is, for example, a difference between defining poverty in any objective or partly objective sense and defining it subjectively – as felt by the individual or by particular social groups. In any objective sense the word has no absolute meaning which can be applied in all societies at all times. Poverty is a relative concept. Saying who is in poverty is to make a relative statement – rather like saying who is short or heavy. But it is also a statement of a much more complex kind than one referring to a unilineal scale of measurement. It refers to a variety of conditions involving differences in home environment, material possessions and educational and occupational resources as well as in financial resources – most of which are measurable, at least in prin-ciple. Income or expenditure as defined in this paper should be regarded as only one of the possible indicators. We need to develop other indicators

---

absent sick from work for over three months increased from 9 per cent in 1953–4 to 10·6 per cent in 1960 (Morris, 1964, p. 11).

of the command of individuals and families over resources. Our frame of reference can be local, national or international society, according to our interests. In saying all this we are saying nothing new. The fact that poverty is essentially a relative concept and essentially one which refers to a variety of conditions and not simply a financial condition has been accepted overtly or implicitly by leading writers on the subject almost as long as poverty studies have been undertaken.

Implications for government information and research

Reports on government surveys of the population still contain far too little social information about the poorest sections of the population. This is true not only of the family expenditure surveys, but also of nutrition surveys (National Food Survey Committee, 1964). Despite searching public criticisms of the analysis of nutritional data the National Food Survey Committee has failed to provide information about families with children, particularly large families, falling short of the standards recommended by the British Medical Association. No government can expect to pursue rational policies in social security and welfare unless information about living conditions, particularly the living conditions of the poor, is regularly collected, analysed and reported.

The first aim should be to develop various standards which indicate need or poverty. Budgets necessary to purchase minimum nutrition, of the kind developed by the United States Department of Agriculture,[11] might be worked out. The environmental, including housing, resources of families might be more carefully assessed, as also the social and other resources, they require to overcome disability.

The second aim should be to collect information regularly and publish annual reports. It would of course be possible to publish a report complementary to that on the Family Expenditure Survey, showing the sources of income, incomes and expenditures of households receiving certain kinds of social benefits, or of particular kinds of household known to have exceptional social and financial problems – fatherless families, large families or the families of the long-term unemployed. The Central Statistical Office has carried out some useful analyses of redistribution, based on the expenditure surveys, but they give emphasis to overall trends rather than the particular circumstances of poor families as related to middle-income or wealthy families.[12] Government sources in the United States are now pub-

11. Though we hope certain technical criticisms might be overcome. See US Department of Agriculture (1962); and Household Food Consumption Service (1955, 1957).

12. See 'The impact of taxes and social service benefits on different groups of households', *Econ. Trends*, Nov. 1962, and 'The incidence of taxes and social service benefits in 1961 and 1962', *Econ. Trends*, Feb. 1964. See also, Nicholson (1965).

lishing very informative analyses of poverty in that country (Orshansky, 1965). Perhaps in time the same might be possible in the United Kingdom.

The third aim should be to carry out some immediate inquiries into the information about the relationship between income and expenditure, as collected in family expenditure surveys. In addition, more needs to be known about non-respondents. We believe that such inquiries would help to ensure that future family expenditure surveys can be reliably used to depict the socio-economic conditions of particular groups of the population.[13]

Implications for policy

One conclusion that can be drawn from both surveys is that national assistance is inefficient. While it is impossible to give precise figures it is clear that substantial numbers in the population were not receiving national assistance in 1953–4 and 1960 and yet seemed, *prima facie*, to qualify for it. In the latter year, for example, there were nearly one million persons who had pensions or other state benefits and whose incomes fell below assistance rates plus rent.

This national evidence is extremely important and confirms what has been concluded from independent studies, particularly of the aged, in recent years (Cole and Utting, 1962; Townsend and Wedderburn, 1965). It is given greater force by the unambiguous statement in the recent report of a Government committee of inquiry into the impact of rates on households: 'We estimate that about half a million retired householders are apparently eligible for assistance but not getting it.'

This is not the place for a searching discussion of reforms in social security. All that we wish to point out is that there is a two-fold implication for social policy of the evidence in this report – not only that a substantial minority of the population in addition to those receiving national assistance live at or below national assistance standards, but also that a substantial minority are not receiving national assistance and yet appear to qualify for it. The legitimacy of the system of national assistance is therefore called into question.

Possibly the most novel finding is the extent of poverty among children. For over a decade it has been generally assumed that such poverty as

13. A number of improvements have been made in the family expenditure surveys in recent years. We understand that a study of *individual* discrepancies in income/expenditure totals is now in hand and that statistical analyses other than those which are already published are passed on to the Ministry of Pensions.

14. This was a conservative estimate made after consultations with the National Assistance Board (The Allen Report, 1965, p. 117 and pp. 221–225). The Government Social Survey carried out a special survey for the Committee in 1963 which was in all major respects identical to the family expenditure survey.

exists is found overwhelmingly among the aged. Unfortunately it has not been possible to estimate from the data used in this study exactly how many persons over minimum pensionable age were to be found among the seven-and-a-half million persons with low income in 1960. However, such data as we have suggest that the number may be around three million. There were thus more people who were not aged than were aged among the poor households of 1960. We have estimated earlier that there were about two-and-a-quarter million children in low income households in 1960. Thus quantitatively the problem of poverty among children is more than two thirds of the size of poverty among the aged. This fact has not been given due emphasis in the policies of the political parties. It is also worth observing that there were substantially more children in poverty than adults of working age.

There is a simple if relatively expensive remedy for the problem of poverty among children – to substantially increase family allowances, particularly for the larger family. Alternatively, part of the problem could be dealt with at relatively low cost by allowing national assistance to be drawn despite the fact that the breadwinner is receiving full-time earnings. Such a proposal would mean over-riding more than a century of conventional wisdom about incentives. However assistance is paid to families receiving full-time earnings in several States in the United States and this policy enjoys the tacit support of the American trade unions (Sinfield, 1965). The acceptance of this principle would make it possible to deal with the problem of poverty among 'wage stopped' families already receiving assistance and among large families with a breadwinner in full-time work. In the case of the latter group, however, there would remain the problem of families who were not prepared to apply to the Board for help.

Summary

In summary, we have in this chapter brought together the statistics about low levels of living which we presented respectively in chapter 3, for 1953–54, and in chapter 4, for 1960. Although we have tried to apply definitions and procedures which would allow the statistics for the two years to be compared, we realize that it is difficult, for technical reasons, to draw firm conclusions. Between 1953 and 1960 the Ministry of Labour surveys suggest that the number of persons living at low levels increased from 7·8 per cent to 14·2 per cent. Of the difference of 6·4 per cent we would estimate that about 1·5 per cent was due to a better representation in the sample of aged persons in 1960 than in 1953 and another 0·5 or 1 per cent to a fuller representation in the sample of national assistance recipients other than the aged. Very little of the difference seems to be due to a change, relative to wages, in the definition of 'low levels of living', but part of it (about

2 per cent) seems to be due to the fact that the definition was based on income in 1960 and expenditure in 1953–4. Nonetheless, some part of the apparent increase from 7·8 to 14·2 per cent seems attributable to (a) the relative increase in the number of old people in the population, (b) a slight relative increase in the number of men in late middle age who are chronically sick, and (c) the relative increase in the number of families with four or more children, at a time when family allowances have increased much less than average industrial earnings and when the wages of some low-paid workers may not have increased as much as average industrial earnings. On the whole the data we have presented contradicts the commonly held view that a trend towards greater equality has accompanied the trend towards greater affluence.

In general, we regard our figures for 1960 to be the more accurate even though we believe that they understate the numbers of the population with low levels of living because of the under-representation of the aged and the sick. We may summarize our findings for that year by saying that about 5–6 per cent of the population were in low income households because wages, even when supplemented by family allowances, were insufficient to raise them above the minimum level. A further 3–4 per cent were in households receiving social insurance benefits (principally pensions) but the latter were insufficient. Many such households would probably be entitled to national assistance but for various reasons had not applied for it. A further 4–5 per cent of the population were in low income households because, under various regulations, they were not entitled to the full scale of national assistance grant or because the minimum we have taken is considerably above the *basic* national assistance scale.

Even if we take a substantially lower base line – the basic assistance scale plus rent – we find that about two million people (3·8 per cent of the population) were living in households with exceptionally low incomes. For about a quarter of them the problem was inadequate earnings and family allowances; for nearly half of them the problem was inadequate social insurance benefits coupled with unwillingness to apply for national assistance, and for the remainder the amount of national assistance being received was apparently inadequate.

In terms of national information we conclude from the evidence that steps should be taken by the government to ensure that regular surveys are made of the living conditions of the poorest households in our society and that reports should be published showing their sources of income and how their social characteristics compare with those of other households.

Finally, we conclude that the evidence of substantial numbers of the population living below national assistance level, and also of substantial numbers seeming to be eligible for national assistance but not receiving it, calls for a radical review of the whole social security scheme. Moreover, the fact that nearly a third of the poor were children suggests the need for a readjustment of priorities in plans for extensions and developments.

References

ALLEN REPORT (1965), *Report of the Committee of Inquiry into the Impact of Rates on Households*, cmnd. 2582, HMSO.

CARTTER, A. M. (1955), *The Re-Distribution of Income in Post-War Britain*, Yale University Press.

COLE, D., and UTTING, J. (1962), *The Economic Circumstances of Old People*, Occasional Papers on Social Administration, no. 4, Codicote Press.

HOUSEHOLD FOOD CONSUMPTION SERVICE (1955), *Food Consumption and Dietary Levels of Households in the US*, Agricultural Research Service.

LYDALL, H. F. (1959), 'The long-term trend in the size distribution of income', *J. Roy. stat. Soc.*, series A, vol. 122, part 1, pp. 1-46.

MORRIS, J. N. (1964), *Uses of Epidemiology*, second edition, Livingstone.

NATIONAL FOOD SURVEY COMMITTEE (1964), *Domestic Food Consumption and Expenditure; 1962*, HMSO.

NICHOLSON, J. L. (1965), *Redistribution of Income in the United Kingdom in 1959, 1957, 1953*, Bowes & Bowes.

ORSHANSKY, M. (1965), 'Counting the poor: another look at the poverty profile', *Soc. Security Bull.*, vol. 28.

PAISH, F. W. (1957), The real incidence of personal taxation', *Lloyds Bank Rev.*, vol. 43, pp. 1-16.

POLITICAL AND ECONOMIC PLANNING (1952), *Poverty: Ten Years After Beveridge*, vol. 19, no. 344.

ROWNTREE, B. S., and LAVERS, G. R. (1951), *Poverty and the Welfare State: A Third Social Survey of York Dealing only with Economic Questions*, Longman.

ROYAL COMMISSION ON TAXATION (1955), *Report of the Royal Commission on Taxation*, cmnd. 9474, HMSO.

SEERS, D. (1951), *The Levelling of Incomes Since 1938*, Blackwell.

SINFIELD, A. (1965), 'Supplementation of earnings by public assistance in the United States', University of Essex, (unpublished).

TITMUSS, R. M. (1962), *Income Distribution and Social Change*, Allen & Unwin.

TOWNSEND, P. (1962), 'The meaning of poverty', *Brit. J. Sociol.*, vol. 13, no. 3, September.

TOWNSEND, P., and WEDDERBURN, D. (1965), *The Aged in the Welfare State*, Occasional Papers on Social Administration, no. 14, Bell.

US Department of Agriculture (1962), *Family, Food Plans and Food Costs*, research report no. 20, Agricultural Research Service.

WEDDERBURN, D. (1962), 'Poverty in Britain today: the evidence', *sociol. Rev.*, vol. 10, no. 3.

Editor's Note

This note briefly describes some of the information about poverty in Britain that has become available since *The Poor and the Poorest* was written.

One of the most important developments since 1965 has been the publication of the results of two government surveys examining the situation of low income groups. The first was that of retirement pensioners carried out by the Ministry of Pensions and National Insurance (1966). The principal findings of this inquiry are set out in Table 1. Nearly three million retirement pensions had incomes (apart from National Assistance) which were below the National Assistance standard (then £3·80 a week for a single person plus rent). Of these, only just over half were receiving National Assistance. After further investigation, the report concluded that some 850,000 retirement pensioners were eligible for National Assistance but were not receiving it.[1] This amply confirms the conclusions drawn by Abel-Smith and Townsend (page 365). Moreover, there is little evidence that this problem has been overcome by the introduction of Supplementary Benefits – (see Atkinson, 1969, chapter 4).

Table 1 **Survey of retirement pensioners June 1965**

	Numbers	Percentage
Income (before National Assistance) below NA scale	2,940,000	47
Receiving NA	1,560,000	25
Not entitled to NA on account of savings	360,000	6
Apparently entitled to NA but not receiving it	990,000	16

Source: Ministry of Pensions and National Insurance (1966, Tables 3.2 and 3.4(2)).
Notes: 1. NA denotes National Assistance.
   2. Because of rounding, columns may not add up to the totals shown.
   3. The figures are adjusted for non-response.

One of the most striking conclusions of *The Poor and the Poorest* concerned poverty among children. This finding was borne out by the report 'Circumstances of families' by the Ministry of Social Security

1. The Ministry paid a second visit to the households apparently entitled to assistance to check their eligibility, and this reduced the figure from 990,000 in Table 1 to 850,000·

(1967) on its survey in June 1966 of families with two or more children receiving family allowances. The principal results of this inquiry are shown in Table 2. Of the 3·9 million families concerned, 280,000 had incomes below the National Assistance scale. Of these, 135,000 were receiving National Assistance, but 15,000 did not receive the full allowance because of the operation of the wage stop. There were, therefore, 160,000 families living below the National Assistance scale. (If the Supplementary Benefit standard introduced in November 1966 were employed, the number would rise to 230,000.) Particularly significant for policy purposes was the fact that 70,000 families fell below the National Assistance scale even though the father was in full-time work.

Table 2 **Survey of families receiving family allowances – June 1966**

Type of family	Families whose resources (excluding NA) were less than NA scale	Children in those families	Corresponding estimates on SB base	
			Families	Children
Father in full-time work	70,000	255,000	125,000	410,000
Father sick	55,000	190,000	60,000	195,000
Father unemployed	40,000	155,000	40,000	155,000
Fatherless families	75,000	205,000	75,000	215,000
Other families	35,000	110,000	45,000	130,000
All families	280,000	910,000	345,000	1,110,000

Source: Ministry of Social Security (1967, Table 2.1).
Notes: 1. NA denotes National Assistance scale in force in June 1966. SB refers to Supplementary Benefit scale introduced in November 1966.
2. Because of rounding, columns may not add up to totals shown.

The problem of family poverty was taken up again by the government in its special analysis of the Family Expenditure Survey published in *Two-Parent Families*. The chief results of this investigation are shown in Table 3. The most important conclusion was that in December 1970 there were around 100,000 families (containing over 300,000 children) being below the Supplementary Benefit level. The report also compared the number of (two-parent) low income families in different years, and concluded that 'the evidence suggests that there may have been a decline in the numbers of such families between December 1966 and 1968, after which the estimates of numbers are stable'. As however, has been pointed out by Townsend (1972), it is doubtful whether any such firm conclusion can be drawn in view of the fact that the 1966 data were not treated in the same way as that for later years, that the estimates for large families for 1968–70

Table 3 'Two-parent families' enquiry

	No. with income below Supplementary Benefit level (with father in full-time employment or wage-stopped)			
	No. of families		No. of children	
	All families	Families with 2 or more children	All families	Families with 2 or more children
As at June 1966	na	72,000	na	253,000
December 1966	na	114,000	na	384,000
December 1968	100,000	73,000	307,000	280,000
December 1969	92,000	76,000	304,000	288,000
December 1970	105,000	73,000	316,000	284,000

Source: Department of Health and Social Security (1971, Table 10 C).
Notes: 1. na denotes not available.
2. The difference between the figures for June 1966 given here and those in Table 2 (70,000 families in work plus 15,000 wage-stopped) is accounted for by the fact that the self-employed are included in Table 2 but excluded here.

were averaged in a rather arbitrary way, and that the self-employed were excluded.

The studies referred to above relate to subgroups of the population and while they cover a large proportion of those people most obviously at risk, they do not provide adequate information about the population as a whole. In 1967-9, Townsend and Abel-Smith carried out a full-scale survey of living standards in the United Kingdom. However, at the time of writing, the results of this survey were not available and the only assessment that can be made of the trends since 1960 for the population as a whole is that based on secondary analyses of the Family Expenditure Survey carried out for 1967 and 1969 by Atkinson. These results, shown in Table 4, do not suggest that poverty has declined dramatically in importance over the

Table 4 Proportion of population with incomes below national assistance/supplementary benefit level

	Year	%
1 Poor and the poorest	1960	3·8
2 Atkinson	1967	3·5
3 Atkinson	1969	3·4

Sources: 1. Reading 19, page 358.
2. Atkinson (1969, p. 37).
3. Atkinson (1971, p. 22).

B. Abel-Smith and P. Townsend 371

1960s. This conclusion is reinforced by a 'minimum' estimate based on the Ministry of Pensions and National Insurance survey of pensioners and the Circumstances of Families survey, showing that in 1966 these two groups alone accounted for 3·7 per cent of the population being below the National Assistance level (Atkinson, 1969, p. 37).

References

ATKINSON, A. B. (1969), *Poverty in Britain and the Reform of Social Security*, Cambridge University Press.
ATKINSON, A. B. (1971), 'Conflict in social security policy', in N. Kaldor (ed.), *Conflicts in Policy Objectives*, Blackwell.
DEPARTMENT OF HEALTH AND SOCIAL SECURITY (1971), Statistical Report Series, no. 14, *Two-Parent Families*, HMSO.
MINISTRY OF PENSIONS AND NATIONAL INSURANCE (1966), *Financial and Other Circumstances of Retirement Pensioners*, HMSO.
MINISTRY OF SOCIAL SECURITY (1967), *Circumstances of Families*, HMSO.
TOWNSEND, P. (1972), 'Politics and the statistics of poverty', *Pol. Q.*, vol. 43, pp. 103–112.

21 Annual Report of the Council of Economic Advisers

Poverty in America

Extract from chapter 2 of the Annual Report of the Council of Economic Advisers, *Economic Report of the President 1964*, Government Printing Office, 1964, pp. 55–73.

[. . .] There will always be some Americans who are better off than others. But it need not follow that 'the poor are always with us'. In the United States today we can see on the horizon a society of abundance, free of much of the misery and degradation that have been the age-old fate of man. Steadily rising productivity, together with an improving network of private and social insurance and assistance, has been eroding mass poverty in America. But the process is far too slow. It is high time to redouble and to concentrate our efforts to eliminate poverty.

Poverty is costly not only to the poor but to the whole society. Its ugly by-products include ignorance, disease, delinquency, crime, irresponsibility, immorality, indifference. None of these social evils and hazards will, of course, wholly disappear with the elimination of poverty. But their severity will be markedly reduced. Poverty is no purely private or local concern. It is a social and national problem.

But the overriding objective is to improve the quality of life of individual human beings. For poverty deprives the individual not only of material comforts but of human dignity and fulfillment. Poverty is rarely a builder of character.

The poor inhabit a world scarcely recognizable, and rarely recognized, by the majority of their fellow Americans. It is a world apart, whose inhabitants are isolated from the mainstream of American life and alienated from its values. It is a world where Americans are literally concerned with day-to-day survival – a roof over their heads, where the next meal is coming from. It is a world where a minor illness is a major tragedy, where pride and privacy must be sacrificed to get help, where honesty can become a luxury and ambition a myth. Worst of all, the poverty of the fathers is visited upon the children.

Equality of opportunity is the American dream, and universal education our noblest pledge to realize it. But, for the children of the poor, education is a handicap race; many are too ill-prepared and ill-motivated at home to learn at school. And many communities lengthen the handicap by providing the worst schooling for those who need the best.

Although poverty remains a bitter reality for too many Americans, its incidence has been steadily shrinking. The fruits of general economic growth have been widely shared; individuals and families have responded to incentives and opportunities for improvement; government and private programs have raised the educational attainments, housing standards, health, and productivity of the population; private and social insurance has increasingly protected families against loss of earnings due to death, disability, illness, old age and unemployment. Future headway against poverty will likewise require attacks on many fronts: the active promotion of a full-employment, rapid-growth economy; a continuing assault on discrimination; and a wide range of other measures to strike at specific roots of low income. As in the past, progress will require the combined effort of all levels of government and of private individuals and groups.

All Americans will benefit from this progress. Our Nation's most precious resource is its people. We pay twice for poverty: once in the production lost in wasted human potential, again in the resources diverted to coping with poverty's social by-products. Humanity compels our action, but it is sound economics as well.

This chapter considers, first, the changing numbers and composition of America's poor. Second, it presents a brief report on the factors that contribute to the continuation of poverty amidst plenty. Although the analysis is statistical, the major concern is with the human problems that the numbers reflect. The concluding part concerns strategy against poverty in the 1960s and beyond.

The sections below will chart the topography of poverty. A few significant features of this bleak landscape deserve emphasis in advance. Poverty occurs in many places and is endured by people in many situations; but its occurrence is nonetheless highly concentrated among those with certain characteristics. The scars of discrimination, lack of education and broken families show up clearly from almost any viewpoint. Here are some landmarks:

1. One fifth of our families and nearly one fifth of our total population are poor.

2. Of the poor, 22 per cent are nonwhite; and nearly one half of all nonwhites live in poverty.

3. The heads of over 60 per cent of all poor families have only grade school educations.

4. Even for those denied opportunity by discrimination, education significantly raises the chance to escape from poverty. Of all nonwhite families headed by a person with eight years or less of schooling, 57 per cent are

poor. This percentage falls to 30 for high school graduates and to 18 per cent for those with some college education.

5. But education does not remove the effects of discrimination: when nonwhites are compared with whites at the same level of education, the nonwhites are poor about twice as often.

6. One third of all poor families are headed by a person over 65, and almost one half of families headed by such a person are poor.

7. Of the poor, 54 per cent live in cities, 16 per cent on farms, 30 per cent as rural nonfarm residents.

8. Over 40 per cent of all farm families are poor. More than 80 per cent of nonwhite farmers live in poverty.

9. Less than half of the poor are in the South; yet a southerner's chance of being poor is roughly twice that of a person living in the rest of the country.

10. One quarter of poor families are headed by a woman; but nearly one half of all families headed by a woman are poor.

11. When a family and its head have several characteristics frequently associated with poverty, the chances of being poor are particularly high: a family headed by a young woman who is nonwhite and has less than an eighth grade education is poor in 94 out of 100 cases. Even if she is white, the chances are 85 out of 100 that she and her children will be poor.

The nature and extent of poverty

Measurement of poverty is not simple, either conceptually or in practice. By the poor we mean those who are not now maintaining a decent standard of living – those whose basic needs exceed their means to satisfy them. A family's needs depend on many factors, including the size of the family, the ages of its members, the condition of their health, and their place of residence. The ability to fulfill these needs depends on current income from whatever source, past savings, ownership of a home or other assets, and ability to borrow.

Needs and resources

There is no precise way to measure the number of families who do not have the resources to provide minimum satisfaction of their *own* particular needs. Since needs differ from family to family, an attempt to quantify the problem must begin with some concept of average need for an average or representative family. Even for such a family, society does not have a clear and unvarying concept of an acceptable minimum. By the standards of contemporary American society most of the population of the world is poor; and most Americans were poor a century ago. But for our society today a consensus on an approximate standard can be found. One such standard is suggested by a recent study, described in a publication of the Social Security Administration, which defines a 'low-cost' budget for a nonfarm family of four and finds its cost in 1962 to have been $3955. The cost of what the study defined as an 'economy-plan' budget was $3165. Other studies have used different market baskets, many of them costing more. On balance, they provide support for using as a boundary, a family whose annual money income from all sources was $3000 (before taxes and expressed in 1962 prices). This is a weekly income of less than $60.

These budgets contemplate expenditures of one third of the total on food, i.e. for a $3000 annual budget for a four-person family about $5 per person per week. Of the remaining $2000, a conservative estimate for housing (rent or mortgage payments, utilities, and heat) would be another $800. This would leave only $1200 – less than $25 a week – for clothing, transportation, school supplies and books, home furnishings and supplies, medical care, personal care, recreation, insurance and everything else. Obviously it does not exaggerate the problem of poverty to regard $3000 as the boundary.

A family's ability to meet its needs depends not only on its money income but also on its income in kind, its savings, its property and its ability to borrow. But the detailed data (of the Bureau of the Census) available for pinpointing the origins of current poverty in the United States refer to money income. Refined analysis would vary the income cut-off by family size, age, location and other indicators of needs and costs. This has not been possible. However, a variable income cut-off was used in the sample study of poverty in 1959 conducted at the University of Michigan Survey Research Center. This study also estimates the overall incidence of poverty at 20 per cent; and its findings concerning the sources of poverty correspond closely with the results based on an analysis of Census data.

A case could be made, of course, for setting the overall income limit either higher or lower than $3000, thereby changing the statistical measure of the size of the problem. But the analysis of the sources of poverty, and of the programs needed to cope with it, would remain substantially unchanged.

No measure of poverty as simple as the one used here, would be suitable for determining eligibility for particular benefits or participation in particular programs. Nevertheless, it provides a valid benchmark for assessing the dimensions of the task of eliminating poverty, setting the broad goals of policy, and measuring our past and future progress toward their achievement.

If it were possible to obtain estimates of total incomes – including non-money elements – for various types of families, those data would be preferable for the analysis which follows. The Department of Commerce does estimate total nonmoney incomes in the entire economy in such forms as the rental value of owner-occupied dwellings and food raised and consumed on farms, and allocates them to families with incomes of different size. Because of statistical difficulties, these allocations are necessarily somewhat arbitrary, and are particularly subject to error for the lower income groups. No attempt is made to allocate them by other characteristics that are meaningful for an analysis of poverty. Of course, the total of money plus nonmoney income that would correspond to the limit used here would be somewhat higher than $3000.

The changing extent of poverty

There were 47 million families in the United States in 1962. Fully 9·3 million, or one fifth of these families – comprising more than 30 million persons – had total money incomes below $3000. Over 11 million of these family members were children, one sixth of our youth. More than 1·1 million families are now raising four or more children on such an income. Moreover, 5·4 million families, containing more than 17 million persons, had total incomes below $2000. More than a million children were being raised in very large families (six or more children) with incomes of less than $2000.

Serious poverty also exists among persons living alone or living in nonfamily units such as boarding houses. In 1962, 45 per cent of such 'unrelated individuals' – five million persons – had incomes below $1500 and, 29 per cent – or more than three million persons – had incomes below $1000. Thus, by the measures used here, 33 to 35 million Americans were living at or below the boundaries of poverty in 1962 – nearly one fifth of our Nation.

The substantial progress made since World War II in eliminating poverty is shown in Figure 1 and Table 1. In the decade 1947–56, when incomes were growing relatively rapidly, and unemployment was generally low, the number of poor families (with incomes below $3000 in terms of 1962 prices) declined from 11·9 million to 9·9 million, or from 32 per cent to 23 per cent of all families. But in the period from 1957 through 1962, when total growth was slower and unemployment substantially higher, the number of families living in poverty fell less rapidly, to 9·3 million, or 20 per cent of all families.

The progress made since Second World War has not involved any major change in the distribution of incomes. The one fifth of families with the highest incomes received an estimated 43 per cent of total income in 1947 and 42 per cent in 1962. The one fifth of families with the lowest incomes received 5 per cent of the total in 1947 and 5 per cent in 1963.

Table 1 Money income of families, 1947 and 1950–62

Year	Median money income of all families (1962 prices)		% of families with money income	
	Dollars	Index 1947 = 100	Less than $3000 (1962 prices)	Less than $2000 (1962 prices)
1947	4117	100	32	18
1950	4188	102	32	19
1951	4328	105	29	17
1952	4442	108	28	17
1953	4809	117	26	16
1954	4705	114	28	17
1955	5004	122	25	15
1956	5337	130	23	14
1957	5333	130	23	14
1958	5329	129	23	14
1959	5631	137	22	13
1960	5759	140	21	13
1961	5820	141	21	13
1962	5956	145	20	12

Sources: Department of Commerce and Council of Economic Advisers.

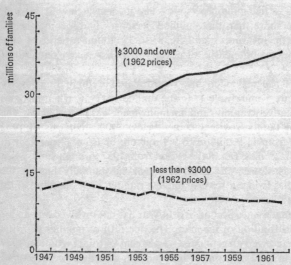

Figure 1   Number of families by family income (Source: Department of Commerce)

Even if poverty should hereafter decline at the relatively more rapid rate of the 1947–56 period, there would still be 10 per cent of the Nation's families in poverty in 1980. And, if the decline proceeded at the slower rate achieved from 1957 on, 13 per cent of our families would still have incomes under $3000 in 1980. We cannot leave the further wearing away of poverty solely to the general progress of the economy. A faster reduction of poverty will require that the lowest fifth of our families be able to earn a larger share of national output.

The composition of today's poor

To mount an attack on poverty we must know how to select our targets. Are the poor concentrated in any single geographical area? Are they confined to a few easily identifiable groups in society? Conclusions drawn from personal observation are likely to be misleading. Some believe that most of the poor are found in the slums of the central city, while others

Table 2 **Selected characteristics of all families and poor families, 1962**

Selected characteristic	No. of families (millions)		% of total	
	All families	Poor families	All families	Poor families
Total	47·0	9·3	100	100
Age of head:				
14–24 years	2·5	0·8	5	8
25–54 years	30·4	3·9	65	42
55–64 years	7·3	1·4	16	15
65 years and over	6·8	3·2	14	34
Education of head:[1]				
8 years or less	16·3	6·0	35	61
9–11 years	8·6	1·7	19	17
12 years	12·2	1·5	26	15
More than 12 years	9·3	0·7	20	7
Sex of head:				
Male	42·3	7·0	90	75
Female	4·7	2·3	10	25
Labor force status of head:[2]				
Not in civilian labor force	8·4	4·1	18	44
Employed	36·9	4·6	78	49
Unemployed	1·7	0·6	4	6
Color of family:				
White	42·4	7·3	90	78
Nonwhite	4·6	2·0	10	22

Table 2 – *continued*

Selected characteristic	No. of families millions		% of total	
	All families	Poor families	All families	Poor families
Children under 18 years of age in family:				
None	18·8	4·9	40	52
One to three	22·7	3·3	48	36
Four or more	5·5	1·1	12	11
Earners in family:				
None	3·8	2·8	8	30
One	21·1	4·3	45	46
Two or more	22·1	2·2	47	23
Regional location of family:[3,4]				
Northeast	11·5	1·6	25	17
North Central	13·1	2·3	29	25
South	13·5	4·3	30	47
West	7·0	1·0	16	11
Residence of family:[4,5]				
Rural farm	3·3	1·5	7	16
Rural nonfarm	9·9	2·7	22	30
Urban	31·9	5·0	71	54

1. Based on 1961 income (1962 prices).

2. Labor force status relates to survey week of March 1963.

3. Based on 1960 residence and 1959 income (1962 prices).

4. Data are from 1960 Census are therefore not strictly comparable with the other data shown in this table, which are derived from *Current Population Reports*.

5. Based on 1959 residence and 1959 income (1962 prices).

Note. Data relate to families and exclude unrelated individuals. Poor families are defined as all families with total money income of less than $3000.

Sources: Department of Commerce and Council of Economic Advisers.

believe that they are concentrated in areas of rural blight. Some have been impressed by poverty among the elderly, while others are convinced that it is primarily a problem of minority racial and ethnic groups. But objective evidence indicates that poverty is pervasive. To be sure, the inadequately educated, the aged and the nonwhite make up substantial portions of the poor population. But as Table 2 shows, the poor are found among all major groups in the population and in all parts of the country.

Using the income measure of poverty described above, we find that 78 per cent of poor families are white. Although one third of the poor families are headed by a person 65 years old and over, two fifths are headed by persons in the 25 to 54 year range. Although it is true that a great deal of poverty is associated with lack of education, almost four million poor families (39 per cent) are headed by a person with at least some education beyond grade school. The data show that less than half the poor live in the South. And the urban poor are somewhat more numerous than the rural poor. In Figure 2 the poor and the non-poor are compared in terms of these and other characteristics.

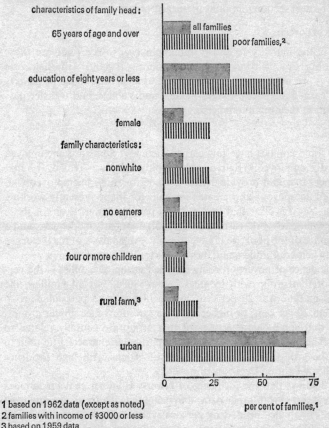

characteristics of family head:

65 years of age and over
 — all families
 — poor families,[2]

education of eight years or less

female

family characteristics:

nonwhite

no earners

four or more children

rural farm,[3]

urban

0   25   50   75

1 based on 1962 data (except as noted)
2 families with income of $3000 or less
3 based on 1959 data

per cent of families,[1]

Figure 2   Characteristics of poor families compared with all families
(Source: Department of Commerce)

Yet there are substantial concentrations of poverty among certain groups. For example, families headed by persons 65 years of age and older represent 34 per cent of poor families. Moreover, they appear among the poor $2\frac{1}{2}$ times as frequently as they appear among all families. The last two columns of Table 2 show five additional major categories of families that appear more than twice as often among the poor as among the total population: nonwhite families, families headed by women, families headed by individuals not in the civilian labor force, families with no wage earners, and rural farm families. Of course, some of these groups overlap considerably; but the data help to identify prospective targets for an antipoverty attack. The next section pinpoints these targets further.

The roots of poverty

Poverty is the inability to satisfy minimum needs. The poor are those whose resources – their income from all sources, together with their asset holdings – are inadequate. This section considers why those in poverty lack the earned income, property income and savings, and transfer payments to meet their minimum needs.

Earned income

Why do some families have low earned incomes? Some are unemployed or partially employed. High overall employment is a remedy of first importance. It would provide earned income for those unemployed who are able to accept jobs and greater earnings for many presently working part-time. Yet it is clear that this is only a partial answer. Even for those able and willing to work, earnings are all too frequently inadequate, and a large number of the poor are unable to work. An analysis of the incidence of poverty helps one understand the reasons for low earnings.

The incidence of poverty for any specified group of families is the percentage of that group with incomes below $3000. For all families, the incidence in 1962 was 20 per cent. An incidence for a particular group higher than 20 per cent, or higher than the rates for other similar groups, suggests that some characteristics of that group are causally related to poverty. The basic cause may not be the particular characteristic used to classify the group. But an examination of groups with high incidence should throw light on the roots of poverty.

Table 3 shows that the incidence of poverty is 76 per cent for families with no earners. From other data, it appears that the incidence rate is 49 per cent for families headed by persons who work part-time. A family may be in either of these situations as a result of age, disability, premature death of the principal earner, need to care for children or disabled family members, lack of any saleable skill, lack of motivation, or simply heavy unemployment in the area.

The problem of another group of families is the low rates of pay found most commonly in certain occupations. For example, the incidence of poverty among families headed by employed persons is 45 per cent for farmers, and 74 per cent for domestic service workers.

Table 3 Incidence of poverty, by characteristics relating to labour force participation, 1962

Selected characteristic	Incidence of poverty (%)
All families	20
Earners in family:	
None	76
One	20
Two	10
Three or more	8
Labor force status of head:[1]	
Not in civilian labor force	50
Employed	12
Unemployed	34
Age of head:	
14–24 years	31
25–54 years	13
55–64 years	19
65 years and over	47
Sex of head:	
Male	17
Wife in labor force	9
Female	48

[1] Status relates to survey week of March 1963.

Note: Data relate to families and exclude unrelated individuals. Poverty is defined to include all families with total money income of less than $3000; these are also referred to as poor families. Incidence of poverty is measured by the per cent that poor families with a given characteristic are of all families having the same characteristic.

Sources: Department of Commerce and Council of Economic Advisers.

The chief reason for low rates of pay is low productivity, which in turn can reflect lack of education or training, physical or mental disability, or poor motivation. Other reasons include discrimination, low bargaining power, exclusion from minimum wage coverage, or lack of mobility resulting from inadequate knowledge of other opportunities, or unwillingness or inability to move away from familiar surroundings.

The importance of education as a factor in poverty is suggested by the fact that families headed by persons with no more than eight years of education have an incidence rate of 37 per cent (Table 4). Nonwhite and rural families show an even higher incidence of poverty. The heads of these families are typically less well educated than average. For example, non-white family heads have completed a median of 8·7 years of school, compared to 11·8 for whites. In 1959 the median education of all males over twenty-five with incomes below $1000 and living on a farm was slightly above seven years in school; those with incomes above $5000 had completed over ten years in school.

[. . .] Some families are forced into poverty by society's own standards. Their potential earners, otherwise able to hold a job, cannot free themselves from the family responsibilities which they must fulfill. Such is the case, for example, with families headed by women with small children.

Table 4 **Incidence of poverty by education, colour and residence, 1962**

Selected characteristic	Incidence of poverty (%)
All families	20
Education of head:[1]	
8 years or less	37
9–11 years	20
12 years	12
More than 12 years	8
Color of family:	
White	17
Nonwhite	44
Residence of family:	
Farm	43
Nonwhite	84
Nonfarm	18

[1] Data relate to 1961, and money income in 1962 prices.
Note: data relate to families and exclude unrelated individuals. Poverty is defined to include all families with total money income of less than $3000; these are also referred to as poor families. The incidence of poverty is measured by the per cent that poor families with a given characteristic are of all families having the same characteristic.
Sources: Department of Commerce and Council of Economic Advisers.

Customary or mandatory retirement at a specified age also limits earnings by some healthy, able-bodied persons. However, retirement is often associated with deteriorating health, and poverty among the aged is greatest at ages over seventy or seventy-five and for aged widows – persons for whom employment is not a realistic alternative.

Property income and use of savings

Some families with inadequate current earnings from work can avoid poverty thanks to past savings – which provide an income and, if necessary, can be used to support consumption. Savings are particularly important for the elderly. More than half of those over 65 have money incomes above

$3000, and many also own homes. Others, although their money incomes are below $3000, have adequate savings that can be drawn upon to support a decent standard of consumption.

But most families with low earnings are not so fortunate. If avoiding poverty required an income supplement of $1500 a year for a retired man and his wife, they would need a capital sum at age sixty-five of about $19,000 to provide such an annuity. Few families have that sum. The median net worth for all spending units (roughly equivalent to the total of families and unrelated individuals) was only $4700 in 1962. For all spending units whose head was sixty-five years or more, the median net worth was $8000. Meeting contingencies caused by illnesses is often a crucial problem for older people. About half of the aged, and about three fourths of the aged poor, have no hospital insurance, although their medical care costs are two-and-a-half times as high as those of younger persons. Their resources are typically inadequate to cover the costs of a serious illness.

The median net worth of the fifth of all spending units having the lowest incomes was only $1000. Much of what property they have is in the form of dwellings. (About 40 per cent of all poor families have some equity in a house.) Although this means that their housing costs are reduced, property in this form does not provide money income that can be used for other current expenses.

Most families – including the aged – whose incomes are low in any one year lack significant savings or property because their incomes have always been at poverty levels. This is clear in the results of the Michigan study already cited. Among the reporting families classified in that study as poor in 1959, 60 per cent had never earned disposable income as high as $3000, and nearly 40 per cent had never reached $2000. The comparable figures for all families were 17 per cent and 10 per cent, respectively. Among the aged poor reporting, 79 per cent had never reached $3000, and fully one half had never earned $2000. While nearly 60 per cent of *all* families have enjoyed peak incomes above $5000, among all poor families only 14 per cent had ever reached that level; and a mere 5 per cent of the aged poor had ever exceeded $5000.

The persistence of poverty is reflected in the large number who have been unable to accumulate savings. The Survey Research Center study found that more than one half of the aged poor in 1959 had less than $500 in liquid savings (bank deposits and readily marketable securities), and they had not had savings above that figure during the previous five years. Less than one fifth of all poor families reported accumulated savings in excess of $500. The mean amount of savings used by poor families in 1959 was $120; and only 23 per cent of the poor drew on savings at all.

It is clear that for most families property income and savings do not provide a buffer against poverty.

Transfer payments and private pensions

Poverty would be more prevalent and more serious if many families and individuals did not receive transfer payments. In 1960, these payments (those which are not received in exchange for current services) constituted only 7 per cent of total family income, but they comprised 43 per cent of the total income of low-income spending units. At the same time, however, only about half of the present poor receive any transfer payments at all. And, of course, many persons who receive transfers through social insurance programs are not poor – often as a result of these benefits.

Transfer programs may be either public or private in nature and may or may not have involved past contributions by the recipient. Public transfer programs include social insurance – such as Unemployment Compensation, Workmen's Compensation, and Old Age, Survivors', and Disability Insurance (OASDI); veterans' benefits; and public assistance programs, such as Old Age Assistance (OAA) and Aid to Families with Dependent Children (AFDC).

Private transfer programs include organized systems such as private pension plans and supplementary unemployment benefits, organized private charities, and private transfers within and among families.

It is important to distinguish between insurance-type programs and assistance programs, whether public or private. Assistance programs are ordinarily aimed specifically at the poor or the handicapped. Eligibility for their benefits may or may not be based upon current income; but neither eligibility nor the size of benefits typically bears any direct relationship to past income. Eligibility for insurance-type programs, on the other hand, is based on past employment, and benefits on past earnings.

The Federal–State unemployment insurance system covers only about 77 per cent of all paid employment and is intended to protect workers with a regular attachment to the labor force against temporary loss of income. Benefits, of course, are related to previous earnings.

While the largest transfer-payment program, OASDI, now covers approximately 90 per cent of all paid employment, there are still several million aged persons who retired or whose husbands retired or died before acquiring coverage. Benefits are related to previous earnings, and the average benefit for a retired worker under this program at the end of 1963 was only $77 a month, or $924 a year. The average benefit for a retired worker and his wife if she is eligible for a wife's benefit is $1565 a year.

Public insurance-type transfer programs have made notable contributions to sustaining the incomes of those whose past earnings have been adequate, and to avoiding their slipping into poverty as their earnings are interrupted or terminated. These programs are of least help to those whose earnings have never been adequate.

Public assistance programs are also an important support to low-income and handicapped persons. Money payments under OAA average about $62 a month for the country as a whole, with State averages ranging from $37 to about $95 a month. In the AFDC program the national average payment per family (typically of four persons) is about $129 a month, including services rendered directly. State averages range from $38 a month to about $197 a month.

Private transfers within and between families are included in the total money income figures used in this chapter only to the extent that they are regular in nature, e.g. alimony or family support payments, and are excluded when they take the form of casual or irregular gifts or bequests. While data are lacking on the value of such gifts, they are clearly not a major source of income for the poor.

Private pensions, providing an annuity, are additional resources for some persons and families. In 1961 the beneficiaries of such plans numbered about two million (as against about twelve million receiving OASDI benefits), and total benefits paid were about $2 billion. While the combination of OASDI and private pensions serves to protect some from poverty, most persons receiving OASDI receive no private pension supplement. In any case, benefits under private pension plans range widely, and since they are typically related to the individual's previous earnings, they are low when earnings have been low.

Thus, although many families do indeed receive supplements to earnings in the form of pensions, social insurance benefits, and incomes from past saving, those families with a history of low earnings are also likely to have little of such supplementary income. And since most poor families have small amounts of property, they cannot long meet even minimum needs by depleting their assets.

The vicious circle

Poverty breeds poverty. A poor individual or family has a high probability of staying poor. Low incomes carry with them high risks of illness; limitations on mobility; limited access to education, information and training. Poor parents cannot give their children the opportunities for better health and education needed to improve their lot. Lack of motivation, hope, and incentive is a more subtle but no less powerful barrier than lack of financial means. Thus the cruel legacy of poverty is passed from parents to children.

Escape from poverty is not easy for American children raised in families accustomed to living on relief. A recent sample study of AFDC recipients found that more than 40 per cent of the parents were themselves raised in homes where public assistance had been received. It is difficult for children to find and follow avenues leading out of poverty in environments where education is deprecated and hope is smothered. This is particularly true when discrimination appears as an insurmountable barrier. Education may be seen as a waste of time if even the well-trained are forced to accept menial labor because of their color or nationality.

The Michigan study shows how inadequate education is perpetuated from generation to generation. Of the families identified as poor in that study, 64 per cent were headed by a person who had less than an eighth grade education. Of these, in turn, 67 per cent had fathers who had also gone no further than eighth grade in school. Among the children of these poor families who had finished school, 34 per cent had not gone beyond the eighth grade; this figure compares with 14 per cent for all families. Fewer than one in two children of poor families had graduated from high school, compared to almost two out of three for all families.

Of two million high school seniors in October 1959 covered by a Census study, 12 per cent did not graduate in 1960. Of these drop-outs 54 per cent had IQs above 90, and 6 per cent were above 110. Most of them had the intellectual capabilities necessary to graduate. The drop-out rate for non-white male students, and likewise for children from households with a nonworking head, was *twice* the overall rate. And it was twice as high for children of families with incomes below $4000 as for children of families with incomes above $6000. Moreover, many of the children of the poor had dropped out before reaching the senior year.

A study of drop-outs in New Haven, Connecticut, showed that 48 per cent of children from lower-class neighborhoods do not complete high school. The comparable figure for better neighborhoods was 22 per cent.

Other studies indicate that unemployment rates are almost twice as high for drop-outs as for high school graduates aged 16–24. Moreover, average incomes of male high school graduates are 25 per cent higher than those of high school drop-outs, and nearly 150 per cent higher than those of men who completed less than eight years of schooling.

There is a well-established association between school status and juvenile delinquency. For example, in the New Haven study cited above, 48 per cent of the drop-outs, but only 18 per cent of the high school graduates, had one or more arrests or referrals to juvenile court.

Low-income families lose more time from work, school and other activities than their more fortunate fellow citizens. Persons in families with incomes under $2000 lost an average of eight days of work in the year 1960–61, compared to 5·4 for all employed persons. They were restricted in activity for an average of 30 days (compared to 16·5 for the whole population) and badly disabled for 10·4 days (compared to 5·8 for the whole population).

In spite of tendencies for poverty to breed poverty, a smaller proportion of our adult population has been poor – and a smaller fraction of American children exposed to poverty – in each succeeding generation. But, at least since the Second World War, the speed of progress has not been equal for all types of families, as is shown in Table 5.

Table 5 **Number of families and incidence of poverty, by selected family characteristics, 1947 and 1962**

Selected characteristic	No. of families			Incidence of poverty (%)[1]		Percentage change in no.
	1947	1962	Percentage change 1947 to 1962	1947	1962	of poor families, 1947 to 1962
	Millions					
All families	37·3	47·0	26	32	20	−22
Earners in family:						
None	2·2	3·8	68	83	76	54
One	21·9	21·1	−4	35	20	−45
Two	9·9	17·0	73	20	10	−13
Three or more	3·3	5·1	56	10	8	29
Labor force status of head:[2]						
Not in civilian labor force	5·5	8·4	52	61	50	23
Unemployed	1·2	1·7	49	49	34	2
Employed	31·9	36·9	16	28	12	−48
Age of head:						
14–24 years	1·8	2·5	39	45	31	−6
25–54 years	25·0	30·4	22	27	13	−41
55–64 years	6·1	7·3	19	32	19	−28
65 years and over	4·4	6·8	54	57	47	27
Sex of head:						
Male	33·5	42·3	26	30	17	−30
Female	3·8	4·7	26	51	48	19
Color of family:						
White	34·2	42·4	24	29	17	−27
Nonwhite	3·1	4·6	46	67	44	−3
Children under 18 years of age in family:						
None	16·2	18·8	16	36	26	−16
One	8·9	8·7	−2	30	17	−46
Two	6·4	8·5	33	27	13	−33
Three or more	5·7	10·9	92	32	17	2

Table 5 – *continued*

Selected characteristic	No. of families			Incidence of poverty (%)[1]		Percentage change in no. of poor families 1947 to 1952
	1947	1962	Percentage change 1947 to 1962	1947	1962	
	Millions					
Regional location of family:[3]						
Northeast	10·1	11·5	14	26	14	−42
North Central	11·5	13·1	14	30	18	−31
South	11·5	13·5	17	49	32	−24
West	5·1	7·0	37	28	15	−26
Residence of family:						
Farm[4]	6·5	3·2	−51	56	43	−62
Nonfarm[5]	30·8	43·8	42	27	18	−5

[1] The incidence of poverty is measured by the per cent that poor families with a given characteristic are of all families having the same characteristic.

[2] Labor force status for April survey week of 1949 and March survey week of 1963. Income data (1962 prices) are for 1948 and 1962.

[3] Income data for 1949 and 1959. Since regional location data are from 1950 and 1960 Censuses, they are not strictly comparable with other data shown in this table, which are derived from *Current Population Reports*.

[4] The 1960 Census change in definition of a farm resulted in a decline of slightly over 1 million in the total number of farm families. Therefore, the incidence figures for 1947 and 1962 may not be strictly comparable.

[5] Since 1959, nonfarm data are not available separately for rural nonfarm and urban.

Note. Data relate to families and exclude unrelated individuals. Poverty is defined to include all families with total money income of less than $3000 (1962 prices); these are also referred to as poor families.

Sources: Department of Commerce and Council of Economic Advisers.

The incidence of poverty has declined substantially for most categories shown in the table. But there are some notable exceptions – families (1) with no earner, (2) with head not in the civilian labor force, (3) with head sixty-five years of age or older, (4) headed by a woman, and (5) on farms. It is also striking that in these classes poverty is high as well as stubborn. Poverty continues high among nonwhites, although there has been a large and welcome decline in this incidence.

With the sole exception of the farm group, the total number of *all* families in each of these categories has remained roughly the same or has increased. Hence the high-incidence groups, including the nonwhites, have come to constitute a larger *proportion* of the poor (Table 6).

Table 6 **Selected characteristics of poor families 1947 and 1962**

Selected characteristic	% of poor families with characteristic	
	1947	1962
Family heads:		
65 years of age and over	20	34
Female	16	25
Nonwhite families	18	22
Rural farm families	30	20[1]
No earners in family	16	30

1. Data are from *Current Population Reports* and are for 1959, based on incomes in 1962 prices. See Table 5, footnote 4, for comparability problem.
Note: Data relate to families and exclude unrelated individuals. Poor families are defined as families with total money income of less than $3000 (1962 prices).
Sources: Department of Commerce and Council of Economic Advisers.

This tabulation shows that certain handicapping characteristics, notably old age, or absence of an earner or of a male family head, have become increasingly prominent in the poor population. This is both a measure of past success in reducing poverty and of the tenacity of the poverty still existing. Rising productivity and earnings, improved education, and the structure of social security have permitted many families or their children to escape; but they have left behind many families who have one or more special handicaps. These facts suggest that in the future economic growth alone will provide relatively fewer escapes from poverty. Policy will have to be more sharply focused on the handicaps that deny the poor fair access to the expanding incomes of a growing economy.

But the significance of these shifts in composition should not be exaggerated. About half of the poor families are still headed neither by an aged person nor by a woman, and 70 per cent include at least one earner. High employment and vigorous economic growth are still of major importance for this group. And it is essential to remember that one third of the present poor are children. For them, improvements in the availability and quality of education offer the greatest single hope of escaping poverty as adults.

22 P. A. Baran and P. M. Sweezy

Monopoly Capitalism and Race Relations

Extract from P. A. Baran and P. M. Sweezy, *Monopoly Capital*, Monthly Review Press, 1966, pp. 257–65.

[. . .] What social forces and institutional mechanisms have forced Negroes to play the part of permanent immigrants, entering the urban economy at the bottom and remaining there decade after decade?[1]

There are, it seems to us, three major sets of factors involved in the answer to this crucially important question. First, a formidable array of private interests benefit, in the most direct and immediate sense, from the continued existence of a segregated sub-proletariat. Second, the socio-psychological pressures generated by monopoly capitalist society intensify rather than alleviate existing racial prejudices, hence also discrimination and segregation. And third, as monopoly capitalism develops, the demand for unskilled and semi-skilled labour declines both relatively and absolutely, a trend which affects Negroes more than any other group and accentuates their economic and social inferiority. All of these factors mutually interact, tending to push Negroes ever further down in the social structure and locking them into the ghetto.

Consider first the private interests which benefit from the existence of a Negro sub-proletariat. (a) Employers benefit from divisions in the labour force which enable them to play one group off against another, thus weakening all. Historically, for example, no small amount of Negro migration was in direct response to the recruiting of strike-breakers. (b) Owners of ghetto real estate are able to overcrowd and overcharge. (c) Middle and upper income groups benefit from having at their disposal a large supply of cheap domestic labour. (d) Many small marginal businesses, especially in the service trades, can operate profitably only if cheap labour is available to them. (e) White workers benefit by being protected from Negro competition for the more desirable and higher-paying jobs. Hence the customary distinction, especially in the South, between 'white' and 'Negro' jobs, the exclusion of Negroes from apprentice programmes, the refusal of

1. 'The Negro population', says the Commission on Race and Housing, 'in spite of its centuries of residence in America, has at present some of the characteristics of an incompletely assimilated immigrant group' (pp. 8–9).

many unions to admit Negroes, and so on.[2] In all these groups – and taken together they constitute a vast majority of the white population – what Marx called 'the most violent, mean and malignant passions of the human breast, the Furies of private interest', are summoned into action to keep the Negro 'in his place'.

With regard to race prejudice, it has already been pointed out that this characteristic white attitude was deliberately created and cultivated as a rationalization and justification for the enslavement and exploitation of coloured labour.[3] But in time, race prejudice and the discriminatory behaviour patterns which go with it came to serve other purposes as well. As capitalism developed, particularly in its monopoly phase, the social structure became more complex and differentiated. Within the basic class framework, which remained in essentials unchanged, there took place a proliferation of social strata and status groups, largely determined by occupation and income. These groupings, as the terms 'stratum' and 'status' imply, relate to each other as higher or lower, with the whole constituting an irregular and unstable hierarchy. In such a social structure, individuals tend to see and define themselves in terms of the 'status hierarchy' and to be motivated by ambitions to move up and fears of moving down.[4] These ambitions and fears are of course exaggerated, intensified, played upon by

2. 'There has grown up a system of Negro jobs and white jobs. And this is the toughest problem facing the Negro Southerner in employment.' Dunbar (1964, p. 457).

3. Among coloured peoples, race prejudice, to the extent that it exists at all, is a defensive reaction to white aggression and therefore has an entirely different significance. It may serve to unify and spur on coloured peoples in their struggles for freedom and equality, but once these goals have been achieved it rapidly loses its *raison d'être*. As Oliver Cox has pointed out: 'Today communication is so far advanced that no people of colour, however ingenious, could hope to put a cultural distance between them and whites comparable to that which the Europeans of the commercial and industrial revolution attained in practical isolation over the coloured peoples of the world. And such a relationship is crucial for the development of that complex belief in biological superiority and consequent colour prejudice which Europeans have been able to attain. Therefore, we must conclude that race prejudice is not only a cultural trait developed among Europeans, but also that no other race could hope to duplicate the phenomenon. Like the discovery of the world, it seems evident that this racial achievement could occur only once (pp. 348–9).' The other side of this coin is, since the coloured races obviously can and will attain cultural and technological equality with whites, that the race prejudice of modern whites is not only a unique but also a transitory historical phenomenon. It needs to be added, however, that completely eliminating it from the consciousness of whites, even in a predominantly non-exploitative (that is, socialist) world, may take decades rather than months or years.

4. The crucial importance of the status hierarchy in the shaping of the individual's consciousness goes far to explain the illusion, so widespread in the United States, that there are no classes in this country, or, as the same idea is often expressed, that everyone is a member of the middle class.

the corporate sales apparatus which finds in them the principal means of manipulating the 'utility functions' of the consuming public.

The net result of all this is that each status group has a deep-rooted psychological need to compensate for feelings of inferiority and envy toward those above by feelings of superiority and contempt for those below. It thus happens that a special pariah group at the bottom acts as a kind of lightning rod for the frustrations and hostilities of all the higher groups, the more so the nearer they are to the bottom. It may even be said that the very existence of the pariah group is a kind of harmonizer and stabilizer of the social structure – so long as the pariahs play their role passively and resignedly. Such a society becomes in time so thoroughly saturated with race prejudice that it sinks below the level of consciousness and becomes a part of the 'human nature' of its members.[5] The gratification which whites derive from their socio-economic superiority to Negroes has its counterpart in alarm, anger, and even panic at the prospect of Negroes' attaining equality. Status being a relative matter, whites inevitably interpret upward movement by Negroes as downward movement for themselves. This complex of attitudes, product of stratification and status consciousness in monopoly capitalist society, provides an important part of the explanation why whites not only refuse to help Negroes to rise but bitterly resist their efforts to do so. (When we speak of whites and their prejudices and attitudes in this unqualified way, we naturally do not mean all whites. Ever since John Brown, and indeed long before John Brown, there have been whites who have freed themselves of the disease of racial prejudice, have fought along with Negro militants for an end to the rotten system of exploitation and inequality, and have looked forward to the creation of a society in which relations of solidarity and brotherhood will take the place of relations of superiority and inferiority. Moreover, we are confident that the number of such whites will steadily increase in the years ahead. But their number is not great today, and in a survey which aims only at depicting the broadest contours of the current social scene it would be wholly misleading to assign them a decisive role.)

The third set of factors adversely affecting the relative position of Negroes is connected with technological trends and their impact on the demand for different kinds and grades of labour. Appearing before a Congressional committee in 1955, the then Secretary of Labor, James P. Mitchell, testified that unskilled workers as a proportion of the labour force

5. At this level of development, race prejudice is far from being reachable by public opinion polls and similar devices of 'sociometrics' which remain close to the surface of individual and social phenomena. Incidentally, we have here another reason for believing that the eradication of race prejudice from whites will be, even in a rational society, a difficult and protracted process.

had declined from 36 per cent in 1910 to 20 per cent in 1950.[6] A later Secretary of Labor, Willard Wirtz, told the Clark Committee (1963, p. 57) that the percentage of unskilled was down to 5 per cent by 1962. Transated into absolute figures, this means that the number of unskilled workers declined slightly, from somewhat over to somewhat under thirteen million between 1910 and 1950, and then plummeted to fewer than four million only twelve years later. These figures throw a sharp light on the rapid deterioration of the Negro employment situation since the Second World War. What happened is that until roughly a decade and a half ago, with the number of unskilled jobs remaining stable, Negroes were able to hold their own in the total employment picture by replacing white workers who were moving up the occupational ladder. This explains why the Negro unemployment rate was only a little higher than the white rate at the end of the Great Depression. Since 1950, on the other hand, with unskilled jobs disappearing at a fantastic rate, Negroes not qualified for other kinds of work found themselves increasingly excluded from employment altogether. Hence the rise of the Negro unemployment rate to more than double the white rate by the early 1960s. Negroes, in other words, being the least-qualified workers are disproportionately hard hit as unskilled jobs (and, to an increasing extent, semi-skilled jobs) are eliminated by mechanization, automation and cybernation. Since this technological revolution has not yet run its course – indeed many authorities think that it is still in its early stages – the job situation of Negroes is likely to go on deteriorating. To be sure, technological trends are not, as many believe, the *cause* of unemployment: that role, as we have tried to show in earlier chapters, is played by the specific mechanisms of monopoly capitalism.[7] But within the framework of this society technological trends, because of their differential impact on job opportunities, can rightly be considered a cause, and undoubtedly the most important cause, of the relative growth of Negro unemployment.

All the forces we have been discussing – vested economic interests, socio-psychological needs, technological trends – are deeply rooted in monopoly capitalism and together are strong enough to account for the fact that

6. *Automation and Technological Change*, Hearings Before the Sub-committee on Economic Stabilization of the Joint Committee on the Economic Report, 84th Congress, 1st Sess., pursuant to Sec. 5(a) of P. L. 304, 79th Congress, 14, 15, 17, 18, 24, 25, 26, 27, and 28 October 1955, p. 264.

7. Under socialism there is no reason why technological progress, no matter how rapid or of what kind, should be associated with unemployment. In a socialist society technological progress may make possible a continuous reduction in the number of years, weeks, and hours worked, but it is inconceivable that this reduction should take the completely irrational form of capitalist unemployment.

Negroes have been unable to rise out of the lower depths of American society. Indeed so pervasive and powerful are these forces that the wonder is only that the position of Negroes has not drastically worsened. That it has not, that in absolute terms their real income and consuming power have risen more or less in step with the rest of the population's, can only be explained by the existence of counteracting forces.

One of these counteracting forces we have already commented upon: the shift out of Southern agriculture and into the urban economy. Some schooling was better than none; even a rat-infested tenement provided more shelter than a broken-down shack on Tobacco Road; being on the relief rolls of a big city meant more income, both money and real, than subsistence farming. And as the nation's *per capita* income rose, so also did that of the lowest income group, even that of unemployables on permanent relief. As we have seen, it has been this shift from countryside to city which has caused so many observers to believe in the reality of a large-scale Negro breakthrough in the last two decades. Actually, it was an aspect of a structural change in the economy rather than a change in the position of Negroes within the economy.

But in one particular area, that of government employment, Negroes have indeed scored a breakthrough, and this has unquestionably been the decisive factor in preventing a catastrophic decline in their relative position in the economy as a whole. Table 1 gives the essential data (all levels of government are included).

Table 1 **Non-white employment in government, 1940–62**
(figures are for April, in thousands)

	1940	1956	1960	1961	1962
Government employees, total	3845	6919	8014	8150	8647
Non-white government employees	214	670	855	932	1046
Non-white as per cent of total	5·6	9·7	10·7	11·4	12·1

Source: United States Department of Labor (1962, p. 8).

Between 1940 and 1962, total government employment somewhat more than doubled, while non-white (as already noted, more than 90 per cent Negro) employment in government expanded nearly five times. As a result non-white employment grew from 5·6 per cent of the total to 12·1 per cent. Since non-whites constituted 11·5 per cent of the labour force at mid-1961, it is a safe inference that Negroes are now more than proportionately represented in government employment.[8]

8. If the data were available to compare income received from government employment by whites and non-whites, the picture would of course be much less favourable for Negroes since they are heavily concentrated in the lower-paying categories. But here

Two closely interrelated forces have been responsible for this relative improvement of the position of Negroes in government employment. The first, and beyond doubt the most important, has been the increasing scope and militancy of the Negro liberation movement itself. The second has been the need of the American oligarchy, bent on consolidating a global empire including people of all colours, to avoid as much as possible the stigma of racism. If American Negroes had passively accepted the continuation of their degraded position, history teaches us that the oligarchy would have made no concessions. But once seriously challenged by militant Negro struggle, it was forced by the logic of its domestic and international situation to make concessions, with the twin objectives of pacifying Negroes at home and projecting abroad an image of the United States as a liberal society seeking to overcome an evil inheritance from the past.

The oligarchy, acting through the federal government and in the North and West through state and local governments, has also made other concessions to the Negro struggle. The armed forces have been desegregated, and a large body of civil rights legislation forbidding discrimination in public accommodations, housing, education and employment, has been enacted. Apart from the desegregation of the armed forces, however, these concessions have had little effect. Critics often attribute this failure to bad faith: there was never any intention, it is said, to concede to Negroes any of the real substance of their demand for equality. This is a serious misreading of the situation. No doubt there are many white legislators and administrators to whom such strictures apply with full force, but this is not true of the top economic and political leadership of the oligarchy – the managers of the giant corporations and their partners at the highest governmental levels. These men are governed in their political attitudes and behaviour not by personal prejudices but by their conception of class interests. And while they may at times be confused by their own ideology or mistake short-run for long-run interests, it seems clear that with respect to the race problem in the United States they have come, perhaps belatedly but none the less surely, to understand that the very existence of their system is at stake. Either a solution will be found which ensures the loyalty, or at least the neutrality, of the Negro people, or else the world revolution will sooner or later acquire a ready-made and potentially powerful Trojan horse within the ramparts of monopoly capitalism's mightiest fortress. When men like Kennedy and Johnson and Warren champion such

---

too there has been improvement. A study made by the Civil Service Commission showed that between June 1962 and June 1963 Negro employment in the federal government increased by 3 per cent and that 'the major percentage gains had been in the better-paying jobs.' (*New York Times*, 4 March 1964).

measures as the Civil Rights Act of 1964, it is clearly superficial to accuse them of perpetrating a cheap political manoeuvre. They know that they are in trouble, and they are looking for a way out.

Why then such meagre results? The answer is simply that the oligarchy does not have the power to shape and control race relations any more than it has the power to plan the development of the economy. In matters which are within the administrative jurisdiction of government, policies can be effectively implemented. Thus it was possible to desegregate the armed forces and greatly to increase the number of Negroes in government employment. But when it comes to housing, education, and private employment, all the deeply rooted economic and socio-psychological forces analysed above come into play. It was capitalism, with its enthronement of greed and privilege, which created the race problem and made of it the ugly thing it is today. It is the very same system which resists and thwarts every effort at a solution.

References

CLARK COMMITTEE (1963), *Nation's Manpower Revolution*, Government Printing Office.

COX, O. (1959), *Caste, Class and Race*, Monthly Review Press.

COMMISSION ON RACE AND HOUSING, (1958), *Where Shall We Live?*, University of California Press.

DUNBAR, L. W. (1964), *Equal Employment Opportunity*, Clark Committee.

UNITED STATES DEPARTMENT OF LABOR (1962), *The Economic Situation of Negroes in the United States*, Bulletin S-3, p. 8.

Further Reading

General

P. A. Baran and P. M. Sweezy, *Monopoly Capital*, Monthly Review Press, 1966, Penguin edition, 1968.

E. Cannan, *Wealth*, third edition, Staples Press, London and New York, 1928.

H. Dalton, *The Inequality of Incomes*, Routledge, 1920.

D. Donnison, 'Liberty, equality and fraternity', *Three Banks Rev.*, no. 88, 1970, pp. 3–23.

R. C. Edwards, M. Reich and T. E. Weisskopf, *The Capitalist System*, Prentice-Hall, 1972.

G. Kolko, *Wealth and Power in America*, Praeger, 1962.

H. P. Miller, *Rich Man, Poor Man*, Crowell; Signet Press, 1964.

S. M. Miller and P. Roby, *The Future of Inequality*, Basic Books, 1970.

J. N. Morgan, *et al.*, *Income and Welfare in the United States*, McGraw-Hill, 1962.

J. Pen, *Income Distribution*, Allen Lane, London, 1971.

W. G. Runciman, *Relative Deprivation and Social Justice*, Routledge & Kegan Paul, 1966.

R. M. Titmuss, *Income Distribution and Social Change*, Allen & Unwin, 1962.

Distribution of income

F. G. Adams, 'The size of individual incomes – socio-economic variables and chance variation', *Rev. of Econ. and Stat.*, vol. 40, 1958, pp. 390–98.

R. G. D. Allen, 'Changes in the distribution of higher incomes', *Economica*, vol. 24, 1957, pp. 138–53.

J. A. Brittain, 'Some neglected features of Britain's income levelling', *Amer. Econ. Assoc., Papers and Proceedings*, vol. 50, 1960, pp. 593–603.

E. C. Budd, 'Postwar changes in the size distribution of income in the US', *Amer. Econ. Rev., Papers and Proceedings*, vol. 60, 1970, pp. 247–60.

D. G. Champernowne, 'A model of income distribution', *Econ. J.*, vol. 63, 1953, pp. 318–51.

Economic Commission for Europe, *Incomes in Postwar Europe*, UN, 1967.

B. F. Haley, 'Changes in the distribution of income in the United States', in J. Marchal and B. Ducros (eds.), *The Distribution of National Income*, New York St Martin's Press and Macmillan, 1968, pp. 3–29.

I. B. Kravis, *The Structure of Income*, University of Pennsylvania Press, 1962.

S. Kuznets, 'Quantitative aspects of the economic growth of nations: part VIII, distribution of income by size', *Econ. Devel. and cult. Change*, vol. 11, 1963, pp. 1–80.

S. Lebergott, 'The shape of the income distribution', *Amer. econ. Rev.*, vol. 49, 1959, pp. 328–47.

H. F. Lydall, 'The long-term trend in the size distribution of income', *J. Roy. Stat. Soc.*, vol. 122, Series A, pt. 1, 1959, pp. 1–37.

J. N. Morgan, 'The anatomy of income distribution', *Rev. econ. Stat.*, vol. 44, 1962, pp. 270–83.

A. R. Prest and T. Stark, 'Some aspects of income distribution in the UK since World War II', *Manchester School*, vol. 35, 1967, pp. 217–43.

K. R. Ranadive, 'The equality of incomes in India', *Bull. Oxford Inst. Econ. Stats.*, vol. 27, 1965, pp. 119–34.

T. Stark, *The Distribution of Personal Income in the United Kingdom 1949–63*, Cambridge University Press, 1972.

Distribution of earnings

G. Becker, *Human Capital*, National Bureau of Economic Research, 1964.

J. Edmonds and G. Radice, *Low Pay*, Fabian Research Series, 270, 1968.

J. R. Hicks, *The Theory of Wages*, 2nd edn., Macmillan, 1963.

H. G. Lewis, *Unionism and Relative Wages in the United States*, University of Chicago Press, 1963.

H. F. Lydall, *The Structure of Earnings*, Oxford University Press, 1968.

J. Mincer, 'The Distribution of Labour Incomes – A Survey', *J. Econ. Lit.*, vol. 8, 1970, pp. 1–26.

National Board for Prices and Incomes, Report 1969, *General Problems of Low Pay*, HMSO, cmnd. 4648, 1971.

M. W. Reder, 'The size distribution of earnings', in J. Marchal and B. Ducros (eds.), *The Distribution of National Income*, International Economic Association, Macmillan, 1968, pp. 583–610.

M. W. Reder, 'A partial survey of the theory of income size distribution', in L. Soltow (ed.), *Six Papers on the Size Distribution of Wealth and Income*, National Bureau of Economic Research, 1969, pp. 205–53.

D. Robinson, 'Low paid workers and incomes policy', *Bull. Oxford Inst. Econ. Stats.*, vol. 29, 1967, pp. 1–29.

G. Routh, *Occupation and Pay in Great Britain 1906–60*, Cambridge University Press, 1965.

H. Staehle, 'Ability, wages, and income', *Rev. Econ. and Stats.*, vol. 25, 1943, pp. 77–87.

A. R. Thatcher, 'The distribution of earnings of employees in Great Britain', *J. roy. stat. Soc.*, Series A, vol 131, Part 2, 1968, pp. 133–70.

H. A. Turner, 'Trade unions, differentials and the levelling of wages',
Manchester School, vol. 20, 1952, pp. 227–82.

Distribution of wealth

A. B. Atkinson, *Unequal Shares – Wealth in Britain*,
Allen Lane, 1972.

H. Campion, *Public and Private Property in Great Britain*, Oxford University
Press, 1939.

F. Lundberg, *The Rich and the Super Rich*, Lyle Stuart, 1968.

M. Meacher, 'Wealth: Labour's Achilles heel', in P. Townsend and
N. Bosanquet (eds.), *Labour and Inequality*, Fabian Society, 1972.

J. R. S. Revell, 'Changes in the social distribution of property in Britain during
the twentieth century', *Actes du Troisième Congrès International d'Histoire
Economique*, Munich, 1965, pp. 367–384.

J. Wedgwood, *The Economics of Inheritance*, Routledge & Kegan Paul, 1929,
Penguin edition 1939.

Distribution by factor shares

P. Davidson, *Theories of Aggregate Income Distribution*, Rutgers University
Press, 1960.

K. Heidensohn, '*The Share of Labour*', *Manchester School*, vol. 37, 1969,
pp. 295–313.

N. Kaldor, 'Alternative theories of distribution', *Rev. econ. Stud.*, vol. 23,
1956, pp. 83–100.

I. B. Kravis, 'Relative income shares in fact and theory', *Amer. econ. Rev.*,
vol. 49, 1959, pp. 917–49.

E. H. Phelps-Brown, and P. E. Hart, 'Share of wages in the national income',
econ. J., vol. 62, 1952, pp. 253–77.

E. H. Phelps-Brown, *Pay and Profits*, Manchester University Press, 1969.

T. Scitovsky, 'A survey of some theories of distribution', in *The Behaviour of
Income Shares*, National Bureau of Economic Research, 1968, pp. 15–31.

R. M. Solow, 'A sceptical note on the constancy of relative shares', *Amer.
econ. Rev.*, vol. 48, 1958, pp. 618–31.

Poverty and racial discrimination

I. Adams, W. Cameron, B. Hill, and P. Penz, *The Real Poverty Report*,
M. G. Hurtig, 1971. (Report on poverty in Canada.)

A. B. Atkinson, *Poverty in Britain and the Reform of Social Security*,
Cambridge University Press, 1969.

A. B. Batchelder, *The Economics of Poverty*, second edition, Wiley, 1972.

D. Bull (ed.), *Family Poverty*, Duckworth, 1971.

D. Caplovitz, *The Poor Pay More: Consumer Practices of Low-Income Families*, The Free Press of Glencoe, 1963.

K. Coates, and R. Silburn, *Poverty: the Forgotten Englishmen*, Penguin, 1970.

M. S. Gordon (ed.), *Poverty in America*, Chandler, 1965.

M. Harrington, *The Other America*, Macmillan, Penguin, 1962.

R. F. Henderson, A. Harcourt and R. J. A. Harper, *People in Poverty: A Melbourne Survey*, Cheshire, 1970.

R. J. Lampman, *The Low Income Population and Economic Growth*, Study Paper 12 for Joint Economic Committee, 86th Congress, US Government Printing Office, 1959.

T. Lynes, *National Assistance and National Prosperity*, Bell, 1962.

D. Marsden, *Mothers Alone: Poverty and the Fatherless Family*, Allen Lane 1969.

M. Orshansky, 'Who's who among the poor: a demographic view of poverty', *Soc. Security Bull.*, vol. 28, no. 7, 1965, pp. 3–27.

S. Rowntree, *Poverty – A Study of Town Life*, Macmillan, 1901.

L. Thurow, *Poverty and Discrimination*, Brookings, 1969.

P. Townsend (ed.), *The Concept of Poverty*, Heinemann, 1970.

US Department of Labour, *Black Americans, – A Chartbook*, US Government Printing Office, 1971.

H. G. Vatter and T. Palm (eds.), *The Economics of Black America*, Harcourt Brace Jovanovich, 1972.

D. Wedderburn, 'Poverty in Britain today – the evidence', *sociol. Rev.*, vol. 10, 1962, pp. 257–82.

M. Wynn, *Family Policy*, Michael Joseph, 1970.

World poverty

D. Horowitz, *The Abolition of Poverty*, Praeger, 1969.

T. Hayter, *Aid as Imperialism*, Penguin, 1971.

G. Ohlin, *Foreign Aid Policies Reconsidered*, OECD, 1966.

G. Myrdal, *Asian Drama*, Twentieth Century Fund, 1968, Penguin, 1969.

G. Ranis (ed.), *The Gap Between Rich and Poor Nations*, Macmillan, 1972.

Redistributive effect of government budget

A. M. Cartter, *The Redistribution of Income in Postwar Britain*, Yale University Press, 1955.

Economic Trends, 'The incidence of taxes and social security benefits', February, 1971.

A. J. Merrett and D. A. G. Monk, 'The structure of UK taxation 1962–3', *Bull. of the Oxford University Inst. of Econ. and Stat.*, vol. 28, 1966, pp. 145–62.

J. L. Nicholson, *Redistribution of Income in the United Kingdom in 1959, 1957 and 1953*, Bowes & Bowes, 1965.

H. Simons, *Personal Income Taxation*, University of Chicago Press, 1938.

A. Webb and J. Sieve, *Income Redistribution and the Welfare State*, Bell, 1971.

Acknowledgements

Permission to reproduce the following readings in this volume is acknowledged to the following sources:

1 Allen & Unwin
2 *International Economic Review*
3 Academic Press Inc.
4 Penguin Books Limited
5 *The Economic History Review*
6 *Lloyds Bank Review*
7 United States Government Printing Office
8 American Economic Association
9 University of Chicago Press
10 National Bureau of Economic Research
11 *Review of Economics and Statistics*
12 American Sociological Association
13 Allen & Unwin
14 *British Journal of Industrial Relations*
15 Basil Blackwell
16 *Review of Economics and Statistics*
17 Allen & Unwin and Harvard University Press
18 *Econometrica*
19 *Economic Journal*
20 G. Bell & Sons Limited
21 United States Government Printing Office
22 Monthly Review Press

Author Index

Abel-Smith, B., 10, 349, 350, 369, 371
Adams, F. G., 193
Aigner, D. J., 51, 63
Aitchison, J., 187
Allen Report, 365
Archibald, G. C., 10
Arnold, M., 17, 18, 19, 21, 26, 33
Arrow, K. J., 52
Atkinson, A. B., 14, 369, 371, 372

Bacon, R., 11
Bagehot, W., 17, 18
Baran, P., 351
Barbor, A. W., 194
Barna, T., 290
Batchelder, A. B., 351
Bateman, J., 96, 339
Baxter, R. D., 87, 92, 94, 97
Becker, G., 351
Beckerman, W., 11
Bellerby, J. R., 149
Benge, E. J., 194
Black, J. D., 149
Blaug, M., 161
Boissevain, C. H., 166
Bollinger, D. L., 289
Bowley, A., 73, 87, 88, 92, 94
Brady, D. S., 111, 116
Bronfenbrenner, M., 8, 10
Brown, J. A. C., 187
Brundage, P. F., 284
Burk, S. L. H., 194
Burns, A. F., 112
Burt, C., 25, 166, 301
Butters, J. K., 289

Campion, H., 243, 246, 248, 252, 253,
    254, 255, 259, 260, 290
Carleton, R. O., 169
Carter, C. O., 301
Cartter, A. M., 136, 290, 353

Chalmers, G., 87
Champernowne, D. G., 167, 187, 305,
    321, 322
Clark, H. F., 181
Cole, D., 86, 365
Colquhoun, P., 85, 86, 87, 92, 93, 94, 96
Commission on Race and Housing,
    392
Copeland, M. A., 128
Council of Economic Advisors, 349,
    350, 378, 380, 383, 384, 390, 391
Cox, O., 393
Crum, W. L., 277

Dalton, H., 8, 46, 49, 51, 54, 55, 78
Daniels, G. H., 243, 246, 248, 252, 253,
    255, 260, 290
Davenant, C., 87, 92
David, M., 39
Davis, H. T., 201
Deane, P. M., 84, 86
Dorfman, R., 36
Dunbar, L. W., 393

Economic Commission for Europe, 65
Educational Policies Commission, 184
Edwards, A. M., 178
Életö, O., 55
Ely R. T., 193
Epstein, L., 35
Erskine May, 17, 18

Ferge, S., 42
Fijalkowski-Bereday, G. Z., 345
Fisher, A. G. B., 184
Fisher, I., 8
Fisher, J., 35
Fitzwilliams, J. M., 114, 118, 120, 121
Friedman, M., 161, 165, 168, 169, 187,
    310
Frigyes, E., 55

Subject Index